Advanced Modelling in Finance
using Excel and VBA

Wiley Finance Series

Operational Risk: Measurement and Modelling
Jack King

Advance Credit Risk Analysis: Financial Approaches and Mathematical Models to Assess, Price and Manage Credit Risk
Didier Cossin and Hugues Pirotte

Dictionary of Financial Engineering
John F. Marshall

Pricing Financial Derivatives: The Finite Difference Method
Domingo A Tavella and Curt Randall

Interest Rate Modelling
Jessica James and Nick Webber

Handbook of Hybrid Instruments: Convertible Bonds, Preferred Shares, Lyons, ELKS, DECS and Other Mandatory Convertible Notes
Izzy Nelken (ed)

Options on Foreign Exchange, Revised Edition
David F DeRosa

The Handbook of Equity Derivatives, Revised Edition
Jack Francis, William Toy and J Gregg Whittaker

Volatility and Correlation in the Pricing of Equity, FX and Interest-Rate Options
Riccardo Rebonato

Risk Management and Analysis vol. 1: Measuring and Modelling Financial Risk
Carol Alexander (ed)

Risk Management and Analysis vol. 2: New Markets and Products
Carol Alexander (ed)

Implementing Value at Risk
Philip Best

Credit Derivatives: A Guide to Instruments and Applications
Janet Tavakoli

Implementing Derivatives Models
Les Clewlow and Chris Strickland

Interest-Rate Option Models: Understanding, Analysing and Using Models for Exotic Interest-Rate Options (second edition)
Riccardo Rebonato

Advanced Modelling in Finance using Excel and VBA

Mary Jackson
and
Mike Staunton

JOHN WILEY & SONS, LTD

Chichester • New York • Weinheim • Brisbane • Singapore • Toronto

Reprinted September, November 2001, February 2002

Other Wiley Editorial Offices

John Wiley & Sons, Inc., 605 Third Avenue,
New York, NY 10158-0012, USA

Wiley-VCH Verlag GmbH, Pappelallee 3,
D-69469 Weinheim, Germany

John Wiley & Sons Australia Ltd, 33 Park Road, Milton,
Queensland 4064, Australia

John Wiley & Sons (Asia) Pte Ltd, 2 Clementi Loop #02-01,
Jin Xing Distripark, Singapore 129809

John Wiley & Sons (Canada) Ltd, 22 Worcester Road,
Rexdale, Ontario M9W 1L1, Canada

British Library Cataloguing in Publication Data

A catalogue record for this book is available from the British Library

ISBN 0 471 49922 6

Typeset in 10/12pt Times by Laser Words, Chennai, India
Printed and bound in Great Britain by Antony Rowe Ltd, Chippenham, Wiltshire
This book is printed on acid-free paper responsibly manufactured from sustainable forestry,
in which at least two trees are planted for each one used for paper production.

Contents

Preface

When asked why they tackled Mount Everest, climbers typically reply "Because it was there". Our motivation for writing Advanced Modelling in Finance is for exactly the opposite reason. There were then, and still are now, almost no books that give due prominence to and explanation of the use of VBA functions within Excel. There is an almost similar lack of books that capture the true vibrant spirit of numerical methods in finance.

It is no longer true that spreadsheets such as Excel are inadequate tools in highly technical and numerically demanding areas such as the valuation of financial derivatives. With efficient code and VBA functions, calculations that were once the preserve of dedicated packages and languages can now be done on a modern PC in Excel within seconds, if not fractions of a second. By employing Excel and VBA, our purpose is to try to bring clarity to an area that was previously covered with black boxes.

What started as an attempt to push back the boundaries of Excel through macros turned into a full-scale expedition into the VBA language within Excel and then developed from equities, through options and finally to cover bonds. Along the way we learned scores of new Excel skills and a much greater understanding of the numerical methods implemented across finance.

The genesis of the book came from material developed for the 'Computer-Based Financial Modelling' elective on the MBA degree at London Business School. The part on equities formed the basis for an executive course on 'Equity Portfolio Management' run annually by the International Centre for Money and Banking in Geneva. The parts on options and bonds comprise a course in 'Numerical Methods' on the MSc in Mathematical Trading and Finance at City University Business School. The book is within the reach of both students at the postgraduate level and those in the latter undergraduate years.

There are no prerequisites for readers apart from a willingness to adopt a pro-active stance when using the book–namely by taking advantage of the inherent 'what-if' quality of the spreadsheets and by looking at and using the code forming the VBA user-defined functions. Since we assume for the most part that asset returns are lognormal and therefore use binomial trees as a central numerical method, our explanations can be based on familiar results from probability and statistics. Comprehension is helped by the use of a common notation throughout, and transparency by the availability of complete solutions in both Excel and VBA forms.

Acknowledgements

Our main debt is to the individuals from the academic and practitioner communities in finance who first developed the theory and then the numerical methods that form the material for this book. In the words of Sir Isaac Newton "If I have seen further it is by standing on the shoulders of giants".

We would also like to thank our colleagues at both London Business School and City University Business School, in particular Elroy Dimson, Elias Dinenis, Paul Marsh and Kiriakos Vlahos.

We would like to thank Sam Whittaker at Wiley for her enthusiasm, encouragement and much needed patience, invaluable qualities for an editor.

Last but not least, we are grateful for the patience of family and friends who have occasionally chivvied us about the book's somewhat lengthy gestation period.

1
Introduction

We hope that our text, Advanced Modelling in Finance, is conclusive proof that a wide range of models can now be successfully implemented using spreadsheets. The models range across the complete spectrum of finance including equities, equity options and bond options spanning developments from the early fifties to the late nineties. The models are implemented in Excel spreadsheets, complemented with functions written using the VBA language within Excel. The resulting user-defined functions provide a portable library of programs with more than sufficient speed and accuracy.

Advanced Modelling in Finance should be viewed as a complement (or dare we say, an antidote) to traditional textbooks in the area. It contains relatively few derivations, allowing us to cover a broader range of models and methods, with particular emphasis on more recent advances.

The major theoretical developments in finance such as portfolio theory in the 1950s, the capital asset pricing model in the 1960s and the Black–Scholes formula in the 1970s brought with them analytic solutions that are now straightforward to calculate. The subsequent decades have seen a growing body of developments in numerical methods. With an intelligent choice of parameters, binomial trees have assumed a central role in the more numerically-intensive calculations now required to value equity and bond options. The centre of gravity in finance now concerns the search for more efficient ways of performing such calculations rather than the theories from yesteryear.

The breadth of the coverage across finance and the sophistication needed for some of the more advanced models are testament to the ability of Excel, the built-in functions contained in Excel and the real programming environment that VBA provides. This allows us to highlight the commonality of assumptions (lognormality), mathematical problems (expectation) and numerical methods (binomial trees) throughout finance as a whole. Without exception, we have tried to ensure a consistent and simple notation throughout the book to reinforce this commonality and to improve clarity of exposition.

Our objective in writing a book that covers the broad range of subjects in finance has proved to be both a challenge and an opportunity. The opportunity has provided us with the chance to overview finance as a whole and, in so doing, to make important connections and bring out commonalities in asset price assumptions, mathematical problems, numerical methods and Excel solutions. In the following sections we summarise a few of these unifying insights that apply to equities, options and bonds with regard to finance, mathematical topics, numerical methods and Excel features. This is followed by a more detailed summary of the main topics covered in each chapter of the book.

1.1 FINANCE INSIGHTS

The genesis of modern finance as a subject separate from economics started with Markowitz's development of portfolio theory in 1952. Markowitz used utility theory to model the preferences of individual investors and to develop a mean–variance approach to examining the trade-off between return (as measured by an asset's mean return) and risk (measured by an asset's variance of return). This subsequently led to the development by Sharpe, Lintner and Treynor of the capital asset pricing model (CAPM), an equilibrium model describing expected returns on equities. The CAPM introduced beta as a measure of diversifiable risk, arguing that the creation of portfolios served to minimise the specific risk element of total risk (variance).

The next great theoretical development was the equity option pricing formula of Black and Scholes, which rested on the ability to create a (riskless) hedge portfolio. Contemporaneously, Merton extended the Black–Scholes formula to allow for continuous dividends and thus also options on commodities and currencies. The derivation of the original formula required the solving of the diffusion (or heat) equation familiar from physics, but was subsequently encompassed by the broader risk-neutral approach to the valuation of derivatives.

1.2   ASSET PRICE ASSUMPTIONS

Although portfolio theory was derived through individual preferences, it could also have been obtained by making assumptions about the distribution of asset price returns. The standard assumption is that equity returns follow a lognormal distribution–equivalently we can say that equity log returns follow a normal distribution. More recently, practitioners have examined the effect of departures from strict normality (as measured by skewness and kurtosis) and have also proposed different distributions (for example, the reciprocal gamma distribution).

Although bonds have characteristics that are different from equities, the starting point for bond option valuation is the short interest rate. This is frequently assumed to follow the lognormal or normal distribution. The result is that familiar results grounded in these probability distributions can be applied throughout finance.

1.3   MATHEMATICAL AND STATISTICAL PROBLEMS

Within the equities part, the mathematical problems concern optimisation. The optimisation can also include additional constraints, exemplified by Sharpe's development of returns-based style analysis. Beta is estimated as the slope coefficient in a linear regression.

Options are valued in the risk-neutral framework as statistical expectations. The normal distribution of log equity prices can be approximated by an equivalent discrete binomial distribution. This binomial distribution provides the framework for calculating the expected option value.

1.4   NUMERICAL METHODS

In the context of portfolio optimisation, the optimisation involves portfolio variance, and the numerical method needed for optimisation is quadratic programming. Style analysis also uses quadratic programming, the quantity to be minimised being the error variance. Although not usually thought of as optimisation, linear regression chooses slope coefficients to minimise residual error. Here optimisation is of a different kind, regression analysis, which provides analytical formulas to calculate the beta coefficients.

Turning to option valuation, the binomial tree provides the structure within which the risk-neutral expectation can be calculated. We highlight the importance of parameter choice by examining the convergence properties of three different binomial trees. Such trees also allow the valuation of American options, where the option can be exercised at any date prior to maturity.

With European options, techniques such as Monte Carlo simulation and numerical integration are also used. Numerical search methods, in particular the Newton–Raphson approach, ensure that volatilities implied by option prices in the market can be estimated.

1.5   EXCEL SOLUTIONS

The spreadsheets demonstrate how Excel can be used as a prototype for building models. Within the individual spreadsheets, all the formulas in the cells can easily be examined and we have endeavoured to incorporate all intermediate calculations in cells of their own. The spreadsheets also allow the hallmark ability to 'what-if' by changing parameter values in cells.

The implementation of all the models and methods occurs twice: once in the spreadsheets and once in the VBA functions. This dual approach serves as an important check on the accuracy of the numerical calculations.

Some of the VBA procedures are macros, normally seen by others as the main purpose of VBA in Excel. However, the majority of the procedures we implement are user-defined functions. We demonstrate how easily these functions can be written in VBA and how they can incorporate Excel functions, including the powerful matrix functions.

The Goal Seek and Solver commands within Excel are used in the optimisation tasks. We show how these commands can be automated using VBA user-defined functions and macros. Another under-used aspect of Excel involves the application of array functions (invoked by the Ctrl+Shift+Enter keystroke combination) and we implement these in user-defined functions. To improve efficiency, our binomial trees in user-defined functions use one-dimensional arrays (vectors) rather than two-dimensional arrays (matrices).

1.6   TOPICS COVERED

There are four parts in the book, the first part illustrating the advanced modelling features in Excel followed by three parts with applications in finance. The three parts on applications cover equities, options on equities and options on bonds.

Chapter 2 emphasises the advanced Excel functions and techniques that we use in the remainder of the book. We pay particular attention to the array functions within Excel and provide a short section detailing the mathematics underlying matrix manipulation.

Chapter 3 introduces the VBA programming environment and illustrates a step-by-step approach to the writing of VBA subroutines (macros). The examples chosen demonstrate how macros can be used to automate and repeat tasks in Excel.

Chapter 4 moves on to VBA user-defined functions, which have a crucial role throughout the applications in finance. We emphasise how to deal with both scalar and array variables–as input variables to VBA functions, their use in calculations and finally as output variables. Again, we use a step-by-step approach for a number of examples. In particular, we write user-defined functions to value both European options (the Black–Scholes formula) and American options (binomial trees).

Chapter 5 introduces the first application part, that dealing with equities.

Chapter 6 covers portfolio optimisation, using both Solver and analytic solutions. As will become the norm in the remaining chapters, Solver is used both in the spreadsheet and automated in a VBA macro. By using the array functions in Excel and VBA, we detail how the points on the efficient frontier can be generated. The development of portfolio theory is divided into three generic problems, which recur in subsequent chapters.

Chapter 7 looks at (equity) asset pricing, starting with the single-index model and the capital asset pricing model (CAPM) and concluding with Value-at-Risk (VaR). This introduces the assumption that asset log returns follow a normal distribution, another recurrent theme.

Chapter 8 covers performance measurement, again ranging from single-parameter measures used in the very earliest days to multi-index models (such as style analysis) that represent current best practice. We show, for the first time in a textbook, how confidence intervals can be determined for the asset weights from style analysis.

Chapter 9 introduces the second application part, that dealing with options on equities. Building on the normal distribution assumed for equity log returns, we detail the creation of the hedge portfolio that is the key insight behind the Black–Scholes option valuation formula. The subsequent interpretation of the option value as the discounted expected value of the option payoff in a risk-neutral world is also introduced.

Chapter 10 looks at binomial trees, which can be viewed as a discrete approximation to the continuous normal distribution assumed for log equity prices. In practice, binomial trees form the backbone of numerical methods for option valuation since they can cope with early exercise and hence the valuation of American options. We illustrate three different parameter choices for binomial trees, including the little-known Leisen and Reimer tree that has vastly superior convergence and accuracy properties compared to the standard parameter choices. We use a nine-step tree in our spreadsheet examples, but the user-defined functions can cope with any number of steps.

Chapter 11 returns to the Black–Scholes formula and shows both its adaptability (allowing options on assets such as currencies and commodities to be valued) and its dependence on the asset price assumptions.

Chapter 12 covers two alternative ways of calculating the statistical expectation that lies behind the Black–Scholes formula for European options. These are Monte Carlo simulation and numerical integration. Although these perform less well for the simple options we consider, each of these methods has a valuable role in the valuation of more complicated options.

Chapter 13 moves away from the assumption of strict normality of asset log returns and shows how such deviation (typically through differing skewness and kurtosis parameters) leads to the so-called volatility smile seen in the market prices of options. Efficient methods for finding the implied volatility inherent in European option prices are described.

Chapter 14 introduces the third application part, that dealing with options on bonds. While bond prices have characteristics that are different from equity prices, there is a lot of commonality in the mathematical problems and numerical methods used to value options. We define the term structure based on a series of zero-coupon bond prices, and show how the short-term interest rate can be modelled in a binomial tree as a means of valuing zero-coupon bond cash flows.

Chapter 15 covers two models for interest rates, those of Vasicek and Cox, and Ingersoll and Ross. We detail analytic solutions for zero-coupon bond prices and options on zero-coupon bonds together with an iterative approach to the valuation of options on coupon bonds.

Chapter 16 shows how the short rate can be modelled in a binomial tree in order to match a given term structure of zero-coupon bond prices. We build the popular

Black–Derman–Toy interest rate tree (both in the spreadsheet and in user-defined functions) and show how it can be used to value both European and American options on zero-coupon bonds.

The final Appendix is a Pandora's box of other user-defined functions, that are less relevant to the chosen applications in finance. Nevertheless they constitute a useful toolbox, including as they do functions for ARIMA modelling, splines, eigenvalues and other calculation procedures.

1.7   RELATED EXCEL WORKBOOKS

Part I which concentrates on Excel functions and procedures and understanding VBA has three related workbooks, AMFEXCEL, VBSUB and VBFNS which accompany Chapters 2, 3 and 4 respectively.

Part II on equities has three related workbooks, EQUITY1, EQUITY2 and EQUITY3 which accompany Chapters 6, 7 and 8 respectively.

Part III on options on equities has four files, OPTION1, OPTION2, OPTION3 and OPTION4 which accompany Chapters 10, 11, 12 and 13 respectively.

Part IV on bonds has two related workbooks, BOND1 and BOND2 which accompany Chapters 14, 15 and 16 as indicated in the text.

The Appendix has one workbook, OTHERFNS.

1.8   COMMENTS AND SUGGESTIONS

Having spent so much time developing the material and writing this book, we would very much appreciate any comments, suggestions and, dare we say, possible corrections and improvements. Please email mstaunton@london.edu or find your way to www.london.edu/ifa/services/services.html or www.business.city.ac.uk/irmi/mstaunton.html.

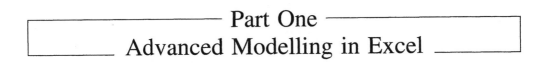
Part One
Advanced Modelling in Excel

2
Advanced Excel Functions and Procedures

The purpose of this chapter is to review certain Excel functions and procedures used in the text. These include mathematical, statistical and lookup functions from Excel's extensive range of functions, as well as much-used procedures such as setting up Data Tables and displaying results in XY charts. Also included are methods of summarising data sets, conducting regression analyses, and accessing Excel's Goal Seek and Solver. The objective is to clarify and ensure that this material causes the reader no difficulty. The advanced Excel user may wish to skim the content or use the chapter for further reference as and when required. To make the various topics more entertaining and more interactive, a workbook AMFEXCEL.xls includes the examples discussed in the text and allows the reader to check his or her proficiency.

2.1 ACCESSING FUNCTIONS IN EXCEL

Excel provides many worksheet functions, which are essentially calculation routines that have been coded up. They are useful for simplifying calculations performed in the spreadsheet, and also for combining into VBA macros and user-defined functions (topics covered in Chapters 3 and 4).

The Paste Function button (labelled *fx*) on the standard toolbar gives access to them. (It was previously known as the function wizard.) As Figure 2.1 shows, functions are grouped into different categories: mathematical, statistical, logical, lookup and reference, etc.

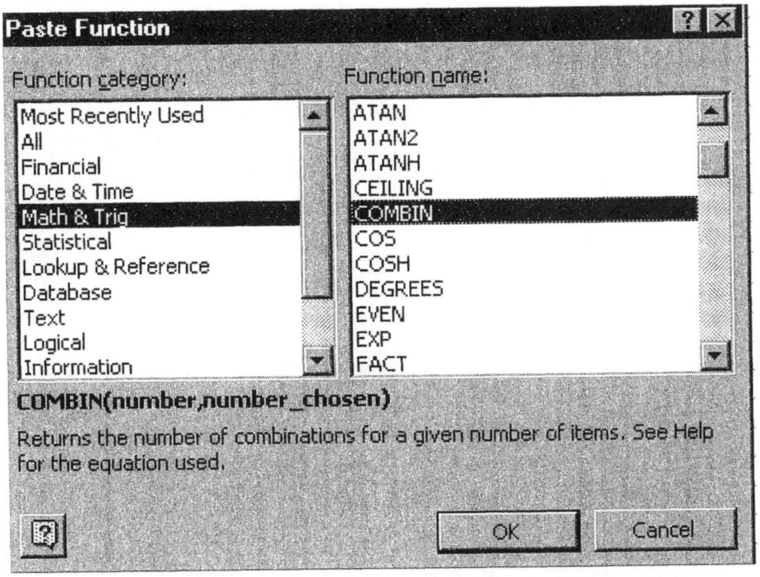

Figure 2.1 Paste Function dialog box showing the COMBIN function in the Math category

Here the Math & Trig function COMBIN has been selected, which produces a brief description of the function's inputs and outputs. For a fuller description, press the Help button (labelled ?).

On clicking OK, the Formula palette appears providing slots for entering the appropriate inputs, as in Figure 2.2. The required inputs can be keyed into the slots (as here) or 'selected' by referencing cells in the spreadsheet (by clicking the buttons to collapse the Formula palette). Note that the palette can be dragged away from its standard position. Clicking the OK button on the palette or the tick on the Edit line enters the formula in the spreadsheet.

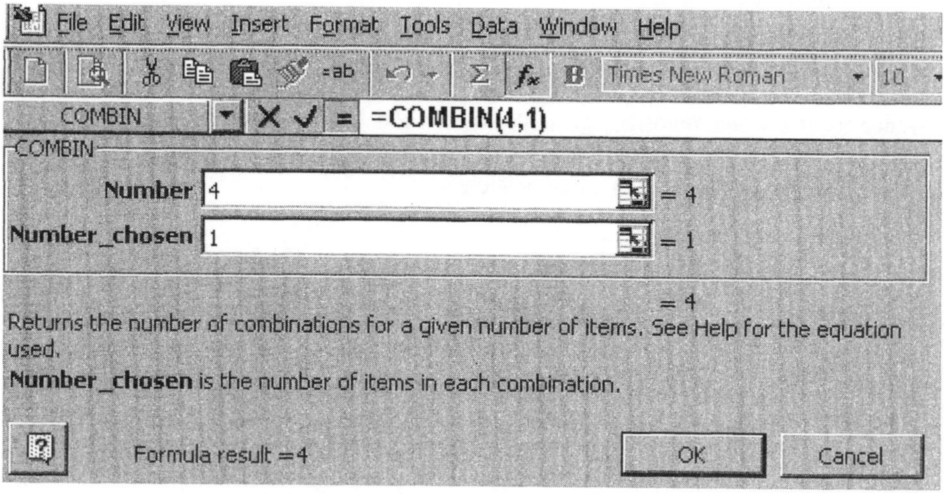

Figure 2.2   Building the COMBIN function in the Formula palette

As well as the Formula palette with inputs for function COMBIN, Figure 2.2 shows the construction of the cell formula on the Edit line, with the Paste Function button depressed (in action). Notice also the Paste Name button (labelled =ab) which facilitates pasting of named cells into the formula. (Attaching names to ranges and referencing cell ranges by names is reviewed in section 2.10.)

As well as all Excel functions, the Paste Function button also provides access to the user-defined category of functions which are described in Chapter 4.

Having discussed how to access the functions, in the following sections we describe some specific mathematical and statistical functions.

2.2   MATHEMATICAL FUNCTIONS

Within the Math & Trig category, we make use of the $EXP(x)$, $LN(x)$, $SQRT(x)$, $RAND()$, $FACT(x)$ and COMBIN(number, number_chosen) functions.

$EXP(x)$ returns values of the exponential function, $\exp(x)$ or e^x. For example:

- $EXP(1)$ returns value of e (2.7183 when formatted to four decimal places)
- $EXP(2)$ returns value of e^2 (7.3891 to four decimal places)
- $EXP(-1)$ returns value of $1/e$ or e^{-1} (0.36788 to five decimal places)

In finance calculations, cash flows occurring at different time periods are converted into future (or present) values by applying compounding (or discounting) factors. With continuous compounding at rate r, the compounding factor for one year is $\exp(r)$, and the equivalent annual interest rate r_a, if compounding were done on an annual basis, is given by the expression:

$$r_a = \exp(r) - 1$$

Continuous compounding and the use of the EXP function is illustrated further in section 2.7.1 on Data Tables.

$LN(x)$ returns the natural logarithm of value x. Note that x must be positive, otherwise the function returns #NUM! for numeric overflow. For example:

- LN(0.36788) returns value -1
- LN(2.7183) returns value 1
- LN(7.3891) returns value 2
- LN(-4) returns value #NUM!

In finance, we frequently work with (natural) log returns, applying the LN function to transform the returns data into log returns.

$SQRT(x)$ returns the square root of value x. Clearly, x must be positive, otherwise the function returns #NUM! for numeric overflow.

RAND() generates a uniformly distributed random number greater than or equal to zero and less than one. It changes each time the spreadsheet recalculates. We can use RAND() to introduce probabilistic variability into Monte Carlo simulation of option values.

FACT(number) returns the factorial of the number, which equals $1*2*3* \ldots *$number. For example:

- FACT(6) returns the value 720

COMBIN(number, number_chosen) returns the number of combinations (subsets of size 'number_chosen') that can be made up from a 'number' of items. The subsets can be in any internal order. For example, if a share moves either 'up' or 'down' at four discrete times, the number of sequences with three ups (and one down) is:

$$\text{COMBIN}(4,1) = 4 \text{ or equally COMBIN}(4,3) = 4$$

that is the four sequences 'up-up-up-down', 'up-up-down-up', 'up-down-up-up' and 'down-up-up-up'. In statistical parlance, COMBIN(4, 3) is the number of combinations of three items selected from four and is usually denoted as $_4C_3$ (or in general, $_nC_r$).

Excel has functions to transpose matrices, to multiply matrices and to invert square matrices. The relevant functions are:

- TRANSPOSE(array) which returns the transpose of an array
- MMULT(array1, array2) which returns the matrix product of two arrays
- MINVERSE(array) which returns the matrix inverse of an array

These fall in the same Math category. Since some readers may need an introduction to matrices before examining the functions, this material has been placed at the end of the chapter (see section 2.13).

2.3 STATISTICAL FUNCTIONS

Excel has several individual functions for quickly summarising the features of a data set (an 'array' in Excel terminology). These include AVERAGE(array) which returns the mean, STDEV(array) for the standard deviation, MAX(array) and MIN(array) which we assume are familiar to the reader.

To obtain the distribution of a moderate sized data set, there are some useful functions that deserve to be better known. For example, the QUARTILE function produces the individual quartile values on the basis of the percentiles of the data set and the FREQUENCY function returns the whole frequency distribution of the data set after grouping.

Excel also provides functions for a range of different theoretical probability distributions, in particular those for the normal distribution: NORMSDIST and NORMSINV for the standard normal with zero mean and standard deviation one; NORMDIST and NORMINV for any normal distribution.

Other useful functions in the statistical category are those for two variables, which provide many individual quantities used in regression and correlation analysis. For example:

- INTERCEPT(known_ y's, known_ x's)
- SLOPE(known_ y's, known_ x's)
- RSQ(known_ y's, known_ x's)
- STEYX(known_ y's, known_ x's)
- CORREL(array1, array2)
- COVAR(array1, array2)

There is also a little known array function, LINEST(known_ y's, known_ x's), which returns the essential regression statistics in array form. Most of these functions are examined in more detail in section 2.11 on regression. Their performance is compared and contrasted with the regression output from the Data Analysis Regression procedure.

In the next section, we explain how to use the FREQUENCY, QUARTILE and various normal functions via examples in the Frequency and SNorm sheets of the AMFEXCEL workbook.

2.3.1 Using the Frequency Function

FREQUENCY(data_array, bins_array) counts how often values in a data set occur within specified intervals (or 'bins'), and then returns these frequencies in a vertical array. The bins_array is the set of intervals into which the values are grouped. Since the function returns output in the form of an array, it is necessary to mark out a range of cells in the spreadsheet to receive the output *before* entering the function.

We explain how to use FREQUENCY with an example set out in the Frequency sheet of the AMFEXCEL workbook. As shown in Figure 2.3, monthly returns and log returns (using the LN function) in columns D10:D71 and E10:E70 have been summarised in rows 4 to 7. Suppose the aim is to get the frequency distribution of the log returns (E10:E71), i.e. the so-called 'data_array'. The objective might be to check that these returns are approximately normally distributed. First, we have to decide on intervals (or bins) for grouping the data. Inspection of the maximum and minimum log returns suggests about 10 to 12 intervals in the range −0.16 to +0.20. The 'interval' values, which have been entered in range G5:G14, act as upper limits when the log returns are grouped into the so-called 'bins'.

	A	B	C	D	E	F	G	H	I	J
2	Returns for months 1 - 62									
3	Summary Statistics:			Returns	Ln Returns		Frequency Distribution:			
4		Mean		1.78%	0.014		interval	freq	%freq	%cum freq
5		St Dev		8.09%	0.080		-0.16			
6		Max		21.23%	0.193		-0.12			
7		Min		-14.21%	-0.153		-0.08			
8							-0.04			
9	Month			Returns	Ln Returns		0.00			
10	Feb-92	1		7.06%	0.0682		0.04			
11	Mar-92	2		-11.54%	-0.1226		0.08			
12	Apr-92	3		7.77%	0.0748		0.12			
13	May-92	4		10.66%	0.1013		0.16			
14	Jun-92	5		-11.72%	-0.1247		0.20			
15	Jul-92	6		-8.26%	-0.0862					
16	Aug-92	7		-2.89%	-0.0293					
17	Sep-92	8		9.93%	0.0947		Total			
18	Oct-92	9		12.65%	0.1191					

Figure 2.3   Layout for calculating the frequency distribution of log returns data

To enter the FREQUENCY function correctly, select the range H5:H15. Then start by typing = and clicking on the Paste Function button (labelled *fx*) to complete the function syntax:

$$=FREQUENCY(E10:E71,G5:G14)$$

After adding the last bracket ')', with the cursor on Excel's Edit line, enter the function by holding down the **Ctrl** then the **Shift** then the **Enter** keys. (You need to use three fingers, otherwise it will not work. If this fails, keep the output range of cells 'selected', press the Edit key (F2), edit the formula if necessary, then press Ctrl+Shift+Enter once again.)

You should now see the function enclosed in curly brackets {} in the cells, and the frequencies array in cells G5:G15. The results are in Figure 2.4. Use the SUM function in cell H17 to check that the frequencies sum to 62.

Interpreting the results, we can see that there were no log returns below −0.16, six values in the range −0.16 to −0.12 and no values above 0.20. (The bottom cell in the FREQUENCY array, G15, contains any values above the bins' upper limit, 0.20.)

Since the FREQUENCY function has array output, individual cells cannot be changed. If a different number of intervals is required, the current array must be deleted and the function entered again.

It helps to convert the frequencies into percentage frequencies (relative to the size of the data set of 62 values) and then to calculate cumulated percentage frequencies as shown in columns I and J in Figure 2.4. The percentage frequency and cumulative percentage frequency formulas can be examined in the Frequency sheet.

	A	B	C	D	E	F	G	H	I	J
2	Returns for months 1 - 62									
3	Summary Statistics:			Returns	Ln Returns		Frequency Distribution:			
4		Mean		1.78%	0.0145		interval	freq	%freq	%cum freq
5		St Dev		8.09%	0.0802		-0.16	0	0%	0%
6		Max		21.23%	0.1925		-0.12	6	10%	10%
7		Min		-14.21%	-0.1533		-0.08	4	6%	16%
8							-0.04	7	11%	27%
9	Month			Returns	Ln Returns		0.00	10	16%	44%
10	Feb-92	1		7.06%	0.0682		0.04	5	8%	52%
11	Mar-92	2		-11.54%	-0.1226		0.08	16	26%	77%
12	Apr-92	3		7.77%	0.0748		0.12	9	15%	92%
13	May-92	4		10.66%	0.1013		0.16	4	6%	98%
14	Jun-92	5		-11.72%	-0.1247		0.20	1	2%	100%
15	Jul-92	6		-8.26%	-0.0862			0	0%	100%
16	Aug-92	7		-2.89%	-0.0293					
17	Sep-92	8		9.93%	0.0947		Total	62		

Figure 2.4   Frequency distribution of log returns with % frequency and cumulative distributions

The best way to display the percentage cumulative frequencies is an XY chart with data points connected by a smooth line with no markers. To produce a chart like that in Figure 2.5, select ranges G5:G14 and J5:J14 as the source data. Note that, to select non-contiguous ranges, select the first range, then hold down the Ctrl key whilst selecting the second and subsequent ranges.

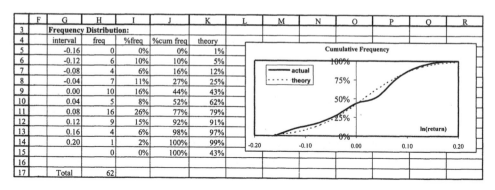

Figure 2.5   Chart of cumulative % frequencies (actual and strictly normal data)

For normally distributed log returns, the cumulative distribution should be sigmoid in shape (as indicated by the dashed line). The actual log returns data shows some departure from normality, possibly due to skewness.

2.3.2   Using the Quartile Function

QUARTILE(array, quart) returns the quartile of a data set. The second input 'quart' is an integer that determines which quartile is returned: if 0, the minimum value of the array; if 1, the first quartile (i.e. the 25th percentile of the array); if 2, the median value (50th percentile); if 3, the third quartile (75th percentile); if 4, the maximum value.

The quartiles provide a quick and relatively easy way to get the cumulative distribution of a data set. For example in cell H22 in Figure 2.6, the entry:

$$QUARTILE(E10:E71,G22)$$

where G22 contains the integer value 1, returns the first quartile. The value displayed in the cell is -0.043, which is the log return value below which 25% of the values in the data set fall. The second quartile, 0.028, is the median and the third quartile, 0.075, is the value below which 75% of the values fall. Figure 2.6 also shows an XY chart of the range H21:I25 with the data points marked. The cumulative curve based on just five data points can be seen to be quite close to the more accurate version in Figure 2.5.

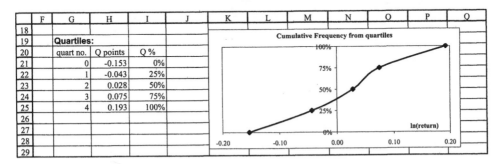

Figure 2.6   Quartiles for the log returns data in the Frequency sheet

The QUARTILE function is used in section 3.5 to illustrate array handling in VBA. A related function, PERCENTILE(array, k) which returns the kth percentile of a data set, is used to illustrate coding an array function in section 4.7.

2.3.3   Using Excel's Normal Functions

Of the statistical functions related to normal distribution, their names all start with the four letters NORM, and some include an S to indicate that the standard normal distribution is assumed.

NORMSDIST(z) returns the cumulative distribution function for the standard normal distribution. NORMSINV(probability) returns values of z for specified probabilities.

The rather more versatile NORMDIST(x, mean, standard_dev, cumulative) applies to any normal distribution. If the 'cumulative' input parameter $= 1$ (or TRUE), it returns values for the cumulative distribution function; if 'cumulative' input $= 0$ (or FALSE), it returns the probability density function.

Figure 2.7 shows the Norm sheet, with entries for the probability density and for the left-hand tail probability in cells C5 and D5 respectively. Both these formulas use the general NORMDIST function with mean and standard deviation inputs set to 0 and 1 respectively. In C5, the last input ('cumulative') takes value 0 for the probability density and in D5 takes value 1 for the left-hand tail probability.

The ordinate values corresponding to left-hand tail probabilities can be obtained from the NORMINV function as shown in cell F5.

To familiarise yourself with these functions, copy the formulas down and examine the results.

In the last section, we obtained a cumulative percentage frequency distribution for log returns. One check on normality is to use the NORMDIST function with the observed mean and standard deviation to calculate theoretical percentage frequencies. This has been done in column K of the Frequency sheet. The resulting frequencies are shown in the Figure 2.5 chart, superimposed on the distribution of actual returns. Some departures from normality can be seen.

	A	B	C	D	E	F	G
2	Excel Normal Functions for N(0, 1)						
3							
4			PDF	CDF		Inv(Normal)	
5		-4.00	0.0001	0.0000		-4.00	
6		-3.00					
7		-2.00			=NORMINV(D5,0,1)		
8		-1.00		=NORMDIST(B5,0,1,1)			
9		0.00	=NORMDIST(B5,0,1,0)				
10		1.00					
11		2.00					
12		3.00					
13		4.00					
14							

Figure 2.7 Excel's general normal distribution functions in the SNorm sheet

Excel provides an excellent range of functions for data summary, and for modelling various theoretical distributions. We make considerable use of them in both the Equity and the Options parts of the text.

2.4 LOOKUP FUNCTIONS

In tables of related information, 'lookups' allow items of information to be extracted on the basis of different lookup inputs. For example, in Figure 2.8 we illustrate the use of the VLOOKUP function which for a given volatility value 'looks up' the Black–Scholes call value from a table of volatilities and related call values. (We shall cover the background theory in Chapter 11 on the Black–Scholes formula.)

In general the function:

VLOOKUP(lookup_value, table_array, col_index_num, range_lookup)

searches for a value in the leftmost column of a table (table_array), and then returns a value in the same row from a column you specify (with col_index_num). By default, the first column of the table must be in ascending order (which implies that range_lookup = 1 (or TRUE)). In fact, if this is the case, the last input parameter can be ignored.

Lookup examples are in the LookUp sheet. To check your understanding, use the VLOOKUP function to decide the commission to be paid on different sales amounts, given the commission rates table in cell range F5:G7. Then scroll down to the Black–Scholes Call Value LookUp Table, illustrated in Figure 2.8.

The lookup_value (for volatility) is in C17 (20%), the table array is F17:G27, with volatilities in ascending order and call values in column 2 of the table array. So the formula in cell D18:

$$=VLOOKUP(C17,F17:G27,2)$$

returns a call value of 9.73 for the 20% volatility.

	A	B	C	D	E	F	G	H
15	Black-Scholes Call Value Lookup Table							
16						Volatility	BS Call Value	
17		Volatility	**20%**			15%	8.63	
18		VLOOKUP				16%	8.84	
19						17%	9.05	
20						18%	9.27	
21		call value	9.73			19%	9.50	
22		MATCH				20%	9.73	
23						21%	9.96	
24						22%	10.19	
25		row	6			23%	10.43	
26		column	2			24%	10.67	
27		INDEX				25%	10.91	
28								

Figure 2.8   Layout for looking up call values given volatility in the LookUp sheet

The lookup_value is matched approximately (or exactly) against values in the first column of the table, a row selected on the basis of match and the entry in the specified column returned. Try experimenting with different volatility values such as 20.5%, 21.5% in cell C17 to see how the lookup function works.

The range_lookup input is a logical value (TRUE or FALSE) which specifies whether you want the function to return exact matches or approximate ones. If TRUE or omitted, an approximate match is returned. If no exact match is found, the next largest value (less than the look_up value) is returned. If FALSE, then VLOOKUP will find an exact match or return the error value #NA.

There is a related HLOOKUP function that works horizontally, searching for matches across the top row of a table and reading off values from the specified row of the table.

MATCH and INDEX are other lookup functions, also illustrated in Figure 2.8. The function MATCH(lookup_value, lookup_array, match_type) returns the relative position of an item in a single column (or row) array that matches a specified value in a specified order (match_type). Note that the function returns a position within the array, rather than the value itself.

If the match_type input is 0, the function returns the position of an exact match, whatever the array order. If the match_type input is 1, the position of an approximate match is returned, assuming the array is in ascending order. Otherwise, with match_type = −1, the function returns an approximate match assuming that the array is in descending order.

In Figure 2.8, the call values in column G are in ascending order. To find the position in the array that matches value 9.73, the formula in D22 is:

$$=MATCH(C21,G17:G27,1)$$

which returns the position 6 in the array G17:G27.

The function INDEX(array, row_num, column_num) returns a value from within an array, the row number and column number having been specified. Thus the row and column numbers in cells C25 and C26 ensure that the INDEX expression in Figure 2.9 returns the value in the sixth row of the second column of the array F17:G27.

	A	B	C	D	E	F	G	H
15	**Black-Scholes Call Value Lookup Table**				=VLOOKUP(C17,F17:G27,2)			
16						Volatility	BS Call Value	
17		Volatility	**20%**			15%	8.63	
18		VLOOKUP		9.73		16%	8.84	
19						17%	9.05	
20						18%	9.27	
21		call value	9.73			19%	9.50	
22		MATCH		6		20%	9.73	
23						21%	9.96	
24				=MATCH(C21,G17:G27,1)		22%	10.19	
25		row	6			23%	10.43	
26		column	2			24%	10.67	
27		INDEX		9.73		25%	10.91	
28								
29				=INDEX(F17:G27,C25,C26)				

Figure 2.9   Function formulas and results in the LookUp sheet

If the array is a single column (or a single row), the unnecessary col_num (or row_num) input is left blank. You can experiment with the way INDEX works on such arrays by varying the inputs into the formula in cell D27.

We make use of VLOOKUP, MATCH and INDEX in the Equities part of the book.

2.5   OTHER FUNCTIONS

When developing spreadsheet formulas, as far as possible we try to develop 'general' formulas whose syntax takes care of related but different cases. For example, the cash flow in any year for any of the bonds shown in Figure 2.10 could be zero, could be a coupon payment or could be a principal plus coupon payment.

	A	B	C	D	E	F	G	H	I
2	**Bond Cashflows**								
3		Bond	Type 1	Type 2	Type 3	Type 4	Type 5		
4		Price	100.0	98.0	95.5	101.0	102.1		
5		Coupon	5	4	3	5	6		
6		Maturity	1	2	2	3	3		
7									
8	**Cash Flows for bonds**		Type 1	Type 2	Type 3	Type 4	Type 5		
9	Initial Cost		**100.0**	98.0	95.5	101.0	102.1		
10	Receipts:								
11	Year	1	**105**	⬅	=IF($B11<C$6,C$5,IF($B11=C$6, 100+C$5,0))				
12	Year	2							
13	Year	3							
14									

Figure 2.10   A general formula with mixed addressing and nested IF functions in Bonds sheet

The IF function gives different outputs for each of two conditions, and a nested IF statement can be constructed to give three outputs (or even more different outputs if further levels of nesting are constructed). The cash flow formula in cell C11 with one level of nesting:

$$=IF(\$B11<C\$6,C\$5,IF(\$B11=C\$6,100+C\$5,0))$$

produces the cash flows for each bond type and in each year when copied through the range C11:H13.

For the type 1 bond, the cash flow depends on the particular year (cell B11) and the bond maturity (C6). If the year is prior to maturity (B11<C6), the cash flow is a coupon payment C5; if maturity has just been reached (B11=C6), the cash flow is principal plus coupon (100+C5); otherwise (B11>C6), the cash flow is zero. The nested IF takes care of the cash flows when the bond is at (or beyond) maturity, and the first condition in the outer IF takes care of the coupon payments.

The formula is written with 'mixed addressing' to ensure that when copied its cell references change appropriately. We write C$6 and C$5 to ensure that when copied down column C, rows 5 and 6 are always referenced for the relevant maturity and premium. However $B11 will change to $B12 and $B13 for the different years. We write $B11, so that when the formula is copied to column D, column B is still accessed for the year, but C$5 and C$6 change to D$5 and D$6.

The additional thought required to produce this general formula is more than repaid in terms of the time saved when replicating the results for a large model.

2.6 AUDITING TOOLS

With cell formulas of any complexity, it helps to have the Auditing buttons to hand, i.e. on a visible toolbar. One way to achieve this from the menubar is via View then Toolbars then Customise. With the Customise dialog box on screen as shown in Figure 2.11, tick the Auditing toolbar, which should then appear.

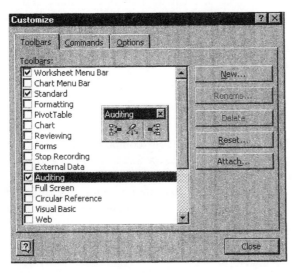

Figure 2.11   Accessing the Auditing toolbar with main buttons

The crucial buttons are those shown in Figure 2.11, namely from left to right, Trace Precedents, Remove All Arrows and Trace Dependents.

Returning to the spreadsheet, select cell C11 and click the Trace Precedents button to show the cells whose values feed into cell C11 as shown in Figure 2.12. (It also shows the cells feeding into F13.) Click Remove All Arrows to clear the lines.

	A	B	C	D	E	F	G
2	Bond Cashflows						
3		Bond	Type 1	Type 2	Type 3	Type 4	Type 5
4		Price	100.0	98.0	95.5	101.0	102.1
5		Coupon	5	4	3	5	6
6		Maturity	1	2	2	3	3
7							
8	Cash Flows for bonds		Type 1	Type 2	Type 3	Type 4	Type 5
9	Initial Cost		100.0	98.0	95.5	101.0	102.1
10	Receipts:						
11	Year	1	105	4	3	5	6
12	Year	2	0	104	103	5	6
13	Year	3	0	0	0	105	106

Figure 2.12   Illustration of Trace Precedents used on the Bonds sheet

The Customise dialog box is where you can tailor toolbars to your liking. If you click the Commands tab, and choose the appropriate category, you can drag tools from the Commands listbox by selecting and dragging buttons onto your toolbars. Conversely, you can remove buttons from your toolbars by selecting and dragging (effectively returning them to the toolbox).

2.7   DATA TABLES

Data Tables help in carrying out a sequence of recalculations of a formula cell without the need to re-enter or copy the formula. The AMFEXCEL workbook contains several examples of Data Tables. We use the calculation of compounding and discounting factors in sheet CompoundDTab to illustrate Data Tables with one input variable, and also with two input variables. A further sheet called BSDTab contains other examples on the use of Data Tables for consolidation.

2.7.1   Setting Up Data Tables with One Input

Figure 2.13 shows the compounding factor for continuous compounding at rate 5% for a period of one year (in cell C10). The equivalent discount factor at rate 5% for one year is in cell D10. The cell formulas for these compounding factors are also shown.

Suppose we want a table of compounding and discounting factors for different time periods, say $t = 1, 2$, up to 10 years. To do this via a Data Table, an appropriate layout is first set up, as shown in row 16 and below.

The formula(s) for recalculation are in the top row of the table (row 16). Thus in D16, the cell formula is simply =C10, which links the cell to the underlying formula in cell C10. Similarly, in E16, the cell formula is =C11. The required list of times for input value t is in column C starting on the row immediately below the formula row. Notice that cell C16 at the intersection of the formula row and the column of values is left blank. The so-called Table Range for the example in Figure 2.13 is C16:E26.

	A	B	C	D	E	F	G
2	Continuous Compounding						
3	Inputs:						
4	Initial value (a)		1				
5	Interest rate-cont (r)		5.0%				
6	Interest rate-p.a.	r_a =exp(r)-1	5.1%				
7	Time (t)		1				
8							
9	Outputs:				=$C$4*EXP($C$5*$C$7)		
10	Compound factor t yrs		1.051				
11	Discount factor t yrs		0.951		=$C$4*EXP(-$C$5*$C$7)		
12							
13			Enter formula(s) for output				
14							
15				compound	discount		
16				1.051	0.951		
17			1				
18	Enter numbers		2				
19	for input variable t		3				
20			4				
21			5				
22			6				
23			7				
24			8				
25			9				
26			10				
27							

Figure 2.13   Layout for Data Table with one input variable in CompoundDTab sheet

Now the spreadsheet is ready for the Data Table calculations, so simply:

- Select the Table range, that is cell range C16:E26
- From the main menu, choose Data then Table
  In dialog box, specify: Column input cell as cell C7
                  then click OK

The results are shown in Figure 2.14, the cells in the table having been formatted to improve legibility. The table cells display as values but actually contain array formulas. These values are *dynamic*, which means they will be re-evaluated if another assumption value, such as the rate r, changes or if individual values of t are changed. Confirm this by changing the interest rate in cell C5 to 6% and watching the cells re-evaluate. To continue, remember to change the interest rate back to 5%.

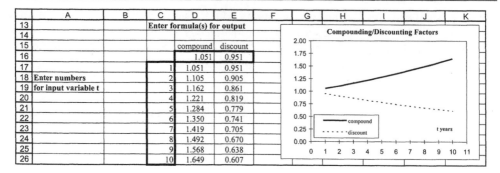

	A	B	C	D	E	F	G	H	I	J	K
13			Enter formula(s) for output								
14											
15				compound	discount						
16				1.051	0.951						
17			1	1.051	0.951						
18	Enter numbers		2	1.105	0.905						
19	for input variable t		3	1.162	0.861						
20			4	1.221	0.819						
21			5	1.284	0.779						
22			6	1.350	0.741						
23			7	1.419	0.705						
24			8	1.492	0.670						
25			9	1.568	0.638						
26			10	1.649	0.607						

Figure 2.14 Data Table with different compounding and discounting factors for different periods

2.7.2 Setting Up Data Tables with Two Inputs

Suppose we wish to calculate discounting factors (from the formula in cell C11) for different rates of interest as well as different time periods. Once again, the appropriate layout for two inputs must be set up before invoking the Data Table procedure. One possible layout is shown in Figure 2.15.

	A	B	C	D	E	F	G	H	I	J
28		Enter formula for output								
29						interest rate r				
30			0.951	3.0%	3.5%	4.0%	5.0%	5.5%	6.0%	
31	Enter numbers		1							
32	for input variables		2							
33			3							
34			4							
35		time t	5							
36			6							
37			7							
38			8							
39			9							
40			10							

Figure 2.15 Layout for Data Table with two input variables in CompoundDTab sheet

Here the Table area is set up to be range C30:I40. Down the first column are the values for the period t (column input variable) for which discount factors are required (col input). Across row 30 are five values for the interest rate r (row input). The top left-hand cell of the table (C30) contains the formula to be recalculated for all the combinations of interest rate and time. The formula in C30 is =C11, which links to the discount factor formula.
    The steps to get the Data Table data are:

- Select the Table range i.e. C30:I40
- From the menu, choose Data then Table
    In dialog box, specify: Column input cell as cell C7
                        Row input cell as cell C5
                        then click OK

The results are displayed in Figure 2.16. Check that the values for the 5% rate tally with those previously calculated in Figure 2.14.

	A	B	C	D	E	F	G	H	I	J
28		Enter formula for output								
29						interest rate r				
30			0.951	3.0%	3.5%	4.0%	5.0%	5.5%	6.0%	
31	Enter numbers		1	0.970	0.966	0.961	0.951	0.946	0.942	
32	for input variables		2	0.942	0.932	0.923	0.905	0.896	0.887	
33			3	0.914	0.900	0.887	0.861	0.848	0.835	
34			4	0.887	0.869	0.852	0.819	0.803	0.787	
35		time t	5	0.861	0.839	0.819	0.779	0.760	0.741	
36			6	0.835	0.811	0.787	0.741	0.719	0.698	
37			7	0.811	0.783	0.756	0.705	0.680	0.657	
38			8	0.787	0.756	0.726	0.670	0.644	0.619	
39			9	0.763	0.730	0.698	0.638	0.610	0.583	
40			10	0.741	0.705	0.670	0.607	0.577	0.549	

Figure 2.16 Data Table with discount factors for different interest rates and periods

Data Tables are extremely useful for doing a range of what-ifs painlessly. The good news is that the tables automatically adapt to changes in the model. The bad news is that if a sheet contains many Data Tables, their continual recalculation can slow down the speed with which the sheet adapts to other entries or modifications. For this reason, it is possible to switch off automatic recalculation for tables.

Note the following points in setting up Data Tables:

- At present, Excel requires the Data Table input cells to be in the same sheet as the table.
- Data Table cells contain formulas of the array type, e.g. the entries in the table cells take the form {=TABLE(C5,C7)} where C5 and C7 are the input cells. Since these are terms of an array, you cannot edit a single formula in a table.
- To rebuild or expand a Data Table, select all cells containing the {=TABLE()} formula with Edit then Clear All or press Delete.
- Changing the input values and other assumption values causes Data Tables to re-evaluate unless the default calculation method is deliberately changed.

In large models for which a long time is spent in recalculation after every entry in the spreadsheet, the automatic recalculation of Data Tables can be switched off if necessary. To do this:

- Choose Tools then Options
- Select the Calculation tab then choose Automatic except Tables

When automatic recalculation is switched off, pressing the F9 key forces a recalculation of all tables.

If you are familiar with the Black–Scholes formula for option valuation, you may wish to consolidate your knowledge of Data Tables by setting up the three tables suggested in the BSDTab sheet. This is equivalent to examining the sensitivity of the Black–Scholes call value to the current share price S, and to various other inputs.

2.8 XY CHARTS

Excel provides many types of charts, but for mathematical, scientific and financial purposes, the XY (Scatter) chart is preferable. Where unambiguous, we refer to this type simply as an XY chart. The important point is that the XY chart has both the X and Y axes numerically scaled. In all other two-axis chart types (including the Line chart), only the vertical axis is numerically scaled, the horizontal X axis being for labels.

Creating an XY chart is handled by the Chart Wizard which proceeds through four steps referred to as Chart Type, Source Data, Chart Options and Chart Location. Given that we shall almost always be creating XY charts, embedded in the spreadsheet, the most important of the four steps is the second, Source Data. The steps are discussed for the results of the Data Table with one input described in section 2.7.1 and illustrated in Figure 2.14. The Data Table results to be charted are in range C17:E26 of the Compound-DTab sheet, column C containing the x values against which columns D and E are to be plotted. Having selected the data to be charted, the steps are:

1. Click the Chart Wizard button on the main toolbar. (It looks like a small bar chart.) In the Step 1 dialog box (in Figure 2.17), choose the 'Chart Type'; here XY (Scatter), subtype smoothed Line without markers. Click the button 'to view sample'. If OK, continue by clicking the Next button.

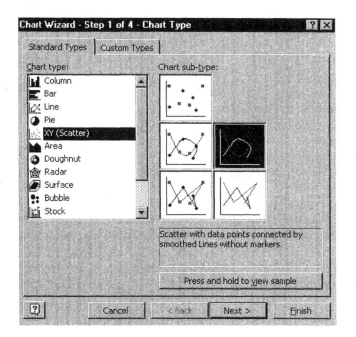

Chart Wizard button

Figure 2.17   Dialog box for specifying the Chart Type

2. In the Step 2 dialog box, check that the correct 'Source Data' is specified on the Data Range sheet, noting that Excel will interpret this block as three column series. Click the Series tab on which the X and Y values are specified for Series1. Click in the Name box and add a name for the currently activated series, either by selecting a spreadsheet cell or by typing in a name (compound). Figure 2.18 shows Series2 being re-named 'discount', the entry in cell E15. Click on the Next button to continue.

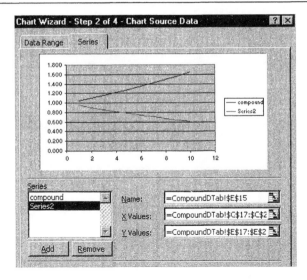

Figure 2.18   Dialog box for specifying the X and Y values in the Source Data

3. In the Step 3 dialog box, set up the 'Chart Options' such as titles, gridlines, appearance or not of legends, etc. For our chart, it is sufficient to add titles and switch off gridlines, as in Figure 2.19. Continue by clicking the Next button.

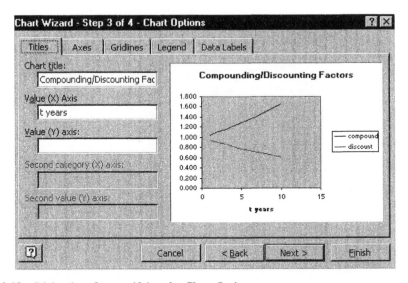

Figure 2.19   Dialog box for specifying the Chart Options

4. In the Step 4 dialog box, decide the 'Chart Location'. A chart can be created either as an object on the spreadsheet (an embedded chart) or on a separate chart sheet. Often it is preferable to have an embedded chart to see the effect in the chart of data changes, as is the case shown here in Figure 2.20.

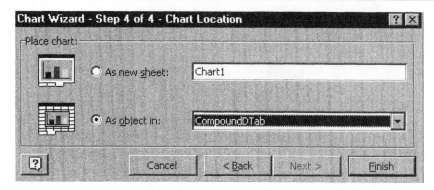

Figure 2.20   Dialog box for specifying the Chart Location

For a more professional look, the raw chart shown in Figure 2.21 needs certain cosmetic work to improve its appearance, the main changes being to Format the Plot area to a plain background (None), to work on the axes via Format Axis, similarly the Titles and Legends. Frequently the scales on axes, the font size for titles, etc. and size of chart area need changing. The plots of the data series may need to show the individual points (which can be achieved by activating the data series and reformatting). By modifying the raw chart, a more finished version such as that shown as part of Figure 2.14 can be achieved.

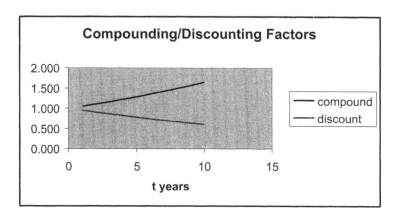

Figure 2.21   Raw chart produced by the Chart Wizard

2.9   ACCESS TO DATA ANALYSIS AND SOLVER

Excel has some additional modules which are available if a full installation of the package has occurred but may be missing if a space-saving installation was done. We use both Solver and the Analysis ToolPak regression routine, so it is worth checking on the Tools menu that both are available. See Figure 2.22 which includes both Solver and Data

Analysis options. If either is missing from the Tools menu, click on the Add-Ins option (also on the Tools menu). Check that Analysis ToolPak, Analysis ToolPak–VBA and Solver are ticked in the Add-Ins dialog box as shown in Figure 2.22, then click OK. As a result, you should see both Solver and Data Analysis on the Tools menu.

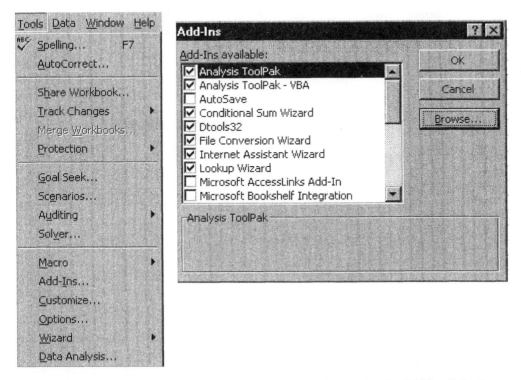

Figure 2.22   Tools menu with Data Analysis and Solver available, also the Add-Ins dialog box

Using Solver is best described in the context of an optimisation problem, so this is postponed until section 6.5 of the Equities part of the book where it is used to find optimum portfolio weights.

Before tackling regression analysis using functions and via the Analysis ToolPak, we briefly look at range names, which are useful for selecting and referencing large ranges of data.

2.10   USING RANGE NAMES

Figure 2.23 shows the top part of returns data for ShareA and Index in the Beta sheet of AMFEXCEL. Our purpose in the next section is to regress the Share returns on the Index returns to see if there is a relationship. To specify the calculation routines, it helps to have 'names' for the cell ranges containing the data, say ShareA for the data range B5:B64 and Index for the index returns in C5:C65.

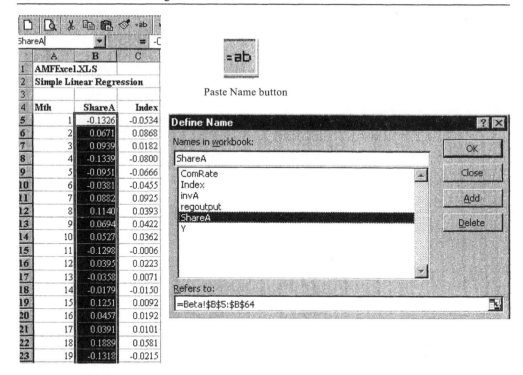

Figure 2.23   Data range with name, the Paste Name button and the Define Name dialog box

If the range to be named is selected, the desired name can be entered in the 'namebox' shown to the left just below the main menu bar, as illustrated in Figure 2.23. Thereafter the name ShareA is attached to range B5:B64 in the Beta sheet. Alternatively, the selected range can be named by choosing Insert then Name then Define, adding the name ShareA in the dialog box that appears (also in Figure 2.23). Thereafter, the returns range can be selected or referenced by name, for example by choosing the name ShareA from the namebox or in functions by using the Paste Name button.

2.11   REGRESSION

We assume that the reader is broadly familiar with simple (two-variable) regression analysis, which we shall employ in the Equities part of the book. Our purpose here is to outline how Excel can be applied to carry out the necessary computations. In fact, there are several ways of doing regression with Excel, the main division being between using Excel functions and applying the regression routine from the Analysis ToolPak. We illustrate these two main alternatives for simple regression using the Share and Index returns data in the Beta sheet of the workbook, first using the Excel functions and second via the Data Analysis Regression procedure. If you are unfamiliar with these functions and procedures, the Beta sheet provides a suitable layout for experimentation.

Excel provides individual functions for the most frequently required regression statistics. Figure 2.24 shows the intercept and slope functions that make up the regression equation and two measures of fit, namely R-squared and the residual standard deviation (labelled STEYX for 'standard error of Y given X'). Since the data ranges have been named, their names can be 'pasted in' to the Function palette using the Paste Name button. The functions are dynamic in that they change if the data (in ranges ShareA and Index) alters.

	E	F	G	H	I
29	**Excel regression functions**				
30					
31	INTERCEPT	-0.0013	=INTERCEPT(ShareA,Index)		
32	SLOPE	1.5065	=SLOPE(ShareA,Index)		
33	RSQ	0.4755	=RSQ(ShareA,Index)		
34	STEYX	0.0595	=STEYX(ShareA,Index)		

Figure 2.24   Excel functions for regression in the Beta sheet

As well as the individual functions, there is also the LINEST array function, which takes as inputs the two columns of returns and outputs the essential regression quantities in array form. Note that it is important to select a suitably sized range for the output before entering the LINEST syntax. Usually for simple regression a cell range of five rows by two columns is required. Figure 2.25 shows the function LINEST(ShareA,Index,,1) being specified in the Function palette, the output range of F40:G44 having been selected. The Const input is left blank and the Stats input ensures that the full array of statistical results is returned.

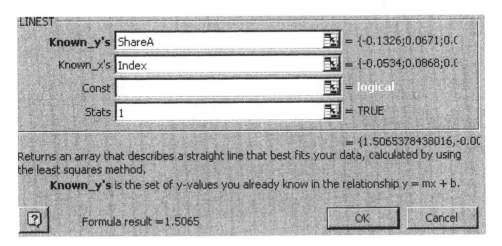

Figure 2.25   Building the LINEST array function in the formula palette

The array output is shown (with annotation) in Figure 2.26. In addition to the slope and intercept (here labelled Beta and Alpha respectively), LINEST also provides the standard errors of estimates and a rudimentary analysis of variance (or ANOVA).

	E	F	G	H	I
38	**Output from Linest (Remember Ctrl+Shift+Enter)**				
39					
40	Beta	1.5065	-0.0013	Alpha	
41	Beta (SE)	0.2077	0.0078	Alpha (SE)	
42	RSQ	0.4755	0.0595	STEYX	
43	F	52.5873	58.0000	N-2	
44	Regression SS	0.1860	0.2051	Residual SS	
45					

Figure 2.26   Array output from the LINEST function used on the returns data in the Beta sheet

Next, we examine the regression routine contained in the Analysis ToolPak. To set this up, choose Tools, then Data Analysis, then Regression, to see the dialog box shown in Figure 2.27. Once again the Y and X ranges can be referenced by selection or if named, by 'pasting in' the names. It is usually more convenient to specify a top left-hand cell for the output range in the data sheet rather than accept the default (of results dumped in a new sheet).

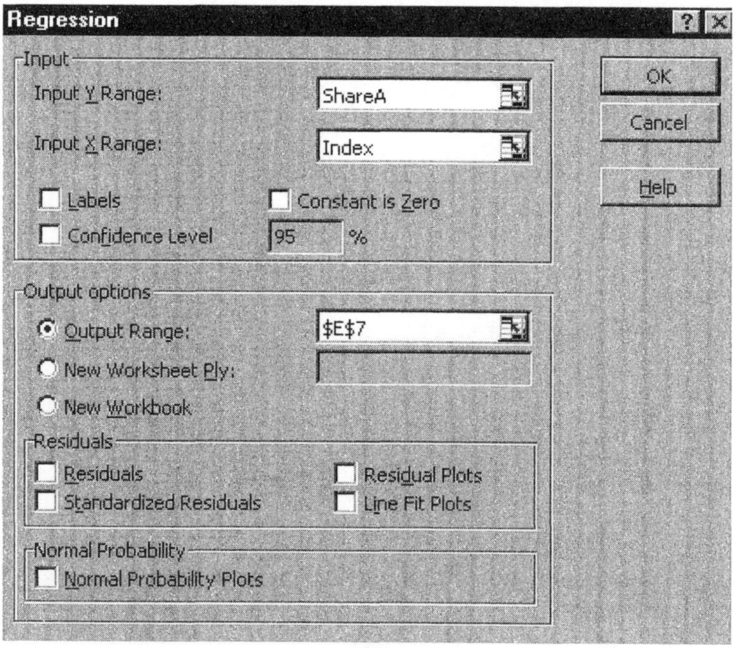

Figure 2.27   Specifying the Analysis ToolPak regression calculations and output option

The results are shown in Figure 2.28, the intercept and slope of the regression equation being in cells F23 and F24. The R-squared and Standard Error (the residual standard deviation) in cells F12 and F13 are measures of fit. The output is static, that is, it is a dump of numbers no longer connected to the original data. If any of the input data changes, the analysis does not adjust, but has to be manually recalculated.

	E	F	G	H	I	J	K
7	SUMMARY OUTPUT						
8							
9	*Regression Statistics*						
10	Multiple R	0.6896					
11	R Square	0.4755					
12	Adjusted R Square	0.4665					
13	Standard Error	0.0595					
14	Observations	60					
15							
16	ANOVA						
17		*df*	*SS*	*MS*	*F*	*Sig F*	
18	Regression	1	0.1860	0.1860	52.5873	1.11E-09	
19	Residual	58	0.2051	0.0035			
20	Total	59	0.3911				
21							
22		*Coefficients*	*Std Error*	*t Stat*	*P-value*	*Lower 95%*	*Upper 95%*
23	Intercept	-0.0013	0.0078	-0.164	0.870	-0.017	0.014
24	X Variable 1	1.5065	0.2077	7.252	0.000	1.091	1.922

Figure 2.28   Results from Analysis ToolPak regression routine shown in the Beta sheet

To illustrate the dynamic nature of functions in contrast, suppose that the index for month 4 was subsequently corrected to value 0.08 (not −0.08 as currently in cell C8). If the entry is changed, the functions in F31:F34 and F40:G44 update instantaneously, so that for example, RSQ drops from 0.4755 to 0.3260. To update the Analysis ToolPak results, the regression must be run again.

The static nature of the output from the Analysis ToolPak routines makes them less attractive for calculation purposes than the parallel Excel functions. Typically, the routines are written in the old XLM macro language from Excel version 4. More importantly, they cannot easily be incorporated into VBA user-defined functions, in contrast to most of the Excel functions.

2.12   GOAL SEEK

Goal Seek is another of Excel's static procedures. This tool produces a solution that matches a formula cell to a numerical target. For example, in Figure 2.29 there is a discrepancy between the market price (in G8) and the Black–Scholes call value (G4) for an option on a share. (The Black–Scholes value depends on the volatility of the share, and always contains an estimate of future volatility.) Suppose we want to know the size of the volatility that will match the two, or equivalently make the difference between the two (in G9) zero. This is an ideal problem for Goal Seek to solve.

To use Goal Seek on the BSDTab sheet, choose Tools then Goal Seek. Fill in the problem specification as shown in Figure 2.30 and click on OK. The solution produced by Goal Seek is shown in Figure 2.31, namely the volatility needs to be 23% for the Black–Scholes formula value to match the market price.

	A	B	C	D	E	F	G
2	**Black-Scholes Option Values**						
3							
4	Share price (S)		100.00		**Black-Scholes Call Value**		9.73
5	Exercise price (X)		95.00		via user-defined function		
6	Int rate-cont (r)		8.00%				
7	Dividend yield (q)		3.00%				
8	Option life (T, years)		0.50		Market value		10.43
9	Volatility (σ)		20.00%		Difference		0.70
10							

Figure 2.29   BS Call value formula and market price in BSDTab sheet

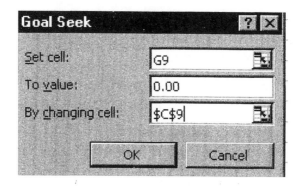

Figure 2.30   Goal Seek settings to find volatility (C9) that matches BS value and market price

	A	B	C	D	E	F	G
2	**Black-Scholes Option Values**						
3							
4	Share price (S)		100.00		**Black-Scholes Call Value**		10.43
5	Exercise price (X)		95.00		via user-defined function		
6	Int rate-cont (r)		8.00%				
7	Dividend yield (q)		3.00%				
8	Option life (T, years)		0.50		Market value		10.43
9	Volatility (σ)		23.00%		Difference		0.00
10							

Figure 2.31   Volatility value produced by Goal Seek making difference (in G9) zero

Goal Seek starts with an initial 'guess', then uses an iterative algorithm to get closer and closer to the solution. Effectively the initial value of the 'changing cell'–here volatility of 20%, is the initial guess. In finding a solution, Goal Seek allows you to vary one input cell, whereas Solver (which is introduced in Chapter 6) allows you to change several input cells.

To consolidate, use Goal Seek in the BSDTab sheet to find the volatility implied by a market price of 9.

2.13   MATRIX ALGEBRA AND RELATED FUNCTIONS

Matrix notation is widely used in algebra, as it provides a compact form of expression for systems of similarly structured equations. Operations with matrices look surprisingly like ordinary algebraic operations, but in particular multiplication of matrices is more complex. Excel contains useful matrix functions, in the Math category, which require a little background knowledge of how matrices behave to get full benefit from them. The following sections explain matrix notation, and describe the operations of transposing, adding, multiplying and inverting matrices. The examples illustrating these operations are in the MatDef sheet of the AMFEXCEL workbook. If you are conversant with matrices, you may wish to jump straight to the summary of matrix functions (section 2.13.7).

2.13.1   Introduction to Matrices

In algebra, rectangular arrays of numbers are referred to as matrices. A single column matrix is usually called a column vector; similarly a single row matrix is called a row vector. In Excel, rectangular blocks of cells are called arrays. All the following blocks of numbers can be considered as matrices:

$$\begin{vmatrix} 2 \\ 4 \end{vmatrix} \quad |6 \quad 7| \quad \begin{vmatrix} -3 & 2 & 7 \\ 2 & 20 & 19 \\ 7 & 9 & 21 \end{vmatrix} \quad \begin{vmatrix} -3 & 2 & 7 \\ 2 & 20 & 19 \\ 7 & 9 & 21 \\ 0 & 13 & 3 \end{vmatrix}$$

where the brackets | | are merely notational. Calling these matrices x, y, A, and B respectively, x is a column vector and y a row vector. Matrix A has three rows and three columns and hence is a square matrix. B is not square since it has four rows and three columns, i.e. B is a 4 by 3 matrix. The numbers of rows, r, and of columns, c, give the dimensions of a matrix sometimes written as $(r \times c)$. For example, if:

$$x = \begin{vmatrix} 2 \\ 4 \end{vmatrix} \text{ and } y = |6 \quad 7|$$

then x has dimensions (2×1) whereas y has dimensions (1×2).

2.13.2   Transposing a Matrix

Transposition of a matrix converts rows into columns (and vice versa). Clearly the transpose of column vector x will be a row vector, denoted as x^T. The spreadsheet extract in Figure 2.32 shows the transposes of column vector x and row vector y.

The TRANSPOSE function applied to the cells of an array returns its transpose. For example, the transpose of the 2 by 1 vector x in cells C4:C5 will have dimensions (1×2). To use the TRANSPOSE function, select the cell range I4:J4 and key in the formula:

$$=\text{TRANSPOSE(C4:C5)}$$

finishing with Ctrl+Shift+Enter pressed simultaneously. The result is shown in Figure 2.32.

	A	B	C	D	E	F	G	H	I	J	K
1	Array Manipulation:										
2									Transposes		
3	array:	dim					array:	dim			
4	x	(2x1)	2				x^T	(1x2)	2	4	
5			4								
6											
7	y	(1x2)	6	7			y^T	(2x1)	6		
8									7		
9		Array Multiplication									
10	xy	(2x2)	12	14			$(xy)^T$	(2x2)	12	24	
11			24	28					14	28	
12											
13	yx	(1x1)	40				$(yx)^T$	(1x1)	40		

Figure 2.32   Matrix operations illustrated in the MatDef sheet

2.13.3   Adding Matrices

Adding two matrices involves adding their corresponding entries. For this to make sense, the arrays being added must have the same dimensions. Whereas **x** and **y** cannot be added, **x** and $\mathbf{y^T}$ do have the same dimensions, 2 by 1, and therefore they can be added, the result being:

$$\mathbf{x} + \mathbf{y^T} = \begin{vmatrix} 2 \\ 4 \end{vmatrix} + \begin{vmatrix} 6 \\ 7 \end{vmatrix} = \begin{vmatrix} 8 \\ 11 \end{vmatrix} = \mathbf{z} \text{ say}$$

To multiply vector **y** by 10 say, every entry of **y** is multiplied by 10. Thus:

$$10\mathbf{y} = 10 * |6 \quad 7| = |60 \quad 70|$$

This is comparable to adding **y** to itself 10 times.

2.13.4   Multiplying Matrices

For two matrices to be multiplied they have to have a common dimension, that is, the number of columns for one must equal the number of rows for the other. The shorthand expression for this is 'dimensional conformity'. For the product **xy** the columns of **x** must match the rows of **y**, (2×1) times (1×2), resulting in a (2×2) matrix as output.

In Figure 2.32, the product **xy** in cells C10:D11 has elements calculated from:

$$\begin{vmatrix} 2 \\ 4 \end{vmatrix} \quad |6 \quad 7| = \begin{vmatrix} 2*6 & 2*7 \\ 4*6 & 4*7 \end{vmatrix} = \begin{vmatrix} 12 & 14 \\ 24 & 28 \end{vmatrix}$$

i.e. the row 1, column 1 element of product **xy** comes from multiplying the individual elements of row 1 of **x** by the elements of column 1 of **y**, etc.

In contrast, the product **yx** has dimensions (1×2) times (2×1), that is (1×1), i.e. it consists of a single element. Looking at product **yx** in cell C13, this element is computed as:

$$|6 \quad 7| \quad \begin{vmatrix} 2 \\ 4 \end{vmatrix} = |6*2 + 7*4| = |40|$$

These results demonstrate that for matrices, **xy** is not the same as **yx**. The order of multiplication is critical.

The MMULT array function returns the product of two matrices, called array1 and array2. So to get the elements of the (2×2) matrix product **xy**, select the 2 by 2 cell range, C10:D11 and key in or use the Paste Function button and build the expression in the Formula palette:

$$=MMULT(C4:C5,C7:D7)$$

remembering to enter it with Ctrl+Shift+Enter.

If ranges C4:C5 and C7:D7 are named **x** and **y** respectively, then the formula to be keyed in simplifies to:

$$=MMULT(x,y)$$

Consider two more arrays:

$$\mathbf{C} = \begin{vmatrix} 12 & 4 \\ 3 & 13 \end{vmatrix} \text{ and } \mathbf{D} = \begin{vmatrix} 16 & 19 & -2 \\ 5 & 12 & 14 \end{vmatrix}$$

The dimensions of **C** and **D** are (2×2) and (2×3) respectively, so since the number of columns in **C** is matched by the number of rows in **D**, the product **CD** can be obtained, its dimensions being (2×3). So:

$$\mathbf{CD} = \begin{vmatrix} (12*16+4*5) & (12*19+4*12) & (-12*2+4*14) \\ (3*16+13*5) & (3*19+13*12) & (-3*2+13*14) \end{vmatrix} = \begin{vmatrix} 212 & 276 & 32 \\ 113 & 213 & 176 \end{vmatrix}$$

However, the product **DC** cannot be formed because of incompatible dimensions (the number of columns in **D** does not equal the number of rows in **C**). In general, the multiplication of matrices is not commutative, so that usually $\mathbf{CD} \neq \mathbf{DC}$, as in this case.

If **C** and **D** are the names of the 2 by 2 and 2 by 3 arrays respectively, then the cell formula:

$$=MMULT(C,D)$$

will produce the elements of the 2 by 3 product array.

2.13.5 Matrix Inversion

A square matrix **I** with ones for all its diagonal entries and zeros for all its off-diagonal elements is called an identity matrix. Thus:

$$\mathbf{I} = \begin{vmatrix} 1 & 0 & 0 & \cdots & 0 \\ 0 & 1 & 0 & \cdots & 0 \\ 0 & 0 & 1 & \cdots & 0 \\ \cdots & \cdots & \cdots & \cdots & \cdots \\ 0 & 0 & 0 & \cdots & 1 \end{vmatrix} \quad \text{is an identity matrix}$$

Suppose **D** is the (2×3) matrix used above, and **I** is the (2×2) identity matrix, then:

$$\mathbf{ID} = \begin{vmatrix} 1 & 0 \\ 0 & 1 \end{vmatrix} * \begin{vmatrix} 16 & 19 & -2 \\ 5 & 12 & 14 \end{vmatrix} = \begin{vmatrix} 16 & 19 & -2 \\ 5 & 12 & 14 \end{vmatrix} = \mathbf{D}$$

Multiplying any matrix by an identity matrix of appropriate dimension has no effect on the original matrix (and is therefore similar to multiplying by one).

Now suppose **A** is a square matrix of dimension n, that is an n by n matrix. Then, the square matrix $\mathbf{A}^{-1}$ (also of dimension n) is called the inverse of **A** if:

$$\mathbf{A}^{-1}\mathbf{A} = \mathbf{A}\mathbf{A}^{-1} = \mathbf{I}$$

For example, if:

$$\mathbf{A} = \begin{vmatrix} -3 & 2 & 7 \\ 2 & 20 & 19 \\ 7 & 9 & 21 \end{vmatrix} \text{ then } \mathbf{A}^{-1} = \begin{vmatrix} -0.175 & -0.015 & 0.072 \\ -0.064 & 0.079 & -0.050 \\ 0.086 & -0.029 & 0.045 \end{vmatrix}$$

and

$$\mathbf{A}\mathbf{A}^{-1} = \mathbf{I} = \begin{vmatrix} 1 & 0 & 0 \\ 0 & 1 & 0 \\ 0 & 0 & 1 \end{vmatrix}$$

Finding the inverse of a matrix can be a lot of work. Fortunately, the MINVERSE function does this for us. For example, to get the inverse of matrix **A** shown in the spreadsheet extract in Figure 2.33, select the 3 by 3 cell range I17:K19 and enter the array formula:

$$=\text{MINVERSE(C17:E19)}$$

You can check that the result is the inverse of **A** by performing the matrix multiplication $\mathbf{A}\mathbf{A}^{-1}$.

	A	B	C	D	E	F	G	H	I	J	K	L	M	N	O	P	Q
16	array:	dim					array:	dim									
17	A	(3x3)	-3	2	7		A⁻¹	(3x3)	-0.175	-0.015	0.072		AA⁻¹	1.00	0.00	0.00	
18			2	20	19				-0.064	0.079	-0.050			0.00	1.00	0.00	
19			7	9	21				0.086	-0.029	0.045			0.00	0.00	1.00	
20																	
21	b	(3x1)	20				x = A⁻¹b	(3x1)	-3.4355								
22			-5						-1.6772								
23			0						1.8640								
24																	

Figure 2.33   Matrix inversion shown in the MatDef sheet

2.13.6 Solving Systems of Simultaneous Linear Equations

One use for the inverse of a matrix is in solving a set of equations such as the following:

$$-3x_1 + 2x_2 + 7x_3 = 20$$

$$2x_1 + 20x_2 + 19x_3 = -5$$

$$7x_1 + 9x_2 + 21x_3 = 0$$

These can be written in matrix notation as $\mathbf{Ax} = \mathbf{b}$ where:

$$\mathbf{A} = \begin{vmatrix} -3 & 2 & 7 \\ 2 & 20 & 19 \\ 7 & 9 & 21 \end{vmatrix} \quad \mathbf{b} = \begin{vmatrix} 20 \\ -5 \\ 0 \end{vmatrix} \text{ and } \mathbf{x} = \begin{vmatrix} x_1 \\ x_2 \\ x_3 \end{vmatrix}$$

The solution is given by premultiplying both sides of the equation by the inverse of $\mathbf{A}$:

$$\mathbf{A}^{-1}\mathbf{A}\mathbf{x} = \mathbf{A}^{-1}\mathbf{b}, \text{ so } \mathbf{I}\mathbf{x} = \mathbf{A}^{-1}\mathbf{b} \quad \text{i.e.} \quad \mathbf{x} = \mathbf{A}^{-1}\mathbf{b}$$

In Figure 2.33, the solution vector $\mathbf{x}$ is obtained from the matrix multiplication function in cell range I21:I23 in the form:

$$=\text{MMULT}(I17:K19,C21:C23)$$

Not every system of linear equations has a solution, and in special cases there may be many solutions. The set $\mathbf{A}\mathbf{x} = \mathbf{b}$ has a unique solution only if the matrix $\mathbf{A}$ is square and has an inverse $\mathbf{A}^{-1}$. In general, the solution is given by $\mathbf{x} = \mathbf{A}^{-1}\mathbf{b}$.

2.13.7 Summary of Excel's Matrix Functions

In summary, Excel has functions to transpose matrices, to multiply matrices and to invert square matrices. The relevant functions are these:

TRANSPOSE(array)	returns the transpose of an array
MMULT(array1, array2)	returns the matrix product of two arrays
MINVERSE(array)	returns the matrix inverse of an array

Because these functions produce arrays as outputs, the size of the resulting array must be assessed in advance. Having 'selected' an appropriately sized range of cells, the formula is keyed in (or obtained via the Paste Function button and built in the Formula palette). It is entered in the selected cell range with the combination of keys Ctrl+Shift+Enter (instead of simply Enter). If this fails, keep the output range of cells 'selected', press the Edit key (F2), edit the formula if necessary, then press Ctrl+Shift+Enter again.

To consolidate, try the matrix exercises in the sheet MatExs.

We make extensive use of the matrix functions in the Equities part of the book, both for calculations in the spreadsheet and as part of VBA user-defined functions.

SUMMARY

Excel has an extensive range of functions and procedures. These include mathematical, statistical and lookup functions, as well as much-used procedures such as setting up Data Tables and displaying results in XY charts.

Access to the functions is handled through the Paste Function button and the function inputs specified on the Formula palette. The use of range names simplifies the specification of cell ranges, especially when the ranges are sizeable. Range names can be used on the Formula palette.

Facilities on the Auditing toolbar, in particular the Trace Precedents, Trace Dependents and Remove Arrows buttons are invaluable in examining formula cells.

It helps to be familiar with the range of Excel functions because they can easily be incorporated into user-defined functions, economising on the amount of VBA code that has to be written.

Care is required in using array functions. It helps to decide in advance the size of the cell range appropriate for the array results. Then having selected the correct cell range, the formula is entered with the keystroke combination Ctrl+Shift+Enter.

The built-in functions are volatile, that is they update if their input data changes. In contrast, procedures such as Goal Seek and Solver and the routines in the Analysis ToolPak are static. The results form a 'data dump' not linked to the originating data. Therefore if the input data changes, the procedures have to be repeated.

3
Introduction to VBA

This chapter introduces the use of VBA and macros within Excel, and attempts to do so in the context of examples where VBA enhances spreadsheet functionality. Whilst not intended as a full introduction to programming in VBA, it argues the case for mastering some VBA, touches on the 'object-oriented' focus of the language, and suggests an incremental approach to mastering the code. Most of the examples in this chapter involve simple code, the first 'hands-on' examples being in section 3.3.3. However, in section 3.6, several applications are developed more fully and some fruitful areas for macros identified. These include subroutines to produce charts, to calculate and display normal probability plots, and to generate the efficient frontier. A related workbook, VBSUB.xls, contains the examples discussed in the chapter and can be used for reference. However, the reader is advised to start by entering code in a new workbook (without opening the VBSUB workbook).

Throughout the book, the VBA coding used for routines is reviewed. The functions and macros developed in subsequent chapters build on the basic foundations laid down in this and the next chapter.

3.1 ADVANTAGES OF MASTERING VBA

Macros form an important part of an experienced user's palette for two main reasons: they are an excellent way to control repeated calculations, and they can be written to assist third-party users who might have less familiarity with spreadsheets. From our perspective, the main objective of mastering VBA is to be able to automate calculations using functions and macros. Spreadsheet models are more robust if complicated sequences of calculations are replaced by function entries. Excel provides an excellent range of functions and VBA can be used to extend that range. In addition, VBA macros are a useful way to produce charts and to automate repeated operations, such as simulation. In both instances, the resulting procedures are programs in VBA, but in the first case, they are user-defined functions and in the second, macros (or subroutines). Whilst the code is largely common to both types of procedure, this chapter focuses on writing macros, whereas Chapter 4 deals solely with user-defined functions.

The programming language used in Excel is called Visual Basic for Applications or VBA for short. The word *basic* confirms that the program is derived from the ancient BASIC mainframe language, which means VBA tends to be relatively inefficient for tasks involving very large volumes of computations. As PCs become ever more powerful and spreadsheets accumulate many features, the boundary between spreadsheets and dedicated computational packages has become blurred. The question to pose at this stage is what is the best way to achieve a task, such as finding the 'efficient frontier', or simulating the performance of a stock, or evaluating the 'eigenvectors' of a matrix. The answer will depend on the aims of the user. The spreadsheet will be slower, but the calculation process will be easier to follow. In contrast, the dedicated package will be faster, but the process of calculation more remote and less comprehensible.

It is important to match your usage of VBA to the task in hand, and to be selective in the parts of VBA that you use, bearing in mind that spreadsheets do not provide the answer to all questions. Using VBA subroutines to automate repetitive tasks is efficient programming; using VBA to create your own simple functions is efficient; but trying to program bullet-proof interaction for a novice user accessing a complex spreadsheet model seems like the road to misery. Whilst seasoned applications programmers can probably tackle this task, the pertinent question is should you? VBA is not a panacea for all programming tasks, and should be used selectively since more efficient computing methods exist for some computationally intensive tasks.

Excel's macro recorder translates user keystrokes into VBA code and can be used to suggest appropriate coding. While it is possible to use the recorder and remain ignorant of the underlying VBA code, the aim of this chapter is to provide some explanations and demonstrate practical applications, thus allowing you to become a more efficient user of the whole Excel package. Probably the best approach at first is to use the recorder to generate rudimentary code, then to selectively edit (or rewrite) the results as you become more familiar with VBA.

It is important to be aware of the distinction between VBA subroutines and functions. Whilst both are distinct, named blocks of source code, the raison d'être of functions is to return values. Typically subroutines accept no inputs, but they carry out a sequence of spreadsheet commands (which may use values from cells in the spreadsheet, and change the values in particular cells). In contrast, functions can accept inputs (or 'arguments'), they carry out a series of predominantly numerical calculations away from the spreadsheet, and return a single value (or a single array). However, for both subroutines and functions, the spreadsheet is the first development tool.

3.2 OBJECT-ORIENTED ASPECTS OF VBA

A few concepts that you need to grasp follow from the fact that VBA is an **'object-oriented'** programming language. Each Excel object represents a feature or a piece of functionality in Excel, e.g. workbooks, worksheets, ranges, charts, scenarios, etc. are all Excel objects as is Excel itself (the Application object). You program in VBA to manipulate the properties and apply methods to Excel objects.

Many statements can be made about objects and VBA, but essentially they can be condensed into four rather cryptic statements. Textbooks and VBA help screens abound with explanations, but overall, these tend to be confusing.

The first statement is *Objects come in collections*. For example, the Workbooks collection consists of all open workbooks, similarly the Worksheets (or Sheets) collection (all the sheets in a workbook), the Scenarios collection (all scenarios associated with a particular sheet), the Charts collection (all the charts on a sheet), etc. However, some objects come as singular objects (i.e. collections of one member only), for example, Excel has only one Application object (itself) and for any cell on the spreadsheet there is only one Font object (although this object has several properties, such as Name, Size, etc.). These are singular objects that are referenced directly, e.g. by simply writing Application. or Font. (the object followed by a 'fullstop'). Individual objects in collections are referenced by indexing the collection either by number (1, 2, 3 . . .) or by name, e.g. Workbooks(1). or Sheets("inputs"). The Range object is by definition a singular object, but notice that it is referenced in a way that is similar to that of a collection, either by name or by address, e.g. Range("data"). or Range("A1:B20").

The second statement is *Objects are arranged in a hierarchy*. The following sequence illustrates the hierarchy of objects in Excel. It shows how the cell range named 'data' in sheet 'inputs' of the Model.xls workbook is referenced via its position in the hierarchy:

```
Application.Workbooks("Model.xls").Sheets("inputs").Range("data")
```

It is not necessary to use the full hierarchy, as long as the identification of the cell range (here named 'data') is unique. If the Model.xls workbook is the active book when the VBA code is executing, then Sheets("inputs").Range("data") is adequate; or referencing the active workbook explicitly:

```
ActiveWorkbook.Sheets("inputs").Range("data")
```

Similarly, if only the Model.xls book is open and the 'inputs' sheet is currently active, then ActiveSheet.Range("data") is adequate and simpler to write.

The third statement is *Objects have properties*. Properties are the attributes of an object, the values or settings that describe the object. VBA can be used either to set a property or to get a property setting. Property values are usually numbers, text, True or False and so on. You can control Excel objects by using VBA to change their properties. An example is:

```
Application.ScreenUpdating = False
```

This line of code stops the Excel screen updating during the running of a macro. ScreenUpdating is a property of the Application object, taking values True/False.

Another pair of examples is:

```
Range("B23").Name = "month2"
Range("B23").Value = 4000
```

which gives cell B23 the name 'month2' and value 4000. The syntax follows the 'Object.Property' style. In these examples, 'Application' and 'Range' refer to objects, whereas 'ScreenUpdating', 'Name' and 'Value' are properties of the objects. The following example takes a setting from a spreadsheet cell, and assigns it to variable 'firstval':

```
firstval = Range("B23").Value
```

The fourth statement is *Objects have methods*. Methods are a set of predefined activities that an object can carry out or have applied to it. Here are some examples of methods applied to Range objects:

Range("A1:B3").Select	which selects the cell range A1:B3
Range("A1:B10").Copy	which copies the cell range A1:B10
Range("storerange").PasteSpecial	which pastes the contents of the Clipboard from the previous command to cell 'storerange'

The syntax follows the 'Object.Method' style. In the above examples, the objects are instances of the 'Range' object while 'Select', 'Copy' and 'PasteSpecial' are methods which act on the objects. Workbook objects and Worksheet objects also have methods, for example:

```
Workbooks("Model.xls").Activate      makes Model.xls the active workbook
Sheets("inputs").Delete               deletes the sheet called 'inputs'
```

There are some minor exceptions to the above explanation. But if you record your code, you never need to worry about the distinction between properties and methods. You can also refer to the Excel Object Browser in the Visual Basic Editor to check the correct syntax to accompany specific objects.

3.3   STARTING TO WRITE VBA MACROS

Mastering any language is a cumulative process, part formal learning of rules, part informal experimenting and testing out coding ideas. VBA code is developed in the Visual Basic Editor, Excel's code writing environment. Since Excel 97, this has been enlarged and enhanced somewhat from the Excel 5/7 version, providing more support for writing code. We start by examining the code for some simple examples. VBA's MsgBox function is introduced as it provides a simple mechanism for displaying calculated values and feeding back simple diagnostic messages. We show how to generate code using the recorder and contrast the results with written code. The advantages of the dual approach of recording and editing are outlined.

3.3.1   Some Simple Examples of VBA Subroutines

A subroutine is a standalone segment of VBA code; it constitutes the basic building block in programming. The subroutine performs actions and consists of a series of VBA statements enclosed by Sub and End Sub statements. Its name is followed by empty parentheses (unless it takes an argument passed to it from another subroutine).

For example, the LinkOne() subroutine links the contents of one cell to another on the active sheet. The code starts with the Sub keyword, followed by the macro name, LinkOne. A comment statement outlines the purpose of the macro. (Text preceded by an apostrophe is ignored in processing, so this is a useful way to add explanatory comments to the code.) The first statement uses the Value property of the Range object, the second the Formula property:

```
Sub LinkOne()
'enters a value in B3, then links cell B4 to B3
Range("B3").Value = 4000
Range("B4").Formula = "=b3"
End Sub
```

The LinkOne routine works on the active sheet. However, if there is ambiguity about the target sheet for these operations, the cell's range reference should be more precise. The subroutine below sets the value of cell B3 in sheet 'Inputs' to 4000. The value in cell B3 is then copied into cell B4 in the same sheet:

```
Sub LinkTwo()
'enters a value in B3, then links cell B4 to B3 on Inputs sheet
Sheets("Inputs").Range("B3").Value = 4000
Sheets("Inputs").Range("B4").Formula = "=b3"
End Sub
```

Or if the actions are to take place on the currently active sheet, ActiveSheet. can be used instead of Sheets("Inputs").

The forgoing examples illustrate the type of code which Excel's recorder would generate in response to actual keystrokes. Contrast it with the code for the subroutine Factorial below. This subroutine computes a factorial (denoted fac) for the number in cell B5 (referred to as num) and enters the result in cell C5. It has two new features. Firstly, the code uses variables, i, fac and num, which subsequently are assigned values. Secondly, the factorial is computed by repeated multiplication in a For...Next loop with index i. (The counter i starts at value 1 and increases by 1 each time it passes through the loop until its value goes above the upper limit, num.)

```
Sub Factorial()
'calculates the factorial of a number in B5
num = Range("B5").Value
fac = 1
For i = 1 To num
    fac = i * fac
Next i
Range("C5").Value = fac
End Sub
```

Other than using and returning values to the spreadsheet, this code is straightforward Basic and has little to do with Excel per se. This type of code must be entered manually.

3.3.2   MsgBox for Interaction

In general, a subroutine gets its input either from spreadsheet cells or from the user (via the screen) and its outputs are either pasted into the workbook or displayed to the user. Two useful display screens are generated by the VBA built-in functions, MsgBox() and InputBox(). The simpler of these, MsgBox(), displays a message on screen then pauses for user response, as is illustrated below:

```
Sub MsgBoxDemo1()
MsgBox "Click OK to continue"
End Sub
```

The message (or 'prompt') is within the quotation marks and must be present. Brackets around the prompt are optional in this simple instance of MsgBox. However, when an answer is required from MsgBox, the brackets are required to indicate that MsgBox is being used as a function. The MsgBox display can be made more useful if a variable is 'concatenated' (or 'chained') on to the prompt using ampersand (&). For example, in the Factorial subroutine, the result could be communicated to the user with the statement:

```
MsgBox "Factorial is "& fac
```

as in the code below. In this version, the user supplies the number via an InputBox. This VBA function pops up a dialog box displaying a message and returns the user's input, here called num. The argument in the InputBox syntax below is the message displayed, also known as the 'prompt'. Here InputBox has brackets to indicate it is being used 'as a function', that is, to return an answer, num. The factorial is built up multiplicatively in a For...Next loop:

```
Sub Factorial()
'calculates the factorial of a number
fac = 1
num = InputBox("Enter number ")
For i = 1 To num
fac = i * fac
Next i
MsgBox "Factorial is "& fac
End Sub
```

We use this simple factorial example to explore elements of programming macros in section 3.4.

3.3.3   The Writing Environment

The Visual Basic Editor (referred to as the VBE) is where subroutines are written, tested out and debugged. We assume Excel's workbook environment, its menu, commands and toolbars are familiar territory. When developing VBA procedures, it helps to have Excel's Visual Basic toolbar visible in the Excel window (shown in Figure 3.1). As with other toolbars, this has buttons which are programmed to carry out sequences of relevant menu commands, here Tools Macro commands such as Run Macro, Record Macro and the VBE (first, second and fourth from left), etc.

Figure 3.1   Excel's Visual Basic toolbar

VBA code is written (or recorded) not in worksheets but in Module sheets. In Excel 97 (and subsequent versions) these appear in a different window, the Visual Basic (VB) window, and the process of developing macros involves switching to and fro between the Excel and VB windows (using the keystroke combinations Alt+Tab or Alt+F11) or the equivalent buttons.

To try this out for yourself, open a new workbook in Excel, choose Tools then Macro then Visual Basic Editor to go to the VB window. (Or simply click the VBE button on the VB toolbar.) The VB window consists of the Project Explorer and the Properties window as well as the Code window (which is not usually present until the workbook has Modules). The Code window is where programs are written and/or keystrokes recorded. From the VB window you can refer to the Excel Object Browser to check the correct VBA syntax to accompany specific objects. (In the VB window, choose View to access the Object Browser, then choose Excel in the top left-hand References textbox.)

The VBE also contains numerous debugging and editing tools that can be accessed from its command bar or via its own specialist toolbars. More detail on the Visual Basic Environment is at the end of the chapter in Appendix 3A (and could be skimmed now).

3.3.4   Entering Code and Executing Macros

VBA code is entered on a Module sheet. To add one to the workbook, on the VB window menu, choose Insert then Module to get a blank module sheet in the Code window. Begin typing in the Code window, for example:

```
Sub MsgBoxDemo()
MsgBox "Click OK to continue"
End Sub
```

At the end of the first statement, when you press Enter, Excel adds the End Sub statement. You may also notice the 'quick information' feature, which assists with the entry of recognisable bits of syntax.

There are several ways to run the subroutine:

- From the Code window, with the pointer positioned anywhere in the body of the routine's code, choose Run then Sub/UserForm (alternatively click the Run button on the VB Standard toolbar underneath the VB window menu).
- From the Excel window, choose Tools then Macro then Macros, then select MsgBoxDemo macro and Run it or click on the VB toolbar Run button.
- You can also execute the macro using a chosen keyboard shortcut (for example, the combination of Ctrl+Shift+G) or, if you're really trying to impress, link the macro to a button on the spreadsheet.

When you run your code, execution may stop if a run-time error occurs. The ensuing dialog box suggests the nature of error, although for novice programmers the comments are somewhat opaque. Having noted the error message, on clicking OK the cursor jumps to the statement containing the error and the subroutine declaration statement is shown highlighted (in yellow). Having corrected the error, to continue execution, click Reset on the Run menu (or the Reset button with a black square) to remove the yellow highlight and run the macro again.

For further practice, enter the Factorial subroutine in the updated form given below. In this version, the loop has been replaced by the Excel function FACT, which calculates factorials. Note that to use Excel's functions in VBA code, it is sufficient to preface the function name FACT with Application. (or WorksheetFunction.):

```
Sub Factorial()
'calculates the factorial of a number
num = InputBox("Enter integer number ", "Calculate Factorial ")
fac = Application.Fact(num)
MsgBox "Factorial is "& fac
End Sub
```

To avoid the memory overflowing, run subroutine Factorial with integer numbers less than 25 say.

Both these simple macros have to be entered manually. However, the code for many operations can be generated by Excel's macro recorder, so next we explore this other approach to macro writing.

3.3.5 Recording Keystrokes and Editing Code

The recorder translates keystrokes into VBA code and has two modes when interpreting cell addresses: its default mode (absolute references) and the relative references mode. Initially you will almost always use the recorder with absolute references, however detail on the alternative mode is given at the end of the chapter in Appendix 3B. As an illustration, a simple macro entering data into cells B8:C10 will be recorded in the absolute (default) mode.

The macro recorder is invoked from the Excel window by choosing Tools, then Macro then Record New Macro. Give the macro a name, say Entries, then click OK. (Alternatively, start recording by clicking the Record Macros button on the VB toolbar.) The Stop Recording button appears on a small toolbar (together with the Relative References button). The Relative References button should not be 'pressed in'.

In the sheet, select cell B8 and enter JAN in B8; move down to B9, enter FEB in B9; move down to B10 and enter Total. Then changing to column C, select C8, enter 300; select C9, enter 400; select C10, entering the formula =SUM(C8:C9) in the cell and click Stop Recording. Click the VBE button to see the code recorded from your keystrokes in the Code window. Hopefully, it should be similar to the code below:

```
Sub Entries()
'entering data using absolute addresses
    Range("B8").Select
    ActiveCell.FormulaR1C1 = "JAN"
    Range("B9").Select
    ActiveCell.FormulaR1C1 = "FEB"
    Range("B10").Select
    ActiveCell.FormulaR1C1 = "Total"
    Range("C8").Select
    ActiveCell.FormulaR1C1 = "300"
    Range("C9").Select
    ActiveCell.FormulaR1C1 = "400"
    Range("C10").Select
    ActiveCell.FormulaR1C1 = "=SUM(R[-2]C:R[-1]C)"
    Range("C11").Select
End Sub
```

When a cell is 'selected', it becomes the ActiveCell (a property of the Application object which returns a range). The entries are made using ActiveCell.FormulaR1C1 to put the entries into cells B8 to C10. When you run the macro, by switching to Excel and clicking the Run Macro button (or from the Code window with Run then Sub/UserForm), notice that the macro always produces the same results, i.e. it always fills the range B8 to C10.

For a VBA novice, the best approach is to record keystrokes to suggest code, then edit to improve, make more concise, and generalise the code. The combination of recording, editing and testing out code is a practical approach. Recorded code can produce excellent results when the actions required consist of sequences of menu commands, as for example in producing a chart of some data, doing a data sort or specifying pivot tables, etc. The recorder produces concise code encapsulating quite complex instructions. In contrast, if the actions recorded are mostly a sequence of cursor moves, the recorder generates very verbose code. The best approach in this instance is to write the code, or record bits and edit the results.

As an illustration, look back at the code generated for the Entries macro. Recorded code always includes much 'selecting' of cells, but when writing code it is not necessary to explicitly select cells to enter data into them. The following edited version of the code performs the same operations but is more concise:

```
Sub ConciseEntries()
'entering data using absolute addresses
    Range("B8").Formula = "JAN"
```

```
  Range("B9").Formula = "FEB"
  Range("B10").Formula = "Total"
  Range("C8").Formula = "300"
  Range("C9").Formula = "400"
  Range("C10").Formula = "=SUM(C8:C9)"
End Sub
```

In fact for a single cell range object, it turns out to be unnecessary to specify the Formula property, so the code is simply:

```
Sub Entries()
'entering data using absolute addresses
  Range("B8") = "JAN"
  Range("B9") = "FEB"
  Range("B10") = "Total"
  Range("C8") = "300"
  Range("C9") = "400"
  Range("C10") = "=SUM(C8:C9)"
End Sub
```

A practical way to tidy up generated code is to comment out (add apostrophes in front of possibly) redundant statements, then test by running the macro to see the effect.

When developing code, it frequently helps to display messages about the stage of processing reached, particular intermediate values in calculations, etc. The VBA MsgBox function is invaluable for this. At the editing stage it helps to add comments concisely describing the action performed by the macro, together with any unusual features or requirements. More importantly, any useful possibilities for generalising the scope of the code should be explored.

For reference, all the macros discussed in this section are stored in ModuleA and can be run from the IntroEx sheet of VBSUB.

Reviewing the Factorial subroutine developed in the previous paragraphs, it is clear that code of this type with its use of variables and a For...Next loop will never result from recording keystrokes. It has to be entered manually. Therefore, some guidelines for conducting this more conventional type of programming are set out in the following section.

3.4   ELEMENTS OF PROGRAMMING

In the financial modelling context, much of the code you will want to write will have as its objective the control of numerical calculations. This involves assigning variables, applying proper control structures on the flow of processing and reporting results. These tasks are common to programming whatever the language. VBA programs differ only in that they often originate from spreadsheet models, where tasks are performed by menu commands and where crucial calculations are in cell formulas, many involving Excel functions. Fortunately, it is easy to incorporate Excel functions in VBA code. Rather than replace the spreadsheet model, VBA programs increment or enhance their functionality. We briefly review a few relevant aspects of programming concerning the use of variables, in particular array variables, structures that control the flow of processing and the use of Excel functions in VBA.

3.4.1 Variables and Data Types

In programming, variables are used to store and manipulate data. Conventionally, data comes in different forms or 'types' and this influences the amount of memory allocated for storage. In most numerical calculation, the main distinctions are between numbers (conventional decimal system numbers otherwise known as scalars), integers, Booleans (True or False), and dates. There are also string variables that hold textual as opposed to numerical information. VBA has a useful data type, variant, which can represent any data type. It is the default data type, which can be useful when a variable's type is uncertain. However, the variant type consumes additional memory, which can affect processing speeds if large amounts of numerical processing are required. There is also an 'object' variable type which can refer to an object such as a range or a worksheet. See Green (1999) for more details of the different data types.

From the viewpoint of novice VBA programmers, it is important to explicitly declare all variables used, as this cuts down errors in coding. This can be forced by ensuring that the Option Explicit statement is included at the top of each Module sheet. (The VBE can be set up to ensure that this happens automatically—via Tools then Options on the VB menu, then checking the 'Require Variable Declaration' code setting.) At run-time, the VBA compiler produces an error message if any undeclared variable is encountered. This is particularly useful in detecting mis-spelt variable names in the code. Declaring the data type (as integer, string, Boolean, etc.) is less important in the financial modelling context, but it can be used as a way of indicating (to the user) a variable's purpose in the program.

Variables are declared with the Dim keyword as shown in the third statement of the Factorial subroutine. Here, the two variables have been declared but not data-typed (as integer say). By default they are variant in type:

```
Sub Factorial()
'calculates the factorial of a number
Dim fac, num
num = InputBox("Enter number ", "Calculate Factorial ")
fac = Application.Fact(num)
MsgBox "Factorial is "& fac
End Sub
```

(As an aside, notice that InputBox(), which returns the user's input, has two input parameters or 'arguments' here. The first argument is the prompt 'Enter number ', the second (optional) argument is the title of the dialog box.)

In summary, all variables used in subroutines should be explicitly declared using the Dim keyword. The statement Option Explicit at the top of a Module sheet ensures that all variables must be declared for the subroutine to work correctly.

3.4.2 VBA Array Variables

Where sensible, variables can be grouped by name into arrays (vectors or matrices). For example, the quartiles of the cumulative distribution of a data set can be represented by the array variable, qvec(). Individual elements of the array are referenced as qvec(0), qvec(1), etc. Using the log returns data discussed in the previous chapter, Figure 3.2 shows the quartiles calculated with the Excel QUARTILE function in cells H21:H25, with the first and last Q points being the minimum and maximum of the data set, -0.043 being the value below which 25% of the data falls, etc. So array qvec() could take its values from the cells in range H21:H25, with qvec(0) taking value −0.153, qvec(1) taking value −0.043, etc.

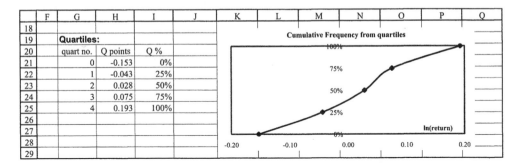

	F	G	H	I	J	K	L	M	N	O	P	Q
18												
19		**Quartiles:**										
20		quart no.	Q points	Q %								
21		0	-0.153	0%								
22		1	-0.043	25%								
23		2	0.028	50%								
24		3	0.075	75%								
25		4	0.193	100%								
26												
27												
28												
29												

Figure 3.2   Quartile values for log returns data as in Data sheet of VBSUB

Extending the idea, array variables can have several dimensions, e.g. the two-dimensional array variable PQmat() could represent a 5 by 2 array consisting of a column of quartiles and a column of the corresponding 'left-hand side' percentages of the distribution. For example, array variable PQmat() could take its values from the 5 by 2 cell range H21:I25 shown in Figure 3.2. Although there are few rules for the names given to array variables, it is helpful to choose names that distinguish between arrays with one dimension (vectors) and two dimensions (matrices). Hence our use of names such as qvec and PQmat.

As with other variables, array variables should be declared before use in the subroutine. By default, VBA numbers its arrays from 0. So the array qvec(), if declared in the statement:

```
Dim qvec(4)
```

will consist of five elements. By extension, the two-dimensional array for two rows and four columns of quartiles and percentages, PQmat(), if declared in the form:

```
Dim PQmat(1,4)
```

will consist of 10 elements, again assuming the default numbering base for arrays is 0.

If you want VBA to use 1 as the lowest index, you must state **Option Base 1** at the start of your Module sheet. If this were done, the array variable qvec(4) would have only four elements, qvec(1), qvec(2), qvec(3) and qvec(4). In fact in most of the VBA procedures developed in this book, the array base is chosen as 1.

The effect of the Option Base setting is illustrated by the following ArrayBase macro. It produces different results according to the Option Base statement at the top of its Module sheet. Since the VBA array function Array() is used to enter the actual array, it is not necessary to specify in advance the dimensions for array variable avec:

```
Sub ArrayBase()
'gives b=20 if Option Base is 1; gives b=30 in absence of Option Base statement
Dim avec, b
avec = Array(10,20,30)
b = avec(2)
```

```
MsgBox "b is "& b
End Sub
```

Often, the number of elements required in an array is not known at the outset, but results from the operations of the macro. This so-called 'dynamic array' does not have a preset number of elements. It is declared with a blank set of brackets, e.g. Dim qvec() or Dim PQmat(). However, before using any non-dimensioned array, a ReDim statement is used to tell VBA how many elements are in the array. In the example below, the named range 'dvec' contains results that are to be stored in array variable cvec. After declaring cvec as an array variable, its dimensions are decided by counting the elements of the named range (dvec), leading to the ReDim statement required before cvec can be used:

```
Sub SelectCount()
're-Dim data array cvec
Dim n, cvec()
Sheets("Data").Range("dvec").Select
n = Selection.Count
ReDim cvec(n)
End Sub
```

Working with arrays in VBA is more complicated than using Excel's array formulas (such as SUM, SUMPRODUCT and the matrix functions). In some cases, array processing can be handled entirely by Excel functions taking array inputs. Note that if individual array elements do not need to be accessed in the code, the array can be referred to by a variable name such as qvec, without the requirement to state its dimensions. However, frequently array processing involves element-by-element operations, which are best handled systematically in a loop. In this case, individual qvec(i) elements have to be identified and typically Dim qvec() and ReDim statements need to be included. The coding requires much more care if errors are to be avoided. There is also ambiguity about the layout of VBA arrays constructed by Excel, in particular as to when they are row vectors and when column vectors. To add possible further confusion, if an array is used as an input to a procedure, Excel numbers the array elements from 1.

3.4.3 Control Structures

In common with other programming languages, VBA provides several control structures to sequence the flow of processing. These include conditional statements such as If...Then...Else, which tests a condition and alters the flow of execution depending on the result of the test; and Select Case, which selects a branch from a set of conditions (or cases). A looping structure allows you to run a group of statements repeatedly. Some loops repeat statements a specific number of times, such as the For...Next loop with its counter which we have already used to calculate the factorial. Other constructions, such as the Do While...Loop, repeat statements until a condition is True (or until a condition is False). We look at simple examples of If...Then in this section, and further examples of the For...Next loop and the Do While...Loop in the following section. Textbooks (such as Green, 1999; Walkenbach, 1999; Wells and Harshbarger, 1997) explain these structures much more extensively and can be referenced for other examples.

As noted in the Factorial subroutine, the VBA interaction function, InputBox, returns the user's input. To make our procedure more robust, wrong inputs should be filtered out and amended inputs requested from the user. One approach is to test the input to check that it is numeric, and to discard it if not. The code below illustrates two uses of the If...Then structure. The first instance is an in-line If...Then with no additional conditions on following code lines. This tests the variable numtype (resulting from a VBA function IsNumeric) and if numtype = True calculates the factorial. The test and ensuing action are contained in a single code line. In the second case, the structure takes the block form of If...Then. If the user input is non-numeric, the user is warned and no calculation takes place. When the conditional statements finish, there is an End If:

```
Sub Factorial()
'calculates the factorial of a number
Dim fac, num, numtype
num = InputBox("Enter number ", "Calculate Factorial ")
numtype = IsNumeric(num)                              'either True or False
If numtype = True Then fac = Application.Fact(num)    'in-line If Then
If numtype = False Then                               'block If Then End If
MsgBox ("Not an integer number. Try again") 'don't proceed
End If
End Sub
```

We make much use of If...Then...Else in Chapter 4 on user-defined functions.

3.4.4   Control of Repeating Procedures

The early version of the factorial subroutine (in section 3.3.1) illustrates the simplest type of repeating procedure, the For...Next loop. As a different example, consider the code for the Quartiles subroutine below. This calculates the quartiles of a data set (taken from a named range, dvec, in the Data sheet of the VBSUB workbook), and displays the results to the user one-by-one in a sequence of dialog boxes. (You may wish to access this sheet of VBSUB to follow the argument in the next paragraphs.)

```
Option Base 0

Sub Quartiles()
'displays quartiles of range named 'dvec'
    Dim i As Integer
    Dim quart                              'to hold the current quartile
    Dim dvec As Variant           'col vec of data
    'fill array variable dvec from spreadsheet range named dvec
    dvec = Worksheets("Data").Range("dvec")

    'calculate quartiles one at a time & display
    For i = 0 To 4
      quart = Application.Quartile(dvec, i)
    MsgBox "Quartile no. "& i & "has value "& quart
    Next i
End Sub
```

Inspection of the current range names in the VBSUB workbook, via the commands Insert then Name then Define shows that the name dvec is attached to the LnReturns data range in column E of the Data sheet. In the code for the Quartiles subroutine, we also use the name dvec for the array variable containing the data set values. To indicate (to us) that dvec is a vector not simply a scalar variable, we declare it as a Variant. Examining the code, we note that after filling array dvec from the spreadsheet cells, the individual quartiles are calculated and displayed element-by-element in the For...Next loop. Note that to use the Excel function QUARTILE in the VBA code, it needs to be prefaced by Application. or WorksheetFunction., as explained in the next section.

The MsgBox prompt has the values of the For...Next counter and the current quartile concatenated, which works, but is not the most satisfactory solution for handling output. We give an improved version of the Quartiles subroutine in section 3.5.

Another useful structure for repeated operations is the Do While...Loop. Repeated operations continue whilst a condition is satisfied and cease when this is not the case. The DelDuplicates subroutine, which searches for and deletes duplicate rows in a database, illustrates the use of the Do While...Loop. Having sorted the database on a specific 'code' field, the entries in the code column are processed row-by-row. If the values of the currentCell and the nextCell are the same, the currentCell row is deleted. Here current-Cell and nextCell are used as object variables, since they reference objects (here Range objects). Because they are object variables, their values have to be assigned with the keyword Set.

```
Sub DelDuplicates()
Dim currentCell, nextCell
Range("database").Sort key1:= Range("code")
Set currentCell = Range("code")
Do While Not IsEmpty(currentCell)
      Set nextCell = currentCell.Offset(1, 0)
      If nextCell.Value = currentCell.Value Then
          currentCell.EntireRow.Delete
      End If
      Set currentCell = nextCell
   Loop
End Sub
```

This subroutine illustrates some of the advantages of VBA's online help. This can be accessed from the VBE, via the Help command and the Help Index. Here the index entry on Delete Method elicited the above subroutine, which provided exactly the operation required. Unfortunately, not all queries posed to VBA's online help are so fruitful, nevertheless, it contains much useful information on syntax. These sections have only touched on a few of the most widely used control structures. Other useful sources for VBA programming techniques are textbooks such as Green (1999), Walkenbach (1999) or Wells and Harshbarger (1997).

3.4.5   Using Excel Functions and VBA Functions in Code

As seen in the Quartiles subroutine, to use an Excel function in a VBA procedure, you need to prefix the function name with Application. In Excel 2000, the function name can be prefixed by WorksheetFunction or Application. For compatibility with earlier versions of Excel, we continue to use Application. In contrast, VBA functions require no prefix, as we have seen with MsgBox, IsNumeric, InputBox, etc. In fact, there are relatively few specific numeric functions built into VBA, currently just Abs, Cos, Exp, Int, Log, Rnd, Sgn, Sin, Sqr and Tan, where Log is the natural log (usually denoted Ln). So some VBA functions are spelt differently from the parallel Excel function (e.g. Sqr in VBA for square root, whereas the Excel function is SQRT). To resolve the conflict, if both a VBA and an Excel function exist for the same calculation, the VBA form must be used rather than the Excel function. (For example, write Log rather than Application.Ln when you require the natural logarithm of some quantity; similarly write Sqr rather than Application.Sqrt.)

3.4.6 General Points on Programming

To conclude this section, some more general advice about the process of tackling a programming project is given. In structured programming, the objective is to write programs that progress in an orderly manner, that are easy to follow and, most important, easy to modify.

It helps to work out on paper the overall application's main stages, breaking the overall task down into distinct and separable subtasks. Then the program can be built in steps, coding and testing a series of self-contained and separate subprograms to accomplish the subtasks. Where possible, it helps to keep the subprogram segments reasonably small. One of the tenets of structured programming is that a code segment should have one entry and one exit point. Program control should not jump into or exit from the middle of code segments. If this practice is adhered to, the process of linking the separate segments of code together is greatly simplified.

Useful programs frequently require updating or modifying in different ways. Program logic is made easier to follow if comments are added when the program is first written. Wherever possible, important constants in the numerical calculations should be para-meterised (explicitly declared) so that they are easy to change if the program is to be used for different circumstances. If code can be written to handle slightly more general situations, it is usually worth the extra effort.

3.5 COMMUNICATING BETWEEN MACROS AND THE SPREADSHEET

Having introduced the use of variables and control structures in programming, this section discusses how VBA macros can obtain inputs directly from the spreadsheet and how results can be returned. It concentrates on the communication between macros and the spreadsheet.

In most cases, a subroutine consists of three parts: input of data, calculations (or manip-ulation of inputs), then output of results. Writing the VBA code for the calculations usually involves conventional programming techniques. The novel aspect of VBA programming is the interaction with the spreadsheet. Taking the three parts separately:

- Input can be from spreadsheet cells or directly from the user via dialog boxes, with the input stored in variables.
- Output can be written to cells or displayed in dialog boxes.
- Calculation can be done in code ('offline'), or by using formulas already in cells or by writing to cells via statements in the VBA subroutine.

The following three versions of the familiar factorial example illustrate combinations of different types of input, calculation and output.

Subroutine Factorial1 gets input from the user, employs the Excel FACT function for the calculation and returns the output via MsgBox. The subroutine does not interact with the contents of the worksheet at all:

```
Sub Factorial1()
Dim fac, num
num = InputBox("Enter number ", "Calculate Factorial ")
fac = Application.Fact(num)
MsgBox "Factorial is "& fac
End Sub
```

In contrast, Factorial2 takes its input from a spreadsheet cell (B5) and returns the factorial answer to another cell (C5):

```
Sub Factorial2()
'gets number from spreadsheet, uses Excel Fact function, returns answer to spreadsheet
Dim fac, num
num = Range("B5").Value
fac = Application.Fact(num)
Range("C5").Value = fac
End Sub
```

As a further variation, in Factorial3 the input number is written to a cell (B6), the factorial formula is written to an adjacent cell with the code:

```
Range("C6").Formula = "=FACT(b6)"
```

and the result displayed back to the user.

```
Sub Factorial3()
'gets number from InputBox, calculates factorial in spreadsheet
' returns answer via MsgBox
    Dim fac, num
    num = InputBox("Enter number ", "Calculate Factorial ")
    Range("B6").Value = num
    Range("C6").Formula = "=FACT(b6)"
    fac = Range("c6").Value
    MsgBox "Factorial is "& fac
End Sub
```

To consolidate, try developing these input–output subroutines with your own formulas and requirements. For reference, the factorial subroutines are all in ModuleF of the VBSUB workbook, and are best run from the IntroEx sheet. When you adapt or write your own subroutines, you may wish to take note of the material in Appendix 3A on the Visual Basic Editor, especially the paragraphs on stepping through and debugging macros.

The process of reading the values of spreadsheet ranges, and writing results to other spreadsheet cells and ranges, is simple if cell-by-cell computation is not required. Suppose the input data is in the spreadsheet range named 'avec', the values of whose cells have to be pasted to another range, with *anchor* cell (the top, left-hand cell) named 'aoutput'. The recorder produces the code in subroutine ReadWrite1, which can be improved by editing out the 'selection' operations, as shown in ReadWrite2:

```
Sub ReadWrite1()                              'recorded macro
    Application.Goto Reference:="avec"
    Selection.Copy
    Application.Goto Reference:="aoutput"
    Selection.PasteSpecial Paste:=xlValues, Operation:=xlNone, SkipBlanks:=_
```

```
      False, Transpose:=False
   Application.CutCopyMode = False
End Sub
```

```
Sub ReadWrite2()                                'edited version
'reads data, writes values to another range
   Range("avec").Copy
   Range("aoutput").PasteSpecial Paste:=xlValues
   Application.CutCopyMode = False              'cancels Copy mode
End Sub
```

The coding becomes a little more complicated if the calculation routine has to be performed on the individual cells of avec. These calculations are likely to be carried out in a repeating loop, and the results pasted one-by-one into an output range. Counting the range avec provides the number of cells in avec to be read and values to be pasted to the output range. Suppose the calculation routine produces the running product of the elements of avec. For the calculation, two variables x and y are used, x for the current element of avec, and y for the current product. Suppose the top cell of the input range, avec, is named 'atop' and the top cell of the output range is named 'aoutput'. The following subroutine reads data cell-by-cell, calculates the product to date and outputs the current product at each step:

```
Sub ReadWrite3()
'reads data cell-by-cell, calculates, writes results
Dim i As Integer, niter As Integer              'niter is counter for iterations
Dim x, y
niter = Range("avec").Count                      'no. of cells in avec
y=1                                              'initial value for product
For i = 1 To niter
   x = Range("atop").Offset(i - 1, 0)
   y = x *y                                       'calculation routine
   Range("aoutput").Offset(i - 1, 0) = y
Next i
Application.CutCopyMode = False
End Sub
```

Offset(i, j) is a most useful method which returns the cell i rows below and j columns to the right of the referenced cell, here Range("atop"). For example, the cell given by Range("atop").Offset(1, 0) is one row below the cell named atop, etc. Initially x takes the value Range("atop").Offset(0, 0), that is the value of Range("atop").

As a final example of communication between macro and spreadsheet, we reconsider the Quartiles subroutine, improving the coding so that the five quartiles are returned as an array to the spreadsheet. The new subroutine, Quartiles1, retains the five quartile values in the array variable qvec() and outputs this to the previously named range qvec1. (The range name qvec1 is attached to range K20:K24 in the Data sheet, as can be confirmed by choosing Insert then Name then Define and inspecting the dialog box.)

In the code below, the array variable qvec(4) is dimensioned to hold the five values. The input and output array variables, dvec (the data set) and qvec1 (the results array), have been declared as Variants to indicate (to us) that they are not simply scalar variables. Since dvec and qvec1 are not accessed element-by-element, their variable declaration Dim statements do not include the brackets (). After filling array dvec from the spreadsheet range dvec, the quartiles array is assembled element-by-element in the For...Next loop. By default, VBA sets up arrays such as qvec() in a worksheet row, so Excel's Transpose function is applied to output the quartiles as a column vector:

```
Option Base 0
Sub Quartiles1()
'pastes 4 by 1 col vector of quartiles into range named 'qvec1'
'requires 2 named ranges in spreadsheet, dvec with data and qvec1
Dim i As Integer
Dim qvec(4)                                      'quartiles array with 5 elements
Dim dvec As Variant                              'col vec of data
Dim qvec1 As Variant                             'results array
   'fill array variable from spreadsheet range
   dvec = Worksheets("Data").Range("dvec")
   'calculate quartiles and assemble as an array
   For i = 0 To 4
      qvec(i) = Application.Quartile(dvec, i)
   Next i
   qvec1 = Application.Transpose(qvec)           'to make a column vector
   'transfer results into spreadsheet range qvec1
   Worksheets("Data").Range("qvec1") = qvec1
End Sub
```

Notice that only one statement is executed in the loop. This illustrates the practice of never putting unnecessary statements in loops. Any statements unaffected by the processing in the loop should always be put outside the loop.

Once again, you should consolidate your understanding by trying out some of these subroutines with your own data and formulas. For reference, the ReadWrite subroutines are in ModuleI and the Quartiles subroutines in ModuleQ of the VBSUB workbook.

This concludes our brief introduction to writing VBA subroutines. For further amplification at this stage, Chapter 2 of Green's (1999) text provides an excellent primer in Excel VBA. The next section contains three further applications, developed and explained at greater length. They represent some realistically useful applications for macros and taken together illustrate further ideas about writing VBA code.

3.6   SUBROUTINE EXAMPLES

In this section, a number of subroutines are developed more fully to illustrate firstly, the process of incremental improvement and secondly, some useful application areas for macros. These examples combine use of the recorder and subsequent code editing. They include subroutines for generating particular types of charts, cumulative frequency and normal probability plots, and repeated optimisation with Solver.

3.6.1   Charts

To start, we develop a subroutine for charting some data such as the cumulative frequency data shown tabulated and plotted out in Figure 3.3.

Suppose the frequency data is in the 'Data' sheet of a workbook in a range named 'chartdata' and the objective is to produce an XY chart with cumulative percentage frequencies on the Y axis. The chart is to be placed as an object on the Data sheet.

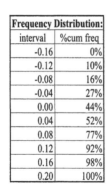

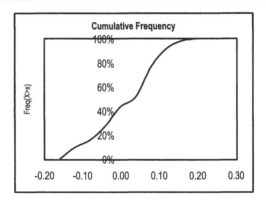

Figure 3.3   Frequency distribution and chart in Data sheet of workbook VBSUB

For a novice VBA user, the code required to manipulate charts is likely to be unknown, so the best approach is to use the recorder to generate the code. The VBA recorder is switched on and the keystrokes required to plot the data in range 'chartdata' are recorded. Wherever possible, use range names (selecting the names from the namebox or clicking the Paste Name button) to specify cell ranges. The code generated for macro here called ChartNew() is likely to be similar to the following:

```
Sub ChartNew()
Charts.Add
    ActiveChart.ChartType = xlXYScatterSmoothNoMarkers          'WizStep1
    ActiveChart.SetSourceData Source:=Sheets("Data").Range("chartdata"), PlotBy:=_
       xlcolumns                                                 'WizStep2
ActiveChart.Location Where:=xlLocationAsObject, Name:="Data"     'WizStep4
    With ActiveChart                                             'WizStep3
        .HasTitle = True                                         'Titles
        .ChartTitle.Characters.Text = "Cumulative Frequency"
        .Axes(xlCategory, xlPrimary).HasTitle = False
        .Axes(xlValue, xlPrimary).HasTitle = True
        .Axes(xlValue, xlPrimary).AxisTitle.Characters.Text = "Freq(X> x)"
    End With
    With ActiveChart.Axes(xlCategory)                            'Gridlines
        .HasMajorGridlines = False
        .HasMinorGridlines = False
    End With
    With ActiveChart.Axes(xlValue)
        .HasMajorGridlines = False
        .HasMinorGridlines = False
    End With
    ActiveChart.HasLegend = False                                'Legend
End Sub
```

(The annotations on the right-hand side above have been added to help explain this somewhat lengthy set of statements. WizStep1 is short for Chart Wizard Step 1, etc.)

The Charts collection in the workbook is augmented by a new chart [Charts.Add] of type XYScatterSmoothNoMarkers [Active.ChartType] taking as source data the cell range named 'chartdata' [ActiveChart.SetSourceData]. The code generated relates closely to the answers given in the first two Chart Wizard steps. In the first step, the chart type is chosen, and in the second, the data range containing the source data is defined and its structure (rows or columns) specified. [The syntax for the method applied to the object ActiveChart is: SetSourceData(Source, PlotBy).] In passing, note that part of the ActiveChart.SetSourceData statement overflows onto the following line. This is indicated in the code by a space followed by underscore (_).

The code line: ActiveChart.Location Where:=xlLocationAsObject, Name:="Data" corresponds to choices made on the fourth wizard screen and ensures that the chart will be located as an embedded object on the Data sheet itself. (If the chart is to be in a separate chart sheet, the code simplifies to ActiveChart.Location Where:=xlLocationAsNewSheet.)

The majority of the subsequent code relates to the choices made in the Wizard's third step, where Chart Options are specified. Notice the useful bit of syntax:

'With... End With'

which Excel's recorder frequently uses when several changes are made to an object, here the ActiveChart object. Hence the code:

```
With ActiveChart
    .HasTitle = True
    .ChartTitle.Characters.Text = "Cumulative Distribution"
    .Axes(xlCategory, xlPrimary).HasTitle = False
    .Axes(xlValue, xlPrimary).HasTitle = True
    .Axes(xlValue, xlPrimary).AxisTitle.Characters.Text = "P(X> x)"
End With
```

defines the various titles, and subsequent code segments define the Gridlines, Axes and Legend in turn.

Much of the code generated by the recorder leaves default settings unchanged and can be edited out to make the macro more concise. A first step is to 'comment out' possibly redundant statements (by adding an apostrophe at the start of the statement), and then to check that the code still works as wished. For example, the following subroutine, ChartNew1 works perfectly well without the comment lines:

```
Sub ChartNew1()
    Charts.Add
    ActiveChart.ChartType = xlXYScatterSmoothNoMarkers
    ActiveChart.SetSourceData Source:=Sheets("Data").Range("chartdata"), PlotBy:=_
        xlColumns
    ActiveChart.Location Where:=xlLocationAsObject, Name:="Data"
    With ActiveChart
        .HasTitle = True
        .ChartTitle.Characters.Text = "Cumulative Frequency"
        .Axes(xlCategory, xlPrimary).HasTitle = False
        .Axes(xlValue, xlPrimary).HasTitle = True
        .Axes(xlValue, xlPrimary).AxisTitle.Characters.Text = "Freq(X> x)"
    End With
    'With ActiveChart.Axes(xlCategory)
    '    .HasMajorGridlines = False
    '    .HasMinorGridlines = False
    'End With
    With ActiveChart.Axes(xlValue)
```

```
        .HasMajorGridlines = False
'       .HasMinorGridlines = False
    End With
    ActiveChart.HasLegend = False
End Sub
```

The code can therefore be reduced to the following:

```
Sub ChartNew2()
'same as ChartNew Macro after removing redundant lines
    Charts.Add
    ActiveChart.ChartType = xlXYScatterSmoothNoMarkers
    ActiveChart.SetSourceData Source:=Sheets("Data").Range("chartdata"), PlotBy:=_
        xlColumns
    ActiveChart.Location Where:=xlLocationAsObject, Name:="Data"
    With ActiveChart
        .HasTitle = True
        .ChartTitle.Characters.Text = "Cumulative Frequency"
        .Axes(xlValue, xlPrimary).HasTitle = True
        .Axes(xlValue, xlPrimary).AxisTitle.Characters.Text = "Freq(X> x)"
    End With
    With ActiveChart.Axes(xlValue)
        .HasMajorGridlines = True
    End With
    ActiveChart.HasLegend = False
    ActiveChart.PlotArea.Select                    'new code added
    Selection.Interior.ColorIndex = xlAutomatic    'remove plot area colour
    ActiveChart.Axes(xlValue).Select
    With ActiveChart.Axes(xlValue)
        .MaximumScale = 1                          'reset max. value on Y axis
    End With
End Sub
```

The code from **ActiveChart.PlotArea.Select** onwards is additional. It ensures that the Y axis scale stops at 1 (or 100%) and removes the default grey colour in the Plot area of the chart.

The various chart macros which can be run with the Data sheet equity returns are in ModuleC of the workbook.

3.6.2   Normal Probability Plot

One useful data visualisation is the so-called normal probability plot. This plot of a set of readings shows whether the variation in the readings can be assumed to be statistically normal. Suppose there are 50 readings. Then the order statistics of a set of 50 normally distributed readings (called norm-scores) are plotted against the standardised values of the readings (called z-scores). If the readings are effectively normal, the points resulting from the two scores will lie more or less on a straight line. An illustrative normal probability plot shown in Figure 3.4 indicates some departures from normality, especially on the tails of the distribution.

At present, Excel does not include this useful plot in its statistical armoury. (The plot referred to as a normal probability plot in the Data Analysis ToolPak Regression option is not a conventional normal probability plot at all, but simply the cumulative distribution of the dependent variable.)

Normal Probability Plot

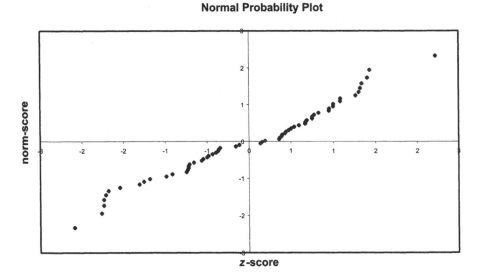

Figure 3.4   A normal probability plot of log returns data

Suppose the readings are in a range named dvec in the Data sheet of the workbook. In the VBA code, an array variable dvec is set up to take the values from the range named dvec. Because we need to process individual array elements, dvec(i), dvec is declared a Variant (and is actually an object variable, specifically a Range object). A second array variable, Znvec, is set up to take vectors of z-scores and norm-scores, one pair of scores for each data value in dvec. These array variables are declared at the beginning of the subroutine NPPlotData.

Since a range variable is referenced by dvec, its values are assigned with the Set keyword, hence:

```
Set dvec = Sheets("Data").Range("dvec")
```

Once dvec has been specified, the number of readings in dvec (say n) can be evaluated and previously declared arrays dimensioned correctly. Hence the statement:

```
ReDim Znvec(n, 2)
```

For each reading in the data set, a z-score and a norm-score are calculated within a For...Next loop. The calculations for the z-score use the Excel AVERAGE and STDEV functions, whereas for the norm-score the calculations involve the Excel RANK function and the inverse standard normal probability function (NORMSINV). The scores are stored in the n by 2 matrix called Znvec, and subsequently output to the named range Znvec in the Data sheet. Once the vectors of scores have been calculated, they can be plotted against each other in an XY chart.

The full code for obtaining the scores for the plot is given below. The penultimate step calls the subroutine ChartNormPlot, which is similar to the chart subroutine developed in section 3.6.1. You can try out the NPPlot macro on the log returns data in the Data sheet of the VBSUB workbook.

```
Option Explicit
Option Base 1

Sub NPPlotData()
 'returns normal probability plot of data from named range dvec

 'declaring variables
 Dim m1, sd1, rank1, c1
 Dim i As Integer, n As Integer
 Dim Znvec() As Variant
 Dim dvec As Variant

 'data input from worksheet
 Set dvec = Sheets("Data").Range("dvec")           'use Set because dvec(i) required
 n = Application.Count(dvec)                        'number of readings
 ReDim Znvec(n, 2)                                  'Znvec dimensioned as n by 2 matrix

 'calculating elements of Znvec array
 m1 = Application.Average(dvec)                     'mean of readings
 sd1 = Application.StDev(dvec)                      'standard deviation of readings
 For i = 1 To n
    Znvec(i, 1) = (dvec(i) −m1) / sd1               'z-score for ith reading
    rank1 = Application.Rank(dvec(i), dvec, 1)
    c1 = (rank1 −3 / 8) / (n + 1 / 4)         'using a continuity correction
    Znvec(i, 2) = Application.NormSInv(c1)          'n-score for ith reading
 Next i

 'output results to range Znvec
 Sheets("Data").Range("Znvec") = Znvec             'matrix of scores output to 'range Znvec
 With Sheets("Data").Range("Znvec")
    .NumberFormat = "0.00"                          'output data formatted
    .Name = "npdata"                                'output range given name npdata
 End With
 ChartNormPlot                                      'subroutine ChartNormPlot called
End Sub
```

The code for the NPPlot subroutine and ChartNormPlot (called from the NPPlotData macro) are stored in ModuleN of the workbook.

3.6.3 Generating the Efficient Frontier with Solver

This application requires a degree of familiarity with portfolio theory and optimisation with Excel's Solver add-in. The reader may prefer to delay inspecting this material until Chapter 6 has been studied.

In looking at portfolios with several risky assets the problem is to establish the asset weights for efficient portfolios, i.e. those that have minimum risk for a specified expected return. It is straightforward to get the optimum weights for a target return with Solver. If the optimisation is repeated with different targets, the efficient portfolios generate the risk–return profile known as the efficient frontier.

For example, Figure 3.5 shows the weights (40%, 50%, 10%) for one portfolio made up of three assets with expected return 2.2%. The target return is 7% and the efficient portfolio is determined by the set of weights that produce this return with minimum standard deviation.

	A	B	C	D	E	F	G	H	I	J
4	**Asset Data**		Exp Ret	Std Dev						
5		TBills	**0.6%**	**4.3%**			Target exp return		**7.0%**	target1
6		Bonds	**2.1%**	**10.1%**						
7		Shares	**9.0%**	**20.8%**						
8										
9	**Correlation Matrix**		TBills	Bonds	Shares		**Portfolio weights:**			
10		TBills	1.00	**0.63**	**0.09**			TBills	40.0%	
11		Bonds	0.63	1.00	**0.23**			Bonds	50.0%	change1
12		Shares	0.09	0.23	1.00			Shares	10.0%	
13										
14	**VCV matrix**		TBills	Bonds	Shares					
15		TBills	0.0018	0.0027	0.0008			Exp Ret	**2.2%**	portret1
16		Bonds	0.0027	0.0102	0.0048			Std Dev	**7.0%**	portsd1
17		Shares	0.0008	0.0048	0.0433					

Figure 3.5   Portfolio weights, expected return and standard deviation of return from Eff1 sheet

To perform this optimisation, Solver requires 'changing cells', a 'target cell' for minimisation (or maximisation) and the specification of 'constraints', which usually act as restrictions on feasible values for the changing cells. In Figure 3.5, we require the weights in cells I10:I12 to be proportions, so the formula in cell I10 of $=1-\text{SUM}(I11:I12)$ takes care of this requirement. For the optimisation, the 'changing cells' are cells I11:I12, named 'change1' in the sheet. The target cell to be *minimised* is the standard deviation of return (I16) named 'portsd1'. There is one explicit constraint, namely that the expected return (cell I15) named 'portret1' equals the target level (in cell I5 named 'target1'). The range names are displayed on the spreadsheet extract to clarify the code subsequently developed for the macro.

Applying Solver once, the optimum weights suggest buying Bonds and Shares and short selling TBills in the proportions shown in Figure 3.6. Cell I15 confirms that this efficient portfolio with minimum standard deviation of 15.7% achieves the required return of 7%.

Changing the target expected return in cell I5 and running Solver again with the same specifications as before would produce another efficient portfolio. Clearly, if the entire efficient frontier is required, the best approach is via a macro. If the optimisation using Solver is recorded, the following type of code is obtained:

```
Sub TrialMacro()
        SolverReset
        SolverAdd CellRef:="$I$15", Relation:=2, FormulaText:="target1"
```

```
        SolverOk SetCell:="$I$16", MaxMinVal:=2, ValueOf:="0", ByChange:="$I$11:$I$12"
        SolverSolve
End Sub
```

	A	B	C	D	E	F	G	H	I	J
2	Efficient Frontier points using Solver (no constraints on weights) Eff1									
3										
4	Asset Data		Exp Ret	Std Dev						
5		TBills	0.6%	4.3%			Target exp return		7.0%	target1
6		Bonds	2.1%	10.1%						
7		Shares	9.0%	20.8%						
8										
9	Correlation Matrix		TBills	Bonds	Shares		Efficient frontier portfolio			
10		TBills	1.00	0.63	0.09			TBills	-5.6%	
11		Bonds	0.63	1.00	0.23			Bonds	35.8%	change1
12		Shares	0.09	0.23	1.00			Shares	69.8%	
13										
14	VCV matrix		TBills	Bonds	Shares					
15		TBills	0.0018	0.0027	0.0008			Exp Ret	7.0%	portret1
16		Bonds	0.0027	0.0102	0.0048			Std Dev	15.7%	portsd1
17		Shares	0.0008	0.0048	0.0433					

Figure 3.6 Optimum portfolio weights for expected return of 7% produced by Solver

The recorded code hints at some of the special VBA functions in the Solver add-in. In particular, the SolverAdd function (for specifying a constraint) has three arguments: the first is a cell reference for the constraint 'LH side', the second an integer code for the relation (2 for =) and the third either a cell reference or a single number. Similarly, the arguments in the SolverOk function specify the particular optimisation problem to be solved.

The recorded code can be improved firstly by writing the functions and their arguments with brackets together with comma delimited arguments, and secondly by employing range names in preference to cell addresses. The Call keyword used with each Solver function highlights the fact that control has been passed to a Function procedure. (Also, it suppresses the value returned by the function.) After editing, the code for the first optimisation is:

```
Sub Eff0()
'to return an efficient portfolio for given target return
        SolverReset
        Call SolverAdd(Range("portret1"), 2, Range("target1"))
        Call SolverOk(Range("portsd1"), 2, 0, Range("change1"))
        Call SolverSolve(True)
        SolverFinish
End Sub
```

The SolverAdd function ensures that the expected return (in the cell named 'portret1') meets the specified target, in cell 'target1'. The SolverOk function controls the optimisation task, ensuring that the entries in cell range 'change1' are such that the portfolio standard deviation (in cell 'portsd1') is minimised. The SolverFinish function is equivalent to selecting options and clicking OK in the Solver Results dialog shown after solution. Effectively, with this statement, the Solver Results dialog box is not displayed under macro control.

The efficient frontier requires the choice of optimal portfolio weights for a range of target returns. Suppose a range of different targets is set up starting with an initial target of 1% (*min_tgt* in general) increasing in steps of 2% (*incr*) as many times as specified (*niter*). The different target returns are produced in a Do While...Loop which repeats *niter* times. For each target return, Solver has to produce optimal weights. The only part of the problem specification that changes on each iteration is the target return. Thus, in the code, most of the Solver specification is set up before the repeated optimisation. Only the SolverChange function that changes the target return sits inside the loop.

```
Sub Eff1()
'   repeated optimisation with given min_target & increment
'   initialisation
    Dim target1: Dim incr
    Dim iter As Integer, niter As Integer
    target1 = Range("min_tgt").Value            'value taken from spreadsheet cell
    incr = Range("incr").Value                  'value taken from spreadsheet cell
    niter = Range("niter").Value                'value taken from spreadsheet cell
    iter = 1                              'initial value for loop counter
'   code to clearout previous results
    ClearPreviousResults                        'a subroutine

'   set up Solver
    SolverReset
    Call SolverAdd(Range("portret1"), 2, Range("target1"))
    Call SolverOk(Range("portsd1"), 2, 0, Range("change1"))
'   repeated part
    Application.ScreenUpdating = False          'turns off screen recalculation
    Do While iter <= niter
        Range("target1").Value = target1        'put current value of target1 in cell
        Call SolverChange(Range("portret1"), 2, Range("target1"))
        Call SolverSolve(True)
        SolverFinish
'       code to copy & paste results in sheet
        ReadWrite                               'a ReadWrite subroutine
        target1 = target1 + incr                'update value of variable target1
        iter = iter +1                          'increment counter
    Loop
    Range("target1").Select
    Application.CutCopyMode = False
    Application.ScreenUpdating = True           'turn screen updating back on
End Sub
```

After writing the code, you can add a description for the macro and assign a keyboard shortcut, just as occurs when you record a macro. To do this, start in the Excel window, choose Tools then Macro then Macros. In the Macro dialog box, select the macro name (Eff1) then click the Options button.

For reference, the macros to generate the efficient frontier are in ModuleS of VBSUB and can be run from the Eff1 sheet. Before you use any macro containing Solver, you must establish a reference to the Solver add-in. With a Visual Basic module active, click References on the Tools menu, then Browse and find Solver.xla (usually in the \Office\Library subfolder).

SUMMARY

VBA is an object-oriented version of the Basic programming language. As well as familiar programming ideas concerning variables and coding, there are also methods and properties for use with Excel objects.

You automate operations in Excel first by writing the code for subroutines and functions in a VBA Module within the workbook, then by running your macros. The Visual Basic Environment provides some tools for debugging macros and access to VBA libraries and online help.

The purpose of VBA subroutines is to carry out actions: in contrast, VBA user-defined functions return values. In the context of financial modelling, we have found that functions are more useful than subroutines. The exceptions are operations that require the production of charts, and automating optimisation tasks using Solver. Subroutines are frequently useful for one-off administrative tasks, which require lots of repetition.

The macro recorder can be used to translate your actions into VBA code. Recording keystrokes in macros is sometimes useful as a starting point, for getting coding clues and insights. Whereas the recorder tends to generate verbose code for simple operations, it can produce highly sophisticated code for many menu-based procedures.

Most Excel functions can be included in VBA macros and there are some special VBA functions for use in macros. This is a useful way of leveraging the knowledge of the experienced Excel model builder.

There are advantages to mastering VBA. The replacement of calculations by functions can lead to more powerful cell formulas and makes calculation sequences more robust and faster. Skilful use of macros to control repeated operations can remove other sources of error from spreadsheet operations.

REFERENCES

Green, J., 1999, *Excel 2000 VBA Programmer's Reference*, Wrox Press Ltd., Birmingham.
Leonhard, W., L. Hudspeth and T. J. Lee, 1997, *Excel 97 Annoyances*, O'Reilly & Associates, Inc., Sebastopol, CA.
Walkenbach, J., 1999, *Excel 2000 Power Programming with VBA*, IDG Books, Foster City, CA.
Wells, E. and S. Harshbarger, 1997, *Microsoft Excel 97 Developer's Handbook*, Microsoft Press.

APPENDIX 3A   THE VISUAL BASIC EDITOR

The Visual Basic Editor was substantially changed for Excel 97 (and later versions) and this appendix details some of its features. It can be activated by pressing the VBE button (on the VB toolbar) or by pressing Alt+F11 in the Excel window. Once activated, you can toggle between the Excel and the Visual Basic windows with Alt+Tab in the usual manner. The Visual Basic Editor can also be opened via the Excel menubar by choosing Tools then Macro then Visual Basic Editor.

The Visual Basic window should look something like that shown in Figure 3.7, which includes a menubar and a toolbar across the top; the Project Explorer and the Properties windows on the left-hand side and the Code window on the right. In the illustration, the

Code window contains the code in Module1, in fact recorded code for the data entry operations described in section 3.3.5.

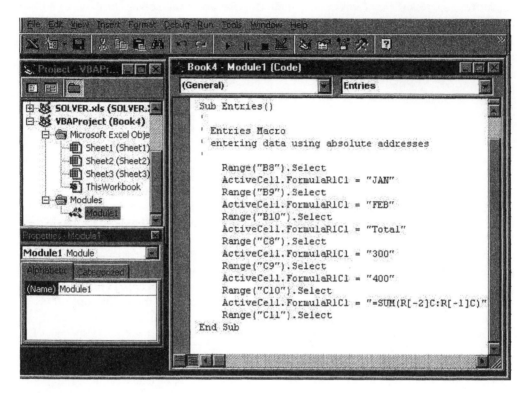

Figure 3.7   Visual Basic window with Project Explorer, Properties and Code windows open

The toolbar and windows described may not be visible when you first activate the Visual Basic Editor. If the toolbar is not visible, use View Toolbars and click once on the Standard option. Similarly, choose View then Project Explorer and View then Properties window to display the two left-hand windows. To display the Code module on the right, double click on the relevant Module (here Module1) in the Project Explorer window.

As the name suggests, the code modules contain the VBA code for procedures. These modules are inserted by choosing Insert then Module from the menubar. (These are Modules, not Class Modules, which are more advanced and will not be covered in this text.) You can insert as many modules as you like in the workbook. One practice is to put related macros into the same module.

The Project Explorer shows the component parts of all the open 'projects'. Its main use is to act as a navigation tool, from which the user can open new modules in which to store code or remove (i.e. delete) a module or to activate the Code windows for existing modules. Selecting a module sheet, the File menu allow you to Remove the module sheet (i.e. delete it) and also to Print out its contents. If you want to copy VBA code from one Module to another, avoid the Export File option. Copying code from one module sheet to another one in the same workbook or any other is best achieved via the Code window with the usual copy and paste operation.

Each Excel object shown in the Project Explorer for a particular 'project' has its own set of 'properties', for example, each worksheet in an active workbook has the 'name' property. These properties can be changed via the Properties window. However, since modifying properties is more relevant for worksheets than for modules, we will not expand on the features of this window further in the context of macros, except to note that the name of each code module can be modified here. (For example, we frequently change the module names to M, 0 and 1, collecting together any macros in ModuleM, functions with base 0 in Module0, and the remaining functions with base 1 in Module1.) In practice, when developing macros, it is more convenient to close the Properties window and possibly the Project Explorer to maximise the size of the Code window.

The Visual Basic window has its own Standard toolbar, as shown in Figure 3.8, with the View Excel button at the left-hand which returns the user to the Excel window. The middle set of buttons concern editing tasks, running and testing out macros, and the right-hand group open other windows such as the Immediate window (for testing individual statements) and the Object Browser (for checking the objects, methods and properties available in VBA). Note in particular the Run Macro button (a right pointing triangle), the Reset button (a square) and the Object Browser (third from the end).

Figure 3.8 Standard toolbar in VB window

There are two types of procedure which we code in VBA: subroutines (or macros) and functions. Only subroutines (or macros) can be recorded. Usually they will require some editing in the Code window and possibly testing using Excel's debugging tools. Since functions cannot be recorded, they must be written in a code module. Therefore the recording tools are of little use in developing functions.

As outlined in the main text, subroutines can be run from the Excel window (via menu commands or by clicking the Run button on the VB toolbar or by using a chosen keyboard shortcut). They can also be run from the Code window (with the pointer positioned anywhere in the body of the routine's code, by clicking the Run button on the VB Standard toolbar underneath the VB window menu). Possibly more user-friendly than either of these ways, subroutines can be attached to buttons. However, since our workbooks rely on functions rather than macros, it is best to refer the reader to other texts for details of attaching macros to buttons. (For example, see Leonhard et al., 1997 for further details on the VBE and developing macros.)

Note that when you try to run subroutines and the VBE intervenes to tell you of an error preventing compilation, macro operation is suspended in so-called 'debug mode', the subroutine name being illuminated in yellow. With the cursor pointing to the offending statement, you can edit simple mistakes, then easily jump out of debug mode via Run

Reset on the Run menu in the VBE command bar or by clicking the Reset button (with the black square). The yellow illumination disappears and the macro can be re-run.

Stepping Through a Macro and Using Other Debug Tools

If your macros don't work as you expect, it helps to step slowly through them operation-by-operation. If you run the macro from the menu, choosing Tools then Macros then selecting the 'macro name', you need to click the **Step Into** button on the Macro dialog box instead of choosing Run. This allows you to step through the macro. Alternatively, provided the cursor is not in a Code window, you can click the **Run** button on the VBA toolbar, choose the macro to be tested then click the **Step Into** button. The VBA Code window opens with the first statement of the chosen macro highlighted (in yellow).

Click the F8 function key (or if visible, the small Step Into button) to move to the next line of code and so on. If you want to see the actions in the spreadsheet window, reduce the size of the VBE window so you can see the Excel sheet underneath or use the Alt+Tab combination to move between windows and watch the macro working line-by-line in the Code window. Click F8 (or the Step Into button) repeatedly to step through the macro. There is a **Step Out** button to escape from step mode. Alternatively, the VBE Editor Window command bar Run menu has a **Reset** choice which gets you out of step or debug mode.

The Debug toolbar in Figure 3.9 contains the Step Into, Step Over and Step Out buttons for proceeding through the macro code. A macro being 'stepped through' line-by-line is said to be in 'break mode'. If the macro calls other secondary routines, the Step Over button executes these secondary routines without stepping through them line-by-line.

Figure 3.9   The Debug toolbar, with Step In, Step Out and Reset buttons shown separately

To illustrate, display the Debug toolbar in the VB window (using View then Toolbars) and try stepping through the Factorial macro (whose code is in ModuleA of the VBSUB workbook). Starting from the IntroEx sheet, choose Tools then Macro then Macros, select the Factorial macro as shown in Figure 3.10, and click the Step Into button. The VB window opens with the first code line of the Factorial macro highlighted (in yellow). Continue stepping through with the Step Into button. When the Input Box asking for the number appears, enter 3 say and click OK. Go on stepping through (checking that the loop is executed three times) until the MsgBox dialog appears with the answer 6.

At any stage, you can jump out of step mode by clicking Reset (or via Run then Reset from the VBE standard command bar).

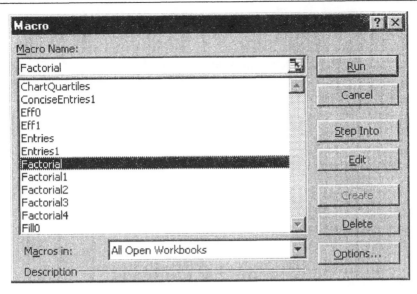

Figure 3.10   Entering step mode for the Factorial macro

As a further illustration, step through the Factorial macro once again after clicking the Locals window button (see the Debug toolbar, fifth button from the right in Figure 3.9). In the new window, the values of variables num, fac and *i* are shown as successive lines of the macro code are executed.

Another useful facility in debugging macros is to insert breakpoints, especially in longer subroutines. When the macro runs, operations cease when a breakpoint is reached. Execution jumps to break mode, and the macro can be explored in step mode. To insert a breakpoint, select the position in the code and click in the adjacent grey margin or simply click the breakpoint button (shown in Figure 3.9 with a small hand). To remove the breakpoint, simply click in the grey margin once again or toggle the breakpoint button. With the Factorial macro, try making the MsgBox statement a breakpoint, then run the macro to check that it runs normally until the point at which the results should be displayed. Then execution changes to 'step mode' for the remaining code lines and macro operations proceed by pressing the F8 key. (Breakpoints can also be used in debugging functions, since they provide a means of changing into step mode to examine the operation of the function code.)

APPENDIX 3B   RECORDING KEYSTROKES IN 'RELATIVE REFERENCES' MODE

The recorder translates keystrokes into VBA code and has two modes when interpreting cell addresses: its default mode (absolute references) and the relative references mode. In section 3.3.5, the macro entering data into worksheet cells was recorded using absolute references. Here, we look at the code generated when recording in relative references mode.

Start with the pointer on cell B8. The macro recorder is invoked from the Excel window by choosing Tools, then Macro then Record New Macro. Give the macro a name, say RelEntries. This time when the Stop Recording button appears on screen, click the Relative References button. It should appear as if 'pressed in'. Then just as before, key in the names of the months. The code when you've finished should look different from the previous macro:

```
Sub RelEntries()
'recorded with relative references
    ActiveCell.FormulaR1C1 = "JAN"
    ActiveCell.Offset(1,0).Range("A1").Select
    ActiveCell.FormulaR1C1 = "FEB"
    ActiveCell.Offset(1,0).Range("A1").Select
    ActiveCell.FormulaR1C1 = "Total"
    ActiveCell.Offset(-2,1).Range("A1").Select
    ActiveCell.FormulaR1C1 = "300"
    ActiveCell.Offset(1,0).Range("A1").Select
    ActiveCell.FormulaR1C1 = "400"
    ActiveCell.Offset(1,0).Range("A1").Select
    ActiveCell.FormulaR1C1 = "=SUM(R[-2]C:R[-1]C)"
    ActiveCell.Offset(1,0).Range("A1").Select
End Sub
```

Try running the macro from different cells in the spreadsheet. The entries are made relative to the pointer position (the ActiveCell referred to as Range("A1")), which itself moves down one row at a time, then to the adjacent column. The Offset method, say Offset(1, 0), returns a range object, the cell in the same column, but one row below relative to the current position. The cell selected is always referenced as "A1" (the ActiveCell), despite the fact that the keystrokes did not involve cell A1 in any way.

To get most assistance from the recorder, it is worth thinking out in advance which mode is likely to be more helpful: absolute or relative references. Usually, it is absolute references, the default mode of recording. However, if you are trying to automate operations that repeat themselves row-by-row down the worksheet, the relative references mode is likely to throw up more clues as to coding. For example, if you want your macro to select a specific cell, perform an action, then select another cell relative to the active cell, record with relative references. However, you need to remember to switch off the Relative References button to return to absolute referencing.

The RelEntries macro can be edited to make it less verbose. Recorded code always includes much 'selecting' of cells, however when writing code, it is not necessary to explicitly select cells to enter data into them. The following edited version of the code performs the same operations but is more concise:

```
Sub ConciseEntries()
'entering data using relative positions
    ActiveCell.FormulaR1C1 = "JAN"
    ActiveCell.Offset(1, 0).FormulaR1C1 = "FEB"
    ActiveCell.Offset(1, 0).FormulaR1C1 = "Total"
    ActiveCell.Offset(-2, 1).FormulaR1C1 = "300"
    ActiveCell.Offset(1, 0).FormulaR1C1 = "400"
    ActiveCell.Offset(1, 0).FormulaR1C1 = "=SUM(R[-2]C:R[-1]C)"
End Sub
```

In fact for a single cell range object, it turns out to be unnecessary to specify the Formula property, so the code is simply:

```
Sub ConciseEntries()
'entering data using relative positions
    ActiveCell.Offset(0, 0) = "JAN"
    ActiveCell.Offset(1, 0) = "FEB"
    ActiveCell.Offset(2, 0) = "Total"
    ActiveCell.Offset(0, 1) = "300"
    ActiveCell.Offset(1, 1) = "400"
    ActiveCell.Offset(2, 1) = "=SUM(R[-2]C:R[-1]C)"
End Sub
```

A practical way to tidy up generated code is to comment out (add apostrophes in front of possibly) redundant statements, then test by running to see the effect.

4
Writing VBA User-defined Functions

As well as automating spreadsheet operations, VBA code can be used to write functions which work in the same way as Excel's 'built-in' functions. Functions are particularly useful when they automate calculation tasks that are required repeatedly. Function calculations are carried out 'off sheet', allowing leaner and cleaner layouts to be devised, and functions are portable so that once programmed they can be copied to other workbooks.

Whereas a VBA subroutine usually performs one or more actions, a VBA function is a set of instructions that returns a single value (similar to the SUM function) or an array of values (like the LINEST function). User-defined functions combine real programming (complete with loops and conditional branching) together with Excel functions (such as NORMSDIST and MMULT).

Functions are simplest to write when they operate on single numerical inputs (scalar inputs) and when they return single cell values. This chapter starts by developing a simple sales commission function with one input and one output to illustrate the steps involved in writing and using functions. Functions with several scalar inputs are written in much the same way. As an illustration, a mathematically more challenging function based on the Black–Scholes option value formula is used. Function writing becomes more exacting when the inputs are arrays rather than single values. To illustrate some aspects of handling arrays, functions for the expected value and variance of a set of cash flows and for the variance of a portfolio of assets are developed. There are further examples where both inputs and outputs are arrays of values. The functions are available in the VBFNS.xls workbook, and the reader is encouraged to experiment with these examples and the exercises set at the end of the chapter.

4.1 A SIMPLE SALES COMMISSION FUNCTION

Suppose rates of commission on sales depend on the month's total sales, the rates being as shown in cells D5:E7 of the spreadsheet in Figure 4.1.

	A	B	C	D	E
1	VBFns1.xls				
2		Sales Commission Function			
3					
4	Sales	Commission		Sales >=	CommRate
5	25000	3000		0	8.0%
6	9999	799.92		10000	10.5%
7	10000	1050		20000	12.0%

Figure 4.1 Commission rates on sales in SalesCom sheet of VBFNS.xls

If cell A5 contains one value for the total sales, then the commission (in cell B5) can be evaluated in several ways, for example, with a formula involving nested IF functions:

=IF(AND(A5>=0,A5<10000),A5*0.08,IF(AND(A5>=10000,A5<20000),

A5*0.105,A5*0.12))

However, if sales commission calculations are frequently performed and many more rates involved, a better approach is to create a user-defined function which can be called just like any other function in Excel. We start by discussing suitable VBA code for the function, and in the next section explain how to write the code and test out the results in a workbook.

Look at the code listed below for a function named Commission, which requires one input (or 'argument'), the monthly sales total denoted Sales. The function is referred to as Commission(Sales) and its output is the commission due. The code is written in a Module sheet as with macros:

```
Option Explicit              'to force variable declaration

Function Commission(Sales)
 'returns commission on sales
 If Sales>=0 And Sales < 10000 Then Commission= 0.08*Sales
 If Sales>= 10000 And Sales< 20000 Then Commission= 0.105*Sales
 If Sales>= 20000 Then Commission= 0.12*Sales
End Function
```

Examining the code line-by-line, the function is declared with the Function keyword, its name Commission, requiring one input, Sales, shown within the brackets. When the function code is executed, a single-valued result is assigned to the function's name Commission. The conditional If... Then statements determine the appropriate commission rate and apply it to the Sales figure. Notice that only one of these statements will be executed, so the function's value is uniquely determined for the particular level of Sales. The code ends with the required statement End Function. Note that statements following an apostrophe sign are explanatory comments and are not executed.

In line with good programming practice, the Option Explicit statement at the beginning of the Module sheet ensures that all variables used in the VBA code must be declared. Here, since the only variables used, Commission and Sales, have been declared implicitly in the opening Function statement, no further declarations are required. (This point is elaborated more fully in section 4.3).

4.2   CREATING COMMISSION(SALES) IN THE SPREADSHEET

To create the Commission function in your spreadsheet, simply insert a Module sheet in the workbook. To do this, choose Tools then Macro then Visual Basic Editor to go to the VB window. With your workbook highlighted in the Project window, choose Insert then Module from the menu. Enter the VBA code for the function in the Code window (ensuring that Option Explicit is declared at the top of the Module sheet).

To test the function out on the spreadsheet, enter a formula such as:

=Commission(25000)

The result should be 3000 (since sales at this level qualify for commission at 12%). Or if the sales figure is in cell A5, use the formula:

=Commission(A5)

As with other Excel functions, the Paste Function button (formerly the function dictionary) can be employed to help enter functions like Commission. All user-created functions are grouped in a category with the name User Defined.

If your function does not work, you may see an error message in the cell (such as #NAME? or #VALUE?) which usually indicates a mismatch between the function and input or that the function name is wrongly entered. Alternatively a Microsoft Visual Basic 'compile error' message may appear, indicating a mistake in your code. In this case, note the nature of the error (frequently 'Variable not defined'), click OK and correct the highlighted error. Then, most important, click the Reset button (with the black square) on the VB Standard toolbar, which will remove the yellow bar from the function name statement. Return to the spreadsheet and re-enter your function (either pressing F2 then Enter or retyping the entry).

Another way to check the working of a function is to use breakpoints in the code and to use the Locals window to observe the numerical values being calculated. For example, make the statement:

If Sales>=0 And Sales<10000

a breakpoint by clicking the statement in the adjacent margin (as described in Appendix 3A). Next return to the SalesCom sheet and re-enter (or refresh) the Commission function. As the function evaluates, the cursor should jump back to the function code, and the sequence of evaluation can be observed by stepping through the remaining code.

Before leaving the VBE, you may wish to rename your Module sheet, as say Module0, in the Properties window (as described in Appendix 3A).

In the next section, we develop some slightly more complex functions with several inputs whose statements involve calls to Excel functions as well as VBA functions. The functions for the Black–Scholes option value formula illustrate additional aspects of writing code for user-defined functions.

4.3 TWO FUNCTIONS WITH MULTIPLE INPUTS FOR VALUING OPTIONS

As yet, Excel does not have a built-in function to calculate the value of an option using the Black–Scholes formula. This allows us to develop a user-defined function suitable for valuing a call, named BSCallValue say. The underlying theory that is the background to the Black–Scholes formula is introduced in Part III of the book. Although at this stage you will not necessarily understand the option value formula, remember that our purpose here is merely to turn the formula into workable VBA code.

The Black–Scholes pricing formula for a European call allowing for dividends is:

$$c = S \exp(-qT)N(d_1) - X \exp(-rT)N(d_2)$$

In the formula, S is the current share price, X the exercise price for the call at time T, r the continuously compounded risk-free interest rate, hence the expression $\exp(-rT)$ for the risk-free discount factor over period T. The continuous dividend yield on the share is denoted q, so that the share price S is replaced by $S\exp(-qT)$ in the valuation formulation. The notation $N(d)$ is used to denote the cumulative standard normal probability of a value less than d. Here d_1 and d_2 are given by:

$$d_1 = [\ln(S/X) + (r - q + \sigma^2/2)T]/[\sigma\sqrt{T}]$$

$$d_2 = [\ln(S/X) + (r - q - \sigma^2/2)T]/[\sigma\sqrt{T}] = d_1 - \sigma\sqrt{T}$$

where σ is the volatility of the share.

The spreadsheet extract in Figure 4.2 shows details of a six-month option on a share with current value $S = 100$, $X = 95$, $r = 8.0\%$, $q = 3\%$ and $\sigma = 20\%$. Expressions d_1 and d_2 are evaluated in cells G8 and G11, from which the cumulative normal probabilities $N(d_1)$ and $N(d_2)$ in cells G9 and G12 are derived, using Excel's NORMSDIST function. These are inputs to the call value cell formula (in G4):

$$=D4*D16*G9-D5*D15*G12$$

which evaluates as 9.73. (The same inputs produce the related put value for the option shown in cell H4.)

The call formula can be programmed into a user-defined function with six inputs (S, X, r, q, T, σ), whose answer is shown in cell G5.

	A	B	C	D	E	F	G	H
2	Black-Scholes Formula							
3							Call	Put
4	Share price (S)			100.00		BS value	9.73	2.49
5	Exercise price (X)			95.00		BSval via fn	9.73	2.49
6	Int rate-cont (r)			8.00%				
7								
8	Dividend yield (q)			3.00%		d_1	0.6102	
9						$N(d_1)$	0.7291	
10	Time now (0, years)			0.00				
11	Time maturity (T, years)			0.50		d_2	0.4688	
12	Option life (T, years)			0.50		$N(d_2)$	0.6804	
13	Volatility (s)			20.00%				
14								
15	Exp (-rT)			0.9608				
16	Exp (-qT)			0.9851				

Figure 4.2   Details of an option and Black–Scholes values for the call and put in BS sheet

The VBA code for the Function BSCallValue(S, X, r, q, tyr, sigma) is set out below. The time to maturity for the option (in years) is denoted tyr and σ is denoted sigma. The calculations in the Black–Scholes formula are sufficiently complex for us to use intermediate variables [denoted DOne and NDOne for d_1 and $N(d_1)$] in coding the function:

```
Option Explicit          'to force variable declaration

Function BSCallValue(S, X, r, q, tyr, sigma)
'     returns Black–Scholes call value (allowing for q=div yld)
```

```
Dim ert, eqt
Dim DOne, DTwo, NDOne, NDTwo
ert = exp(-r * tyr)                'exp is the VBA function for 'e'
eqt = exp(-q * tyr)                'dividend yield effect
DOne = (log(S/X)+(r-q + 0.5*sigma^2)*tyr)/(sigma*sqr(tyr))
DTwo = (log(S/X)+(r-q – 0.5*sigma^2)*tyr)/(sigma*sqr(tyr))
NDOne = Application.NormSDist(DOne)
NDTwo = Application.NormSDist(Dtwo)
BSCallValue = (S*eqt*NDOne - X*ert*NDTwo)
End Function
```

The statement **Option Explicit** at the top of the module sheet forces the declaration of all variables used in calculating the function. To comply, the 'Dim' statement declares the six variables (ert, eqt, DOne, DTwo, NDOne, NDTwo). Descriptive names have been chosen for the variables, e.g. DOne for d_1 and NDOne for $N(d_1)$, etc. to link the code to the conventional notation for the options formula. The variable **ert** is the discount factor for converting payoffs at maturity to present values: in algebraic terms, $\exp(-rT)$. The variable **eqt** is the dividend yield effect on the current share price, algebraically $\exp(-qT)$. Note that the input variables (such as S, X, etc.) are automatically declared in the Function command itself, so should not be included in Dim statements.

Despite the unwieldy appearance of the code, the calculation is relatively simple. Notice that the three expressions 'exp', 'log' and 'sqr' are built-in VBA functions for 'e', natural logs (ln) and square-root respectively. Where both VBA and Excel functions exist for the same expression, the VBA function must be used rather than the corresponding Excel function. When Excel functions are used in the code, they must be prefaced with **Application.** or **WorksheetFunction**. Hence:

NDOne = Application.NormSDist(DOne)

uses the Excel function NORMSDIST.

Thus, the formula:

$$=\text{BSCallValue}(100, 95, 8\%, 3\%, 0.5, 20\%)$$

evaluates to 9.73. (The formula in cell G5 displaying the value 9.73 takes its inputs from the cells in column B.)

Turning to the corresponding BS valuation formula for a European put, the put–call parity relationship ensures that the value of a European put is given by:

$$p = -S\exp(-qT)N(-d_1) + X\exp(-rT)N(-d_2)$$

with d_1 and d_2 as before. The only difference from the previous call formula is the change of sign from positive to negative for the d_1 and d_2 arguments in the cumulative normal probability expressions and the reversed signs for the two terms in the Black–Scholes formula. By adding a further argument, iopt (with value 1 for a call and -1 for a put) the VBA code for a call can be generalised to cover valuation of either European option, call or put.

The code for function BSOptValue with seven inputs (including iopt set to 1 or -1) is given below. If iopt $= -1$, NDOne becomes $N(-d_1)$, NDTwo becomes $N(-d_2)$, and the signs of the two terms in the BS equation have altered since iopt $= -1$. Confirm in the spreadsheet that for a put, BSOptValue$(-1, 100, 95, 8\%, 3\%, 0.5, 20\%)$ equals 2.40 [whereas BSOptValue$(1, 100, 95, 8\%, 3\%, 0.5, 20\%)$ returns 9.73 as before]:

```
Function BSOptValue(iopt, S, X, r, q, tyr, sigma)
'  returns the Black-Scholes value (iopt=1 for call, -1 for put, q = div yld)
'  uses fns BSDOne and BSDTwo
   Dim ert, eqt, NDOne, NDTwo
   ert = exp(-r * tyr)
   eqt = exp(-q * tyr)
   NDOne = Application.NormSDist(iopt * BSDOne(S, X, r, tyr, sigma))
   NDTwo = Application.NormSDist(iopt * BSDTwo(S, X, r, tyr, sigma))
   BSOptValue = iopt * (S* eqt* NDOne - X * ert * NDTwo)
End Function
```

```
Function BSDOne(S, X, r, q, tyr, sigma)
'  returns the Black - Scholes d1 value
   BSDOne = (log(S/X) + (r-q +0.5*sigma^2)*tyr)/(sigma*sqr(tyr))
End Function
```

```
Function BSDTwo(S, X, r, q, tyr, sigma)
'  returns the Black-Scholes d2 value
   BSDTwo = (log(S/X)+(r-q - 0.5*sigma^2)*tyr)/(sigma*sqr(tyr))
End Function
```

Note that the intermediate quantities, DOne and DTwo, have been coded as functions in their own right and are simply called from the 'master' function. The object is to modularise the VBA code making its operation more transparent and allowing errors in coding to be pinned down more accurately.

In summary, functions are VBA procedures which return values, their code being enclosed in between the keywords Function and End Function. Following the Function keyword, the name of the function is declared followed by a list of inputs in brackets. A series of VBA statements follow and when the function has run, the name returns the output:

```
Function name (input1, input2, . . .)
[statements]
[name = expression]
End Function
```

In good VBA programming, it is preferable to head each Module sheet with the Option Explicit statement, which forces formal variable declaration. Note that whereas all variables created and used in computing the function should be declared with Dim statements, variables that are function inputs do not need to be declared. If Excel functions are required in the code, they must be referred to with the Application. or the Worksheet-Function. prefix.

4.4 MANIPULATING ARRAYS IN VBA

Unfortunately, there is a step change in the complexity of coding functions with array input and output. Therefore before developing such functions, it is worth considering how arrays are handled in Excel. In many instances, familiar Excel functions such as SUM, AVERAGE, STDEV, SUMPRODUCT and NPV can be employed to take care of the array handling. In other cases, additional safeguards are required to code array handling so that it performs as intended. In particular:

- In the absence of suitable built-in functions, it may be necessary to process individual array elements, so repeated operations in a loop are required. If so, the number of elements in the array must be counted, and this is easily achieved with code such as Application.Count(avec) using the Excel COUNT function.

- It is important to be clear about the numbering of arrays. If the Option Base declaration is omitted, the elements number from 0 (the default). If the Option Base 1 statement is included at the top of the module, the array elements number from 1 as is usual in Excel operations.

- When matrix operations such as matrix multiplication are required, care must be taken in checking dimensional conformity. (By conformity we mean that the number of columns in matrix **A** must equal the number of rows in matrix **B** for the matrix product **AB** to be defined and evaluated.) Coding statements may need to be included to ensure that input arrays are in the correct format (row vector or column vector) for any matrix manipulation.

Some simple functions are included in Appendix 4A to explain how arrays are handled in VBA with an emphasis on manipulating matrices.

Array handling is illustrated in the next two sections, both explicitly in processing individual items in the arrays as in the variance function in section 4.5 and implicitly by using Excel's matrix multiplication and other array functions in section 4.6.

4.5 EXPECTED VALUE AND VARIANCE FUNCTIONS WITH ARRAY INPUTS

Suppose that the cash flows from an investment are uncertain, having five possible levels, the probabilities of each level being as shown in the first column of Figure 4.3. Evaluating the Expected Value of the cash flows requires each cash flow to be multiplied by its probability, as shown in column D, before the products are summed.

	A	B	C	D	E
2	Expected Values				
3					
4	Probs p(i)	Cflows Cf(I)	Devs	p(I)*Cf(i)	p(i) * Dev^2
5	0.05	-500	-1250	-25	78125
6	0.2	100	-650	20	84500
7	0.5	700	-50	350	1250
8	0.2	1300	550	260	60500
9	0.05	2900	2150	145	231125
10	Expected Values			750	
11	Variance				455500
12	Std Dev				674.9

Figure 4.3 Cash flows with their probabilities in the ExpValues sheet of VBFNS workbook

A concise formula which encapsulates this method uses the Excel function:

SUMPRODUCT(B5:B9,A5:A9)

In passing note that the two arrays in SUMPRODUCT must both be column vectors (as here) or both row vectors. Also note that this formula is not appropriate for returning expected values if the second of the arrays (A5:A9 here) does not sum to one as probabilities should.

The spreadsheet calculations for variance are less compact, requiring each probability to be multiplied by the squared deviation of the cash flow from its mean, as indicated in column E. So it is an advantage to have VBA functions for the variance (and for simplicity for the expected value of the cash flows as well), since with functions the element-by-element calculations are performed 'off-sheet'. The two functions, WVariance and ExpVal, have as inputs the two arrays whose contents combine to produce the expected value, the cash flows array vvec and the probabilities array pvec.

The code for the ExpVal(vvec, pvec) function centres on using Excel functions SUM, COUNT and SUMPRODUCT. Since the Excel functions deal with all array handling for this function, the code is straightforward. The initial If... Then conditional statement strips out cases when the expected value cannot be sensibly computed, i.e. when the elements of array pvec do not sum to one or when the two arrays do not have the same number of elements. In these cases the function returns the value −1:

```
Function ExpVal(vvec, pvec)                       'returns expected value for
2 arrays
If Application.sum(pvec) <> 1 Or _
    Application.Count(vvec) <> Application.Count(pvec) Then
    ExpVal = -1
    Exit Function
ElseIf pvec.Rows.Count <> vvec.Rows.Count Then vvec = Application.Transpose(vvec)
End If
ExpVal = Application.SumProduct(vvec, pvec)
End Function
```

For the SUMPRODUCT function to work, both input arrays should be vectors of the same type, row or column vectors. If the inputs are not of the same form, vvec is transposed.

The VBA code for the WVariance function requires individual elements of the arrays to be handled. The **Option Base 1** declaration at the top of the module sheet ensures that array elements number from 1 (as opposed to the default 0). As in the ExpVal function, conditional branching filters out the cases when the elements of pvec do not sum to unity and when the two arrays have different numbers of elements:

```
Option Base 1          'makes array numbering start from 1


Function WVariance(vvec, pvec)                    'calculates variance
Dim expx                                          'Expected Value of x
Dim i As Integer
If Application.sum(pvec) <> 1 Or _
    Application.Count(vvec) <> Application.Count(pvec) Then
        WVariance = -1
        Exit Function
End If
expx = ExpVal(vvec, pvec)                         'using the ExpVal function
WVariance = 0
For i = 1 To Application.Count(pvec)
    WVariance = WVariance + pvec(i)*(vvec(i) - expx)^2
Next i
WVariance = Application.Sum(WVariance)
End Function
```

Once again, the If... Then conditional statement strips out cases when the variance cannot be sensibly computed. The variance is built up incrementally using a For... Next loop as shown above. Notice that squared deviations are expressed in the form: (vvec(i) - expx)^2, where $\exp x$ is the expected value of the cashflows, vvec(i). This quantity is evaluated using the VBA function ExpVal, that we have just created, hence in VBA code:

$$expx = ExpVal(vvec, pvec)$$

As the loop counter i increases on each loop, the variance is incremented by adding one pvec(i)*(vvec(i)–expx)^2 term.

As an exercise, develop the code for a function to evaluate the Standard Deviation of the cash flows. Remember to use the VBA built-in function, Sqr, rather than the Excel function. It would be sensible to include a test that the WVariance function is giving a meaningful numeric output (i.e. that it is non-negative) before taking its square root. (VBA code for the standard deviation is given as a solution to Exercise 4 at the end of the chapter.)

If your function does not work, you may need to add some well-positioned MsgBox functions to indicate intermediate values. For example, if the probability in cell A5 of Figure 4.3 is changed from 0.05 to 0.5 say, the sequence of processing can be checked by inserting a suitably worded message box (MsgBox "Got here") immediately before the statement Exit Function.

Another approach is to test the procedure by calling it from a subroutine. Run-time errors display as usual, and you can also use the debugger to track down the problem. For example, the macro CheckFn sets up the arrays vvec and pvec, then calls the Function WVariance. The debugger will pop up error boxes if there are errors in the code:

```
Sub CheckFn()
'calls WVariance function
'needs named ranges vvec, pvec in spreadsheet
Dim vvec As Variant, pvec As Variant
Set vvec = Range("vvec")
Set pvec = Range("pvec")
Range("B22").Value = WVariance(vvec, pvec)
End Sub
```

It is worth adding a brief description of what the function does, so that it appears when you access the function in the function dictionary. To do this, start in the VB environment with the relevant Module sheet active. Then access the Object Browser which allows you to look at the methods and properties of Excel's various objects. With the current workbook name displayed in the Libraries part, choose the Module sheet where your function code resides, and select your function in the Members window. On the right mouse button, one option is Properties, whose dialog box allows you to add a brief description of your function. Finally, click OK to close the dialog box. Check that your description appears when you access the function via the Paste Function button.

4.6 PORTFOLIO VARIANCE FUNCTION WITH ARRAY INPUTS

Functions to calculate the mean and variance of returns for portfolios are easy to develop. To illustrate the process, a simple spreadsheet formulation using Excel functions is explained, then the cell formulas are coded in VBA to produce the corresponding functions.

The spreadsheet in Figure 4.4 contains risk and return information for three assets, A, B and C, and shows the results of constructing a portfolio with equal amounts of each of the three assets. The asset returns are in cells C5:C7, a column vector referred to with range name **e** in the spreadsheet formula and in the VBA code referred to as retsvec. The portfolio is made up of the three assets in the proportions set out in cells E5:E7, a second column vector with range name **w** in the spreadsheet formulas and referred to as wtsvec in the VBA code.

	A	B	C	D	E	F	G
2	**Portfolio Risk & Return**						
3			e		w		Portfolio
4	**Asset Data**		Exp Ret	StDevRet	weights		ExpRet
5		A	8%	4%	33.3%		9.3%
6		B	15%	5%	33.3%		StDev
7		C	5%	1%	33.3%		2.57%
8					100%		
9							
10	Correlations		1	0.5	-0.2		
11			0.5	1	-0.1		
12			-0.2	-0.1	1		
13							
14	**VCV Matrix V**		A	B	C		
15		A	0.0016	0.0010	-0.0001		Variance
16		B	0.0010	0.0025	-0.0001		=w^{T}Vw
17		C	-0.0001	-0.0001	0.0001		0.07%

Figure 4.4   Risk and return for portfolio of three assets in PFolio sheet

The expected portfolio return (in cell G5) is the weighted sum of the expected returns on each of A, B and C (in fact, 0.093 or 9.3%). The formula in G5 using the named ranges **w** and **e** is the Excel function SUMPRODUCT(**e**,**w**), which gives the weighted return, provided the number of elements in each of the column vectors is the same.

The variance–covariance matrix for the three assets can be calculated cell-by-cell from the correlations (C10:E12) and the individual asset return standard deviations (in cells D5:D7). The resulting matrix of cells (C15:E17) contains the individual variances of returns for assets A, B and C on the diagonal and also the covariances for all pairs of assets in the off-diagonal cells. Suppose this variance–covariance matrix is given the range name **V**. Together with the weights array, it forms the basis for calculating the portfolio variance, essentially a matrix multiplication of form $\mathbf{w}^T\mathbf{V}\mathbf{w}$ where $\mathbf{w}^T$ is the transpose of the weights vector **w**. The formula in cell G17 for variance combines the Excel functions TRANSPOSE for transposing an array and MMULT for matrix multiplication. It is written as:

$$MMULT(TRANSPOSE(\mathbf{w}), MMULT(\mathbf{V},\mathbf{w}))$$

(Since this is an array function, in entering the formula into cell G17, remember to press the keystroke combination Ctrl+Shift+Enter.)

For Excel's MMULT function to work, the dimensions of any pair of adjacent matrices being multiplied must conform, i.e. the number of columns in the first matrix must equal the number of rows in the second matrix. Here TRANSPOSE(**w**) is a 1 by 3 row vector, and MULT(**V**,**w**) is a 3 by 1 column vector, so matrix multiplication is possible, giving the single cell value of 0.0007 (or 0.07%). So for this portfolio, the risk in return is $\sqrt{0.0007} = 0.0257$ (or 2.57%).

It is simple to write the code for the portfolio return function, called PFReturn(wtsvec, retsvec):

```
Option Base 1

Function PFReturn(wtsvec, retsvec)          'returns weighted return for PortFolio
If Application.Count(wtsvec) <> Application.Count(retsvec) Then
    PFReturn = "Counts not equal"
Exit Function
Elself retsvec.Rows.Count <> wtsvec.Rows.Count Then
    wtsvec = Application.Transpose(wtsvec)
End If
PFReturn = Application.SumProduct(retsvec, wtsvec)
End Function
```

The second function, PFVariance(wtsvec, vcvmat), has a more complex code:

```
Function PFVariance(wtsvec, vcvmat)              'calculates PF variance
    Dim nc As Integer, nr As Integer
    Dim v1 As Variant
    nc = wtsvec.Columns.Count
    nr = wtsvec.Rows.Count
    If nc > nr Then wtsvec = Application.Transpose(wtsvec)
    v1 = Application.MMult(vcvmat, wtsvec)
    PFVariance = Application.SumProduct(v1, wtsvec)
End Function
```

The function has vector and matrix inputs and requires VBA statements that satisfy the conformity requirements for matrix multiplication. We would prefer the function to work when the weights array is a row vector as well as when it is a column vector. To achieve this, the dimensions of the array are determined. Variables nr and nc (representing the number of rows and columns) for the weights array wtsvec are declared as integers. For the matrix multiplication to work, the weights vector must be a column vector, hence the statement:

```
If nc > nr Then wtsvec = Application.Transpose(wtsvec)
```

A temporary vector v1 is used in the matrix multiplication, so it is declared up front as a variant. As mentioned in Section 3.4.1, this is a flexible data type that can be of any form, scalar or array or matrix. Here v1 stores the 3 by 1 column vector $\mathbf{Vw}$. One convenient way of evaluating $\mathbf{w^T Vw}$ in VBA is to use the SUMPRODUCT function to multiply the elements of the two 3 by 1 column vectors $\mathbf{w}$ and $\mathbf{Vw}$. Hence the penultimate statement line of code:

```
PFVariance = Application.SumProduct(v1, wtsvec)
```

which returns a scalar value to PFVariance.

The code for the PFVariance function centres on ensuring that the Excel MMULT function evaluates properly. Because the user enters the function arguments, the code needs to adjust them where necessary to enforce matrix conformity. However, since the MMULT and SUMPRODUCT functions handle all the array computations, it is not necessary to declare dimensions for array v1 in the code or to process individual elements. This keeps the code somewhat simpler.

Although the spreadsheet illustrates results for a three-asset portfolio, the two functions have the advantage of working with arrays of any size.

4.7 FUNCTIONS WITH ARRAY OUTPUT

All the functions described so far return values to individual cells (i.e. scalar output). Sometimes, we want functions to return arrays of values, similar to the LINEST function which returns a 5 by $(k + 1)$ array of regression results for a data set with k explanatory variables. Generally, functions with array output are a little more difficult to code in VBA because of the need to correctly configure and construct arrays. In addition, the user needs clues as to the appropriate range to be selected for formula entry using the function. The function name can be used to suggest vector or matrix output, and the function description in the function dictionary can include the dimensions of the output. In the code, the variable names and variable type declarations can indicate whether vectors are manipulated element-by-element or as a whole.

The approach is illustrated with an example from descriptive statistics: summarising the distribution of a data set with percentiles. The objective is to obtain from a function the vector or matrix of computed values.

Suppose the data comprises a large set of price data, such as that shown in the first column of the sheet Data in Figure 4.5 and named dvec. Note that only 12 prices out of the 120 values in the data set are displayed in the figure.

The prices below which 10% of the values lie, 20% lie, 30% lie, etc. are called the 'deciles' of the distribution. They are simply special cases of the percentiles of the cumulative distribution. Just as the average of the data array called dvec can be evaluated with an Excel function, the PERCENTILE function produces the various percentiles. When the 0% value or minimum price is included, there are 11 deciles. These are displayed in Figure 4.5 together with the relevant percentages. When plotted, the 11 by 2 array of values displays the shape of the cumulative distribution of the data. Hence the objective is to code a function that returns an 11 by 2 matrix of values.

	A	B	C	D
1	VBFns.xls			
2	**Data for Summary**			
3				
4	count	120		
5	mean	250.10		
6	stdev.	1.04		
7				
8	dvec		deciles	percent
9	249.1		247.40	0%
10	250.8		248.69	10%
11	250.1		249.18	20%
12	252.1		249.60	30%
13	247.9		249.90	40%
14	250.7		250.10	50%
15	251.2		250.44	60%
16	249.8		250.73	70%
17	251.9		251.00	80%
18	251.8		251.40	90%
19	250.0		252.60	100%
20	248.8			

Figure 4.5   Data with summarising deciles from the DecilesMat function

The code for this function, DecilesMat(dvec), is set out below. Since the dimensions of the array are known, the array variable can be declared from the start with these dimensions (Dim decmat(11, 2)). The first column holds the decile values, obtained from the Excel PERCENTILE function; the second column holds the relevant percentages, 0%, 10%, 20%, etc.

Option Base 1

```
Function DecilesMat(dvec)
'returns 11 by 2 array of deciles ready for X-Y plot
Dim i As Integer
Dim decmat(11, 2) As Variant        'output array
   For i = 0 To 10
     decmat( i + 1, 1) = Application.Percentile(dvec, 0.1 * i)
     decmat( i + 1, 2) = 0.1 * i
   Next i
   DecilesMat = decmat
End Function
```

To apply the function, an 11 by 2 cell range is selected, the array formula is typed or entered via the function dictionary specifying the relevant data set, then the keystroke combination Ctrl+Shift+Enter to enter the matrix of values.

4.8   USING EXCEL AND VBA FUNCTIONS IN USER-DEFINED FUNCTIONS

As we have already seen, standard Excel functions such as COUNT and SUMPRODUCT can be used in VBA code when prefaced with Application. or WorksheetFunction. Until recently, a useful 'List of Worksheet Functions available to Visual Basic' could be accessed via the Excel Visual Basic Help. However, it has proved illusive to locate in recent upgrades of Excel. When last viewed, although most could be used in VBA code, not all the standard functions were listed. Incorporating Excel functions where possible both capitalises on the user's knowledge of Excel and reduces the task of coding functions reliably.

In addition, VBA provides a range of built-in functions as does the Analysis ToolPak, and their usage is briefly outlined in the following paragraphs.

4.8.1   Using VBA Functions in User-Defined Functions

VBA functions such as MsgBox, InputBox, etc. are used without any prefix. There are a handful of Excel functions that are duplicated by standard VBA functions, such as the Excel SQRT function duplicated by the Sqr function in VBA. In writing functions, the VBA function must be used in preference to its Excel double.

VBA has a tiny number of maths functions as follows: Abs, Atn, Cos, Exp, Log, Randomize, Rnd, Sgn, Sin, Sqr and Tan. You can confirm this by browsing the VBA library in the Object Browser from within the VB Editor, then choosing the Math functions. All except Randomize have Excel equivalents–the corresponding Excel functions, in those cases where the names are different, are ATAN, LN, RAND, SIGN and SQRT.

There are also several 'conversion' functions available in VBA: useful ones are Fix, Hex, Int and Oct. If you enter the function in lower case letters you should see the function name capitalised automatically if VBA recognises the function.

To summarise, VBA functions must be used in preference to their Excel equivalents. They are used in VBA code without the Application. prefix.

4.8.2 Add-Ins

The Analysis ToolPak (ATP) containing additional functions such as COUPDAYS, LCM and MULTINOMIAL is an add-in to Excel. If the Tools menu in Excel does not contain the Data Analysis option then (as described in section 2.9) the Analysis ToolPak must be installed. Following installation you should be able to see the ATP functions written in upper case in the function dictionary.

To use ATP functions in VBA module sheets you must do two things:

1. In Excel, use the Tools then Add-Ins command to install the Analysis ToolPak–VBA. The VBA equivalent functions will then appear as duplicates in the function dictionary, though in *mixed case*.
2. From within the VB environment, use the Tools then References command to link to the ATPVBAEN.xla file. (This file was added in during step 1.) ATP functions can now be used in VBA code just like standard VBA functions (i.e. without the Application. prefix). Without the reference, VBA will not recognise the functions.

4.9   PROS AND CONS OF DEVELOPING VBA FUNCTIONS

In reflecting on the advantages and disadvantages of developing functions for spreadsheet calculations, the following points are worth making.

Pros

When compared to spreadsheet calculations and complex cell formulas, functions have the advantage of compressing extensive calculations into one cell. Provided it is programmed accurately and intelligibly named, the user-defined function can pack considerable power into a single cell. Entering functions into cells is less error prone than entering complex cell formulas. If the functions and arguments are clearly and sensibly named, they are easier for semi-expert users to deal with than complex formulas. To ensure user confidence in functions, it is most important that the VBA code is clearly annotated and documented.

Functions also have the advantage of portability, since they can be used in any workbook, provided their VBA code can be accessed. The best way to make function code (in ModuleA1, book A say) available to another workbook (book B) is to copy the required code to a Module sheet in B (ModuleB1 say). Note that activating the Code window for ModuleA1 then copying and pasting to ModuleB1 in the usual manner achieves this. Do not attempt to 'export' the Module sheet from the Project Explorer window. With portability in mind, it is sensible to group the code for related functions into the same module sheet, for example, ModuleB1 in VBFNS contains code for all the Black–Scholes related functions.

Functions are also extendable (e.g. a function written for a portfolio of three assets holds for any number of assets). With a little ingenuity, they can be generalised (e.g. the addition of the iopt argument in the BSOptValue Function means the function can be used for puts as well as calls).

Sometimes, the existence of a function means that complicated structures do not need to be constructed in the spreadsheet. For example, there is no need to replicate the binomial tree structure for different numbers of steps if the number of binomial steps is an argument in the function. (See Appendix 4B where the development of a function for option valuation via a binomial tree is described.)

Cons

Some people mention the need to grapple with VBA as a disadvantage of user-defined functions. However, it should be emphasised that familiarity with only a small subset of VBA is needed for coding functions. The syntax and control structure required for function writing are essentially Basic programming. This is the traditional programming not the object-oriented part of the VBA language.

Impossible Tasks for Functions

Some operations cannot be programmed into functions. Short of rewriting the linear programming code in VBA, or inserting temporary dummy sheets, optimisations using Solver cannot be written as functions. Similarly, operations that require actions like constructing a chart or formatting the colour of a cell depending on its numerical value are not easily achievable with functions.

Following the Summary section, Appendix 4A illustrates several aspects of using Excel's matrix functions to manipulate arrays. Then in Appendix 4B functions for binomial tree valuation of options are described. Some simple exercises on function writing follow, together with brief solution notes.

SUMMARY

Developing VBA functions capitalises on the user's knowledge of spreadsheets and of Excel's functions. Programming is involved, but at a straightforward and intuitively obvious level.

In contrast to subroutines that perform actions with objects, VBA functions are procedures which return values, any calculations involved being carried out 'off-sheet'. A key distinction is that Function procedures are 'passive', that is, the code within the function cannot manipulate ranges.

Most of Excel's extensive range of built-in functions can also be included in user-defined functions: in the VBA code, they are referenced by name with the prefix **Application.** or **WorksheetFunction.** VBA also provides a range of its own functions, which need no prefix, and can be referenced in the Object Browser.

User-defined functions take arguments, which can be numerical values, single cell inputs and array inputs. Function arguments are implicitly declared in the Function statement, and therefore need not be explicitly declared. All other variables used in the function code should be declared and data-typed where appropriate.

Functions can return single values or arrays of values. Generally, functions that handle array input and return arrays of values are more difficult to code.

User-defined functions are used in the spreadsheet either by typing in their names and arguments or via the Paste Function button. They are listed in the function dictionary in the User-Defined category. It is possible to briefly document what the function does and what inputs are required, so that some helpful text appears in the Function Dictionary dialog box when the function is entered.

In the case of complex functions, it is sensible to adopt a modular approach, building a series of intermediate functions, which individually can be tested out.

APPENDIX 4A   FUNCTIONS ILLUSTRATING ARRAY HANDLING

The first example, Function ArrayDemo1, illustrates the use of Excel's matrix multiplication and inversion functions. For the function to work, both Amat1 and Amat2 must be square matrices and of the same dimensions. Because all processing of the individual elements of the matrices is taken care of by Excel functions, the code is particularly straightforward. The product of the matrix multiplication, named Amat12 to indicate that it is a matrix, is declared as a variant to reinforce the fact that it is non-scalar in type and dimension:

```
Function ArrayDemo1(Amat1, Amat2)
  'uses the MMult and MInverse array functions
  Dim Amat12 As Variant
  Amat12 = Application.MMult(Amat1, Amat2)
  ArrayDemo1 = Application.MInverse(Amat12)
End Function
```

If a matrix and vector are to be multiplied together, it is important that the dimensions conform. If Amat1 is a 3 by 3 matrix and avec a 3 by 1 column vector, if the matrix is 'post'multiplied by the vector, the result is a 3 by 1 column vector. Function ArrayDemo2, with inputs avec and Amat1, produces a column vector:

```
Function ArrayDemo2(avec, Amat1)
  'multiplying matrix (Amat1) and col vector (avec)
  ArrayDemo2 = Application.MMult(Amat1, avec)
End Function
```

Alternatively, if the vector is transposed into a row vector, it could 'pre'multiply the matrix, Amat1, but the result would be different, in fact a 1 by 3 row vector. The third line of code would need to be modified to read as:

```
ArrayDemo2 = Application.MMult(Application.Transpose(avec), Amat1)
```

In general we code functions such that they behave in a comparable manner to Excel functions. That is, we require functions with array input to accept either row or column arrays. Where the function returns an output vector, the output is a row vector. Function ArrayDemo3 returns a row vector, whatever the form of the input avec (i.e. whether avec is a row or column vector). If avec is a column vector, its rows will exceed its columns in number, and this condition will cause the vector to be transposed into a row vector. Otherwise it is already in the correct format. Function ArrayDemo3 returns a row vector, whatever the input vector:

```
Function ArrayDemo3(avec)
  'returning a row vector, whatever the input
  Dim nr As Integer, nc As Integer
  nr = avec.Rows.Count
  nc = avec.Columns.Count
  If nr > = nc Then avec = Application.Transpose(avec)
```

```
   ArrayDemo3 = avec
End Function
```

The next function, ArrayDemo4, illustrates how arrays can be set up element-by-element within VBA code. The important point to note is that these constructed arrays are row vectors by default. For this reason, the matrix multiplication operation should work as coded and a row vector will be returned:

```
Option Base 1

Function ArrayDemo4(Amat1)
   'VBA sets up array avec as row array
   Dim avec(3) As Variant
   avec(1) = 3
   avec(2) = 4
   avec(3) = 5
   ArrayDemo4 = Application.MMult(avec, Amat1)
End Function
```

Alternatively, if the penultimate line of code is:

```
ArrayDemo4 = Application.MMult(Amat1, Application.Transpose(avec))
```

a different matrix multiplication operation will return a column vector with different values.

The Option Base 1 statement at the top of the module sheet ensures that the array elements number from 1 as is usual in Excel operations. If the Option Base declaration is omitted, the elements number from 0 (the default) (and the subsequent matrix multiplication will fail because of non-conformity). Here, the Option Base statement ensures that elements in array avec are simply avec(1), avec(2) and avec(3), and that there is no avec(0).

Where no suitable Excel array functions exist for the required manipulation of arrays, element-by-element processing in a loop may be unavoidable. If so, the number of elements in the array must be counted and this is easily achieved with code such as Application.Count(avec). (For an array created within a user-defined function, the number of elements can also be evaluated using the UBound (and LBound) properties of an array.)

APPENDIX 4B   BINOMIAL TREE OPTION VALUATION FUNCTIONS

The Black–Scholes formula gives values for straightforward European calls and puts. An alternative numerical approach to option valuation, which can be applied to a wide range of options, is the binomial tree method. This approach approximates the development of share prices over the option life by a series of linked probabilistically-determined binomial steps (at which incremental share movements are restricted to up and down movements of known size). This binomial tree structure produces a share price tree with a spread of ending prices and a cluster of paths through the tree of differing frequency. For each ending node in the tree, the option on the share can be valued and, using the probabilistic structure of the tree, the option payoff can be discounted back to get its present value.

	A	B	C	D	E	F	G	H	I
2	CRR Option Valuation								
3									
4	Share price (S)			100.00		Cox, Ross & Rubinstein			
5	Exercise price (X)			95.00					
6	Int rate-cont (r)			8.00%		dt	0.0556		
7						erdt	1.0045		
8	Dividend yield (q)			3.00%		ermqdt	1.0028		
9						u	1.0483		
10	Time now (0, years)			0.0000		d	0.9540		
11	Time maturity (T, years)			0.5000		p	0.5177		
12	Option life (T, years)			0.5000		p*	0.4823		
13	Volatility (s)			20.0%					
14							European		American
15	Steps in tree (n)			9		via CRRtree	9.63		
16	iopt			1		via fn	9.63		9.63
17	option type			Call		BS value	9.73		

Figure 4.6   Option valuation via CRR binomial tree method

The spreadsheet in Figure 4.6 shows details of the call option evaluated previously (with the Black–Scholes function BSOptValue in cell G17) together with the components of a nine-step binomial tree. The life of the option ($T = 0.5$ years) is split into nine time steps each of length δt (here 0.0556 years). The objective is to develop a second option valuation function, this time based on the tree valuation method. To understand the VBA code, it is important to understand how valuation occurs in the binomial tree and hence a short digression into the mechanics of the approach is in order. However, in the function to be developed, computation of the binomial tree and the option payoffs at maturity are all contained in the code of the function itself.

The values of the share price up and down multipliers (u and d) and the associated probabilities p and p^* used at each step are due to Cox, Ross and Rubinstein (CRR). Their formulas ensure that the resulting share price tree is consistent with the geometric diffusion process considered by practitioners to be realistic for share price processes. The detailed formulas for u, d, p and p^* need not concern us here, but when applied to the starting price and repeated for all nine steps, these give rise to the share price tree shown in Figure 4.7 below.

	A	B	C	D	E	F	G	H	I	J	K
17	Binomial Tree Valuation										
18	Share										
19		0	1	2	3	4	5	6	7	8	9
20	9										152.85
21	8									145.81	139.09
22	7								139.09	132.69	126.58
23	6							132.69	126.58	120.75	115.19
24	5						126.58	120.75	115.19	109.89	104.83
25	4					120.75	115.19	109.89	104.83	100.00	95.40
26	3				115.19	109.89	104.83	100.00	95.40	91.00	86.81
27	2			109.89	104.83	100.00	95.40	91.00	86.81	82.81	79.00
28	1		104.83	100.00	95.40	91.00	86.81	82.81	79.00	75.36	71.89
29	0	100.00	95.40	91.00	86.81	82.81	79.00	75.36	71.89	68.58	65.43
30											

Figure 4.7   Nine-step share price tree using CRR parameters

Starting at value 100, one step later the two possible prices are 104.83 ($100u$) and 95.40 ($100d$). After nine steps, a share that has i up moves (and $(9 - i)$ down moves) will have value $100u^i d^{9-i}$, or more generally for an n-step tree:

$$S_{in} = Su^i d^{n-i}$$

It follows that the 10 payoffs of the associated option at expiry, as shown in cells K49:K58 of Figure 4.8, are given by the formulas:

$$\max[S_i - X, 0] \quad \text{for } i = 0, 1, \ldots, 9 \text{ and } S = 100, X = 95$$

For example, for nine up movements the option value is:

$$\max[100(1.048)^9 - 95, 0] = 57.85$$

The last operation is to value this vector of cells, K49:K58, weighting each by its probability of occurrence and discounting back to time 0. This involves 'rolling back' the terminal option payoffs, using the up and down probabilities, p and p^*, and discounting to get values at step 8 in time, and so on back to their present value. For example at step 8, the option value in cell J50 is $[57.85p + 44.09p^*]/1.0045 = 50.99$. The steps are displayed numerically in Figure 4.8, so that the final option value via binomial valuation is shown in cell B58 (9.63 as compared with the Black–Scholes value of 9.73).

	A	B	C	D	E	F	G	H	I	J	K
47	Option Value										
48		0	1	2	3	4	5	6	7	8	9
49	9										57.85
50	8									50.99	44.09
51	7								44.47	37.89	31.58
52	6							38.29	32.00	25.97	20.19
53	5						32.41	26.41	20.65	15.13	9.83
54	4					26.84	21.10	15.60	10.32	5.25	0.40
55	3				21.65	16.27	11.24	6.67	2.81	0.20	0.00
56	2			16.98	12.13	7.79	4.15	1.50	0.11	0.00	0.00
57	1		12.96	8.76	5.23	2.52	0.80	0.05	0.00	0.00	0.00
58	0	9.63	6.15	3.42	1.50	0.42	0.03	0.00	0.00	0.00	0.00

Figure 4.8 Rolling back and discounting option values

The VBA code for the BinOptVal function, based on the CRR tree, is shown below. The statement **Option Base 0** at the top of the Module sheet is strictly speaking unnecessary. It merely confirms that for this function, all arrays number from 0, which is the default numbering anyway. The function has eight inputs, including **nstep**, the number of steps in the tree. For the moment, the function returns the value of a European option (with **iopt = 1** for a call, **iopt = –1** for a put). At the end of the section, we note how straightforward it is to extend the function code to cover American options as well as the simpler European versions:

```
Option Base 0                          'arrays number from 0

Function BinOptVal(iopt, S, X, r, q, tyr, sigma, nstep)     'code for European Options
```

'returns binomial option value, European only, where iopt = 1 for call, -1 for put

```
Dim delt, erdt, ermqdt, u, d, p, pstar
Dim i As Integer, j As Integer
Dim vvec As Variant
ReDim vvec(nstep)     'known size of vector

'calculate parameters
delt = tyr / nstep                        'length of time step
erdt = Exp(r * delt)                      'compounding factor
ermqdt = Exp((r-q) * delt)                'drift term
u = Exp(sigma * Sqr(delt))                'up multiplier
d = 1 / u                                 'down multiplier
p = (ermqdt - d) / (u - d)                'up prob
pstar = 1 - p                             'down prob

'calculating vector of option values after n steps
For i = 0 To nstep
vvec(i) = Application.Max(iopt*(S*(u^i)*(d^(nstep-i))-X), 0)
Next i
'calculating conditional payoffs & discounting back step-by-step
For j = nstep - 1 To 0 Step -1
  For i = 0 To j
                vvec(i) = (p*vvec(i + 1) + pstar*vvec(i))/erdt
  Next i
Next j
BinOptVal = vvec(0)
End Function
```

The valuation process centres on vector array vvec(), declared as a variant type. For nstep =9, vvec() has 10 values, vvec(0) to vvec(9), as ensured by the dimensioning statement ReDim vvec(9), in general vvec(nstep).

After declaring variables, the CRR tree parameters for the up and down price movements are assigned. For the call option shown in Figure 4.6, the initial values of vvec() are vvec(0) = 57.85, vvec(1) = 44.09, ... vvec(9) = 0, i.e. the option payoffs shown in K49:K58 of Figure 4.8. In the VBA code, these values are derived from formulas of the form:

$$\max[S(u^i d^{(\text{nstep}-i)}) - X, 0] \quad i = 0, 1, 2, \ldots, \text{nstep}$$

The statements producing the initial vvec() array are:

```
For i = 0 To nstep
  vvec(i)=Application.Max(iopt*(S*(u^i)*(d^(nstep-i))-X), 0)
Next i
```

The subsequent five lines of code drive the process of working backwards through the tree, valuing and discounting:

```
For j = nstep - 1 To 0 Step -1
  For i = 0 To j
    vvec(i) = (p*vvec(i+1)+pstar*vvec(i))/erdt
  Next i
Next j
```

Examining the code, at each backwards step (j value), the vvec() array is recalculated, replacing redundant values with new values as the option is valued. This has the advantage of limiting storage requirements to a single vector with only $(n + 1)$ elements. Thus for the nine-step tree, when $j = 8$, vvec() is re-evaluated, the entries changing to vvec(0) = 50.99, vvec(1) = 37.89, etc. and when finally $j = 0$, vvec(0) becomes 9.63. (In the spreadsheet in contrast, working backwards through the tree from step 9 to step 0 requires us to display 10 vectors of values, see Figure 4.8). Thus, the present value of the option is contained in vvec(0) when $j = 0$.

Using this function to evaluate the call via a nine-step tree as in cell G15, we have:

$$\text{BinOptVal}(1, 100, 95, 8\%, 3\%, 0.5, 20\%, 9)$$

which returns the value 9.63. In general the closeness of the binomial tree option valuation to the Black–Scholes value should improve as the number of steps increases. For example, BinOptVal(1, 100, 95, 8%, 3%, 0.5, 20%, 50) evaluates as 9.74. The proximity of binomial valuation to the Black–Scholes value can be checked out by constructing a Data Table on the function, varying the number of steps, nstep.

Figures 4.6, 4.7 and 4.8 show the binomial tree valuation of a call. If the option is a put, input parameter iopt $= -1$, and the VBA function statements producing the initial vvec() array:

```
For i = 0 To nstep
  vvec(i)=Application.Max(-1*(S*(u^i)*(d^(nstep-i))-X), 0)
Next i
```

give terminal outcomes for the put. Check that for a put:

$$=\text{BinOptVal}(-1, 100, 95, 8\%, 3\%, 0.5, 20\%, 9)$$

evaluates as 2.40 as compared with 2.49 for the Black–Scholes value.

American options in contrast to European ones allow the possibility of early exercise, that is, exercise before the option matures. It has been shown that early exercise is never preferable for American calls (in the absence of dividends), so their valuation is exactly the same as European calls. However, for American puts, early exercise is frequently more valuable than waiting until maturity. To adjust the VBA code in the valuation function, BinOptVal, one additional input parameter (iea $= 1$ for European, iea $= 2$ for American) is introduced and just one additional line of code is required:

```
'for Amer options, allowing for early exercise at each step
If iea=2 Then vvec(i)=Application.Max(vvec(i), iopt*(S*(u^i)*(d^(j-i))-X))
```

The full code for this generalised binomial valuation function, which works for both European and American calls and puts, is set out below:

```
Function BinOptVal(iopt, iea, S, X, r, q, tyr, sigma, nstep)
'returns binomial option value (iopt = 1 for call, -1 for put;
'iea=1 for euro, 2 for amer)

  Dim delt, erdt, ermqdt, u, d, p, pstar
  Dim i As Integer, j As Integer
  Dim vvec As Variant
  ReDim vvec(nstep)        'known size of vector
  'calculate parameters
  delt = tyr / nstep                    'length of time step
  erdt = Exp(r * delt)                  'compounding factor
```

```
    ermqdt = Exp((r-q) * delt)              'dividend yield effect

    u = Exp(sigma * Sqr(delt))              'up multiplier
    d = 1 / u                               'down multiplier
    p = (erdt - d) / (u - d)                'up prob
    pstar = 1 - p                           'down prob
    'calculating vector of option values after 9 steps
    For i = 0 To nstep
        vvec(i) = Application.Max(iopt*(S*(u^i)*(d^(nstep - i))-X), 0)
    Next i
    'calculating conditional payoffs & discounting back step-by-step
        For j = nstep-1 To 0 Step -1
            For i = 0 To j
            vvec(i) = (P * vvec(i + 1) + pstar * vvec(i)) / erdt
    'for Amer options, allowing for early exercise at each step
            If iea = 2 Then vvec(i) = Application.Max(vvec(i),
                iopt*(S*(u^i)*(d^(j-i))-X))
            Next i
        Next j
    BinOptVal = vvec(0)
End Function
```

Previously, the value of the European put, with characteristics given in Figure 4.6, evaluated as 2.40, whereas its American counterpart evaluated as 2.54 on the nine-step tree.

EXERCISES ON WRITING FUNCTIONS

1. Financial Arithmetic
Develop VBA functions for the following simple financial arithmetic calculations:

   i.   FutureValue(P, r, n, t), a function that returns the future value of investment P, after t years, given interest at rate of return r p.a., compounded n times a year.

  ii.   Function AnnPercentRate(rf, f), a function that returns the annual effective rate of compounding interest at rate rf, f times p.a.

 iii.   Function APRCont(r), a function that returns the annual effective rate equivalent to continuous compounding at rate r p.a.

2. Sum and SumProduct Functions
Develop code for a function that behaves in the same manner as the Excel SUM function. The function should sum all numerical values in an array.

Also write a function to emulate Excel's SUMPRODUCT(array1, array2) which calculates the product of the elements of two arrays. It should give an error message if the arrays are of different size.

3. Net Present Value Function
Develop code for a function that behaves in the same manner as Excel's NPV function that requires two inputs, the first an array of cash flows and the second the discount rate, e.g. Function NetPV(cvec, rate).

4. Standard Deviation of Cash Flows (section 4.5)
Develop code for a function to evaluate the standard deviation of a set of cash flows (vvec) with different probability weights (pvec) as discussed in section 4.5. Remember to use the VBA built-in function, Sqr, rather than the Excel function.

5. PayBack Function

The spreadsheet shows cash flows over five years for an investment proposal. After an outflow at the start, the cumulated cash flows turn positive during the third year, the time at which this happens being known as the project's payback period (here 2.4 years).

The intermediate calculations determining the payback period are set out in the work-sheet. They centre on cumulating cash flows at yearly intervals and testing to determine the time at which the cumulative sum first turns positive. Develop a Payback Function, say PayBack(cvec) that returns the payback period for any array of cash flows.

	A	B	C	D
1	VBFns1.xls			
2		**Payback Function**		
3		Proposal A		
4	year	Cashflow	Cum Cflow	
5				
6	0	**-100**	-100	=B6
7	1	35	-65	=B7+C6
8	2	45	-20	
9	3	55	35	
10	4	60	95	
11	5	60	155	
12				
13	NPV		64.8	
14	IRR		37.2%	
15	**Payback Period**		2.4	
16				
17	Discount Rate		**15%**	

SOLUTION NOTES FOR EXERCISES ON FUNCTIONS

1. Financial Arithmetic Functions

Function FutureValue(P, r, n, t)
'returns future value of P, compounded at annual rate r
'n times a year, for t years

```
  FutureValue = P * (1 + r / n)^(n * t)
End Function
```

Function AnnPercentRate(rf, f)
'returns annual effective rate of compounding at rate rf, f times p.a.
```
  Dim APR
  APR = (1 + rf)^f-1
  AnnPercentRate = APR
End Function
```

Function APRCont(r)
'returns annual effective rate of compounding continuously at rate r p.a.
```
  APRCont = Exp(r) - 1
End Function
```

2. Code for SUM()

Option Base 1

Function SumArray(avec)
'VBA version of Excel's SUM function

```
Dim n as integer: Dim i as Integer
Dim total
total = 0
n=Application.Count(avec)
For i = 1 to n
total = total + avec(i)
Next i
SumArray = total
End Function
```

Code for SUMPRODUCT()

```
Option Base 1

Function ProdArray(xvec, yvec)
'VBA version of Excel's SUMPRODUCT function
   Dim i, imax, j, jmax
   imax = Application.CountA(xvec) 'counts all elements in 1st array
   jmax = Application.CountA(yvec) 'counts all elements in 2nd array
   If imax = jmax Then
      ProdArray = 0
      For i = 1 To imax
      If Application.IsNumber(xvec(i)) And Application.IsNumber(yvec(i)) Then _
         ProdArray = ProdArray + xvec(i) * yvec(i)
      Next i
   Else ProdArray = "Counts don't match"
   End If
   ProdArray = ProdArray
End Function
```

3. NPV Code

```
Option Base 1

Function NetPV(cflowvec, rate)
Dim i as Integer
NetPV=0
For i = 1 to Application.Count(cflowvec)
NetPV=NetPV + cflowvec(i)/(1+rate)^(i-1)
Next i
NetPV = NetPV
End Function
```

4. Code for Standard Deviation of Cash Flows

```
Option Base 1

Function StdDev(vvec, pvec)
   If Application.Count(vvec) = Application.Count(pvec) Then
      StdDev = Variance(vvec, pvec)
      If IsNumeric(StdDev) And StdDev <> - 1 Then        'IsNumeric(arg1) VBA Fn
         StdDev = Sqr(StdDev)                            'Sqr(arg1) is VBA Math Fn
   Else
         StdDev = -1
      End If
   Else
      StdDev = "Counts not equal"
   End If
   StdDev = StdDev
End Function
```

5. Payback Function

The code for the function is given below and three features are highlighted in turn.

Firstly, the elements in the array, cvec, require unambiguous numbering. Here, Option Base 1 ensures that elements in array cvec can be referred to as cvec(1), cvec(2), the final one being cvec(6) having value 60. There is no cvec(0).

Secondly, the function has been made more robust by using the If... Then... Else syntax at the start to strip out those exceptional cases when Payback cannot be evaluated. (For example, when the first cash flow is positive, cvec(1) > = 0, or when the cumulative sum of all the cash flows remains negative, Application.Sum(cvec)<0, the function is displayed as '−1').

Thirdly, the array input, cvec, is processed element-by-element, the individual cash flows being added one-by-one to get the cumulative cash flow sum, denoted by variable csum. This happens in the For...Next loop in which the individual cash flows are cumulated one-by-one, as i increments up to its maximum value (Application.Count(cvec))—here up to at most six times. When variable csum first becomes positive, the flow of processing jumps out of the For...Next loop (Exit For) and Payback period is evaluated.

A little care is needed to identify exactly which the 'ith' cash flow term is that turns csum from negative to positive. In this example, when $i = 4$, csum changes from -20 to $+35$, the last negative csum being -20 at the end of year 2. The exact payback time in years is therefore 2 years plus fraction 20/55, that is 2.4 years.

VBA Code for Payback Function

Option Base 1

```
Function Payback(cvec)
'calculates payback period, i.e. no. of years (to 1 dpl)
'initial cash flow must be negative

  Dim csum                    'csum = cumulative cash flow
  Dim i As Integer
  If cvec(1) >= 0 Or Application.sum(cvec) < 0 Then
    Payback = -1
  Else
    csum = 0
    For i = 1 To Application.Count(cvec)
      csum = csum + cvec(i)
      If csum > 0 Then
        Exit For
      End If
    Next i
    csum = csum-cvec(i)
    Payback = Application.Round(i-2-csum/cvec(i),1)
  End If
End Function
```

Part Two
Advanced Modelling in Equities

5
Introduction to Equities

In Part II of the book we look at equities. The coverage of relevant topics is spread over the following three chapters: Chapter 6 on portfolio optimisation, Chapter 7 on asset pricing and Chapter 8 on performance measurement and attribution. In this introductory chapter, we briefly summarise the finance theory covered in the Equities part of the book and introduce the range of numerical methods implemented in the spreadsheets that accompany the text.

The development of mean–variance portfolio theory in the fifties by Harry Markowitz provided the genesis of finance as an academic subject, separate from but related to economics. Markowitz pointed out the crucial distinction between the risk of individual equities and the contribution of an individual equity to portfolio risk. One important feature of mean–variance portfolio theory was the identification of return and risk with mean and variance. By linking the variation in returns to the normal distribution, much classical statistical analysis was available to implement finance theory. Following on from portfolio theory in the sixties came the capital asset pricing model (CAPM), a single-factor model of expected equity returns, introducing beta as an important measure of portfolio risk. In the aftermath of the CAPM various measures of portfolio performance were suggested. Subsequent developments incorporated multiple-factor models for portfolio returns, the latest example of which is Sharpe's style analysis for performance attribution in the early 1990s. The topics outlined in the following three chapters include risk–return representation, portfolio risk and return, the efficient frontier, the single-index model, CAPM, traditional performance measures, style analysis and Value-at-Risk (VaR).

The three associated workbooks (EQUITY1.xls, EQUITY2.xls and EQUITY3.xls) follow the chronological development of equity portfolio management, whilst also revealing the recurrence of important ideas across different areas of the subject. Portfolio theory has at times been constrained by the lack of computing power. At the present time, with Excel and high specification PCs, this is less of a constraint (though some applications involve the handful of asset classes rather than the thousands of individual equities).

The main numerical technique used in the next three chapters is a form of optimisation known as quadratic programming. This technique can be implemented using Excel's Solver add-in. We show how to structure a range of different portfolio optimisation problems and produce optimal weights by correctly applying Solver. Repeated application of the quadratic programming algorithm is used to generate the efficient frontier in Chapter 6, and to perform style analysis in Chapter 8. The second numerical technique used in the context of equities is regression. In Chapter 7 we show how Excel's regression functions can be adapted to estimate beta coefficients. At a more mundane level, much of the computation in estimating risk and returns from asset data can be handled via Excel's statistical functions. We also use VBA macros to automate the use of Solver in Chapters 6 and 8, and to show how charts can be produced efficiently.

The three main topics covered in the EQUITY1.xls, EQUITY2.xls and EQUITY3.xls workbooks all involve optimisation problems with quadratic objective functions: portfolio risk (frontier portfolios), the sum of squared residuals (beta estimates) and the error variance (style analysis). Though some of the simpler problems have analytic solutions, as a rule, optimisation problems are typically solved using an iterative search process that seeks to find the optimal solution. In Excel, this search process is handled by the Solver add-in. In particular, the use of Solver is illustrated in the EF2 sheet in EQUITY1 and the Style sheets in EQUITY3.

Equities are important in themselves but also as a preparation for the valuation of options on equities covered in Part III of the book.

6
Portfolio Optimisation

In this chapter, we look at a single individual investor and explore how he can solve the problem of portfolio optimisation. The background theory and many practical examples are set out in Bodie et al. (1996, Chapters 6 and 7). We concentrate on spreadsheet implementation of calculation procedures, and include an exploration of the underlying generic portfolio problem types. For establishing the weights for risky portfolios, the main workhorse is Excel's Solver, whereas for the allocation between risky and risk-free assets in the generic portfolio problems, user-defined functions for spreadsheet formulas are preferable. Sections 6.1 and 6.2 cover important preliminaries for risky portfolios. Sections 6.3 to 6.5 concentrate on determining optimal portfolio weights. In section 6.6, the risk–return trade-off and risk aversion are introduced with the ensuing sections 6.7 to 6.9 applying spreadsheets to the generic portfolio problems. The chapter concludes with fuller details on the user-defined functions and macros developed to assist portfolio analysis in the associated workbook, EQUITY1.xls.

6.1 PORTFOLIO MEAN AND VARIANCE

The mean–variance model of portfolio choice is well described and explained in finance textbooks (for example Bodie et al., 1996, Chapter 7 on Optimal Risky Portfolios). Markowitz reduced the optimisation problem to that of finding mean–variance efficient portfolios, with efficient points having the highest expected return for a given level of risk. Throughout this chapter, risk will be measured by portfolio variance (or more strictly by its square root, the standard deviation of portfolio returns). We use two ideas in developing the portfolio models for a set of assets:

- the mean and variance of returns for the portfolios;
- the parallel representation of portfolios in risk–return space.

We assume throughout that the portfolio must be fully invested by imposing the restriction that the weights of the holdings in different assets (w_i) must add up to 100%.

Given any set of risky assets and a set of weights that describe how the portfolio investment is split, the general formulas for n assets are:

Portfolio return: $\qquad E(r_p) = \sum w_i E(r_i)$

Portfolio variance: $\quad Var(r_p) = \sigma_p{}^2 = \sum \sum w_i w_j \operatorname{cov}(i, j) \quad$ where $\operatorname{cov}(i, i) = \sigma_i{}^2$

where $E(r_i)$ denotes the expected return for the ith asset, and σ_i is the risk (standard deviation of returns) for the ith asset. The elements $\operatorname{cov}(i, j)$ make up the so-called variance–covariance matrix of the assets. As its formula shows, portfolio variance is a quadratic function of the portfolio weights. The portfolio risk, as measured by its standard deviation, is the square root of the variance.

Working in a spreadsheet, it helps to have expressions for portfolio return and risk that are easy to 'enter'. Since the summed formulas above are most unsuitable for cell entry, we adopt two alternative approaches: (i) cell formulas based on Excel's vector and matrix multiplication and (ii) user-defined functions, which can be accessed in the workbook.

Looking first at explicit cell formulas, if the expected returns and the portfolio weights are represented by column vectors (denoted $\mathbf{e}$ and $\mathbf{w}$ respectively, with row vector transposes $\mathbf{e}^T$ and $\mathbf{w}^T$), and the variance–covariance terms by matrix $\mathbf{V}$, then the expressions can be written as simple matrix formulas. They can easily be implemented with Excel array functions:

	matrix notation	*Excel formula*
Portfolio return:	$\mathbf{w}^T\mathbf{e}$	=SUMPRODUCT(w,e)
Portfolio variance:	$\mathbf{w}^T\mathbf{V}\mathbf{w}$	=MMULT(TRANSPOSE(w), MMULT(V,w))

Figure 6.1 illustrates these calculations for three asset classes (TBills, Bonds and Shares). These represent the performance of US asset classes between 1926 and 1992, and have been calculated by applying the Excel STDEV and AVERAGE functions to the historic annual percentage returns data. The current portfolio is split 40%:50%:10% between the three asset types. If the expected returns (C5:C7) and the weights (I10:I12) have range names $\mathbf{e}$ and $\mathbf{w}$ respectively and the variance–covariance matrix (C15:E17) is named $\mathbf{V}$, the above Excel formulas give the portfolio return and variance. Thus, the portfolio with the 40%:50%:10% split has an expected return of 2.2% (cell I15) and risk 7.0% (cell I16), the latter obtained by taking the square root of the variance of 0.0049 (cell I18).

	A	B	C	D	E	F	G	H	I	J
2	Risk & return with three assets									
3										
4	Asset Data		Exp Ret	Std Dev						
5		TBills	0.6%	4.3%			Target exp return		7.0%	
6		Bonds	2.1%	10.1%						
7		Shares	9.0%	20.8%						
8										
9	Correlation Matrix		TBills	Bonds	Shares		Portfolio weights			
10		TBills	1.00	0.63	0.09			TBills	40.0%	
11		Bonds	0.63	1.00	0.23			Bonds	50.0%	
12		Shares	0.09	0.23	1.00			Shares	10.0%	
13						=SUMPRODUCT(w,e)				
14	VCV matrix		TBills	Bonds	Shares					
15		TBills	0.0018	0.0027	0.0008			Exp Ret	2.2%	
16		Bonds	0.0027	0.0102	0.0048			Std Dev	7.0%	
17		Shares	0.0008	0.0048	0.0433					
18								Variance	0.0049	
19										
20						=MMULT(TRANSPOSE(w),MMULT(V,w))				
21										
22		=C11*VLOOKUP(C$14,$B$5:$D$7,3,FALSE)*VLOOKUP($B16,$B$5:$D$7,3,FALSE)								
23										

Figure 6.1   Risk and return calculations for a portfolio of three assets

The input data for these calculations include the variance–covariance matrix for the three sets of returns. The elements of this matrix are calculated from the correlations between each pair of asset classes (cells C10:E12) and the standard deviations (D5:D7). In passing, notice the general formula illustrated in Figure 6.1 for obtaining each element of the variance–covariance matrix, namely:

$$=C11*VLOOKUP(C\$14,\$B\$5:\$D\$7,3,FALSE)*$$

$$VLOOKUP(\$B16,\$B\$5:\$D\$7,3,FALSE)$$

Here, the element is the covariance of TBills and Bonds: the corresponding correlation is in cell C11 and the two relevant standard deviations (for TBills and Bonds) are obtained by two vertical lookups on the range B5:D7 which includes asset labels and standard deviations.

The second approach with respect to computation of portfolio risk and return is to write user-defined functions in VBA. If the vectors of expected returns and portfolio weights are denoted by variables *retvec* and *wtsvec*, and the variance–covariance matrix by *vcvmat* then functions denoted PortfolioReturn(*retvec*, *wtsvec*) and PortfolioVariance(*wtsvec*, *vcvmat*) can be coded to return the required measures. Portfolio risk is the square root of the value returned by the PortfolioVariance function. Details of the coding of these functions are in the section called User-Defined Functions in Module1. For those unfamiliar with Excel's matrix functions, the user-defined functions provide much simpler expressions to enter in cells.

Our development of mean–variance portfolio theory in sections 6.2 to 6.5 uses three assets, but is easily extended to allow much larger numbers of possible assets.

6.2 RISK–RETURN REPRESENTATION OF PORTFOLIOS

Throughout the section on equities, the overriding theme will be the dual ideas of return and risk. Figure 6.2 shows the representation of portfolios in terms of their risk (on the x axis) and return (on the y axis). The chart shows the position of the three individual asset classes together with portfolios based on the assets. For example, the most risky asset class, Shares, is positioned in the top to the right (risk = 20.8%, return = 9.0%) in contrast to TBills which is nearer to the origin (risk = 4.3%, return = 0.6%).

The current portfolio in Figure 6.1, which consists mostly of TBills and Bonds (with some Shares), is shown in Figure 6.2 with the label 'Fig1 PF'. Although this particular portfolio has an expected return of 2.2%, slightly different weights give a minimum risk portfolio with the same expected return. Minimum risk portfolios are also called efficient and the locus of these portfolios is called the efficient frontier. Thus portfolios with the best combinations of weights lie along the efficient frontier, where a target return is achieved with minimum risk. In the chart, these efficient portfolios or *frontier* portfolios are labelled as the *unconstrained frontier*. Notice that the frontier contains a unique minimum variance, and hence overall there is a minimum variance portfolio. Currently the portfolio weights must sum to one but are unconstrained by any further conditions, hence the terminology 'unconstrained frontier'.

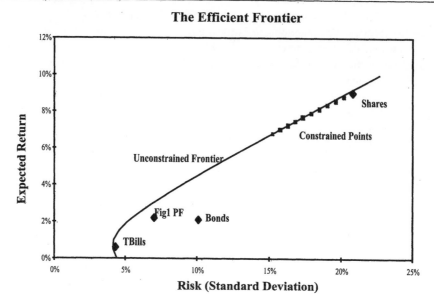

Figure 6.2   Risk–return representation of portfolios

In the following sections, we start by identifying individual points on the efficient frontier and then, in due course, generate the whole frontier. The final stage is to impose
constraints on the holdings of individual asset classes (which in turn confine the return
of the portfolio to a single range) and then to find the position of the constrained frontier
points. Note that, although the scale of the chart does not allow us to confirm this visu-
ally, the constrained points will always lie on or slightly to the right of the unconstrained
frontier.

If there are no additional constraints on the weights for the individual assets, frontier
portfolios can be obtained from formulas outlined by Huang and Litzenberger (1988,
section 6.4). However, generating efficient portfolios using Solver is easier to explain,
so this approach is described first, and then extended to the case when the weights on
individual asset classes are constrained. Finally, methods are suggested for generating the
entire efficient frontier.

6.3   USING SOLVER TO FIND EFFICIENT POINTS

Given the same asset data set out in Figure 6.3, suppose we want to construct an efficient
portfolio producing a target return of 7%. The problem is to find the split across the
assets that achieves the target return whilst minimising the variance of return. This is
a standard optimisation problem amenable to Excel's Solver, which contains a range of
iterative search methods for optimisation. Since portfolio variance is a quadratic function
of the weights, we will be using Solver for quadratic programming.

	A	B	C	D	E	F	G	H	I	J
2	Using Solver to reproduce Unconstrained Frontier Portfolios									
3										
4	Asset Data		Exp Ret	Std Dev						
5		TBills	0.6%	4.3%			Target exp return		7.0%	target1
6		Bonds	2.1%	10.1%						
7		Shares	9.0%	20.8%			(Ctrl + Shift + U to run Macro)			
8										
9	Correlation Matrix		TBills	Bonds	Shares		Frontier portfolio weights			
10		TBills	1.00	0.63	0.09			TBills	40.0%	
11		Bonds	0.63	1.00	0.23			Bonds	50.0%	change1
12		Shares	0.09	0.23	1.00			Shares	10.0%	
13										
14	VCV Matrix		TBills	Bonds	Shares					
15		TBills	0.0018	0.0027	0.0008			Exp Ret	2.2%	portret1
16		Bonds	0.0027	0.0102	0.0048			Std Dev	7.0%	portsd1
17		Shares	0.0008	0.0048	0.0433					

Figure 6.3   Sheet EF1 (in EQUITY1.xls) ready for optimisation

The algebraic structure of problems amenable to solution with quadratic programming is documented fully in Eppen et al. (1998), as is the use of Excel's Solver. Therefore, we confine ourselves to a brief explanation of how to operate Solver for this portfolio problem using the layout in Figure 6.3. Notice the various range names attached to cells, e.g. change1 for cells I11:I12, portret1 for I15, etc.

Solver requires 'changing cells', a 'target cell' for minimisation and the specification of 'constraints', which act as restrictions on feasible values for the changing cells. Notice that the condition on full investment can be achieved by putting the formula:

$$=1-SUM(I11:I12)$$

in cell I10. So the 'changing cells' for the optimisation are cells I11:I12 or, using the range name, change1. The target cell to be minimised is the standard deviation of return (I16), named portsd1. There is one explicit constraint, namely that the expected return (cell I15), named portret1, must at least equal the target level (in cell I5), named target1. (Note: The range names are particularly useful in specifying the Solver parameters and again later in writing the VBA macros to automate the optimisation.)

The steps with Solver are:

1. Invoke Solver by choosing Tools then Options then Solver.
2. Specify in the Solver Parameter Dialog Box:
    the Target cell (I16) to be optimised
    specify *max* or *min*, as shown in Figure 6.4 and
    the changing cells (I11:I12).
3. Choose Add to specify the constraints then OK (Figure 6.4 below on the right). This constraint ensures that I15 must meet the target (cell I5).
4. Click on Options and ensure that Assume Linear Model is not checked.
5. Solve and get the results in the spreadsheet.

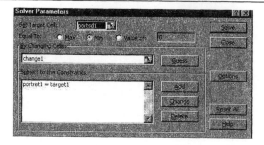
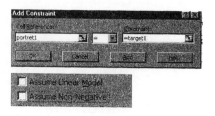

Figure 6.4   Setting up Solver to minimise variance

Applying Solver, the optimum weights suggest positive holdings of Bonds and Shares and a negative holding of TBills in the proportions shown in the sheet in Figure 6.5. Cell I15 confirms that this efficient portfolio with minimum standard deviation of 15.7% achieves the required return of 7%. Changing the target expected return in cell I5 and invoking Solver again with the same specifications as before produces another efficient portfolio. (The reader should confirm this by changing the target return in I5 from 7% to say 3% and then invoking Solver to get the new portfolio weights. Another exercise is to determine the weights for the unique minimum variance portfolio. If the constraint portret1=target1 shown in Figure 6.4 is deleted, Solver gives the weights for this special case–expected return 0.7%, risk 4.1%.)

Since there are no constraints on the weights assigned to individual assets, negative holdings are possible, which is also known as short selling. Indeed for our example in Figure 6.5, the frontier portfolio with an expected return of 7% contains a negative holding of 5.6% in TBills. This means that the portfolio entails borrowing a proportion of the portfolio value, thus incurring an interest charge to offset against the expected returns from the positive holdings in the other two assets.

	A	B	C	D	E	F	G	H	I	J
2	Using Solver to reproduce Unconstrained Frontier Portfolios									
3										
4	Asset Data		Exp Ret	Std Dev						
5		TBills	0.6%	4.3%			Target exp return		7.0%	target1
6		Bonds	2.1%	10.1%						
7		Shares	9.0%	20.8%			(Ctrl + Shift + U to run Macro)			
8										
9	Correlation Matrix		TBills	Bonds	Shares		Frontier portfolio weights			
10		TBills	1.00	0.63	0.09			TBills	-5.6%	
11		Bonds	0.63	1.00	0.23			Bonds	35.8%	change1
12		Shares	0.09	0.23	1.00			Shares	69.8%	
13										
14	VCV Matrix		TBills	Bonds	Shares					
15		TBills	0.0018	0.0027	0.0008			Exp Ret	7.0%	portret1
16		Bonds	0.0027	0.0102	0.0048			Std Dev	15.7%	portsd1
17		Shares	0.0008	0.0048	0.0433					

Figure 6.5   The unconstrained frontier portfolio with 7% expected return

So far, optimal portfolio weights have been obtained by minimising portfolio risk. An alternative approach is to determine portfolio weights to maximise expected return for a specified level of risk. Although these appear to be different problems for Solver, the optimum weights correspond to portfolios lying on the efficient frontier as in the minimisation formulation.

6.4   GENERATING THE EFFICIENT FRONTIER (HUANG AND LITZENBERGER'S APPROACH)

If there are no constraints on individual asset weights, the efficient frontier can also be produced elegantly from algebra. Although some of the more advanced textbooks (such as Elton and Gruber, 1995) demonstrate this through the iterative solution of a set of simultaneous equations, there is a better approach. Huang and Litzenberger (denoted HL) have described how to find two points on the frontier, and then to generate the whole of the frontier from these points (by applying a result due to Black). This section builds on their algebraic approach, the calculation sequence being explained using matrices, to generalise the approach to portfolios with many (i.e. more than three) assets. The context of the following description is spreadsheet implementation with Excel's array functions. This section is of a somewhat more advanced level and may be deferred on first reading until the remainder of the chapter has been understood.

Sheet EF1HL shown in Figure 6.6 includes named ranges to improve the clarity of the formulas in the cells. The vector of expected returns (C5:C7) is named $\mathbf{e}$, the vector of weights (I5:I7) is named $\mathbf{w}$ and the unit vector in A24:A26 is named $\mathbf{u}$. The variance–covariance matrix in C15:E17 is named $\mathbf{V}$. As explained earlier, the portfolio variance is written in matrix form as $\mathbf{w}^T\mathbf{V}\mathbf{w}$ and is evaluated with Excel's matrix multiplication functions in cell I11.

The HL method for finding efficient portfolios requires the inverse of the variance–covariance matrix, which is written as $\mathbf{V}^{-1}$. Excel's MINVERSE function for matrix inversion does the actual calculation. The array formula to enter into the 3 by 3 cell range, H15:J17, is:

$$=\text{MINVERSE(C15:E17)}$$

Note that for array functions, having selected the cell range for the formulas and entered the appropriate formula, the keystroke combination Ctrl+Shift+Enter must be pressed to complete the entry. (If no array formula brackets {} appear in the cell, then press F2 and try again.)

In order to find two frontier portfolios (labelled $\mathbf{g}$ and $\mathbf{g+h}$), Huang and Litzenberger start by calculating four scalar quantities (A, B, C and D). The first three, A, B and C, are products of vectors and matrices and the fourth, D, depends on the previous three:

$$A = \mathbf{u}^T\mathbf{V}^{-1}\mathbf{e} \quad B = \mathbf{e}^T\mathbf{V}^{-1}\mathbf{e} \quad C = \mathbf{u}^T\mathbf{V}^{-1}\mathbf{u} \quad D = BC - A^2$$

If we define two intermediate column vectors $\mathbf{l} = \mathbf{V}^{-1}\mathbf{e}$ and $\mathbf{m} = \mathbf{V}^{-1}\mathbf{u}$, shown in the sheet in cells C24:C26 and D24:D26, the matrix multiplication expressions simplify to:

$$A = \mathbf{u}^T\mathbf{l} \quad B = \mathbf{e}^T\mathbf{l} \quad C = \mathbf{u}^T\mathbf{m}$$

The single cell formula for A in cell G23: =MMULT(TRANSPOSE($\mathbf{u}$), $\mathbf{l}$) involves the MMULT array function, so it must be entered as an array formula (similarly the formulas for B and C). Since the calculations for A, B, C and D all result in scalars, there is no need to 'select' an area greater than a single cell for any of them.

	A	B	C	D	E	F	G	H	I	J	K
2	Using Algebra to reproduce Unconstrained Frontier Portfolios										
3											
4	Asset Data		Exp Ret	Std Dev			Portfolio Weights				
5		TBills	0.6%	4.3%				TBills	33.3%		
6		Bonds	2.1%	10.1%				Bonds	33.3%		
7		Shares	9.0%	20.8%				Shares	33.3%		
8											
9	Correlation Matrix		TBills	Bonds	Shares					via fn	
10		TBills	1.00	0.63	0.09			Exp Ret	3.90%	3.90%	
11		Bonds	0.63	1.00	0.23			Variance	0.0080		
12		Shares	0.09	0.23	1.00			Std Dev	8.95%	8.95%	
13											
14	VCV Matrix		TBills	Bonds	Shares		VCV inverse				
15		TBills	0.0018	0.0027	0.0008			901.51	-246.92	10.80	
16		Bonds	0.0027	0.0102	0.0048			-246.92	171.13	-14.52	
17		Shares	0.0008	0.0048	0.0433			10.80	-14.52	24.53	
18											
19											
20	Finding weights, g and h, to generate points on the frontier										
21											
22		uvec		l	m					g	h	g+h
23						A	3.97				
24		1		1.20	665.40	B	0.20		124.0%	-1851.9%	-1727.9%
25		1		0.81	-90.30	C	595.91		-20.5%	805.2%	784.6%
26		1		1.97	20.82	D	104.15		-3.5%	1046.7%	1043.2%
27											
28								Exp Ret	0.0%	100.0%	100.0%
29								Std Dev	4.4%		237.6%
30											
31	Generating Frontier Portfolios, using g and h										
32											
33	Target expected return			7.0%							
34											
35		weights				via fn					
36			TBills	-5.6%	-5.6%		Exp Ret	7.0%			
37			Bonds	35.8%	35.8%		Std Dev	15.7%			
38			Shares	69.8%	69.8%						

Figure 6.6   Huang and Litzenberger's direct analytical solution

There are further formulas for the asset weights that represent the two points on the envelope, namely portfolio **g** (with an expected return of 0%) and portfolio **g+h** (with an expected return of 100%). These can be expressed as:

$$\mathbf{g} = [B\mathbf{m} - A\mathbf{l}]/D \quad \mathbf{h} = [C\mathbf{l} - A\mathbf{m}]/D$$

Before typing in the formula for **g**, a (3×1) column vector of cells must be selected, because this is an array formula. Similar remarks apply to the entry of the array formula for **h**. The weights for the two frontier portfolios are shown in cells I24:I26 and K24:K26 of Figure 6.6.

Thus the weights making up vector **g** (124%, -20.5%, -3.5%) for TBills, Bonds and Stocks respectively give a portfolio on the frontier with expected return 0%. Similarly, the weights making up vector **g+h** give a second frontier portfolio with expected return 100%. Using the vectors **g** and **h**, a linear combination of them in the form **g+h***T can be constructed to give the weights for a portfolio on the frontier producing any specified expected return, T. For instance, looking at rows 33 to 38 in Figure 6.6, an expected return of 7% can be achieved with a portfolio containing -5.6% in TBills, 35.8% in Bonds and 69.8% in Stocks (cells D36:D38). That is, the minimum risk portfolio with an expected return of 7% consists of holding a mixture of Bonds and Stocks whilst short selling TBills. This result from HL's approach is identical to the result in Figure 6.5 for Solver optimisation with no constraints on weights.

Other points on the frontier can be evaluated using the array expression $\mathbf{g}+\mathbf{h}^*T$ by supplying different values for the expected return, T. In this way the efficient frontier can be generated. For example, in Excel a Data Table with a range of expected returns from 0% to 10% as inputs and portfolio risk and return as outputs can be used as the basis for an XY (Scatter) chart. In Figure 6.2, the points labelled as the 'Unconstrained Frontier' come from such a Data Table.

As is evident, the spreadsheet manipulations required to evaluate the weights for the two efficient portfolios are complex. This is the ideal situation for a VBA user-defined function to simplify formula entry. In section 6.10, the code to implement Huang and Litzenberger's approach is explained. The function HLPortfolioWeights has four arguments: *expret*, *retvec* *vcvmat* and *rf* (here $= -1$). Argument *expret* is the expected return of the frontier portfolio for which the weights are required, *retvec* is the vector of expected returns and *vcvmat* the variance–covariance matrix. The function returns an array of the appropriate portfolio weights. In Figure 6.6, weights from this user-defined function are shown in cells E36:E38 alongside the weights obtained from spreadsheet manipulation.

6.5   CONSTRAINED FRONTIER PORTFOLIOS

If there are constraints on the holdings of individual assets (for example that weights must be non-negative), the analytical solution approach no longer applies. However, Solver will produce the optimum set of weights. To distinguish these from the previous case, we call the resulting portfolio a 'constrained' frontier portfolio. In the first extract of sheet EF2 in Figure 6.7, possible portfolio weights are in cells H8:J8 (named portwts2), with minimum weights in the row above and maximum weights in the row below (named portmin2 and portmax2 respectively). These constraints can then be incorporated into the problem presented to Solver as shown in Figure 6.8.

	A	B	C	D	E	F	G	H	I	J
2	Using Solver to generate the Constrained Frontier									
3										
4	Asset Data		Exp Ret	Std Dev			Constraints on Frontier Portfolio Weights			
5		TBills	0.6%	4.3%						
6		Bonds	2.1%	10.1%				TBills	Bonds	Shares
7		Shares	9.0%	20.8%			portmin2	0.0%	0.0%	0.0%
8							portwts2	7.4%	20.0%	72.6%
9	Correlation Matrix		TBills	Bonds	Shares		portmax2	10.0%	20.0%	100.0%
10		TBills	1.00	0.63	0.09					
11		Bonds	0.63	1.00	0.23			Exp Ret	7.0%	portret2
12		Shares	0.09	0.23	1.00			Std Dev	15.8%	portsd2
13										
14	VCV Matrix		TBills	Bonds	Shares					
15		TBills	0.0018	0.0027	0.0008					
16		Bonds	0.0027	0.0102	0.0048		(Ctrl + Shift + C to run Macro)			
17		Shares	0.0008	0.0048	0.0433			niter2	11	
18								priter2	9.2%	

Figure 6.7   Optimisation allowing for constraints on the portfolio weights, sheet EF2

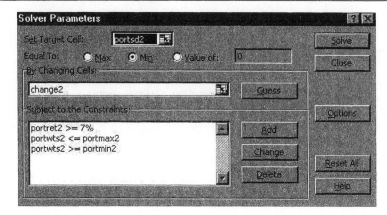

Figure 6.8   Setting up Solver with constraints on values for the weights

The frontier portfolio found by Solver has 7.4% in TBills, 20.0% in Bonds and 72.6% in Shares. This frontier portfolio with an expected return of 7.0%, but now constrained to have non-negative holdings, a maximum of 10% in TBills and 20% in Bonds, has a standard deviation of 15.8%. This compares to a standard deviation of only 15.7% in the unconstrained case, illustrating the point that typically the addition of constraints produces a solution that is inferior to the unconstrained case.

By repeating the use of Solver for a number of different target expected returns we can generate a series of points on the constrained frontier (see Figure 6.9). The mechanics of the macro are described in section 6.12. With the constraints on weights detailed above, the minimum and maximum portfolio expected returns are 6.8% and 9.0% respectively. [The reader should check these figures by applying Solver to find the weights to minimise (maximise) expected return.] Assuming 11 optimisations, this range of returns is split up into 11 target returns and Solver is used 11 times to find frontier portfolios whose returns lie in the feasible range (between 6.8% and 9.0%).

	A	B	C	D	E	F	G	H	I
21	**Constrained Frontier Portfolios**								
22				TBills	Bonds	Shares		Std Dev	Exp Ret
23			effwts2						
24				10.0%	20.0%	70.0%		15.2%	6.8%
25				7.4%	20.0%	72.6%		15.8%	7.0%
26				4.7%	20.0%	75.3%		16.3%	7.2%
27				2.1%	20.0%	77.9%		16.8%	7.4%
28				0.0%	19.3%	80.7%		17.3%	7.7%
29				0.0%	16.1%	83.9%		17.9%	7.9%
30				0.0%	12.9%	87.1%		18.5%	8.1%
31				0.0%	9.7%	90.3%		19.0%	8.3%
32				0.0%	6.4%	93.6%		19.6%	8.6%
33				0.0%	3.2%	96.8%		20.2%	8.8%
34				0.0%	0.0%	100.0%		20.8%	9.0%

Figure 6.9   Weights for constrained frontier portfolios

The portfolios in Figure 6.9 appear labelled Constrained Points in Figure 6.2, the last one being identical to investing only in Shares.

In summary, the most general technique for determining weights for risky portfolios is to apply optimisation using Solver, essentially a numerical iterative process. However, if there are no constraints on the values of the weights (other than that they sum to unity), HL's analytical approach provides formulas for the optimal weights which can be implemented via user-defined functions described in section 6.10.

6.6 COMBINING RISK-FREE AND RISKY ASSETS

This section, together with sections 6.7, 6.8 and 6.9, contains additional material pertinent to the problem of choosing portfolios from risky assets. However, it is essentially theoretical, and could be regarded as appendix material. Its main importance is that we develop the formulas to solve the 'three generic portfolio problems' (as described in Taggart, 1996) and provide user-defined functions. These functions provide solutions to support ideas in Chapters 7 and 8. We introduce the concept of a risk-free asset (that is an asset with zero risk) in order to complete the path towards the development of the capital asset pricing model in the next chapter.

Having discussed portfolios with three (or more) risky assets and shown how to select efficient combinations which are expected to generate specified target returns with minimum risk, we briefly explore how risk and return in investment should be balanced. This risk–return trade-off is a major factor in deciding how to split investment between a portfolio of risky assets and a risk-free asset. The ideas are developed in the context of three generic portfolio problems:

- One–combining a risk-free asset with a risky asset
- Two–combining two risky assets
- Three–combining a risk-free asset with a risky portfolio

The spreadsheet approaches are illustrated in the sheet labelled Generic.

We require a way of measuring an individual's trade-off between risk and return and borrow the concept of the utility function from economics. Let us suppose that individuals have utility functions of the form:

$$U = E(r_p) - 0.5A\sigma_p^2$$

The higher the value of the risk aversion coefficient A for the investor the larger is the penalty from portfolio risk that is subtracted from the portfolio's expected return. Experiments have found the typical value of A to lie between 2 and 4, and we have chosen $A = 3$ for our illustrations.

Since the development in the following sections is in terms of two assets, the general formulas for portfolio return and risk given in section 6.1 are restated here for two assets, namely:

Portfolio return: $E(r_p) = w_1 E(r_1) + w_2 E(r_2)$

Portfolio variance: $\text{Var}(r_p) = \sigma_p^2 = w_1^2 \sigma_1^2 + w_2^2 \sigma_2^2 + 2w_1 w_2 \text{cov}(1, 2)$

where the covariance of the two assets $\text{cov}(1, 2)$ can equally well be expressed in terms of their correlation using $\text{cov}(1, 2) = \text{corr}(1, 2)\sigma_1 \sigma_2$. The risk-free asset has return denoted r_f with zero variance and zero covariances with the risky assets. The portfolio risk is the square root of the variance.

6.7 PROBLEM ONE–COMBINING A RISK-FREE ASSET WITH A RISKY ASSET

The first of the generic portfolio problems, Problem One, involves one risk-free asset (asset0) and one risky asset (asset1) with returns assumed to be uncorrelated. The details are shown in Figure 6.10: the risk-free rate is 1% and asset1 has risk and return somewhat similar to the Bonds that featured in the earlier portfolio. By varying the weight invested in asset1 (cell H14) in a range from 0% to 100% we can generate the straight line linking the risk–return point for asset0 to the risk–return point for asset1. This line is shown in Figure 6.11.

	A	B	C	D	E	F	G	H	I	J	K
2	Generic Portfolio Problems										
3											
4	Problem One : risk-free asset and 1 risky asset										
5											
6	Asset Data		Exp Ret	Std Dev			Risk aversion coefficient (A)				3.00
7		asset 0	1.0%	0.0%							
8		asset 1	2.1%	10.1%							
9											
10	Corr Matrix		asset 0	asset 1			Optimal Portfolio			utility	0.0120
11		asset 0	1.00	0.00							
12		asset 1	0.00	1.00				weights			
13							asset 0	64.1%		return	1.40%
14	VCV Matrix		asset 0	asset 1			asset 1	35.9%		std dev	3.63%
15		asset 0	0.0000	0.0000			asset 1 via fn	35.9%			
16		asset 1	0.0000	0.0102							

Figure 6.10 Spreadsheet calculations for Problem One, sheet Generic

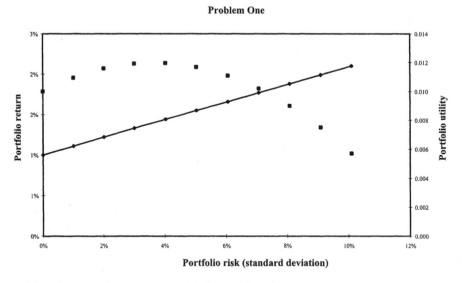

Figure 6.11 Utility and return versus risk for Problem One

Individual investors will choose a particular point on the line depending on the value of their risk aversion coefficient (in cell K6). Figure 6.11 includes the utility curve for portfolios with different proportions of asset1 assuming a risk aversion coefficient of 3 (shown as a series of separate boxes and linked to the right-hand scale of the chart). The utility starts at 0.01 (with 100% invested in asset0) and increases steadily as the proportion invested in asset1 increases until the optimal point is reached, declining thereafter to a utility value of 0.006 with 100% invested in asset1.

The optimal point on the line corresponds to that of maximum utility, which occurs when the weight for asset1 (in cell H14) is evaluated from the formula:

$$w_1{}^* = [E(r_1) - r_f]/A\sigma_1{}^2$$

In this example, the optimal portfolio will have 36% (35.9%) invested in the risky asset to produce a utility value of 0.012 (that is, a certainty equivalent return of 1.2%). A user-defined function called Prob1OptimalRiskyWeight has been developed to provide this weight (as in cell H15). It is described in section 6.11.

Note also that the proportion of the optimal investment put into the risky asset (as opposed to asset0) depends on the investor's degree of risk aversion. An investor with a higher risk aversion coefficient (of say 4) would reduce his proportion of risky assets in his optimal portfolio to 27%.

6.8   PROBLEM TWO–COMBINING TWO RISKY ASSETS

In Problem Two both assets are risky. In our illustration, their returns are weakly positively correlated, just as was the case for the Bonds and Shares in the earlier portfolio example. The details are set out in Figure 6.12 with correlation 0.23 in cell D25.

	A	B	C	D	E	F	G	H	I	J	K
18	Problem Two : 2 risky assets and no risk-free asset										
19											
20	Asset Data		Exp Ret	Std Dev			Risk aversion coefficient (A)				3.00
21		asset 1	2.1%	10.1%							
22		asset 2	9.0%	20.8%			Minimum Variance Portfolio			utility	0.0151
23									weights		
24	Corr Matrix		asset 1	asset 2			asset 1	87.7%		return	2.95%
25		asset 1	1.00	0.23			asset 2	12.3%		std dev	9.77%
26		asset 2	0.23	1.00							
27							Optimal Risky Portfolio			utility	0.0333
28	VCV Matrix		asset 1	asset 2					weights		
29		asset 1	0.0102	0.0048			asset 1	35.2%		return	6.57%
30		asset 2	0.0048	0.0433			asset 2	64.8%		std dev	14.70%
31							asset 1 via fn	35.2%			

Figure 6.12   Spreadsheet calculations for Problem Two, sheet Generic

By varying the weight invested in asset1, we can trace the outline or frontier (see the continuous line in Figure 6.13). The resulting curve linking the risk–return points represented by combinations of the two risky assets demonstrates the benefit of diversification. For example, if an investor starts with a portfolio wholly invested in asset1 then he can increase the return of his portfolio by swapping part of his portfolio into asset2. The risk of his portfolio will also be reduced by this swap despite the fact that asset2, on its own, is a riskier asset than asset1.

This process of swapping from asset1 to asset2 reduces portfolio risk until the point represented by the minimum variance portfolio is reached with 87.7% in asset1 and a portfolio standard deviation of 9.77%. The formula for the minimum variance portfolio does not depend on the risk aversion coefficient and can be viewed as the asset holdings of an investor completely averse to risk.

The minimum variance portfolio value for w_1 can be shown to be:

$$[\sigma_2{}^2 - \rho_{12}\sigma_1\sigma_2]/[\sigma_1{}^2 + \sigma_2{}^2 - 2\rho_{12}\sigma_1\sigma_2]$$

For convenience, this weight for asset1 is referred to as w_1^{mv} (87.7% in cell H24), the weight for asset2 being simply $(1 - w_1^{mv})$. So if 87.7% of the portfolio is in asset1, the combination has minimum risk (9.77%). Note that this is lower than the risk for each asset considered individually.

Investors who are willing to accept more risk will reduce their holdings in asset1 and increase their holdings in asset2. For an investor with a risk aversion coefficient of 3, Figure 6.13 shows the utility (displayed as discrete points linked to the right-hand axis) rising until the risk is approximately 15%. The investor will be prepared to accept more risk until the proportion in asset1 falls to 35.2% with a portfolio standard deviation of 14.7%.

Again, by algebraic manipulation, the expression for the optimal risky weight for asset1 can be derived as:

$$w_1^{opt} = w_1^{mv} + [E(r_1) - E(r_2)]/[A(\sigma_1{}^2 + \sigma_2{}^2 - 2\rho_{12}\sigma_1\sigma_2)]$$

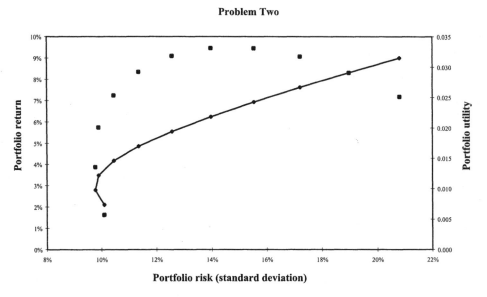

Figure 6.13   Utility and return versus risk for Problem Two

This holding (in cell H29) gives the optimal risky portfolio. The formula for the optimal portfolio weight consists of the minimum variance weight plus an additional term. This additional component depends on the risk aversion coefficient and can be viewed as the investor's speculative demand. The optimal risky portfolio has a utility value of 0.033 (this corresponds to a certainty equivalent return of 3.3%).

Once again, the optimal portfolio weight is most easily calculated via a user-defined function. The function Prob2OptimalRiskyWeight which provides the weight is outlined in section 6.11.

6.9 PROBLEM THREE—COMBINING A RISK-FREE ASSET WITH A RISKY PORTFOLIO

The last of the generic problems focuses on combining the risky portfolio with the risk-free asset. Problem Three is solved in two stages. First, the optimal combination of the risky assets is decided (which is a special case of Problem Two). Second, the split between the risk-free asset and the optimal risky portfolio is decided (essentially Problem One). See Figure 6.14 for details.

First, ignoring the risk-free option, the optimal split between assets1 and 2 is decided. In the previous section the 35%:65% split was roughly optimal when we considered just risky assets. Suppose the optimal risky portfolio, R say, has expected return $E(r_R)$ and standard deviation σ_R, the weight on asset1 being F_1. We want to choose F_1 to maximise the return-to-risk ratio for this portfolio R when combined with the risk-free asset in the second stage, i.e. choose F_1 to maximise:

$$[E(r_R) - r_f]/\sigma_R$$

With a little algebra (or alternatively, geometrical inspection, as in Bodie, it can be shown that the slope of the line joining the portfolios on the efficient frontier to the risk-free asset is greatest when the line is tangential to the frontier. For the weights at the tangential point, the algebra uses excess returns (i.e. the excess over the risk-free rate) and defines $E(R_1) = E(r_1) - r_f$, similarly $E(R_2)$. The resulting formula for the optimal portfolio weight is:

$$F_1{}^{opt} = [\sigma_2{}^2 E(R_1) + cov(1, 2)E(R_2)]/\{\sigma_2{}^2 E(R_1)$$
$$+ \sigma_1{}^2 E(R_2) - cov(1, 2)[E(R_1) + E(R_2)]\}$$

where $E(R_1)$, $E(R_2)$ are expected returns in excess of r_f.

Notice that the optimal risky portfolio weight does not depend on the risk aversion coefficient, but does depend on the risk-free rate.

	A	B	C	D	E	F	G	H	I	J	K	L
33	Problem Three : risk-free asset and 2 risky assets						Solved in 2 stages					
34							Stage 1	Optimal Risky Portfolio ('revised' Problem2)				
35	Asset Data		Exp Ret	Std Dev	Excess ret			*Independent of A*				
36		asset 0	1.00%	0.00%			Stage 2	Optimal Portfolio (using Problem1)				
37		asset 1	2.1%	10.1%	1.10%			*Depends on A*				
38		asset 2	9.0%	20.8%	8.00%							
39							**Optimal Risky Portfolio**			utility	0.0292	
40	Corr Matrix	asset 0	asset 1	asset 2				weights				
41		asset 0	1.00	0.00	0.00		asset 1	10.5%		return	8.28%	
42		asset 1	0.00	1.00	0.23		asset 2	89.5%		std dev	18.89%	
43		asset 2	0.00	0.23	1.00		asset 1 via fn	10.5%				
44												
45	VCV Matrix	asset 0	asset 1	asset 2			**Risk aversion coefficient (A)**				3.00	
46		asset 0	0.0000	0.0000	0.0000		**Optimal Portfolio**			utility	0.0347	
47		asset 1	0.0000	0.0102	0.0048			weights				
48		asset 2	0.0000	0.0048	0.0433		asset 0	32.0%				
49							opt risky	68.0%				
50							opt risky via fn	68.0%				
51									via fn			
52							asset 0	32.0%	32.0%	return	5.95%	
53							asset 1	7.1%	7.1%	std dev	12.84%	
54							asset 2	60.8%	60.8%			

Figure 6.14   Spreadsheet calculations for Problem Three, sheet Generic

With this formula in cell H41, the weight of 10.5% implies that in the risky portfolio the investment is split 10.5% to 89.5% between asset1 and asset2.

In the second stage, the risk-free asset is combined with the optimal risky portfolio from the first stage solution to maximise utility. Hence, as in section 6.8, the risky portfolio has weight $[E(r_R) - r_f]/[A\sigma_R^2]$, the remainder being in the risk-free asset. Note that these portfolio weights do depend on the risk aversion coefficient.

The resulting optimal portfolio, now with 68.0% in the risky portfolio and 32% in the risk-free asset, has increased utility from 0.0292 after the first stage to 0.0347. [Note that the optimal risky proportion can also be obtained from the function Prob1OptimalRiskyWeight (see cell H50).]

Splitting the 68% investment into the original assets, we get the proportions in cells H52:H54. Once again, a user-defined function which provides the vector of weights for the overall optimal portfolio called Prob3OptimalWeightsVec is outlined in section 6.11 (see cells I52:I54).

In the chart in Figure 6.15, the curved frontier represents all the possible combinations of asset1 and asset2. Given the existence of the risk-free asset, the unique optimal portfolio occurs where the line linking the risk-free asset to the risky portfolio's frontier is tangential. (The 'revised' Problem Two determines this 'tangential' point on the frontier.) The line tangential to the frontier starts from a holding of 100% in the risk-free asset, then falls to 0% (at the tangent point), then continues up to a holding of 150% in the optimal risky portfolio and a negative holding of minus 50% in the risk-free asset. (Remember that there are no constraints on the weights for holdings in the risk-free asset.) The second stage (and the solution to Problem Three) involves deciding which position on this tangent line would be chosen as the investor's optimal portfolio. Again, the utility is plotted as a series of points. It appears to be at a maximum for our chosen risk aversion coefficient when the risk is around 12.5%.

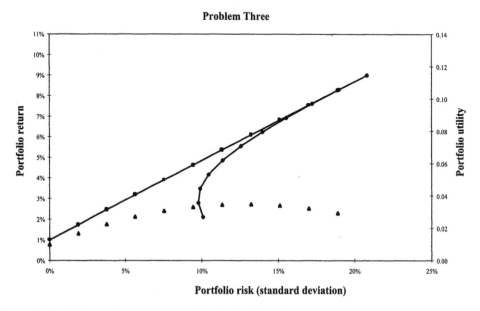

Figure 6.15   Utility and return versus risk for Problem Three

It is now a relatively small step from Problem Three to the development of the capital asset pricing model in the next chapter–the main hurdle is to in some way aggregate the beliefs of the individual investors and so produce a theory of asset pricing.

6.10   USER-DEFINED FUNCTIONS IN Module1

The Module1 sheet contains the code for the user-defined functions applied in workbook Equity1. They provide an insight into the handling of arrays within user-defined functions–array inputs, array functions, calculations with both scalars and arrays and finally returning array outputs. For example, the code for the PortfolioReturn function is:

```
Function PortfolioReturn(retvec, wtsvec)
    returns the portfolio return
    If Application.Count(retvec) = Application.Count(wtsvec) Then
        If retvec.Columns.Count <> wtsvec.Columns.Count Then
            wtsvec = Application.Transpose(wtsvec)
        End If
        PortfolioReturn = Application.SumProduct(retvec, wtsvec)
    Else
        PortfolioReturn = -1
    End If
End Function
```

The above code illustrates how to check the dimensions of arrays involved in calculations. The SumProduct function returns a scalar but requires that the two arrays share the same dimensions. This is achieved by checking that the arrays, retvec and wtsvec, have the same number of elements and then transposing the wtsvec array if the number of columns in each array differs. If the arrays have different numbers of elements the function returns the error value of -1. The need for checking dimensions also arises from allowing the user-defined function to accept input arrays as either column or row vectors.

The HLPortfolioWeights function (whose code is available in Module1) is notable for the care needed when handling array functions. One important aspect is being aware of the dimensions of the arrays within the function. In VBA one-dimensional arrays are stored as row vectors and, in a similar way, one-dimensional arrays returned from user-defined functions to the spreadsheet will also be row vectors. We will follow this convention by ensuring that our user-defined functions return VBA single-dimension arrays into Excel in the form of row vectors. However our preference within user-defined functions is to adopt the alternative convention that vectors should be column vectors. For example, the variables uvec and retvec are transposed if necessary to ensure that they are column vectors.

Intermediate variables resulting from array functions also need to be treated with care:

```
Dim l As Variant, m As Variant
    l = Application.MMult(vinvmat, retvec)
    m = Application.MMult(vinvmat, uvec)
```

Since the variables **l** and **m** are themselves arrays derived from an array function, they both need to be declared as variants but, as they will be used as inputs to array functions, without a specific dimension. Within the MMult calculation, vinvmat is an $[n, n]$ matrix and retvec is an $[n, 1]$ vector. Thus the resulting array will be an $[n, 1]$ (column) vector.

The next minor hurdle to overcome concerns the calculation of the four scalars a, b, c and d. The scalar d is calculated from the other three scalars, each of which is the result of an array function. For instance, a is calculated from the unit vector array uvec and the array 1:

$$a = \text{Application.Sum(Application.MMult(Application.Transpose(uvec), 1))}$$

The MMult calculation multiplies together a $[1, n]$ (row) vector with an $[n, 1]$ (column) vector and thus returns a $[1, 1]$ array (a scalar). Within Excel this doesn't create any difficulties, but in VBA we need to use the Sum function to convert the array result into a scalar.

The final consideration is how to handle mixed-mode calculations involving scalars with individual elements of arrays. In Excel this is handled without concern, as shown in cells I24:I26 for the **g** vector. However, in VBA this is best done within a loop:

```
Dim wtsvec() As Variant
n = Application.Count(retvec)
ReDim wtsvec(n)
For i = 1 To n
    gi = b * m(i, 1) - a * l(i, 1)
    hi = c * l(i, 1) - a * m(i, 1)
    wtsvec(i) = (gi + hi * expret) / d
Next i
```

Since wtsvec is calculated element-by-element we can declare it as a Variant(), but it needs to be subsequently dimensioned using the ReDim statement. Within the loop we can multiply scalars times the individual elements of the array.

6.11   FUNCTIONS FOR THE THREE GENERIC PORTFOLIO PROBLEMS IN Module1

The Prob1OptimalRiskyWeight function, with four inputs, is a straightforward conversion of the formula outlined in section 6.7 into VBA code. The required inputs are the return and risk of the risky asset (r1 and sig1), the risk-free rate (rf) and the risk aversion coefficient (rraval):

```
Function Prob1OptimalRiskyWeight(r1, rf, sig1, rraval)
   'returns risky optimal weight when combined with risk-free asset
   Prob1OptimalRiskyWeight = (r1 - rf) / (rraval * sig1 ^ 2)
End Function
```

The following function called Prob2OptimalRiskyWeight, which can be used for Problems Two and Three, has seven inputs in all: r1, r2, sig1 and sig2 are the returns and standard deviations for the two risky assets; rraval is the investor's risk aversion coefficient, and the risk-free rate rf . The risk-free rate is set equal to zero for Problem Two:

```
Function Prob2OptimalRiskyWeight1(r1, r2, rf, sig1, sig2, corr12, rraval)
   'returns optimal weight for risky asset1 when combined with risky asset2
   'for case with no risk-free asset, enter value of rf <= 0
   Dim cov12, var1, var2, minvarw, w, xr1, xr2
   cov12 = corr12 * sig1 * sig2
   var1 = sig1 ^ 2
   var2 = sig2 ^ 2
   'first look at case with no risk-free asset
   If rf <= 0 Then
      minvarw = (var2 - cov12) / (var1 + var2 - 2 * cov12)
      w = minvarw + (r1 - r2) / (rraval * (var1 + var2 - 2 * cov12))
```

```
'then look at case with risk-free asset
Else
   xr1 = r1 - rf
   xr2 = r2 - rf
   w = xr1 * var2 - xr2 * cov12
   w = w / (xr1 * var2 + xr2 * var1 - (xr1 + xr2) * cov12)
End If
Prob2OptimalRiskyWeight1 = w
End Function
```

The code for the optimal weight is written in terms of the covariance (denoted cov12). The variable minvarw is the minimum variance weight w_1^{mv} and variable w is the value w_1^{opt} which produces the maximum utility portfolio.

For Problem Three, the function uses the functions for solving Problem One and Two. As its name suggests, the Prob3OptimalWeightsVec function returns the three optimal weights in an array. The complete code is shown below followed by an explanation of some steps:

```
Function Prob3OptimalWeightsVec(r1, r2, rf, sig1, sig2, corr12, rraval)
   'returns optimal weights for risk-free asset and 2 risky assets
   'uses Prob2OptimalRiskyWeight fn
   'uses Prob1OptimalRiskyWeight fn
   Dim w0, w1, w2, rr, sigr
   w1 = Prob2OptimalRiskyWeight1(r1, r2, rf, sig1, sig2, corr12, rraval)
   w2 = 1 - w1
   rr = w1 * r1 + w2 * r2
   sigr = Sqr((w1 * sig1)^2 + (w2 * sig2)^2 + 2 * w1 * w2 * corr12 * sig1 * sig2)
   w0 = 1 - Prob1OptimalRiskyWeight(rr, rf, sigr, rraval)
   w1 = (1 - w0) * w1
   w2 = (1 - w0) * w2
   Prob3OptimalWeightsVec = Array(w0, w1, w2)
End Function
```

Ignoring the risk-free asset, the problem reduces to Problem Two and the split between assets1 and 2 is calculated:

```
w1 = Prob2OptimalRiskyWeight1(r1, r2, rf, sig1, sig2, corr12, rraval)
w2 = 1 - w1
```

From these weights the return and risk of the risky portfolio can be calculated:

```
rr = w1 * r1 + w2 * r2
sigr = Sqr((w1 * sig1)^2 + (w2 * sig2)^2 + 2 * w1 * w2 * corr12 * sig1 * sig2)
```

These quantities are inputs in determining the weight for the risk-free asset (essentially a Type One problem). Hence the use of the Prob1OptimalRiskyWeight function.

6.12   MACROS IN ModuleM

The macros to generate the efficient frontier using Solver are contained in this module sheet. Solver is an add-in to Excel and, unless it appears on the Tools menu, needs to be installed. Additionally, to use the Solver functions in VBA, the module sheet must include a reference to the SOLVER.xla add-in file:

```
Sub EffFrontier1()
   SolverReset
   Call SolverAdd(Range("portret1"), 2, Range("target1"))
   Call SolverOk(Range("portsd1"), 2, 0, Range("change1"))
   Call SolverSolve(True)
   SolverFinish
End Sub
```

The EffFrontier1 macro contains a single application of Solver. The SolverAdd function adds the single constraint needed (where the value 2 represents the equality constraint) then the SolverOk function sets up the problem (here the value 2 ensures minimisation). The SolverSolve function solves the problem (the True parameter hides the results screen) then the SolverFinish function retains the final solution values in the spreadsheet.

Strictly speaking, the Call word is not strictly necessary, but we prefer to include it when a subroutine requiring parameters is used in the code. The parameters must then be in brackets when using this syntax.

The EffFrontier2 macro is rather more complicated in that it generates the complete efficient frontier using repeated applications of the Solver function within a loop. The number of repeats is predetermined. The most important lesson is to minimise the code contained in the loop. The Solver problem is set up outside the loop, with the Solver-Change function changing the right-hand side of the constraint (the target expected return) inside the loop. Within the loop, the results of each Solver iteration are copied to a range in the spreadsheet using the PasteSpecial command. The code for the loop is as follows:

```
Do While iter <= niter
   Call SolverSolve(True)
   SolverFinish
   Range("portwts2").Copy
   Range("effwts2").Offset(iter, 0).PasteSpecial Paste:=xlValues
   Range("priter2") = Range("priter2").Value + pradd
   'amend portret constraint in Solver
   Call SolverChange(Range("portret2"), 2, Range("priter2"))
   iter = iter + 1
Loop
```

The initial part of the macro uses Solver twice, first to calculate the minimum portfolio return achievable with the given constraints (with the value of 2 in the SolverOk function) and then to calculate the maximum return (with the value of 1 in the SolverOk function). The range between these two returns is divided into the chosen number of target returns and the frontier portfolio weights determined and stored for each return.

```
SolverReset
'first calculate portfolio min return given constraints
Call SolverAdd(Range("portwts2"), 3, Range("portmin2"))
Call SolverAdd(Range("portwts2"), 1, Range("portmax2"))
Call SolverOk(Range("portret2"), 2, 0, Range("change2"))
Call SolverSolve(True)
SolverFinish
prmin = Range("portret2").Value
'then calculate portfolio max return given constraints
Call SolverOk(Range("portret2"), 1, 0, Range("change2"))
Call SolverSolve(True)
SolverFinish
```

SUMMARY

The theory of portfolio optimisation developed by Markowitz underpins the whole Equities part of the book. We show how the basic formulas for portfolio mean and variance with two assets can be easily extended, using the array functions in Excel, to cover many assets. The array functions allowing matrix multiplication and inversion allow us to implement Huang and Litzenberger's analytic solution to generate the efficient frontier. This is illustrated in spreadsheet form as well as within user-defined functions.

Although the theory is important, its practical implementation requires numerical methods, such as Solver. We demonstrate that the solution obtained by Solver agrees with the HL analytic solution for the unconstrained case and show how to use Solver when there are constraints on the holdings of individual assets. Again, we illustrate the use of Solver both in spreadsheet form and using macros (for repeated applications).

In the next chapter, we cover the next crucial development in finance theory, the capital asset pricing model and the role of beta. We go on to use the lognormal distribution of equity returns in forecasting horizon wealth and Value-at-Risk for individual shares and portfolios.

REFERENCES

Bodie, Z., A. Kane and A. J. Marcus, 1996, *Investments*, 3rd edition, Richard D. Irwin, Englewood Cliffs, NJ.

Elton, E. J. and M. J. Gruber, 1995, *Modern Portfolio Theory and Investment Analysis*, John Wiley & Sons, Chichester.

Eppen, G. D., F. J. Gould, C. P. Schmidt, J. H. Moore and L. R. Weatherford, 1998, *Introductory Management Science, Decision Modelling with Spreadsheets*, 5th edition, Prentice Hall, New Jersey.

Huang, C. and R. Litzenberger, 1988, *Foundations for Financial Economics*, North Holland, New York.

Taggart, R. A., 1996, *Quantitative Analysis for Investment Management*, Prentice Hall, New Jersey.

7
Asset Pricing

We move from examining individual investors (a micro view) to the markets for assets and looking at the behaviour of all investors (a macro view). The crucial difference is the move from making statements about individuals to the drawing of conclusions about the behaviour of investors as a whole. It is this different focus that allows us to make statements about the pricing of financial assets. The capital asset pricing model (CAPM) was developed in the sixties by finance academics. It developed out of the mean–variance portfolio analysis described in the previous chapter. An important conclusion was that market prices reflect only part of a portfolio's risk. The part that is priced, the market-related risk, is measured by beta. The background to the CAPM is extensively discussed in Bodie et al. (1996), Chapter 8.

This chapter opens with the single-index model and illustrates the calculation of associated risk measures, in particular the estimation of betas and variance–covariance matrices from the returns of individual assets. The central numerical technique is regression, which is applied to estimate the beta of an asset, i.e. the return on the asset relative to the return on the market. The betas for a set of assets are useful in their own right to describe the relative responsiveness of assets to the market. However, they also facilitate the calculation of covariances via the single-index model. The EQUITY2.xls workbook contains implementations of the various estimation procedures and a range of user-defined functions have been developed to reduce the computational burden of the procedures.

In the previous chapter, we developed the mean–variance model of Markowitz assuming a utility function to describe the preferences of individual investors. In that analysis, the distribution of asset returns was ignored. We can, as an alternative, generate exactly the same theoretical results from the mean–variance model by assuming that asset returns are lognormally distributed whilst ignoring the preferences of individuals.

If log returns can be assumed to be normally distributed, we can derive analytic answers for both Value-at-Risk and the forecasting of horizon wealth. In this chapter, we include examples of both these techniques. In a sense, we reap the benefit of Markowitz's insight that return and risk can be associated with the mean and variance of the normal distribution and thus can use familiar results from the field of statistics. Also, since it is vital to manoeuvre easily between normal and lognormal moments of asset returns, we give practical illustrations to reinforce the theory linking the two distributions.

7.1 THE SINGLE-INDEX MODEL

The single-index model provides a useful way of building our understanding of return and risk en route to asset pricing models. The model posits a linear relationship between returns on share i and returns on an index, I say. Using R_i and R_I to denote returns in excess of the risk-free rate for the share i and the index I respectively, the equation is written:

$$R_i = \alpha_i + \beta_i R_I + e_i$$

where α_i and β_i are parameters in the model, such that the return on the share is made up of a systematic part $(\alpha_i + \beta_i R_I)$ and a residual part e_i. The systematic part consists of α_i, the share's return if the excess return on index I is zero and $\beta_i R_I$, the return related to movement in index I. So β_i is the share's responsiveness to movements in the index. The residual return, e_i, is not related to the index and is specific to share i. It is assumed to be similar to a random error term, with zero expectation, i.e. $E(e_i) = 0$ so that the expected excess return on share i is given by:

$$E(R_i) = \alpha_i + \beta_i E(R_I)$$

If the index is a stock market index (such as the FTSE100 in the UK or the S&P500 in the US), then the systematic component of return is 'market-related' and the residual component 'firm-specific'. The beta parameter is the share's sensitivity to the market.

Using excess returns for an individual share and for an index (say with returns for 60 months) we can estimate the parameters α_i and β_i using regression. This technique also provides an estimate of $\sigma(e_i)^2$, the variance of the residuals.

The single-index model can also be used to decompose risk (as measured by variance, in line with the previous chapter). The variance of returns on share i can be split into two separate components, the first measuring systematic risk and the second measuring risk that is specific to the individual share:

$$\text{Var}(R_i) = \sigma_i{}^2 = \beta_i{}^2 \sigma_I{}^2 + \sigma(e_i)^2$$

This result greatly simplifies the calculation burden of obtaining variance–covariance matrices, as we shall see in section 7.4.

7.2   ESTIMATING BETA COEFFICIENTS

To estimate betas, it is best to work with log returns (in fact log of excess returns). The sheet Beta illustrates how the beta coefficient for a share is estimated by regression using monthly returns on ShareA and Index (columns B and C in Figure 7.1). Here, the index is the FTSE100 and there are 60 monthly returns for both ShareA and Index. The beta (strictly speaking, the 'unadjusted' beta) is simply the slope estimate from the regression of share excess returns on index excess returns.

	A	B	C	D	E	F	G	H	I	J
2	Estimating Beta Coefficients using Ln Xs Returns									
3										
4	Mth	ShareA	Index		Fitted	Residuals		Excel regression functions		
5										
6	1	-0.1326	-0.0534		-0.0817	-0.0509		INTERCEPT	-0.0013	
7	2	0.0671	0.0868		0.1295	-0.0624		SLOPE	1.5065	
8	3	0.0939	0.0182		0.0261	0.0678		RSQ	0.4755	
9	4	-0.1339	-0.0800		-0.1218	-0.0121		STEYX	0.0595	
10	5	-0.0951	-0.0666		-0.1016	0.0065				
11	6	-0.0381	-0.0455		-0.0698	0.0317		Alpha	-0.0013	
12	7	0.0882	0.0925		0.1381	-0.0499		Alpha (SE)	0.0078	
13	8	0.1140	0.0393		0.0579	0.0561				
14	9	0.0694	0.0422		0.0623	0.0071		Beta	1.5065	
15	10	0.0527	0.0362		0.0533	-0.0006		Beta (SE)	0.2077	
16	11	-0.1298	-0.0006		-0.0022	-0.1276				
17	12	0.0395	0.0223		0.0323	0.0072		Sp Risk from STEYX		
18	13	-0.0358	0.0071		0.0094	-0.0452		Monthly	5.95%	
19	14	-0.0179	-0.0150		-0.0239	0.0060		Annualised	20.60%	
20	15	0.1251	0.0092		0.0126	0.1125		via fn	20.60%	

Figure 7.1   Regression of returns on ShareA on market index to estimate beta

Excel provides a number of alternative ways to estimate the slope coefficient. The formula in cell I7 =SLOPE(B6:B65,C6:C65) uses Excel's SLOPE function to estimate beta (β_i). Similarly, the INTERCEPT function (in cell I6) calculates the intercept (α_i) for the regression equation. Substituting the estimates of α_i and β_i into the equation gives:

$$\text{'Fitted' return} = -0.0013 + 1.5065 \text{ (index return)}$$

Column E contains the 'fitted' values for each index return and column F shows the 'residuals', i.e. actual returns from which the 'fitted' returns have been differenced. The size of the residuals is captured in the residual standard error (cell I9) with another Excel function, STEYX, which has the same inputs as the SLOPE function. Figure 7.2 shows share returns plotted against index returns with the above regression line superimposed. The scatter of returns about the line (and hence not related to the index) is called the specific risk of the share. It is the best estimate of the quantity earlier denoted by $\sigma(e_i)$.

Beta Regression

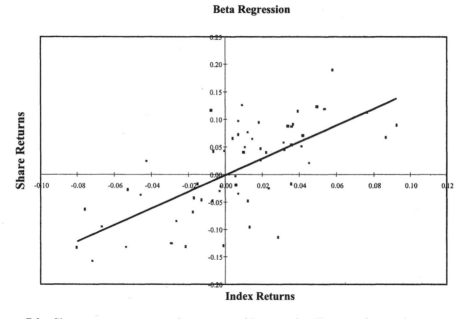

Figure 7.2   Share returns versus market returns with regression line superimposed

Another way to generate all the regression results (albeit in a static form) is to use the commands Tools then Data Analysis then Regression, to get the summary output below cell K6 in Figure 7.3. The intercept and slope are in cells L22:L23 and the residual standard error is in cell L12.

A more concise set of regression results is produced by Excel's LINEST function. This function has the advantage of giving results still dynamically linked to the data, rather than the static data dump produced by the Regression command. LINEST is an array formula, here with five rows and two columns, so a 5 by 2 cell range must be selected prior to entering the formula:

=LINEST(B6:B65,C6:C65,TRUE,TRUE)

to get the array of regression results (not forgetting the subsequent Ctrl+Shift+Enter keystroke combination). These are displayed in range O6:P10 of Figure 7.3 and explanatory labels have been attached in columns N and Q.

Individual items in the LINEST array can be accessed using the INDEX function (see cells I11, I12, I14 and I15). For instance, in cell I14, the beta coefficient is obtained using the formula:

$$=\text{INDEX(LINEST(B6:B65,C6:C65,TRUE,TRUE),1,1)}$$

The standard error of the beta coefficient, in cell I15, is obtained using the formula:

$$=\text{INDEX(LINEST(B6:B65,C6:C65,TRUE,TRUE),2,1)}$$

Specific risk (expressed as an annualised standard deviation) is given in cell I19 (from STEYX) and also in cell I23 (from the sum of squared residuals divided by $n - 2$) as can be confirmed in the Beta sheet. The annualised risk measures are simply the monthly measures multiplied by $\sqrt{12}$.

	K	L	M	N	O	P	Q
4	Output from Tools / Data Analysis / Regression			Output from Linest			
5							
6	SUMMARY OUTPUT			Beta	1.5065	-0.0013	Alpha
7				Beta (SE)	0.2077	0.0078	Alpha (SE)
8	*Regression Statistics*			RSQ	0.4755	0.0595	STEYX
9	Multiple R	0.6896		F	52.5873	58.0000	N-2
10	R Square	0.4755		Regression SS	0.1860	0.2051	Residual SS
11	Adjusted R Square	0.4665					
12	Standard Error	0.0595					
13	Observations	60					
14							
15	ANOVA						
16		*df*	*SS*	*MS*	*F*	*Significance F*	
17	Regression	1	0.1860	0.1860	52.5861	0.0000	
18	Residual	58	0.2051	0.0035			
19	Total	59	0.3911				
20							
21		*Coefficients*	*Standard Error*	*t Stat*	*P-value*	*Lower 95%*	*Upper 95%*
22	Intercept	-0.0013	0.0078	-0.1628	0.8712	-0.0169	0.0144
23	X Variable 1	1.5062	0.2077	7.2516	0.0000	1.0905	1.9220

Figure 7.3   Output from Analysis ToolPak Regression command

In routine beta estimation, the usual practice is to 'adjust' the beta before it can be used as a forecast measure. In the sheet, the beta of 1.51 is a sample estimate from 60 monthly observations. The adjustment assumes that the value-weighted true beta of the population *over all shares* must be equal to 1.00 and that high sample betas are likely to be lower in the period we are trying to forecast, and vice versa for low sample betas. Therefore sample betas are adjusted towards the population mean of 1.0. The scale of adjustment depends on the size of the variance of the sample beta (calculated as the square of the standard error of the sample beta) relative to the size of the variance of the population beta (assumed to be 0.3^2). The ratio is called the mean reversion factor. In our example, set out in Figure 7.4, the sample beta from the regression (1.51) is adjusted by a mean reversion factor of 32%, which moves it towards the population mean. The result is an adjusted beta shown in cell O31 of 1.34. The mean reversion factor is also used to adjust the standard error of the sample beta. As the spreadsheet extract shows, user-defined functions provide an easy way to implement this adjustment of the sample betas.

	H	I	J	K	L	M	N	O
27	Adjusting sample beta for mean reversion							
28								
29	Population beta			1.00		Sample beta		1.51
30	Population beta (SE)			0.30				
31						Adjusted beta		1.34
32	v1 (variance of sample beta)			0.04		via fn		1.34
33	v2 (variance of population beta)			0.09				
34								
35	mean reversion factor			32%		Sample beta (SE)		0.21
36								
37						Adjusted beta (SE)		0.17
38						via fn		0.17

Figure 7.4 Adjusting sample beta for use in forecasting

7.3   THE CAPITAL ASSET PRICING MODEL

In the previous chapter, we developed the theory underlying portfolio optimisation to what we called Problem Three, where an individual chooses how to combine the risk-free asset with an optimal risky portfolio. The CAPM rests on the premise that there is only one optimal risky portfolio and that the single portfolio is the market portfolio, in which all shares are held with weights equal to the proportion of the total market they represent. We have moved from the micro view of the single investor to the macro view of all investors, allowing us to make statements about asset pricing. The CAPM says that beta, a share's covariance with the market, is the only factor that is priced by the market. On the other hand, investors should not expect to be rewarded for bearing specific risk, since the CAPM says that for all shares the expected value of the intercept α will be zero.

The CAPM is a theory about the expected returns on an asset in relation to expected market returns. It suggests that for a fully diversified investor, the only factor affecting the expected excess return on share i, $E(R_i)$, is the systematic risk of the share (as measured by its beta, β_i). The expected value of α for all shares is zero. This can be expressed as:

$$E(R_i) = \beta_i E(R_M)   \text{ since } E(\alpha_i) = 0$$

where β_i is defined as $\text{cov}(R_i, R_M)/\sigma_M^2$ and $E(R_M)$ is the expected excess return on the market. The quantity $\beta_i E(R_M)$ is often referred to as the 'CAPM benchmark' for return.

The CAPM can be deduced from the solution to Problem Three, by supposing that there is a risky asset x which is outside the market portfolio. Problem Three is then solved algebraically such that the weight held in asset x is zero. In the previous chapter, we developed portfolio theory by assuming that investors had 'quadratic' utility functions [that is, of the form $U = E(r_p) - 0.5A\sigma_p^2$]. The CAPM theory can also be developed without the concept of utility but with an alternative assumption–that the distribution of asset returns is (log) normal. We discuss how tenable this alternative assumption is by examining the pattern of returns for a typical share in section 7.5.

7.4   VARIANCE–COVARIANCE MATRICES

In selecting risky portfolios in the last chapter, we attempted to minimise portfolio variance. To determine portfolio variance, we used a variance–covariance matrix for three assets but started with the standard deviations and correlations of the assets. In contrast, the sheet VCV contains returns data (in fact, log excess returns) for eight shares and calculates the correlation matrix and then the variance–covariance matrix of their returns. The calculations are achieved by employing the user-defined CorrMatrix function which incorporates Excel's CORREL function and the VCVMatrix function which uses Excel's COVAR function. The code for both is quite straightforward and can be accessed via the Module1 sheet. The resulting variance–covariance matrix with eight variances and 28 distinct covariances is shown in Figure 7.5.

	L	M	N	O	P	Q	R	S	T
16	VCV Matrix								
17									
18		UBS	CS	Zurich Ins	Winterthur	Roche	Sandoz	Ciba-Geigy	Swissair
19	UBS	0.0042	0.0036	0.0035	0.0032	0.0016	0.0023	0.0025	0.0025
20	CS	0.0036	0.0057	0.0033	0.0035	0.0019	0.0027	0.0029	0.0026
21	Zurich Ins	0.0035	0.0033	0.0050	0.0043	0.0019	0.0024	0.0028	0.0022
22	Winterthur	0.0032	0.0035	0.0043	0.0054	0.0017	0.0028	0.0030	0.0020
23	Roche	0.0016	0.0019	0.0019	0.0017	0.0035	0.0021	0.0024	0.0022
24	Sandoz	0.0023	0.0027	0.0024	0.0028	0.0021	0.0041	0.0030	0.0012
25	Ciba-Geigy	0.0025	0.0029	0.0028	0.0030	0.0024	0.0030	0.0044	0.0027
26	Swissair	0.0025	0.0026	0.0022	0.0020	0.0022	0.0012	0.0027	0.0074

Figure 7.5   Variance–covariance matrix for returns on eight related shares in sheet VCV

For an n-asset problem, the VCV matrix would contain approximately $n^2/2$ different cells. This can create considerable computational effort and additional difficulties in the forecasting of VCV matrices, when there are a large number of possible assets involved. The single-index model, as used by Sharpe, reduces the number of required inputs from an impossible order n^2 to a relatively manageable order n. Sharpe assumes that there is no covariance between assets other than that due to their common link to the market (the single-index). Thus this model does not capture additional covariance between assets due to common effects such as sharing the same industry.

To use the single-index VCV approach, we require estimates of beta β_i and the specific risk $\sigma(e_i)$ for each of the shares together with the variance of the market index σ_M^2. The off-diagonal elements in the matrix are estimated using the formula:

$$\sigma_{ij} = \beta_i \beta_j \sigma_M^2$$

The diagonal elements use the risk decomposition from the single-index model:

$$\sigma_i^2 = \beta_i^2 \sigma_M^2 + \sigma(e_i)^2$$

To create the matrix using a single formula we use the HLOOKUP function to extract the betas and specific risks from the input data, together with an IF statement to add the residual variance for the diagonal elements. Referring to Figure 7.6, the formula in cell M41 reads as follows:

=$M$36*HLOOKUP($L41,$M$32:$T$34,2,FALSE)*HLOOKUP(M$40,$M$32:T

34,2,FALSE)+IF($L41=M$40,HLOOKUP($L41,$M$32:$T$34,3,FALSE)^2,0)

In the first term, the initial HLOOKUP finds β_i by matching the share name in column L while the second HLOOKUP finds β_j by matching the share name in row 40. The IF statement then tests for diagonal elements (where the share names from row and column match) and, where appropriate, adds the residual variance. Although the formula is long, note how the IF statement is placed to make the formula a little more understandable by referring only to the additional element in the formula.

	L	M	N	O	P	Q	R	S	T
30	Input Data for Single-Index Model VCV								
31									
32		UBS	CS	Zurich Ins	Winterthur	Roche	Sandoz	Ciba-Geigy	Swissair
33	Beta	1.13	1.26	1.13	1.11	0.91	1.05	1.16	1.04
34	SpRisk (Mth)	0.0383	0.0478	0.0480	0.0526	0.0416	0.0421	0.0397	0.0721
35									
36	Mkt Variance	0.0022							
37									
38	VCV (Single-Index) Matrix								
39									
40		UBS	CS	Zurich Ins	Winterthur	Roche	Sandoz	Ciba-Geigy	Swissair
41	UBS	0.0042	0.0031	0.0028	0.0027	0.0022	0.0026	0.0028	0.0025
42	CS	0.0031	0.0057	0.0031	0.0030	0.0025	0.0029	0.0032	0.0028
43	Zurich Ins	0.0028	0.0031	0.0051	0.0027	0.0022	0.0026	0.0028	0.0025
44	Winterthur	0.0027	0.0030	0.0027	0.0054	0.0022	0.0025	0.0028	0.0025
45	Roche	0.0022	0.0025	0.0022	0.0022	0.0035	0.0021	0.0023	0.0020
46	Sandoz	0.0026	0.0029	0.0026	0.0025	0.0021	0.0042	0.0026	0.0024
47	Ciba-Geigy	0.0028	0.0032	0.0028	0.0028	0.0023	0.0026	0.0045	0.0026
48	Swissair	0.0025	0.0028	0.0025	0.0025	0.0020	0.0024	0.0026	0.0075

Figure 7.6   Variance–covariance matrix estimated from betas for the single-index model

By comparing the values in Figures 7.5 and 7.6, note how the single-index VCV matrix underestimates the original VCV for the covariances between shares in the same industry. (The assets in the order shown consist of two banks, then two insurance companies then three chemical companies.)

The user-defined function, VCVSingleIndexMatrix, which merely requires the returns data as input, automates the calculation of betas and specific risks and returns the single-index matrix. It can be seen starting at cell M55. Details of the code for the function are given in section 7.8.

7.5 VALUE-AT-RISK

In this section, we examine the concept of Value-at-Risk (VaR), implemented for equities as an analytic calculation derived from the assumed lognormal distribution of returns.

Empirical observation of share returns shows that they typically demonstrate some skewness. However, rescaling returns by taking their logs (usually 'natural' logs) gives a more symmetrical spread of values. So when compared with returns, log returns are usually more symmetric and tend to follow the normal distribution. When log returns are normally distributed, the distribution of returns is said to be lognormal. Although it is frequently possible to overlook the distinction between the lognormal and the normal distribution in some instances (such as dealing with daily returns or with assets of low volatility), in accurate work the difference cannot be ignored. It is important to at least understand the difference between the two cases. One broad distinction is that academic users prefer to use log returns in their analyses whilst commercial software typically uses ordinary (raw) returns and assumes these are normally distributed. Another variation in what is termed 'returns data' is that excess returns (the return after differencing off the risk-free rate) are preferred as the basis for analysis. Essentially, the crucial thing is to know what variant of the underlying share price returns data is being assumed in any analysis.

Strictly speaking, some check should be made on 'returns' data to ensure that it is approximately normally distributed. An easy approach is to produce a normal probability plot, for example for ShareA log returns (column B) of the Beta sheet. The methodology of normal probability plots is described in Chapter 3 (section 3.6.2). The resulting plot of ShareA log returns is shown in Chart1 of the EQUITY2.xls workbook.

Using the normal distribution of log returns, we can define a lower-tail value for a portfolio of assets below which there is a known chance that the asset value will fall. This lower tail value is called the Value-at-Risk or VaR. Essentially the measure is a translation from the volatility of equity returns into the appropriate percentile of the normal distribution function.

As well as the mean and variance of the monthly log returns, which we denote as M and V, we also need to find the mean of the returns data which has a lognormal distribution (denoted by $M1$). Since the moments of the returns distribution are required in this and the following section, they have been summarised in Figure 7.10 later, the crucial linking formula being that $M1 = \exp(M + 0.5V)$.

If the distribution of the monthly log returns on an asset is normal, with mean M and variance V, then over time δt the distribution is also normal, but with mean $M\delta t$ and variance $V\delta t$. From the standard normal distribution, we know there is a 5% chance of being 1.64 standard deviations or more below the mean, that is of being:

$$[M\delta t - 1.64\sqrt{(V\delta t)}]$$

or lower. Similarly, there is a 2.5% chance of being 1.96 standard deviations below and so forth. The 'z-value' (here $z = 1.645$) determines the area in the lower tail of the distribution (here 5%). If the asset starts with value S, then after δt months there will be a 5% chance that its value will be as low as:

$$S[M\delta t - 1.64\sqrt{(V\delta t)}]$$

which is the VaR for the asset. Strictly speaking this is the *absolute* VaR. If only the volatility is captured (and the expected return $SM\delta t$, is ignored), the VaR measure is called *relative*.

VaR is an attempt to estimate the downside risk of an asset or portfolio with a single number, where the VaR represents the maximum loss expected of the asset given an appropriate percentile (say 5%) and time period (say one month). In the real world, VaR is used by the major investment banks as an aggregate measure of the daily downside risk of their trading portfolios. These portfolios are likely to contain the whole gamut of financial assets such as options, bonds and futures as well as equities. Of necessity, the illustration here is chosen with equity portfolios in mind and the complications that arise when calculating VaR for other assets are not addressed.

Calculation of VaR is illustrated for the portfolio of eight Swiss shares, whose returns are displayed in the VCV sheet. We use the monthly log excess returns for the eight shares, as shown in Figure 7.7. In rows 8 and 10 the mean and variance of the monthly log returns are calculated for each asset from the 60 log returns readings in column C through to column J. For example for UBS, the mean [evaluated from formula =AVERAGE(C13:C72)] is in cell W8 and the variance [formula =VARP(C13:C72)] is in cell W10. The formula for the relative VaR uses the asset value for UBS (from cell W6), the UBS variance (from cell W10), in conjunction with the selected time interval (one month from cell W15) and the number of standard deviations or 'z-value' (in cell W19). The relative VaR estimate (in cell W21) can be interpreted as saying that there is only a 5% probability that a holding of UBS shares with a current value of 1000 will lose 105.59 or more in value over the course of the next month. The relative VaR assumes that the asset has an expected return over the period that is small enough to be ignored (as will typically be the case when considering daily VaRs).

The absolute VaR incorporates the expected return on the asset (here 1.21% over the month for UBS from the calculation of $M1$ in cell W12) and subtracts this typically positive amount for long positions from the relative VaR. The expected return ($M1$ in cell W12) uses the formula linking the moments of lognormal and normal returns explained in section 7.7. In our example the absolute VaR of 93.50 in cell W24 is thus smaller than the relative VaR. The share with the lowest VaR estimates of the group is Roche, which of course given our simple formula will have had the smallest variance.

	V	W	X	Y	Z	AA	AB	AC	AD
2	Estimating VaR using Lognormal Distribution								
3									
4		UBS	CS	Zurich Ins	Winterthur	Roche	Sandoz	Ciba-Geigy	Swissair
5									
6	Asset value (S)	1000.0	1000.0	1000.0	1000.0	1000.0	1000.0	1000.0	1000.0
7									
8	Return (M) lnS	0.0100	0.0047	0.0007	-0.0036	0.0200	0.0071	0.0002	-0.0001
9									
10	Variance (V)	0.0041	0.0056	0.0050	0.0053	0.0034	0.0041	0.0044	0.0073
11									
12	Exp ret (M1) S	1.21%	0.75%	0.32%	-0.09%	2.20%	0.92%	0.24%	0.36%
13									
14									
15	Time months (δt)	1							
16									
17	Conf level (c)	95.00%							
18									
19	'z-value'	1.64							
20									
21	VaR Asset Rel	105.59	122.97	115.83	119.77	96.29	104.80	108.80	140.68
22	via fn	105.59	122.97	115.83	119.77	96.29	104.80	108.80	140.68
23									
24	VaR Asset Abs	93.50	115.43	112.63	120.68	74.31	95.64	106.40	137.10
25	via fn	93.50	115.43	112.63	120.68	74.31	95.64	106.40	137.10
26									
27									
28	Estimating Portfolio VaR using Lognormal Distribution								
29									
30	Var Port Rel	702.70							
31	via fn	702.70							
32									
33	Var Port Abs	658.67							
34	via fn	658.67							

Figure 7.7   Calculations for Value-at-Risk for the eight Swiss shares in sheet VCV

It is straightforward to estimate the VaR for a portfolio (here assumed to have equal amounts invested in the eight shares) from the VaRs for the individual shares, in conjunction with the correlation matrix of the individual returns. The relative VaR for the portfolio in cell W30 is 702.70, compared to the sum of the individual VaRs totalling 914.73, thus demonstrating the diversification benefits of holding assets in portfolios. As indicated in Figure 7.7, we provide user-defined functions to calculate the various VaR measures.

7.6 HORIZON WEALTH

In the following section, working with log returns for an asset with mean M and variance V, we set out the linking formulas for the moments of the associated lognormal distribution of returns. The linking formulas are:

$$M1 = \exp(M + 0.5V) \quad \text{and} \quad M2 = \exp(2M + 2V)$$

In the Forecast sheet, we show how to use these relationships to estimate future wealth at some future time, say T years hence, always presuming that past performance can be projected into the future. In doing so, we assume that the historic returns (of form $1 + r$) are effectively independent and follow a lognormal distribution. Future wealth is defined as the product of successive returns and hence will also be lognormally distributed. Figure 7.8 shows an extract from the Forecast sheet.

Let W_1 be wealth at the end of one year into the future, wealth at the start (W_0) being assumed to be one. We use the moments of this lognormally distributed quantity to find the parameters for the normal distribution of $\text{Ln}(W_1)$ in order to forecast future wealth.

	A	B	C	D	E	F	G	H	I	J	K
2	Generating probabilistic forecasts (Ibbotson & Sinquefield)										
3											
4	Returns (1+r)			Ln Returns (1+r)				Forecast Distribution			
5											
6	M1	1.0917		M	0.0715			Current Wealth (W$_0$)			1.00
7	M2	1.2310		V	0.0324			Forecast Horizon (nyr)			20
8								Percentile (pctile)			60%
9	Lognormal distribution			Normal distribution							
10											
11	E (R$_{0,1}$)	9.17%		E (R$_{0,1}$)	9.17%	N (M,V)		z =NORMSINV(pctile)			0.25
12											
13											
14	E (R$_{0,n}$)	7.50%		E (R$_{0,n}$)	7.50%	N (M,V/n)		Forecast Wealth (pctile)			5.12
15								via fn			5.12
16											
17	E (R$_{0,\infty}$)	7.41%		E (R$_{0,\infty}$)	7.41%	N (M,0)		Forecast Return (pctile)			8.51%
18								via fn			8.51%

Figure 7.8 Forecast wealth calculations in sheet Forecast

The series of 70 past annual relative returns in column B of the spreadsheet has a first moment of 1.0917 and a second moment of 1.2310 (cells B6 and B7). From the linking relationships between $M1$ and $M2$ and M and V, we have:

$$M = 2\ln(M1) - 0.5\ln(M2)$$
$$V = -2\ln(M1) + \ln(M2)$$

giving values of 0.0715 and 0.0324 for M and V (in cells E6 and E7 respectively in Figure 7.8). Using our assumption that log returns are normally distributed, the various distributions of forecast returns with their parameters are set out in column F, the variance of forecast returns varying inversely with horizon period. The forecast return of 7.41% for an infinite horizon compares with the geometric mean of returns of 7.23%. The forecast returns for different horizon periods in column E from the parameters of the normal distribution are replicated in column B using the first two moments of the lognormal distribution.

From the normal distribution, we can also go on to draw the complete distribution of forecast wealth for different horizon periods. Different percentiles of its level (for example the upper 95% level) are given by the formula with so-called 'z-values':

$$\mathrm{Ln}(W_T) = MT + 1.64\sqrt{(VT)}$$

where 1.64 is the number of standard deviations below which 95% of the wealth values lie. In general, the 'z-values' as in K11 of Figure 7.8 can be obtained from the Excel function NORMSINV(pctile) where the percentile is in cell K8.

Given a forecast horizon of T years and the appropriate 'z-value', we can then forecast future wealth percentiles using the equation:

$$W_T = W_0 \exp(MT + z\sqrt{V}\sqrt{T})$$

Figure 7.9 below shows the actual wealth generated over the 70 years together with forecast wealth for the 20 years ahead, the median level (50%) as well as the upper 95% and lower 5% percentiles of the wealth distribution.

Forecast of Horizon Wealth

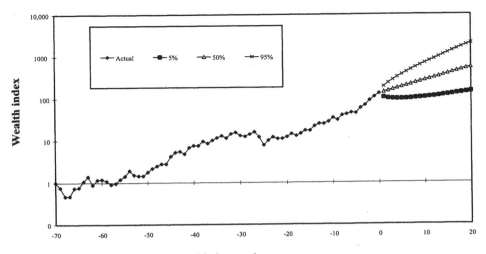

Figure 7.9   Illustration of horizon wealth forecasting

7.7   MOMENTS OF RELATED DISTRIBUTIONS SUCH AS NORMAL AND LOGNORMAL

The table in Figure 7.10 should be read carefully, as the distinction between returns and log returns is often ignored in textbooks and understanding the difference between parameters from the lognormal and normal returns is vital, not only when dealing with equities but in other important areas such as options.

Asset	Returns	Log Returns
Distribution	Lognormal	Normal
First moment	$M1$	M
Second moment	$M2$	V
First moment link	$M1 = \exp(M + 0.5V)$	$M = 2\ln(M1) - 0.5\ln(M2)$
Second moment link	$M2 = \exp(2M + 2V)$	$V = -2\ln(M1) + \ln(M2)$

Figure 7.10   Links between moments of normal and lognormal distributions

We can characterise a distribution through its moments about the mean (as for the normal distribution in the above table) or equivalently through its moments about zero (as for the lognormal distribution). The first moment of any distribution is its mean (denoted $M1$ or simply M), while the second moment (about the mean) is the variance, V as opposed to the second moment about zero, $M2$. In Excel, we can calculate $M2$ by dividing the SUMSQ function of the returns by the number of returns.

This equivalence allows us to translate parameters between the normal and lognormal distributions. Let us assume that the log returns have a normal distribution with mean M and variance V. Then we can find the moments about zero ($M1$ and $M2$) of the corresponding lognormal distribution for returns using the links given at the bottom of the second column in the table. We can reverse this process by finding formulas for the mean and variance of the normal distribution (M and V) in terms of the moments about zero of the corresponding lognormal distribution using the links given at the bottom of the third column in the table.

7.8   USER-DEFINED FUNCTIONS IN Module1

Many of the functions in this module involve straightforward transfers of the formulas from the spreadsheets into VBA. This is true of the ISHorizonWealth function and all the functions whose names start with Portfolio. There are two useful functions CorrMatrix and VCVMatrix for calculating the correlation matrix and the variance–covariance matrix, the only input being a matrix of returns data (retsmat). Both functions systematically select two columns of the returns matrix, apply Excel functions (CORREL and COVAR here) to calculate the measures, then store the result in the output matrix.

One further point about the VCVMatrix code should be mentioned here. When calculating the VCV matrix we use sample measures (such as the VAR function) rather than population measures (such as the VARP function). Rather confusingly, the COVAR function in Excel is a population measure and so must be multiplied by $n/(n-1)$ to get the sample measure.

The most ingenious function in the module is the function that returns the single-index VCV matrix. It has two inputs: the matrix of returns (retsmat) and the market returns vector (mktvec). The code for this is given in full below. Notice the declaration of variables such as rvec() as arrays whose dimensions are later set in ReDim statements when the size of the input matrix has been determined.

```
Function VCVSingleIndexMatrix(retsmat, mktvec)
'   returns nxn sample single-index variance-covariance matrix
'   uses PortfolioBeta fn
'   uses PortfolioSpecificRisk fn
    Dim vmkt, bi, sri
    Dim i As Integer, j As Integer, nc As Integer, nr As Integer
    Dim rvec() As Variant, bvec() As Variant, srvec() As Variant, Vcvmat() As Variant
    nc = retsmat.Columns.Count
    ReDim Vcvmat(nc, nc)
    ReDim bvec(nc)
    ReDim srvec(nc)
    nr = retsmat.Rows.Count
    ReDim rvec(nr)
'   first calculate the inputs (betas, specific risks and market variance)
    For j = 1 To nc
      For i = 1 To nr
         rvec(i) = retsmat(i, j)
      Next i
      bvec(j) = PortfolioBeta(rvec, mktvec)
      srvec(j) = PortfolioSpecificRisk(rvec, mktvec, 1)
    Next j
    vmkt = Application.Var(mktvec)
'   then cycle through vcv matrix
    For i = 1 To nc
      bi = bvec(i)
      sri = srvec(i)
      For j = i To nc
        If j = i Then
           Vcvmat(i, j) = (bi^2) * vmkt + (sri^2)
        Else
           Vcvmat(i, j) = bi* bvec(j)* vmkt
           Vcvmat(j, i) = Vcvmat(i, j)
        End If
      Next j
    Next i
    VCVSingleIndexMatrix = Vcvmat
End Function
```

In the first If... Then loop where j refers to the jth asset and i to the ith return, the beta and specific risk are evaluated for each asset using other user-defined functions. The second If... Then loop inserts the variance and covariance expressions based on the betas and specific risks into the appropriate slot in the VCV matrix.

SUMMARY

The contribution of the single-index model is to divide the view of risk from the previous chapter into two: one part that comes from the influence of the index or market portfolio and a second part that is specific to individual shares or assets. We apply the single-index model to facilitate the estimation of variance–covariance matrices as well as to provide beta coefficients through regression. As always, we show the calculations, here involving regression and matrix multiplication, both in the spreadsheet and in user-defined functions.

The near similarity of the algebra underlying the single-index model and the capital asset pricing model should not prevent us from appreciating just how big a step the development of the CAPM was. In its most literal form, the CAPM says that only market-related risk is rewarded.

Although the CAPM can be developed from individual utility and the generic portfolio problems in the previous chapter, it is more straightforward to focus on the equivalent assumption that log returns on shares follow a normal distribution. We use this assumption of normality to illustrate how to forecast the distribution of future wealth from past returns and also to illustrate the calculation of Value-at-Risk.

In the next chapter, we look at the performance measurement of active investment strategies using both single-index and multi-index passive benchmarks.

REFERENCES

Bodie, Z., A. Kane and A. J. Marcus, 1996, *Investments*, 3rd edition, Richard D. Irwin, Englewood Cliffs, NJ.

8
Performance Measurement and Attribution

The broad objective of performance measurement is to assess and compare the performance (past returns) of different investment strategies. Our main emphasis in this chapter will be on the choice between passive and active investment strategies when assembling a portfolio of risky assets. The secondary emphasis will be on choosing the level of risk-free assets to complement the chosen risky portfolio.

Under a pure passive investment strategy, an investor holds a portfolio that is an exact copy (by component shares and weights) of the market index. The passive investor does not rely on superior information and, apart from rebalancing when the constituents of the index change, there is no trading. The passive investor is rewarded for bearing market risk and will achieve the market return less the unavoidable trading costs.

In contrast, under an active investment strategy the investor's portfolio differs from the market index by having different weights in some or all of the shares in the market index. The active investor relies on having superior information and is prepared to incur much greater trading costs than the passive investor. In practice, only a few active investors outperform the returns from passive investment in the long term, since they bear specific risk and incur greater trading costs. With the increasing complexity of active strategies, the need for more sophisticated benchmarks and performance measurement is becoming ever more vital.

This chapter reviews the earliest ideas about performance measurement from the 1960s as well as the very latest ideas in performance attribution from the 1990s. All the approaches use asset returns, which is advantageous because this data is readily available for individual equities and investment funds. Conventional performance measurement was developed at the same time as the theories on asset pricing described in the previous chapter. Hence the Sharpe ratio uses as a return 'benchmark' the return on the risk-free asset, whereas the other three measures use a CAPM (single-index) benchmark. Another approach from the seventies, the Treynor–Black 'active–passive' model (Treynor and Black, 1973), blends an active portfolio of shares viewed as mispriced with a passive index portfolio to create an optimal risky portfolio. This approach builds on the so-called generic portfolio problems discussed in Chapter 6. Portfolio performance assessment and the Treynor–Black model are both discussed in Bodie et al. (1996), Chapter 24. However, the most recent technique of performance attribution, called style analysis, is not covered in Bodie et al. Style analysis was developed by Sharpe (1992) and uses a multi-index model as the return benchmark.

The four conventional performance measures involve the ratio of the fund's return relative to a return benchmark divided by a chosen measure of risk (such as volatility, beta or residual risk). The measures are illustrated in the spreadsheets of EQUITY3.xls and have also been developed as user-defined functions. Similarly, the spreadsheet implementation of the Treynor–Black 'active–passive' model uses functions, in this case the user-defined functions already developed for the generic portfolio problems. Style analysis, like the task of finding the constrained efficient frontier, uses Excel's Solver to carry out quadratic programming. It has two extensions: obtaining confidence intervals for the style weights (here also implemented using Solver) and exposure analysis, a rolling-period style analysis which shows how a fund's style changes over time. Since many repetitions of style analysis are required, exposure analysis is best implemented in Excel macros.

8.1 CONVENTIONAL PERFORMANCE MEASUREMENT

The conventional measures of performance rank investment strategies by looking at historic return and risk. These measures are now somewhat dated since they use only a single-index benchmark, and they all suffer from a lack of statistical precision and power. It is probably better to view them as more of a lesson in history than current best practice.

The sheet 4Measures looks at the performance measures that were developed in the late 1960s in the aftermath of the CAPM. The measures are defined as follows:

Sharpe's measure $[r_p - r_f]/\sigma(r_p)$

Treynor's measure $[r_p - r_f]/\beta_p = \text{constant} + \alpha_p/\beta_p$

Jensen's measure $\alpha_p = r_p - \{r_f + \beta_p[r_m - r_f]\}$

Appraisal ratio $\alpha_p/\sigma(e_p)$

In the above r_p and $\sigma(r_p)$ are the average return and standard deviation of return for a portfolio, α_p and β_p the CAPM parameters for the portfolio in its relationship with the market, $\sigma(e_p)$ the specific risk of portfolio returns (i.e. the standard deviation of returns not related to the market), and r_f the return on the riskless asset. These measures are calculated using historic (or 'ex-post') data in the hope that such historic measures will contain some predictive ('ex-ante') ability.

The Sharpe measure divides the excess return by the portfolio risk (standard deviation of portfolio returns). Treynor's measure divides excess return by systematic risk, β_p. Jensen's measure is simply α_p, the difference in portfolio return over that predicted by the CAPM given the market return, referred to above as 'mispricing'. The Appraisal ratio divides α_p by the portfolio's non-systematic risk.

	A	B	C	D	E	F	G	H	I	J
2	Performance Measurement									
3										
4		Excess Returns				Four Performance Measures				
5										
6		Mean	29.00%	22.00%				ShareA		Index
7										
8		Total Risk (Mth)	42.00%	30.00%		Sharpe		0.6905		0.7333
9		Spec Risk (Mth)	18.00%	0.00%						
10						Treynor		0.2417		0.2200
11		Alpha	0.10%	0.00%						
12						Jensen		0.10%		0.00%
13		Beta	1.20	1.00						
14						Appraisal		0.0057		
15		Corr (Share, Index)		0.69						

Figure 8.1 Performance measures in the 4Measures sheet

The mean return, alpha, beta, etc. shown in columns C and D of Figure 8.1 have been evaluated from monthly excess returns for an individual share and the market index. (Note that instead of returns from a share we could equally have chosen a portfolio.) The share's positive alpha in cell C11 (and hence Jensen measure in H12) suggest it produces more return than expected under the CAPM. It follows that its Appraisal ratio in cell H14 is also positive. Treynor's measure can also be expressed as a constant plus α_p/β_p, where the constant is the excess return on the market portfolio. However, in our example the alpha value is not enough to compensate for the share's greater total risk than the index, and so the share's Sharpe measure is inferior to that for the index.

The choice of risk measure in the denominator to a large extent determines the purpose for which each measure should be used. For example, the Sharpe measure should be used only to assess the performance of the total investment portfolio (since it ignores correlation with the market). The Treynor and Jensen measures should be used only to assess investments that form a small part of the total investment portfolio. The Appraisal ratio should be used only to distinguish between alternative active investments to be added to a core passive portfolio. These single-index performance measures must be used with caution and are generally inferior to the multi-index performance measures (such as style analysis) that we cover later in this chapter.

8.2   ACTIVE–PASSIVE MANAGEMENT

In practice, many investment managers assume that most shares are fairly valued, but that some are overpriced and some are underpriced. In the light of the CAPM, the extent to which a share is mispriced is measured by its alpha value.

Treynor and Black developed a model for portfolio managers who focus on a portfolio of mispriced shares, thereby assuming that share markets are not entirely efficient. First, they showed how the optimal active portfolio can be blended with the passive market portfolio to create the optimal risky portfolio. Second, they detailed how the optimal risky portfolio can then be combined with the risk-free asset to give the optimal portfolio. These two steps correspond to combining two risky assets and then a risk-free and a risky asset as outlined in our treatment of the generic portfolio problems (Problem Two and Problem One in sections 6.8 and 6.7 respectively). The Treynor–Black approach uses the Appraisal ratio of performance measurement and underlies the 'core-satellite' approach to investment management that is making a comeback.

	A	B	C	D	E	F	G	H	I
2	**Active-Passive Exercise (Treynor-Black)**								
3									
4	Risk-free rate	7.0%							
5	Equity risk premium	8.0%							
6	Equity market risk	20.0%							
7	RRA value (A)	3.0							
8									
9	**A: Find Optimal Active Portfolio**								
10									
11		Exp Rew			Beta	Spec Risk		Rew / Var		Weight
12	Share 1	1.0%			1.13	13.0%		0.592		98.2%
13	Share 2	1.5%			1.13	16.0%		0.586		97.2%
14	Share 3	-2.0%			1.04	25.0%		-0.320		-53.1%
15	Share 4	-0.5%			0.91	14.0%		-0.255		-42.3%
16									
17	**Optimal Active Portfolio**	3.7%			1.27	24.8%		0.603		

Figure 8.2   Treynor–Black's model in the AP sheet

The example shown in Figure 8.2 contains details of four shares that the portfolio manager thinks are mispriced. For example, share 1 is expected to have a 1.0% excess return in the next year (over and above the return expected under the CAPM). The first task is to create the optimal active portfolio, given the expected rewards, beta and specific risk estimates for the four mispriced shares. Treynor–Black argue that we should maximise the Appraisal ratio for the active portfolio. They show that this is equivalent to having holdings for the individual shares that are proportional to their individual expected reward divided by specific variance. These ratios are in cells G12:G15, their total sum is in cell G17 and hence the weights for the four shares in the optimal active portfolio are calculated in cells I12:I15. For example, share 1 has a weight of 98.2% (=G12/G17) in the optimal active portfolio. Combining the four constituents with these weights, the optimal active portfolio has an expected excess return of 3.7%, a beta of 1.27 and specific risk of 24.8% (assuming that the specific risks of the chosen shares are independent).

The second task is to combine the optimal active portfolio with the passive market portfolio (the latter having an excess return equal to the equity risk premium in cell B5, and total risk equal to the equity market risk in cell B6). Here we can apply the solution to generic portfolio Problem Two (described in section 6.8). This focused on combining two risky assets, but the methodology can be applied equally to combining portfolios. Thus the weight for the active portfolio displayed in cell I23 of Figure 8.3 uses the formula:

$$=\textbf{Prob2OptimalRiskyWeight1(B24,E24,B4,B29,E29,B31,B7)}$$

	A	B	C	D	E	F	G	H	I	J
20	B: Find Optimal Risky Portfolio									
21										
22		Active			Passive		Solve Prob2 : optimal risky weights			
23	Return above CAPM	3.7%		Return above Rf	8.0%		w active		32.8%	
24	Return	20.9%			15.0%		w passive		67.2%	
25										
26	Beta	1.27			1.00		Optimal risky portfolio			
27							Xs return		9.9%	
28	Spec risk	24.8%			0.0%		Return		16.9%	
29	Total risk	35.5%			20.0%		Alpha		1.2%	
30							Beta		1.09	
31	corr(a,p)	0.72					Spec risk		8.1%	
32							Total risk		23.3%	
33										
34			Sharpe ratio		0.40		Sharpe ratio		0.43	

Figure 8.3   Finding the optimal risky portfolio in the AP sheet

The function has as inputs the return and risk for the two portfolios (B24, E24, B29, E29), the correlation between them (B31), the risk-free rate (B4) and the risk aversion coefficient (B7). It shows that 32.8% of the investment in risky assets should be in the active portfolio. In passing, note that the optimal risky portfolio has a Sharpe ratio greater than that for the passive portfolio, that is it provides more reward for risk.

The final task is to split the total investment between the optimal risky portfolio and the risk-free asset. Again the solution to this problem has been met before, this time generic portfolio Problem One (in section 6.7). The weight for the optimal risky portfolio in Figure 8.4, cell B41, uses the formula:

$$=\textbf{Prob1OptimalRiskyWeight(I28,B4,I32,B7)}$$

where the function inputs are the return and risk on the optimal risky portfolio (I28, I32), the risk-free rate (B4) and the investor's risk aversion coefficient (B7). Here the proportion invested in risky assets is under two-thirds (61.2%).

	A	B	C	D	E	F	G	H	I	J
37	C: Find Optimal Portfolio									
38										
39	Solve Prob1 : split between risk-free and risky									
40	Risk-free	38.8%								
41	Risky	61.2%								
42										
43							Optimal portfolio			
44	Risk-free	38.8%					Xs return		6.1%	
45	Share 1	19.7%					Return		13.1%	
46	Share 2	19.5%					Alpha		0.7%	
47	Share 3	-10.7%					Beta		0.67	
48	Share 4	-8.5%					Spec risk		5.0%	
49	Passive	41.1%					Total risk		14.2%	

Figure 8.4 Deciding the risky–risk-free proportions in the Treynor–Black model, AP sheet

The active and passive portfolios are illustrated on the risk–return chart in Figure 8.5. Blending the active and passive portfolios produces the portfolios on the frontier between them. The optimal risky portfolio occurs where the straight line from the risk-free asset (7% return) is tangential to this frontier. The risk aversion coefficient influences the position on the line of the final optimal portfolio, which in our example includes 38.8% of risk-free investment.

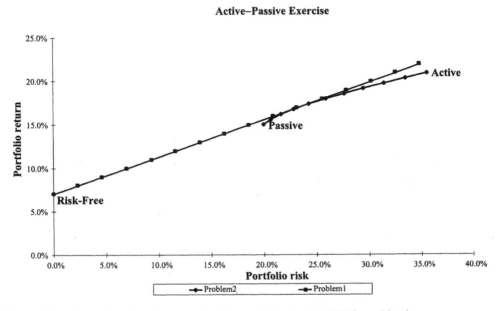

Figure 8.5 Chart sheet for Treynor–Black's model in the EQUITY3 workbook

8.3   INTRODUCTION TO STYLE ANALYSIS

Style analysis is a more recent returns-based approach to measuring the performance of an investment fund. Sharpe (1992) pioneered it in the early nineties by developing an 'asset class factor model' to distinguish the performance of different funds with respect to 'style' and 'selection'. Style analysis can also be viewed as reverse engineering the asset mix in a portfolio.

Investment funds create portfolios that are invested across a number of different national sectors (such as equities, bonds and bills) and, possibly, international sectors (such as currencies, foreign equities and commodities). Within each sector, funds can also hold different amounts of individual assets. Typically, there is no information available to external investors about the detailed choice of assets a particular fund holds. Since different sectors perform differently, it is difficult to separate out the contribution to return made by sector choice on the one hand, or asset choice within sectors on the other hand. However, data on the returns of quoted funds (such as unit and investment trusts) is available and can be used to carry out style analysis.

The objective of style analysis is to construct a benchmark portfolio, from a set of known indices (for which returns are available), against which to compare the performance of an investment fund's actively-managed portfolio. Ideally, the indices should reflect activity in different asset classes, they should be mutually exclusive and exhaustive, and their assets publicly quoted so that they can be tracked 'passively'. (For example, Sharpe used 12 indices to cover the range of investment options available to US funds. The indices were chosen to have as little overlap as possible.)

The equation underlying style analysis for the ith investment fund using n passive indices, where the returns from the indices are denoted $f_1, f_2, \ldots f_n$, is:

$$r_i = [b_{i1}f_1 + b_{i2}f_2 + \cdots + b_{in}f_n] + e_i$$

where r_i is the return on the ith fund, b_{ij} is the weight of the ith fund in the jth index, and e_i is the non-factor component of the return.

Rearranging this multi-index model of returns as the difference between the fund return and the return due to the indices gives:

$$e_i = r_i - [b_{i1}f_1 + b_{i2}f_2 + \cdots + b_{in}f_n]$$

where the bracketed part can be regarded as the return on a weighted portfolio.

Sharpe suggests choosing the weights b_{ij} to minimise the so-called 'tracking error' e_i, or rather to minimise the variance of e_i, a quadratic expression in the weights. Since they make up a portfolio, the weights are constrained to sum to 100% with the individual weights normally lying between 0% and 100%. (However this latter condition can be modified for funds that are allowed to hold assets short.) The weights determined by optimisation are called the style weights and, when combined with the indices, form the benchmark portfolio. We say that the fund with optimised style weights for the different indices is of the same style as the investment fund.

Choosing the style weights to minimise the tracking error over the estimation period can be achieved by quadratic programming. The Solver routine in Excel (from Tools then Solver) allows the analysis to be performed quickly and easily in a spreadsheet.

A useful way to evaluate the effectiveness of style analysis is to calculate the proportion of variance in fund returns 'explained' by the selected style model. This is similar to the conventional R-squared measure in regression, and is calculated for the ith fund as:

$$1 - [\text{Var}(e_i)/\text{Var}(r_i)]$$

Sharpe uses his approach to compare the styles for different investment funds, using the same set of indices from which different benchmark portfolios are estimated. In the following sections, we concentrate on just one fund, establish its style and characteristics. We then examine how the style weights change over time, reflecting changes in the fund's exposure to the different asset classes.

8.4   SIMPLE STYLE ANALYSIS

The Style1 sheet in the EQUITY3 workbook contains monthly returns for a fund and eight passive indices. The top part of the worksheet is illustrated in Figure 8.6. The task is to find weights, in the range D16:J16, that minimise the error variance in cell M6. The task is accomplished using the Solver routine in Excel. Notice that cell C16 contains the expression 1−SUM(D16:J16) which ensures that the style weights sum to unity.

As a preliminary, we have to complete the formulas for the style (in cells L21:L80) and the tracking error (in cells M21:M80). The formula for the style for month 1 (cell L21):

$$=\text{SUMPRODUCT}(\$C\$16{:}\$J\$16,C21{:}J21)$$

multiplies the arrays of style weights and index returns via the SUMPRODUCT function.

	A	B	C	D	E	F	G	H	I	J	K	L	M
1	Equity3.XLS												
2	Style Analysis												
3		Solver - Style Model											
4										Mean Error			-0.0076
5		Target cell	M5							EV*10,000			6.4398
6		Changing cells	D16..J16							Error Variance			0.0006
7		Constraints	C15..J15 >= 0							Active Std Deviation			2.54%
8			C17..J17 <= 1										
9										Asset Variance		0.0027	
10										Style R-sqd		76.2%	
11													
12		Style Weights											
13			Index1	Index2	Index3	Index4	Index5	Index6	Index7	Index8			
14													
15		min	0.0%	0.0%	0.0%	0.0%	0.0%	0.0%	0.0%	0.0%			
16		weight	0.0%	15.8%	46.8%	1.4%	13.2%	0.0%	6.3%	16.5%			
17		max	100.0%	100.0%	100.0%	100.0%	100.0%	100.0%	100.0%	100.0%			
18													
19	Mth	FundA	Index1	Index2	Index3	Index4	Index5	Index6	Index7	Index8		Style	Error
20													
21	1	-0.020	0.008	-0.032	0.043	0.032	0.097	0.110	0.026	0.111		0.048	-0.068

Figure 8.6   Simple style analysis in Style1 sheet

The first error term (in cell L21) is simply the difference between the fund return in cell B21 and the style return. Once the formulas for style and error have been copied down through the rest of the data, the error variance in cell M6 can be evaluated with the function for sample variance:

$$=VAR(M21:M80)$$

Since frequently this value is very small (here 0.0006), we have added a scaled error variance value (multiplied by 10,000) in cell M5 which helps to improve the precision of the optimisation.

With the addition of constraints on the weights in rows 15 and 17 labelled min and max, we can use Solver to minimise the scaled error variance in cell M5. The Solver specification is set out at the top of Figure 8.6, which also contains the resulting style weights. This optimisation can be achieved manually using command Tools then Solver or automatically via a subroutine containing direct calls on the various component functions within Solver. The relevant macro called Style1 in ModuleM is explained briefly in section 8.8. The macro can also be invoked by pressing the Ctrl+Shift+S key combination simultaneously.

The Style1 macro also produces a chart showing resulting style weights that minimise the error variance for the fund and the chosen indices. This shows that for the period examined the fund performed as if invested with weights of 57.8% in index 3, 14.2% in index 5, 7.6% in index 4 and so on. The chosen style explained 95.6% of the fund returns variability. In summary, the style weights for a particular fund generate a passive benchmark portfolio covering the returns for a chosen period against which to compare the performance of active fund managers.

8.5   ROLLING-PERIOD STYLE ANALYSIS

The style identified in the previous analysis is effectively the average of potentially changing styles used over the estimation period. One additional form of analysis is to carry out a number of style analyses covering a succession of periods in order to see how consistent the estimated style is over time. This rolling-period form of style analysis is sometimes known as exposure analysis.

In Figure 8.7, style analysis has been performed using returns for the first 24 months, then for months 7–30, and so on, giving us a time series of seven style analyses (separate analyses, although each has 18 observations in common with the previous one).

The main change in spreadsheet operation is to ensure that the error variance is evaluated for the appropriate range of error terms for each of the individual style analyses. For this, we use the INDEX command in its reference form to select starting and ending cell references within the variance formula, based on the starting month in cell J6 and the ending month in cell J7. The formula for the error variance in cell M23 used for each separate style analysis is:

$$=VAR(INDEX(\$M\$38:\$M\$97,J6,1):INDEX(\$M\$38:\$M\$97,J7,1))$$

With the values of 1 in cell J6 and 24 in cell J7, this is equivalent to the formula VAR(M38:M61).

	A	B	C	D	E	F	G	H	I	J	K	L	M
2		Rolling Period Style Analysis - Exposure											
3			Solver - Exposure Model										
4													
5			Target cell		M22			ExpObs		24			
6			Changing cells		D33..J33			SMonth		37			
7			Constraints		C32..J32 >= 0			EMonth		60			
8					C34..J34 <= 1								
9		Exposure Weights											
10			Index1	Index2	Index3	Index4	Index5	Index6	Index7	Index8			
11													
12		exp1	4.0%	69.8%	18.1%	0.0%	0.0%	4.2%	0.0%	3.9%		mths 1-24	
13		exp2	14.4%	47.8%	25.1%	1.6%	2.7%	0.0%	0.0%	8.4%		mths 7-30	
14		exp3	0.0%	10.2%	36.3%	14.5%	4.8%	0.0%	12.4%	21.8%		mths 13-36	
15		exp4	0.0%	2.7%	40.5%	10.6%	16.0%	0.0%	13.3%	16.8%		mths 19-42	
16		exp5	1.2%	0.0%	29.4%	0.0%	29.6%	6.0%	9.7%	24.2%		mths 25-48	
17		exp6	0.0%	0.0%	37.5%	0.0%	26.0%	6.6%	10.3%	19.6%		mths 31-54	
18		exp7	0.0%	6.7%	49.3%	3.3%	24.0%	9.7%	6.9%	0.0%		mths 37-60	

Figure 8.7 Style exposure model analysis in Style2 sheet

The repeated application of the style analysis is best automated via a macro. In the Style2 macro in the ModuleM sheet, Solver is first set up with the appropriate target cell, changing cells and constraints. Within each Solver repetition, we choose the range for the error variance, use Solver to minimise the error variance and then copy the calculated weights to the output range. The time series of style analyses weights can then be charted as shown in Figure 8.8. The macro can be called by pressing the Ctrl+Shift+E key combination simultaneously.

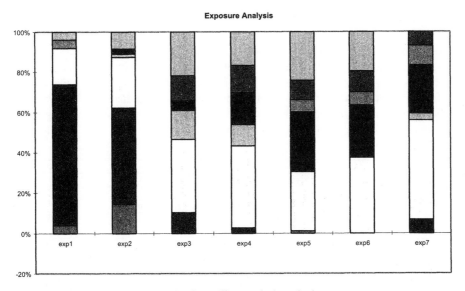

Figure 8.8 Changing style weights in the rolling-period analysis

We can use the exposure weights (estimated say over the previous 24 months) as a passive benchmark against which to compare the performance of the active fund for the current month. At the end of the current month we can compare the return from the active fund against the return from its exposure benchmark, and the resulting difference in performance is known as the selection return for the month. This selection return measures both the impact from selecting shares within the style sectors as well as the impact of changes in weights allocated to different sectors made by the active fund during the month. Thus, for example, a fund might have a positive impact from being overweight in shares that outperformed within its sector but a negative impact from increasing its exposure to sectors that underperformed. By carrying out this procedure over a number of months, the cumulative selection return for the active fund is obtained. Sharpe illustrates how to test the significance of the average selection return using a t-test.

8.6   CONFIDENCE INTERVALS FOR STYLE WEIGHTS

So far, we have estimated style weights (both on a simple basis and on a rolling basis) but we have no idea of how to find whether the estimated style weights differ significantly from zero. To do this, in line with longstanding procedures underlying statistical estimation, we need to calculate standard errors to correspond with the estimated style weights.

In an ideal world, the indices used in style analysis would be independent and thus have returns that were uncorrelated with the returns of any of the other indices. In practice, the indices needed to cover the range of possible asset classes will fall short of the ideal and will sometimes have high correlations with other indices. What we would like to do is to eliminate indices from the style analysis if they are too similar to other indices (substitutes) in order that the remaining subset of indices differ as much as possible (i.e. they provide complements). For instance, we might start with eight indices and by dropping, in turn, four of the more closely related indices we would end up with the four most complementary indices for our eventual style analysis.

One way of judging whether indices are substitutes or complements is to generate a correlation matrix for the returns 'generated' from the different possible style indices. Indices that are easiest to replicate using other indices will be highly correlated with other indices. For instance, in Figure 8.9 below, indices 3, 6 and 8 have correlations above 0.5 with four of the seven other indices. Conversely, indices that are most difficult to replicate will have low correlations with other indices. For instance, indices 1 and 2 have correlations below 0.25 with all the other indices.

	O	P	Q	R	S	T	U	V	W	X
3	Correlation Matrix for Style Index Returns									
4										
5		Index1	Index2	Index3	Index4	Index5	Index6	Index7	Index8	
6		1.00	0.22	0.19	-0.01	0.16	-0.04	-0.06	-0.13	Index1
7		0.22	1.00	0.11	0.10	-0.09	-0.24	0.15	-0.15	Index2
8		0.19	0.11	1.00	0.86	0.53	0.63	0.19	0.62	Index3
9		-0.01	0.10	0.86	1.00	0.48	0.58	0.24	0.61	Index4
10		0.16	-0.09	0.53	0.48	1.00	0.61	0.34	0.52	Index5
11		-0.04	-0.24	0.63	0.58	0.61	1.00	0.31	0.63	Index6
12		-0.06	0.15	0.19	0.24	0.34	0.31	1.00	0.14	Index7
13		-0.13	-0.15	0.62	0.61	0.52	0.63	0.14	1.00	Index8

Figure 8.9   Correlation matrix of style index returns

Style analysis is a development of constrained linear regression and, as such, it should be possible to find confidence intervals for the style weights. This can be done by estimating the style of each chosen index in terms of the other indices (as first described by Lobosco and DiBartolomeo, 1997). The style is estimated without constraints on individual weights (though the weights must sum to 100%), thus giving an unexplained volatility for each index. This is compared to the active standard deviation of the style model for the fund to give standard errors (and hence confidence intervals) for the estimated style weights. See Figures 8.10 and 8.11.

	A	B	C	D	E	F	G	H	I	J	K	L	M
2	Confidence Intervals for Style Weights (see Lobosco & DiBartolomeo, 1997)												
3		Solver - Style Model for Confidence Intervals											
4													
5		Target cell		M6						EV*10,000			34.1653
6		Changing cells		E14..J14						Error Variance			0.0034
7		Constraints								Active Std Deviation			5.85%
8													
9	j *	8								Aset Variance		0.0071	
10										Style R-sqd		52.1%	
11													
12		Style Weights											
13			Index1	Index2	Index3	Index4	Index5	Index6	Index7	Index8			
14	Weight			18.6%	-29.5%	23.0%	41.4%	22.8%	34.0%	-10.3%			
15													
16	Index ASD		2.27%	2.47%	2.69%	2.74%	4.21%	4.21%	5.27%	5.85%			
17													
18													
19	Mth	Indexj*		Index2	Index3	Index4	Index5	Index6	Index7	Index8		Style	Error
20													
21	1	0.111		0.008	-0.032	0.043	0.032	0.097	0.110	0.026		0.091	0.020

Figure 8.10   Confidence intervals for style coefficients in Style3 sheet

We need to build a spreadsheet that can automatically divide the matrix of index returns into two: returns for the chosen single index, j^*, in column B; and returns for the remaining indices in columns D to J. The single index is isolated by using the value of j^* in cell B10 in combination with the INDEX command, here used in the array form to return the value of a chosen cell within the array of returns. This is achieved with this formula in cell B21:

$$=INDEX(\$P\$21:\$W\$80,A21,\$B\$9)$$

The best way to then divide the remaining indices is by writing a user-defined function, StyleSubMatrix, that is described in greater detail in sheet Module1.

The spreadsheet is now set up to use Solver in a fashion similar to the Style1 sheet, though without the constraints on individual weights. This is automated for a single use in the Style3 macro (called by the Ctrl+Shift+J key combination) and for the collection of eight style indices in the Style4 macro (Ctrl+Shift+K). These macros are explained in greater detail in the ModuleM sheet.

	AA	AB	AC	AD	AE	AF	AG	AH	AI
3	Confidence Intervals for Style Weights								
4									
5	Active Std Deviation for Style			2.54%					
6	Observations			60					
7	Non-zero style weights			6					
8									
9		Index1	Index2	Index3	Index4	Index5	Index6	Index7	Index8
10									
11	Weight	0.0%	15.8%	46.8%	1.4%	13.2%	0.0%	6.3%	16.5%
12	non-zero	0	1	1	1	1	0	1	1
13									
14	Index ASD	2.27%	2.47%	2.69%	2.74%	4.21%	4.21%	5.27%	5.85%
15									
16	Weight (SE)	15.36%	14.10%	12.96%	12.74%	8.29%	8.28%	6.61%	5.96%
17									
18	T-statistic	0.00	1.12	3.61	0.11	1.59	0.00	0.96	2.76

Figure 8.11   Confidence intervals for style coefficients in Style3 sheet

The resulting active standard deviations for the individual indices are then used to estimate standard errors for the style weights obtained from the original style analysis of the fund. The formula for the standard error in cell AB16 is:

$$=\$AD\$5/(AB14*SQRT(\$AD\$6-\$AD\$7-1))$$

The index ASD (from cell AB14) is used as the divisor for the standard error. An index that has a high ASD is very difficult to replicate using the other indices and so should have a lower standard error. This is achieved by dividing the estimated weight by the appropriate index ASD. The formula also depends on the number of observations used for the original style analysis and the number of non-zero style weights.

Using the t-statistics, we can then refine the style analysis by dropping indices from the style analysis with t-statistic values insignificantly different from zero (say below 2 at the 95% confidence interval).

Style analysis is much needed. Since the development of the theory underlying the CAPM (and the associated conventional performance measures) in the 1960s, there has been a continuing avalanche of research into finding anomalies observed in asset pricing markets. Differential performance (good over some periods, bad over other periods) has been ascribed to a whole raft of active strategies at differing times. The 1980s saw the documentation of the small firm effect as well as strategies based on dividend yield or price-earnings ratios. The 1990s followed with the market-to-book ratio and momentum. Hot on the heels of the discovery of possible anomalies has come the development of passive benchmarks, especially in the US and the UK, to mimic active strategies. Style analysis is currently the most important of these, as it produces multi-index passive benchmarks against which to compare the performance of the current mix of anomaly-led active strategies.

8.7   USER-DEFINED FUNCTIONS IN Module1

The module contains functions for the four performance measures that are relatively straightforward transfers of the spreadsheet formulas into code.

The function to delete a single column from the matrix of returns and return the reduced dimension matrix is used in computing confidence intervals for the style coefficients. In essence, the function creates a duplicate copy of the original matrix column-by-column, skipping the column to be deleted (using the jadj dummy variable):

```
Function StyleSubMatrix(indxmat, jstar)
'  returns style index returns matrix less column j*
   Dim i As Integer, j As Integer, jadj As Integer, nr As Integer, nc As Integer
   Dim Submat() As Variant
   nr = indxmat.Rows.Count
   nc = indxmat.Columns.Count
   ReDim Submat(nr, nc - 1)
   jadj = 0
   For j = 1 To nc - 1
     If j > = jstar Then jadj = 1
     For i = 1 To nr
       Submat(i, j) = indxmat(i, j + jadj)
     Next i
   Next j
   StyleSubMatrix = Submat
End Function
```

8.8   MACROS IN ModuleM

The quadratic programming formulation for style analysis is slightly simpler than that required to produce an efficient portfolio. Both formulations include upper and lower bounds for the weights, but for style analysis there is no equality constraint equivalent to satisfying the target return. The Style1 subroutine is primarily a simple application of Solver with direct use of the individual Solver functions. Constraints are added using the SolverAdd function, while the problem is set up using the SolverOk function:

```
Sub Style1()
   Range("change1").Value = 0.1
   Range("A1").Select
   SolverReset
   Call SolverAdd(Range("constraint1"), 3, "con1min")
   Call SolverAdd(Range("constraint1"), 1, "con1max")
   Call SolverOk(Range("target1"), 2, 0, Range("change1"))
   Call SolverSolve(True)
   SolverFinish
   Call Chart1
   Application.ScreenUpdating = True
End Sub
```

The Chart1 subroutine was developed with the macro recorder while using the ChartWizard to create a chart on a new sheet. The final two lines of code show values as data labels and suppress the background colour of the chart. These lines of code were added using the macro recorder as a better alternative than searching through reference books or the Help function. Note that the subroutine can be used in its own right, but is also called in the Style1 subroutine:

```
Sub Chart1()
  Charts.Add
  ActiveChart.ChartWizard Source:=Sheets("Style1").Range("chart1s"),_
    Gallery:=xlColumn, Format:=6, PlotBy:=xlRows,_
    CategoryLabels:=1, SeriesLabels:=0, HasLegend:=2, Title:=_
    "Style Analysis", CategoryTitle:="", ValueTitle:="", ExtraTitle _
    :=""
  ActiveChart.ApplyDataLabels Type:=xlShowValue, LegendKey:=False
  ActiveChart.PlotArea.Interior.ColorIndex = xlNone
End Sub
```

The Style2 subroutine is merely the repeated application of the Solver function. Note how after the initialisations Solver is set up before the loop. Within the loop, the call to SolverSolve estimates the next style analysis and then the estimated weights are copied to the output range. Notice also how the use of Offset in the Range("exp0").Offset(iter, 1) statement cycles through the output range:

```
Sub Style2()
  Dim iter As Integer, niter As Integer, rstep As Integer
  Range("exp17").ClearContents
  Range("change2"). Value = 0.1
  Range("A1").Select
  SolverReset
  Call SolverAdd(Range("constraint2"), 3, "con2min")
  Call SolverAdd(Range("constraint2"), 1, "con2max")
  Call SolverOk(Range("target2"), 2, 0, Range("change2"))
  rstep = 6
  niter = 7
  iter = 1
  Do While iter <= niter
  Range("smonth2").Value = 1 + (iter - 1) * rstep
  Call SolverSolve(True)
  SolverFinish
  Range("constraint2").Copy
  Range("exp0").Offset(iter, 1).PasteSpecial Paste:=xlValues
  iter = iter + 1
  Loop
  Call Chart2
  Application.ScreenUpdating = True
End Sub
```

The subsequent subroutines, Style3 and Style4, use similar techniques to those already explained.

SUMMARY

This chapter looks at performance measurement through two different lenses. The first, a distant lens, adapts the theory from the previous chapter to provide conventional measures of performance. The second, a much closer lens, uses a multi-index model to provide the more sophisticated benchmark underlying style analysis.

The conventional performance measures provide a simple ranking of portfolios based on their historic return and risk. They are straightforward to calculate in the spreadsheet but are based on a single-index (CAPM) benchmark and lack statistical power and precision.

The active–passive model developed by Treynor and Black deviates from the CAPM in assuming that security analysts expect differential performance from a number of shares. The main task is to blend the active portfolio with the market portfolio in order to create an optimal risky portfolio. We show how the generic portfolio problems developed in Chapter 6 can be used to solve the active–passive model.

The decades since the development of the CAPM have seen a relentless volume of empirical testing in the search for additional factors beyond beta that might be rewarded. Close on the heels of potential mispricing (such as size or market-to-book ratios) has come the development of more specialised indices (such as large cap, small cap, value or growth). These facilitate the development of multi-index models and, following on, allow the creation of better passive benchmarks for performance measurement.

We illustrate the technique of style analysis, which allows such multi-index models in the measurement of active investment strategies. The technique uses quadratic programming (as in Chapter 6) and is implemented using Solver in the spreadsheet as well as in macros. Style analysis can be carried out over a single period but, more usefully, on a rolling basis, allowing us to capture changes in the style pattern over time.

In contrast to the conventional performance measures, with style analysis we can incorporate statistical inference. We show how to place confidence intervals around the estimated style weights, using a modified version of the standard style analysis. It is also possible to test whether the selection return over time for an active fund has statistical significance.

The path from the theory of portfolio optimisation and asset pricing in the 1950s and 1960s to style analysis in the 1990s is reinforced by a common link. For it was Sharpe who developed both the CAPM and style analysis. It is this combination of theory and practical applications, illustrated in the accompanying spreadsheets, that completes our picture of equities.

REFERENCES

Bodie, Z. A. Kane and A. J. Marcus, 1996, *Investments*, 3rd edition, Richard D. Irwin, Englewood Cliffs, NJ.

Lobosco, A. and D. DiBartolomeo, 1997, "Approximating the Confidence Intervals for Sharpe Style Weights", *Financial Analysts Journal*, **July/Aug**, 80–85.

Sharpe, W. F., 1992. "Asset Allocation: Management Style and Performance Measurement", *Journal of Portfolio Management*, **Winter**, 7–19.

Treynor, J. and F. Black, 1973, "How to Use Security Analysis to Improve Portfolio Selection". *Journal of Business*, **46**, 66–86.

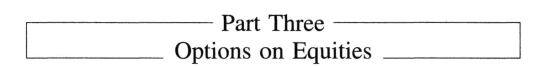

Part Three
Options on Equities

Introduction to Options on Equities

The importance of options cannot be overstated. Since the publication of Fischer Black and Myron Scholes' initial paper on the valuation of options in 1973, a plethora of financial products has been developed and traded throughout the world. In addition, the theory has been extended to cover not only equities but bonds and even real assets.

A call option is the right to buy an asset at an agreed exercise price. A put option is the right to sell an asset at a given exercise price. European options allow exercise only at the expiry of the option. American options allow exercise at or before the expiry date. Whereas the Black–Scholes pricing formula values European options, most traded options are American options.

The Options part of the book is structured differently from the Equities part. This chapter contains an overview of the concepts and theory which will be drawn on in the following four chapters. The objective of option pricing is to value these derivatives and subsequent chapters tackle different approaches to valuation. The appropriateness of different approaches in part depends on the type of option considered and whether the Black–Scholes formula or an extension can be applied. If not, there are alternative numerical methods that can be tried. This chapter attempts to introduce the main ideas which will be fleshed out in the spreadsheet models of the subsequent four chapters. Since the concepts are interlinked and used in several places in the text, they are introduced 'up-front' and expanded in the appropriate chapters.

The different pricing approaches are illustrated in the spreadsheets of the workbooks OPTION1, 2, 3 and 4. Small-scale examples are used to display the calculations, and the calculation routines also encoded in user-defined functions. Frequently the functions can be generalised with a parameter reflecting the problem size (e.g. number of steps in binomial tree, number of simulation trials). This proves to be a very powerful way of automating very large calculation sequences.

The chapter starts with a little history about the development of option pricing, then introduces the Black–Scholes formula, followed by the main ideas concerning hedge portfolios and risk-neutral valuation. Features of options such as whether they are European or American, volatility estimation and the relationship of call values and put values are skimmed. Lastly, the role of numerical methods in option valuation is discussed. The main methods of valuation include the use of binomial trees (the subject of Chapter 10) and also simulation (dealt with in Chapter 12). Chapter 11 concentrates on Black–Scholes, and Chapter 13 is devoted to approaches to be used when some of the assumptions (normality of log returns say) break down.

As with Equities, the emphasis in the text is on understanding and implementing current ideas about options in spreadsheets. Rather than cover all the background theory on options, we refer the reader to standard texts (such as Hull, 2000 and Bodie et al., 1996) for the details. For example, the basic definitions of simple options, their payoff diagrams and put–call parity are described in Hull, Chapters 1 and 7, and Bodie et al., Chapter 19. The basic ideas of option valuation are explained in Bodie et al., Chapter 20, whereas the same material is covered to a more advanced level in Hull, Chapters 9, 10 and 11.

9.1 THE GENESIS OF THE BLACK–SCHOLES FORMULA

Fischer Black (1989) has written a short article describing how he and Myron Scholes came up with their famous formula, and we highlight a few points from it in order to re-emphasise its crucial contribution to modern finance. The key insight behind their analysis is that you can create a hedge portfolio by combining a certain fraction of a share with an option. The term 'hedge' means that over a short period of time the value of the portfolio will remain the same whether the share price rises or falls, since changes in the value of the option will compensate for changes in the share price. Another term used for the hedge portfolio is the riskless portfolio.

Following the publication of papers describing the capital asset pricing model in 1965, a number of academics tried to apply the CAPM to assets other than shares, including bonds, corporate cash flows and particularly warrants. At that time (1969) the market for warrants (long-term options issued by companies) was much more developed than the fledgling market in over-the-counter short-term options.

These academics were trying to value warrants by estimating the expected value of the warrant at expiry and discounting it to the present, despite ignorance of the expected return on the share and the appropriate discount rate. Black had discovered that the warrant value depended on the total risk of the share but did not appear to depend on the expected return of the share.

Working together, Black and Scholes discovered that the expected return on the share could be taken as equal to the risk-free interest rate under certain conditions and, as a consequence, that the expected payoff on the option should be discounted using the same rate. Their draft paper, dated October 1970, containing the famous Black–Scholes formula was sent to the *Journal of Political Economy* and promptly rejected! After intervention by Merton Miller and Gene Fama, the paper was accepted in August 1971, conditional on further revisions. It finally appeared in the May/June 1973 issue of the *Journal of Political Economy*. Also in 1973, surely more than a coincidence, the Chicago Board Option Exchange was created, with trading in call options on shares in 16 companies.

With hindsight, the Black–Scholes formula itself may look relatively uncomplicated now, but its pervasiveness throughout the whole of the option pricing literature and its recognition in the Nobel Prize for Economics awarded to Myron Scholes and Robert Merton in October 1997 is testament enough. Sadly Black died in 1996 and thus could not share in the award.

Having briefly outlined the history of the Black–Scholes research, we move on to look at the actual formula.

9.2 THE BLACK–SCHOLES FORMULA

The Black–Scholes analysis provides a valuation formula for straightforward European options, that can be adapted to value a range of other options. (As already stated, the special feature of European options is that they can only be exercised at maturity.) The analysis assumes that log returns of the share underlying the option are normally distributed as in the Equities chapters. Suppose the option on a share (currently priced at

S) is a call which can only be exercised when the call matures after time period T, the exercise price being X. The payoff from the call at time T is:

$$\max(S_T - X, 0)$$

where S_T represents the share price at time T, i.e. it is a random variable with a probability distribution.

The standard assumptions are that the share price follows a stochastic process with a multiplicative sequence of moves of variable size or, more exactly, what is known as *geometric Brownian motion*. (This model of the share price process is very plausibly explained in Hull's Chapter 10 on the behaviour of stock prices.) Mathematically speaking, this means that the random variable S_T can be written in a stochastic equation of the form:

$$S_T = S \exp(Y_T) = S \exp(\mu_T + \varepsilon \sigma_T)$$

where random variable Y_T is normally distributed and random variable ε has a standard normal distribution, with zero mean and standard deviation equal to one. Y_T has mean μ_T and standard deviation σ_T, where:

$$\mu_T = (\mu - 0.5\sigma^2)T \quad \text{and} \quad \sigma_T = \sigma\sqrt{T}$$

with μ the rate of return on the share and σ the share's annualised volatility. Since Y_T is identical to $\ln(S_T/S)$, the variable $\ln(S_T/S)$ is also normally distributed, which is equivalent to saying that log share returns are normally distributed.

In the Black–Scholes analysis, the call to be valued is combined with a fraction of the share to form the hedge portfolio, which is constructed to be risk-free. Thus the hedge portfolio must earn the risk-free rate of return. The algebra leads on to a partial differential equation (familiar in applied mathematics and known as the diffusion or heat equation). The differential equation is solved to give the Black–Scholes formula.

The Black–Scholes value for a European call option, c, on a share that does not pay any dividends is:

$$c = SN(d_1) - X \exp(-rT)N(d_2)$$

In the formula, S is the current share price, X the exercise price for the call at time T, r the continuously compounded risk-free interest rate, hence the expression $\exp(-rT)$ for the risk-free discount factor over period T. The notation $N(d)$ is used to denote the cumulative standard normal probability distribution function for value d. Here d_1 and d_2 are given by:

$$d_1 = [\ln(S/X) + (r + 0.5\sigma^2)T]/\sigma\sqrt{T}$$

$$d_2 = [\ln(S/X) + (r - 0.5\sigma^2)T]/\sigma\sqrt{T}$$

We examine the Black–Scholes formula and extensions of the analysis more fully in Chapter 11. In the meantime, notice that the rate of return on the share, μ, does not appear in the formula. The reason for this is apparent when we have understood the significance of the so-called hedge portfolio.

9.3 HEDGE PORTFOLIOS

One surprising aspect of the Black–Scholes formula is that the expected return of the share is not included in the formula. However, this is explained by the implicit creation of a hedge portfolio and the inclusion of the risk-free interest rate in the formula instead. But what exactly is meant by the term 'hedge portfolio'?

The Black–Scholes call formula can also be written in the form:

$$c = hS - B \quad \text{where } h = N(d_1) \text{ and } B = X \exp(-rT)N(d_2)$$

The portfolio on the right-hand side, consisting of a fraction of a share and borrowing, exactly replicates the call option on the left-hand side. (This variant gives rise to the term 'replicating-portfolio'.) The Black–Scholes formula shows that the value of the call must be the same as the net investment in the replicating portfolio.

An alternative rearrangement of the Black–Scholes formula, $B = [hS - c]$, produces the hedge portfolio for the call option. Buying a fraction h of the share and selling (or writing) the call creates a hedge portfolio with a fixed value of B. We have replaced $N(d_1)$ with h, and thus see that $N(d_1)$–known as the hedge ratio–is the fraction of a share required to hedge the price risk in writing the call.

To illustrate, let us assume that the change in share price for one time period can be modelled simply as a jump of known size up or down–a simple one step binomial process. For example, if at time $t = 0$ the share has current price 100 (S), let us assume that at time $t = 1$ the share price will either move up to 115 (a relative increase of $u = 1.15$) or down to 95 (a relative decrease of $d = 0.95$). If the call has an exercise price of 100 at time $t = 1$, the respective payoffs on the call will be either 15 (if the share moves up) or 0 (if the share goes down), as illustrated in Figure 9.1.

Notice that we do not know the probabilities of the share moving up or down. However, a hedge portfolio consisting of buying 0.75 of the share and selling one call will produce a guaranteed payoff of 71.25. (The payoff is 0.75*115 − 15 if the share moves up; 0.75*95 if down.) The value of the hedge portfolio is independent of the ultimate share price, that is, it is risk-free, and so must earn the risk-free rate of return for the period, say 5%. To convert payoffs at $t = 1$ back to their value at time $t = 0$ the one-period discount factor is 1/1.05. Equating the portfolio net investment (0.75*100 − c) with the discounted payoff (71.25/1.05 = 67.86) allows us to solve for the option value, c (which evaluates to 7.14).

To summarise, from the Black–Scholes analysis, we have derived both the appropriate hedge ratio ($h = 0.75$) for creating the hedge portfolio and the option value ($c = 7.14$).

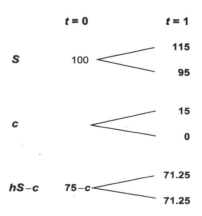

Figure 9.1   One-step binomial trees modelling change in share price

Generalising from the example of Figure 9.1 with the notation in Figure 9.2, the portfolio will have the same payout at time $t = 1$ if $huS - c_u = hdS - c_d$, i.e. if:

$$h = (c_u - c_d)/[S(u - d)]$$

So the hedge ratio measures change in the option price relative to change in the share price.

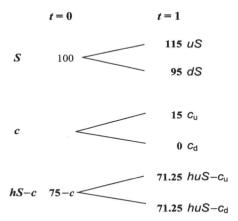

Figure 9.2   General notation for one-step tree for share, call and hedge portfolio

9.4   RISK-NEUTRAL VALUATION

The existence of hedge portfolios allows us to use the risk-neutral valuation method for calculating option values. In a risk-neutral world, one can pretend that investors are indifferent to risk and thus all assets (not just hedge portfolios as in the Black–Scholes analysis) can be valued by discounting their expected payoffs. Note that we are not saying that all assets are equally risky or indeed risk-free, but simply that we can apply a valuation method *as if* investors were indifferent to risk.

The value of an option is equal to its expected payoff in a risk-neutral world discounted at the risk-free interest rate, which can be written as:

$$c = \exp(-rT)E^Q[\max(S_T - X, 0)]$$

where $E^Q[]$ denotes expectation with respect to the risk-neutral probability measure Q. We can see this more clearly by writing the Black–Scholes formula for a call in a slightly different way, as:

$$c = \exp(-rT)[S \exp(rT)N(d_1) - XN(d_2)]$$

The expression inside the square brackets represents the expected payoff of the option. $N(d_2)$ is the probability that the call option will be exercised in a risk-neutral world.

As we shall see, the calculation of the discounted expectation of the option value, in a risk-neutral world, crops up repeatedly in the following chapters. For example, in Chapter 10, the binomial tree provides the structure on which the expectation is calculated and in Chapter 12, both Monte Carlo simulation and numerical integration techniques provide alternative vehicles for calculating the expectation.

9.5 A SIMPLE ONE-STEP BINOMIAL TREE WITH RISK-NEUTRAL VALUATION

We now illustrate how valuation takes place in a risk-neutral world, where we assume for simplicity that the share price can be modelled as a simple one-step binomial process as in the previous illustration. In a risk-neutral world, all assets would have the same expected return, and so the share and a bond should give the same expected return. However a bond is an asset that produces a certain fixed return, here say 5%, irrespective of the return on the share. Suppose that the share has a return of 15% if its price goes up or −5% if the price falls. Here the idea is to find the implicit probabilities of the 'up' and 'down' returns such that the overall return on the share tallies with that on the bond.

The expected return of an asset is the sum of all possible returns, where each possible return is weighted by its probability. Denoting the 'up' probability by p, the expected return on the share is given by:

$$(15\%)p + (-5\%)(1 - p)$$

which depends on the value of p. However, if $p = 0.5$, the share will have an expected return of 5%, exactly the same as the bond. We call this value, $p = 0.5$, the implied 'up' probability for risk-neutral valuation.

Generalising this argument with the notation of Figure 9.2, if share price S at time $t = 0$ moves up to uS or down to dS at $t = 1$ with probability p of an 'up' move, the expected price at $t = 1$ is:

$$uSp + dS(1 - p)$$

where u and d are the relative changes in the share price. If the one-period risk-free rate is r, then for risk-neutral valuation, we require:

$$[uSp + dS(1 - p)]/(1 + r) = S \quad \text{i.e.} \quad p = [(1 + r) - d]/[u - d]$$

(Strictly speaking, for time period τ, the discount factor would be $\exp(-r\tau)$ rather than simply $1/(1 + r)$, so the implied probability would be given by $p = [\exp(r\tau) - d]/[u - d]$.)

Having obtained the implied probabilities, we use these to obtain risk-neutral valuations of other assets. The call value is just the present value (or discounted value) of the probability-weighted payoffs for the option. The call has an exercise price of 100 and thus will have a payoff of 15 when the share price is 115, and a payoff of 0 when the share price is 95. Thus the expected payoff for the option is just $0.5^*(15) = 7.5$. Discounting this expected payoff at the risk-free rate, using the one-period discount factor used previously of $1/1.05$, gives a call value of 7.14. This is the same as the value obtained when using the hedge portfolio approach.

This risk-neutral approach applies to all assets, and not just risk-free assets. The corresponding present value for the share is $[(115)^*0.5 + (95)^*0.5]/1.05 = 100.0$ (thank goodness!).

Clearly, a multi-step tree would be an improvement, giving a better spread of terminal values (S_T) and hence a closer match to the share price distribution. For example, if the option life is three months, a two-step tree would generate three distinct terminal values, a nine-step tree would give 10 distinct values and in general an n-step tree gives $(n + 1)$ distinct values. For a nine-step tree, the individual time steps would represent one-third of a month. We would want the size of the individual binomial steps, the probability of up (or down) moves and the cumulative change in price level over the nine steps to tally with our overall model of the distribution of share price return after three months. With the terminal values having binomial probabilities, if the number of steps were increased, the discrete binomial distribution would approximate to a continuous normal distribution. The objective is to match the steps in the discrete binomial tree to the underlying probabilistic process with its multiplicative sequence of moves outlined earlier, that is, to match the geometric Brownian motion assumed for share prices.

In terms of modelling share price changes over time, a multi-step binomial tree can be constructed to approximate to the normal distribution underlying the Black–Scholes analysis. Since trees are vital in valuing a wide range of options, the basic approach of binomial tree valuation is discussed in some depth in the next chapter.

9.6 PUT–CALL PARITY

The Black–Scholes formula has been stated for a call. As well as call options there are put options, which provide the right to sell an asset at the exercise price X. The payoff from the put at maturity after time T is:

$$\max(X - S_T, 0)$$

For European options (which can only be exercised at maturity) there is a well-known relationship, called put–call parity, linking the values of put options and call options on the same share (current value S) with the same exercise price X. It says that:

$$c + X \exp(-rT) = p + S$$

where p (in this formula) is the put value. The right-hand portfolio of a put and a share completely replicates the left-hand portfolio of a call and borrowing. This means formulas for call values can be easily modified to provide formulas for associated put values. Thus the Black–Scholes pricing formula for a European put option on a share that does not pay any dividends can be shown to be:

$$p = -SN(-d_1) + X \exp(-rT)N(-d_2)$$

Notice that the hedge ratio for a put is based on $-(N(-d_1)) = (N(d_1) - 1)$, which is always negative, whereas the hedge ratio for a call, based on $N(d_1)$, is always positive.

Rather than use separate expressions for puts and calls, we prefer instead to rely on the asymmetry between the payoffs and hence on the values for calls and puts. Where possible, we allow spreadsheets and VBA functions to value both types of options by using the integer parameter 'iopt' with a value of 1 for calls and -1 for puts. This seems a much better approach than duplicating all the call formulas with only a slight change to provide put formulas.

9.7 DIVIDENDS

The original Black–Scholes formula did not include dividends, but Merton adapted the formula to allow for shares with dividends, also extending the Black–Scholes formula to value options on other assets such as currencies. Merton's approach requires the dividends process to be modelled via a continuous dividend yield at rate q per annum. It simply involves replacing the initial value of the share S by $S \exp(-qT)$ in the original Black–Scholes valuation formula, and also in the associated d_1 and d_2 terms.

In the risk-neutral world, a share that pays no dividends has an expected return of r, the risk-free rate. A share with a dividend yield has the same total expected return r, but it is now split into a return of rate $(r - q)$ for the share and q from the continuous dividend yield. Dividends thus reduce the value of a call since the share received if the option is exercised is a wasting asset as dividends are flowing out. Conversely, the value of a put is increased by dividends since a wasting asset is given up at exercise.

9.8   AMERICAN FEATURES

An American option can be exercised at or prior to the maturity date of the option. This provides the practical need for binomial tree methods which easily accommodate possible early exercise. In contrast, the Black–Scholes approach is limited to valuing European options, where there is no early exercise.

Whether early exercise increases option value is partly linked to the question of dividends. For instance, it may be optimal to exercise an American put early, even if there are no dividends on the underlying share. Such a put could also be exercised early after a sufficiently large fall in the share price or when interest rates are high. It is never optimal to exercise an American call on a non-dividend-paying share; though with dividends, it may be optimal to exercise early to capture a sufficiently large dividend.

The binomial tree method provides the value of the American option by comparing the value of the European version of the option with the value of intermediate exercise for each node in the tree. Thus, the binomial method provides the optimal exercise strategy for the American option as well as its value. Valuation of American options is included in the latter part of Chapter 10.

9.9   NUMERICAL METHODS

The calculation of statistical expectation is at the heart of all numerical methods of option valuation. Binomial trees provide an important insight into the mechanics behind the Black–Scholes formula, taking advantage of the close relationship between the normal and the binomial distribution as the number of steps in the tree increases. The modelling of the share price process with a tree allows option payoffs to be calculated at intermediate points in the option's life. This, combined with the 'backwards' nature of the option valuation process, ensures that American options can be valued easily. In fact, binomial trees constitute the main workhorse in providing accurate and efficient valuation for standard American options. Chapter 10 concentrates on binomial trees, examining different ways of constructing trees, how options are valued in the trees and the relative accuracy of the different trees with respect to the benchmark Black–Scholes formula.

The binomial tree method can also be viewed as a very efficient way of generating a comprehensive collection of different predetermined paths for the share price to follow. Binomial trees sacrifice information (e.g. the particular share price paths to reach a specific terminal node) for substantial efficiency gains.

For path-dependent options, other numerical methods tend to be used, most typically Monte Carlo simulation. For standard options, Monte Carlo simulation uses random drawings from the normal distribution to generate a particular share price at maturity. Monte Carlo simulation suffers in comparison with the binomial tree method for standard options, since a far larger number of paths need to be simulated using random numbers (to achieve the precision from trees). Efficiency can be improved by using 'antithetic variates' or 'quasi-random' numbers in the simulation, the latter producing significant efficiency gains. However, for more complicated options, Monte Carlo simulation contains information on intermediate share prices along the simulated path, and thus can be profitably applied to value exotic options where the option payoff depends on the particular path taken by the asset price. Chapter 12 concentrates on Monte Carlo simulation.

Numerical methods extend the range of the underlying Black–Scholes analysis from only European options to American options (via binomial trees) and to path-dependent options (via Monte Carlo simulation). Since the mid-eighties, personal computers have grown enormously in power and spreadsheets such as Excel include built-in functions to calculate probabilities associated with cumulative normal distributions. Nearly all the analytic solutions given in the spreadsheets of Chapters 10 to 13 evaluate almost instantaneously. For example, in Chapter 10 the binomial tree valuations (even with 1000 steps) can be done in under 15 seconds and a Monte Carlo simulation for a standard option with 10,000 trials can be done using Excel in under 45 seconds. Both the binomial trees (especially using the Leisen and Reimer method) and the Monte Carlo simulation provide accurate and efficient solutions to the valuation of the great majority of standard options.

9.10   VOLATILITY AND NON-NORMAL SHARE RETURNS

The final chapter on options (Chapter 13) focuses on volatility, the most important aspect of valuation, and includes current approaches to dealing with non-normal asset distributions.

Reviewing the Black–Scholes formula, the only parameter that is not directly available is the future volatility of the share price. Although historic share prices can be used to give a forecast of future volatility, the market's best guess regarding future volatility is embedded in or implied by the option's market value. So it can be derived using the Black–Scholes formula in the reverse direction. The implied volatility is that level of volatility that makes the Black–Scholes option value equal to the market option price. Option trading is therefore primarily concerned with volatility estimates. If a trader believes that the true volatility will be greater than the implied volatility, then he believes that the option is undervalued by the market (and vice versa).

The Black–Scholes formula is based on the assumption that log share returns are normally distributed. In practice, the distribution of actual returns can differ from exact normality with regard to skewness and kurtosis. This has some impact in applying binomial tree valuation methods. In Chapter 13, we examine some ways of tackling non-normality, in particular, Rubinstein's approach for adapting the standard binomial tree to allow for differences from exact normality.

SUMMARY

A call option is the right to buy an asset at an agreed exercise price. A put is the right to sell an asset at a given exercise price. European options allow exercise only at the expiry of the option, whereas American options allow exercise at or before the expiry date.

The value of an option on a share depends on the current stock price, the exercise price, the time to maturity, the stock price volatility, the risk-free interest rate (and any dividends to be received before the option expires).

The simple one-step binomial tree provides a first look at option valuation. With a replicating portfolio, both the hedge ratio and the option value can be determined. No assumptions are required about the probabilities of the share moving up or down.

The Black–Scholes pricing formula is an analytical formula for valuing European options, the main assumption being that log returns on the share are normally distributed.

In the Black–Scholes analysis, the option to be valued is combined with a fraction of the underlying share to form a hedge portfolio. The fraction or hedge ratio ensures that the hedge portfolio is risk-free, the changes in the option value offsetting the changes in the share value.

Black–Scholes option valuation analysis can also be viewed as the determination of 'implied' or 'risk-neutral' probabilities that enable risk-neutral valuation to take place. Using these probabilities, the option value is equal to its expected payoff (in the risk-neutral world) discounted at the risk-free interest rate.

REFERENCES

Black, F., 1989, "How We Came Up With The Option Formula", *Journal of Portfolio Management*, **Winter**, 4–8.
Bodie, Z., A. Kane and A. J. Marcus, 1996, *Investments*, 3rd edition, Richard D. Irwin, Englewood Cliffs, NJ.
Hull, J. C., 2000, *Options, Futures and Other Derivatives*, Prentice Hall, New Jersey.

10
Binomial Trees

Binomial trees are introduced first because they provide an easy way to understand the Black–Scholes analysis. The binomial tree provides a convenient way to model the share price process using a discrete binomial distribution to approximate the normal distribution of log returns assumed in the Black–Scholes analysis.

Since we can create hedge portfolios, we value options as if we are in a risk-neutral world. There remains the calculation of the expected value of the option payoff. We compare and contrast three different ways of configuring the binomial tree using different parameter choices for the tree (referred to as JR, CRR and LR trees according to their inventors: Jarrow and Rudd; Cox, Ross and Rubinstein; Leisen and Reimer). Each involves different combinations of incremental price changes and probabilities for the tree. Starting with European options, valuation via the JR tree is outlined, and then the better-known CRR tree is described. After discussing the convergence of the valuation approximations derived from trees to the underlying Black–Scholes value, the lesser known LR tree is outlined. Choosing between the different combinations of parameters may seem rather esoteric, but the best choice of parameters (LR) turns out to be much more efficient than the other choices. Experimentation with the different models for European options suggests that the LR tree provides values that match the Black–Scholes values very closely, using only a small number of steps.

Binomial tree valuation comes into its own when pricing American options, where the option may be exercised at intermediate dates, not just at maturity. We show how to adapt the CRR tree to include American features. Chapter 9 and the first part of Chapter 16 of Hull's (2000) textbook on options provide background on binomial valuation methods for both European and American options. However, the exposition is entirely based on CRR trees.

10.1 INTRODUCTION TO BINOMIAL TREES

The binomial tree is an extension of the one-step binomial process, introduced in the previous chapter, to several steps. For example, if the tree has nine sequential steps, at each step the share can move either up or down and its relative position after nine steps is determined by the sequence of up and down steps. We can think of the binomial tree with nine steps as containing the 512 ($=2^9$) possible paths from an initial share price to the end points. There is only a single path to each of the extreme share price nodes (the highest and lowest share price values), but 126 possible paths to each of the two central share price nodes. Although the share price tree has 10 distinct outcomes, values in the middle of the spread are more probable than the extremes. This clustering of paths towards the middle results in a probability distribution for the terminal share price that approximates to the bell curve better known as the normal distribution. In addition, the fact that the paths recombine in the binomial tree to a small number of distinct outcomes gives the method its relative efficiency as compared with simulation.

Turning to option valuation, the tree can be thought of as a sample of 512 paths where the option payoff at the end of a path is weighted by the probability of the particular end point occurring. If the option cannot be exercised early, summing the product of the option payoff and probability over all the end points produces the expected payoff when the option expires. This expectation is then discounted to give the option value (i.e. its present value). Because risk-neutral valuation is used, the discount factor reflects the risk-free rate and the time to maturity of the option.

The binomial tree can be configured in different ways according to a set of parameters for probabilities of up and down steps, and step size. Two of the three sets of parameter choices are relatively well known. The JR tree is characterised by equal probabilities for up and down price multipliers (thus $p = 0.5$). The CRR tree models the share price process such that the product of up and down price multipliers (denoted u and d) equals one. Thus $d = 1/u$ for the CRR tree. These parameter choices generate different share price trees, but neither is affected by the option's exercise price.

The third choice is little known and deserves greater recognition. The LR tree uses precise binomial estimates of the $N(d_1)$ and $N(d_2)$ elements of the Black–Scholes formula. The share price tree at maturity is centred on the exercise price and this eliminates the non-satisfactory convergence of option values seen with the other two tree types as the number of steps increases. The LR tree is best described as the Black–Scholes analysis in a tree.

Implementations of binomial trees are contained in the OPTION1.xls workbook. There are examples of small-scale price trees for all three tree types to illustrate the computations. These spreadsheet implementations underlie the coding of VBA functions which provide option values for larger trees, without the need to display intermediate nodes in the sheet.

10.2   A SIMPLIFIED BINOMIAL TREE

The first sheet in the OPTION1 workbook (named JRBinomial) shows how terminal values and probabilities are obtained for a simple nine-step binomial tree with equiprobable up and down steps of equal size. The tree structure is deliberately simple to focus on the spreadsheet layout, the main formulas, and how the mean and variance of the terminal price are evaluated. This example also illustrates how an approximate standard normal distribution can be generated from a simple nine-step binomial tree.

The extract from the JRBinomial sheet in Figure 10.1 shows imaginary price movements from the starting value of 0 (in cell B18) for a nine-step binomial tree. At each step, the price is equally likely to move up or down by an amount 1/3 ($=1/\sqrt{9}$) shown in cell C5. The cells in column K represent the 10 distinct terminal values of the price change after nine steps. The values are obtained by adding together the sequence of nine up and down steps, each individually of size 1/3. Their actual probabilities of occurrence can be derived from associated binomial probabilities. The choice of the parameters for each step (that is, the equal 'up' or 'down' step size of $1/\sqrt{9}$ and $p = 1/2$) ensures that the distribution of terminal position has mean 0 and variance 1 (as required for the standard normal distribution). In this way, we can model the share price change as the continuous limit of a simpler discrete-time binomial random walk.

	A	B	C	D	E	F	G	H	I	J	K
1	Option1.XLS										
2	Adapted JR Binomial Distribution										
3											
4		nstep	9								
5		step size	0.33								
6		p	0.50								
7											
8		0	1	2	3	4	5	6	7	8	9
9	9										3.00
10	8									2.67	2.33
11	7								2.33	2.00	1.67
12	6							2.00	1.67	1.33	1.00
13	5						1.67	1.33	1.00	0.67	0.33
14	4					1.33	1.00	0.67	0.33	0.00	-0.33
15	3				1.00	0.67	0.33	0.00	-0.33	-0.67	-1.00
16	2			0.67	0.33	0.00	-0.33	-0.67	-1.00	-1.33	-1.67
17	1		0.33	0.00	-0.33	-0.67	-1.00	-1.33	-1.67	-2.00	-2.33
18	0	0.00	-0.33	-0.67	-1.00	-1.33	-1.67	-2.00	-2.33	-2.67	-3.00

Figure 10.1 Terminal values for nine-step binomial tree in sheet JRBinomial

The layout of the tree has been compressed to fit within a square grid, thus allowing a single formula in cell C18 to generate the remainder of the tree (given the initial value in B18). Price increases correspond to diagonal moves in an upward direction, while price decreases correspond to lateral moves along a particular row. Thus the values in row 18 decrease by 1/3 at each step, whereas each upward diagonal change is an increase of 1/3. The formula in cell C18 uses an IF condition to distinguish between 'on' and 'off' leading diagonal positions. If 'on-diagonal', the price one place lower on the diagonal is incremented by one step; if 'off-diagonal', the price one place to the left is reduced by one step. The relative aspect of the price cell is handled by the OFFSET function. The formula in cell C18 is:

$$=IF(\$A18<C\$8,OFFSET(C18,0,-1)-\$C\$5,OFFSET(C18,1,-1)+\$C\$5)$$

After the IF condition, the first formula represents price falls as each cell has a value lower than the cell to its immediate left (same row) by the step size (cell C5). For price increases each cell on the leading diagonal has a value higher than the previous cell on the diagonal by the same step size. The OFFSET command has the cell reference followed by the number of rows then by the number of columns.

Since up and down moves in the tree are equally likely (and hence all individual sequences of up and down moves equally likely), the probability distribution underlying the binomial tree is directly related to the number of possible paths that can be taken to reach a particular terminal position. The number of paths in cell G22 (in Figure 10.2) uses the formula =COMBIN($C$4,C22), where $C$4 is the number of steps and C22 is the number of up steps. The formula for the binomial probability in cell I22 uses the formula =G22*($C$6^$C$4), where $C$6 is the probability of an up move, since each path has the same probability of $1/2^9 = 1/512$. The distribution does indeed have zero mean and variance one (see cells I33 and I34).

	B	C	D	E	F	G	H	I	J	K
20		# of up steps		End price		# paths		Binomial probs		
21										
22		9		3.00		1		**0.002**		
23		8		2.33		9		0.018		
24		7		1.67		36		0.070		
25		6		1.00		84		0.164		
26		5		0.33		126		0.246		
27		4		-0.33		126		0.246		
28		3		-1.00		84		0.164		
29		2		-1.67		36		0.070		
30		1		-2.33		9		0.018		
31		0		-3.00		1		0.002		
32										
33							mean	0.000		
34							st dev	1.000		

Figure 10.2   Probability distribution of the end price in sheet JRBinomial

This simple example is the foundation for the JR binomial tree in the next section that models the share price process, which in turn determines option payoffs. There are two main modifications: allowing the up and down moves to be incremented multiplicatively, not additively, and rescaling the range of terminal positions (here with mean 0 and variance 1) to match the required mean and volatility of share price returns.

10.3   THE JR BINOMIAL TREE

In this section, we value an option using a nine-step binomial tree configured according to the Jarrow and Rudd (JR) parameters. The process requires firstly the construction of the share price tree to identify the terminal share values, the calculation of the associated option values and lastly the evaluation of the discounted value of their expectation. The details of the option are given first, the choice of parameters underlying the tree is discussed next and finally its construction with Excel formulas is described.

We assume that the current share price S is 100, its volatility σ is 20% (on an annualised basis), and that the option is a European call with an exercise price X of 95 and with 0.5 years to maturity. We also assume that the underlying share has a dividend yield of 3% and that the continuously compounded risk-free rate r is 8% (equivalent to an annual interest rate of 8.33%). Since there are nine steps, each time step has length $0.5/9 = 0.0556$ years (δt say). To facilitate comparison of different binomial trees, we will use this same example in later sections of the chapter. The upper part of the JREuro sheet contains these details together with the parameters to generate the tree, as shown in Figure 10.3.

As in the simplified binomial tree, up and down moves in the JR tree are equiprobable, i.e. $p = 0.5$. The individual moves up and down at each step are determined by share price multipliers u and d, chosen such that the mean and variance after n steps match those required for share price returns.

	A	B	C	D	E	F	G	H	I	J	K
1	Option1.XLS										
2	JR European Option Value										
3											
4	Share price (S)			100.00		Jarrow & Rudd				BS	JR
5	Exercise price (X)			95.00							
6	Int rate-cont (r)			8.00%		δt	0.0556		M	4.6202	4.6202
7						erdt	1.0045		V	0.0200	0.0199
8	Dividend yield - cont (q)			3.00%							
9						u	1.0500		M1	102.532	102.531
10	Time now (0, years)			0.00		d	0.9555		M2	10725.1	10724.4
11	Time maturity (T, years)			0.50		p	0.5000				
12	Option life (τ, years)			0.50		p*	0.5000				
13	Volatility (σ)			20.00%							
14											
15	Steps in tree (n)			9		JR value	9.75				
16	iopt			1							
17	option type			Call		BS value	9.73				

Figure 10.3   Option details and JR parameters for binomial tree (sheet JREuro)

The share price process in the JR tree superimposes a risk-neutral drift term and a second term based on volatility on the simple binomial tree. The drift term chosen by Jarrow and Rudd, combined with equiprobable up and down moves, ensures that the share has an expected rate of return of $(r - q)$ when valued in the risk-neutral world. On each step, the expected value of the price multiplier is $\exp[(r - q)\delta t]$, the up move no longer equalling the down move. Since the annual volatility measure σ is a standard deviation, the volatility term $\sigma\sqrt{(\delta t)}$ incorporates the square root of the step size. The second term in the model ensures that the variance on an individual step is $\sigma^2 \delta t$ and hence after n steps or over time T, the variance of log share price is $\sigma^2 T$. Expressed algebraically, the JR tree parameters are:

$$\ln u = (r - q - 0.5\sigma^2)\delta t + \sigma\sqrt{\delta t} \quad \text{or} \quad u = \exp[(r - q - 0.5\sigma^2)\delta t + \sigma\sqrt{\delta t}]$$

$$\ln d = (r - q - 0.5\sigma^2)\delta t - \sigma\sqrt{\delta t} \quad \text{or} \quad d = \exp[(r - q - 0.5\sigma^2)\delta t - \sigma\sqrt{\delta t}]$$

For log share prices, the up and down moves ($\ln u$ and $\ln d$) are incremented additively, leading to a log price tree. To get a share price tree, each move is incremented multiplicatively using factors u and d to scale the previous price up or down.

In Excel, the formula for the 'up' share price multiplier u in cell G9 uses the EXP function:

$$=\text{EXP}((D6-D8-0.5*D13^2)*G6+D13*SQRT(G6))$$

and includes the drift and volatility components for a step.

The 'down' price multiplier d in cell G10 has a negative sign instead of a positive sign before the volatility component.

	A	B	C	D	E	F	G	H	I	J	K
19	Share										
20			0	1	2	3	4	5	6	7	8	9
20												155.16
21	9									147.77	141.20
22	8								140.73	134.47	128.49
23	7							134.02	128.07	122.37	116.93
24	6						127.64	121.96	116.54	111.36	106.41
25	5					121.56	116.15	110.99	106.06	101.34	96.84
26	4				115.77	110.62	105.70	101.01	96.51	92.22	88.12
27	3			110.25	105.35	100.67	96.19	91.92	87.83	83.93	80.20
28	2		105.00	100.33	95.87	91.61	87.54	83.65	79.93	76.38	72.98
29	1	100.00	95.55	91.31	87.25	83.37	79.66	76.12	72.74	69.50	66.41
30	0										

Figure 10.4   Nine-step share price tree using JR parameters (sheet JREuro)

In the share price tree of Figure 10.4, rows correspond to the number of 'up' moves (denoted by state i where i goes from 0 to 9) and columns to steps (step j where j goes from 0 to 9). Algebraically, the share price for state i after j steps, $S_{i,j}$, is modelled as a product of the initial share price S and the up and down share price multipliers for the numbers of up and down moves. For example, starting with $S_{0,0} = S = 100$, one step later the two possible prices are: $S_{0,1} = dS_{0,0} = 95.55$, $S_{1,1} = uS_{0,0} = 105.00$, etc. Hence after n steps:

$$S_{i,n} = u^i d^{n-i} S$$

The formula is essentially recursive, so that at each step the new prices depend only on the previous price and a price multiplier, for example, $S_{i,j+1} = dS_{i,j}$. This can be accomplished most efficiently in Excel, by copying the single formula in cell C30, which is set out below:

=IF($A30<C$20,$G$10*OFFSET(C30,0,−1),IF($A30=C$20,$G$9*OFFSET

(C30,1,−1),""))

The cell formula is very similar to the formula used in the previous section, except that multipliers G10 ('down') and G9 ('up') *multiply* the previous price. The condition on the cell's position is amplified by adding an additional nested IF statement to allow a third possibility. Cells above the leading diagonal (for which $A30>C$20$) are filled with the empty cell formula "". This cell formula in C30, when copied, generates the rest of the tree (and can be extended to create larger trees). By looking at the share values in the middle cells for an even number of time steps (D29, F28, ...) you can see that the modal share price drifts up over time in the JR tree. [Strictly, this is only true if $(r - q - 0.5\sigma^2)$ is greater than zero, which it usually is.]

As the call option is European, we are only concerned with the share prices at the end of step 9 in column K. From these terminal prices $(S_{i,9})$ we derive the call payoffs for each of the 10 prices from the relationship:

$$V_{i,9} = \max[S_{i,9} - X, 0] \quad \text{for} \quad i = 0, 1, \ldots, 9$$

where X is the exercise price for the option. These are shown in cells K49 to K58 of the JREuro sheet and range from 60.16 for nine up moves to 0. Note that non-zero payoffs occur when four or more moves are up: with fewer than four, the option is not exercised.

The remaining task is to calculate the expected value of the call payoff and discount it using the risk-free rate. For this, the binomial probabilities of each of the call payoffs are required, and these are identical to those used in the simple binomial tree. They are set out in cell range K35:K44, the general formula in K44 being:

=COMBIN($D$15,A44)*$G$11^$D$15

where the last two terms give the probability of any sequence of steps $(1/2^9)$ and the Excel COMBIN function gives the number of paths for each payoff. The 10 terminal payoff values and their probabilities taken from sheet JREuro are set out below:

State	9	8	7	6	5	4	3	2	1	0
Option payoff	60.16	46.20	33.49	21.93	11.41	1.84	0	0	0	0
Probability		0.002	0.018	0.070	0.164	0.246	0.246	0.164	0.070	0.018	0.002

The expected value of the option payoff involves weighting each call payoff with its probability and then discounting back at the risk-free rate to ensure risk-neutral valuation.

Thus, the formula in cell G15 for the call value after discounting is:

$$=\text{EXP}(-\text{D6*D12})\text{*SUMPRODUCT}(\text{K35:K44,K49:K58})$$

where EXP($-$D6*D12) is the discount factor for the risk-free rate over 0.5 years.

Thus the nine-step JR tree produces a call value of 9.75 (compared with the Black–Scholes value of 9.73 in cell G17 of Figure 10.3). Hopefully, if the number of steps increases, the tree valuation will converge to the Black–Scholes value. (This topic will be discussed further in section 10.6.) In passing, note that the Black–Scholes value in cell G17 is evaluated from the user-defined VBA function, BSOptionValue, the code being stored in the Module1 sheet. Explanation of the coding is deferred until Chapter 11, where the Black–Scholes formula is discussed in detail.

The JR share price tree that our option valuation is based on consists of the following 10 values, together with the probabilities of each price:

State	9	8	7	6	5	4	3	2	1	0
Share price	155.16	141.20	128.49	116.93	106.41	96.84	88.12	80.20	72.98	66.41
Probability	0.002	0.018	0.070	0.164	0.246	0.246	0.164	0.070	0.018	0.002

The above distribution of share returns is approximately lognormal. Using the table of prices and probabilities, it is easy to calculate the first two moments of the distribution, $M1$ and $M2$ (in cells K9 and K10). From $M1$ and $M2$, the mean and variance (M and V) of the associated normal distribution of log share price are obtained from the formulas (in section 7.7). These moments are shown in Figure 10.3, column K. $M1$ and $M2$ for the JR tree are derived from the terminal share prices in range K21:K30, and M and V from the formulas using $M1$ and $M2$. The JR tree summary values can be compared with the mean and variance of log share price required by the Black–Scholes model. As can be seen, the correspondence between the underlying theoretical values and the values produced by the binomial tree mechanism is good.

You may like to confirm that $M1$, the mean share price, has grown from $S = 100$ by a growth factor of 1.02531, which is equal to $\exp[(r-q)T]$.

The JREuro model can also be used to value a put. By entering -1 as the value for the 'iopt' parameter in cell D16 (in Figure 10.3), the call can be changed into a put. The share price tree is the same as for the call. However, the option payoffs have non-zero values only when the share price falls below the exercise price X. By incorporating a further parameter (iopt $= 1$ for a call, -1 for a put), we can use the general relationship for payoffs for puts or calls:

$$V_{i,9} = \max[\text{iopt}^*(S_{i,9} - X), 0] \quad \text{for} \quad i = 0, 1, \ldots, 9$$

The JR tree is discussed in Wilmott et al. (1996).

10.4   THE CRR TREE

The next two sheets in OPTION1 use the CRR tree. As the CRREuro sheet shows, the layout of the tree is identical to the JR tree, the difference being the share price values in the tree and the probabilities below. The CRRTheory sheet illustrates the theory at the heart of the binomial valuation method, showing the binomial distribution function that approximates to the normal distribution function. The formulas in this sheet allow us to examine how the CRR tree value for European options converges as the number of steps in the tree is increased.

Better known than the JR tree, Cox, Ross and Rubinstein (hereafter CRR) propose an alternative choice of parameters that also create a risk-neutral valuation environment. The price multipliers, u and d, depend only on volatility σ and on δt, not on drift:

$$\ln u = \sigma\sqrt{\delta t} \quad \ln d = -\sigma\sqrt{\delta t}$$

These parameters reflect the volatility of the price change over the step of length δt, but not any overall change in level. In Excel, the formula for u in cell G9 in Figure 10.5 is:

=EXP(D13*SQRT(G6))

In cell G10, the formula for d is simply $1/u$.

	A	B	C	D	E	F	G	H	I	J	K
2	CRR European Option Value										
3											
4	Share price (S)			100.00		Cox, Ross & Rubinstein				BS	CRR
5	Exercise price (X)			95.00							
6	Int rate-cont (r)			8.00%		δt	0.0556	M		4.6202	4.6202
7						erdt	1.0045	V		0.0200	0.0199
8	Dividend yield - cont (q)			3.00%		ermqdt	1.0028				
9						u	1.0483	M1		102.532	102.532
10	Time now (0, years)			0.00		d	0.9540	M2		10725.1	10723.5
11	Time maturity (T, years)			0.50		p	0.5177				
12	Option life (τ, years)			0.50		p*	0.4823				
13	Volatility (σ)			20.00%							
14											
15	Steps in tree (n)			9		CRR value	9.63				
16	iopt			1							
17	option type			Call		BS value	9.73				

Figure 10.5 Option details and CRR parameters for CRR tree (in CRREuro sheet)

Focusing on the resultant share price tree in Figure 10.6, the absence of drift in the share price is evident in the modal (central) values. Look at prices for an even number of steps (D29, F28, . . .). The CRR tree is centred on the current share price, S.

	A	B	C	D	E	F	G	H	I	J	K
19	Share										
20		0	1	2	3	4	5	6	7	8	9
21	9										152.85
22	8									145.81	139.09
23	7								139.09	132.69	126.58
24	6							132.69	126.58	120.75	115.19
25	5						126.58	120.75	115.19	109.89	104.83
26	4					120.75	115.19	109.89	104.83	100.00	95.40
27	3				115.19	109.89	104.83	100.00	95.40	91.00	86.81
28	2			109.89	104.83	100.00	95.40	91.00	86.81	82.81	79.00
29	1		104.83	100.00	95.40	91.00	86.81	82.81	79.00	75.36	71.89
30	0	100.00	95.40	91.00	86.81	82.81	79.00	75.36	71.89	68.58	65.43

Figure 10.6 Nine-step share price tree using CRR parameters (in CRREuro sheet)

To offset the absence of a drift component in u and d, the probability of an up move in the CRR tree is usually greater than 0.5 to ensure that the expected value of the price increases by a factor of $\exp[(r - q)\delta t]$ on each step. The formula for p is:

$$p = (b - d)/(u - d) \quad \text{where } b = \exp[(r - q)\delta t]$$

In our example, the probability of an up move is 0.5177 (cell G11) and hence of a down move 0.4823 (in cell G12), the resultant expected price change factor being 1.0028 (in cell G8).

From the CRR price tree, the call payoffs can be evaluated as for the JR tree. In the final call valuation step, the key formula in cell G15 for the discounted expected call payoff uses the same formula as in the JR tree. The CRR tree with nine steps values the call at 9.63 compared to 9.75 for the JR tree (and the Black–Scholes exact value of 9.73).

As for the JR tree, the CRR tree can be used to value a put by changing the iopt value in cell D16 to -1. Notice that dividends affect only the probabilities in the CRR model, not the share price values, whereas in the JR tree it is vice versa.

10.5   BINOMIAL APPROXIMATIONS AND BLACK–SCHOLES FORMULA

In the spreadsheets so far we have seen the closeness of the option values derived using binomial trees to the Black–Scholes values. The CRRTheory sheet tries to reinforce the link by showing how the continuous normal distribution functions, $N(d)$, in the Black–Scholes result can be replaced by discrete binomial distribution functions. These binomial approximations hold for European options. They involve the so-called 'complementary' binomial distribution function Φ, which is one minus the usual distribution function. Each of the $N(d)$ terms in the Black–Scholes formula can be replaced with a term based on the complementary binomial distribution function Φ.

Figure 10.7 shows the same call option from the previous section, with two new parameters defined. The quantity a (in cell E14) represents the minimum number of up moves required for the call to end 'in-the-money', that is, for the terminal share value to exceed X. Looking back to the CRR tree in Figure 10.6 and in particular at cell K26, it is clear that four up moves produce a terminal share price of 95.40, just above the exercise price of 95. In fact, the value of 4 in cell E14 has been generated by the formula given by Cox and Rubinstein (1985).

	A	B	C	D	E	F	G	H
1	Option1.XLS							
2	Theory behind Binomial Trees							
3								
4	Share price (S)	100.00		Cox, Ross & Rubinstein			Black-Scholes	
5	Exercise price (X)	95.00						
6	Int rate-cont (r)	8.00%		δt	0.0556			
7				erdt	1.0045			
8	Dividend yield - cont (q)	3.00%		ermqdt	1.0028			
9				u	1.0483			
10	Time now (0, years)	0.00		d	0.9540			
11	Time maturity (T, years)	0.50		p	0.5177			
12	Option life (τ, years)	0.50		p'	0.5412			
13	Volatility (σ)	20.00%						
14				a	4			
15	Steps in tree (n)	9					d1	0.6102
16				Φ [a:n,p']	0.8202		N (d1)	0.7291
17	CRR Euro Value	9.63					d2	0.4688
18	via fn	9.63		Φ [a:n,p]	0.7797		N (d2)	0.6804
19								
20	BS Call Value	9.73						

Figure 10.7   CRRTheory sheet showing the binomial approximations for $N(d)$

The other new parameter, p' in cell E12, is a modified probability, given by the formula:

$$p' = pu/\exp[(r - q)\delta t]$$

where the quantity $\exp[(r - q)\delta t]$ is in cell E8.

The concise CRR binomial option pricing formula is written as:

$$c = S\exp(-qT)\Phi[a{:}n, p'] - X\exp(-rT)\Phi[a{:}n, p]$$

Distribution functions are generally defined in terms of the probabilities in the left-hand tail of the distribution, whereas the complementary distribution function refers to the right-hand tail. Thus the formula in cell E16 of the CRRTheory sheet is calculated as the complementary binomial distribution evaluated for $(a - 1)$, that is:

=1−BINOMDIST(E14−1,B15,E12,TRUE)

To test this approximation, you can confirm that the call value of 9.63 in cell B17 (CRRTheory sheet), which uses the formula, agrees with that derived in cell G15 of the CRREuro sheet.

10.6   CONVERGENCE OF CRR BINOMIAL TREES

So far the binomial trees considered have been limited to nine time steps (purely for space considerations). However, it is of interest to explore the accuracy of option values derived from binomial trees where the time to maturity remains fixed but where the number of time steps used in the tree is increased. An easy way to do this, without the need to build larger and larger trees, is to use the concise analytic option pricing formula introduced in the previous section and illustrated in the CRRTheory sheet. This binomial formula can be compared with the true Black–Scholes option value to explore the pattern of convergence as the number of time steps in the tree increases.

One illuminating approach is to set up a Data Table which evaluates the concise CRR option pricing formula (cell B17) and the Black–Scholes value (cell B20) for different numbers of steps (cell B15) and to graph the results. See Figure 10.8.

To effect this, set up a Data Table in the range J4:L12 say. Put the formulas:

=B20 in K4   and   =B17 in L4

to link these cells to the two formula cells. In cells J5 to J12, set out different numbers of steps, say from 16 to 128 in increments of 16. From the Excel menu, specify the Data Table range as J4:L12, and the Column input cell as B15 to get the table of values. Plot the Data Table output as an XY chart. You should see the CRR-based value oscillating around the Black–Scholes value as the number of steps increases.

The observed oscillation in values as the number of steps increases, which also applies for valuations based on the JR tree, occurs because the tree parameters are not linked to the option's exercise price in any way. When the exercise price is the same as the initial share price (i.e. the value in cell B5 is changed to 100), the oscillation is replaced by uniform convergence. However, this is a special case.

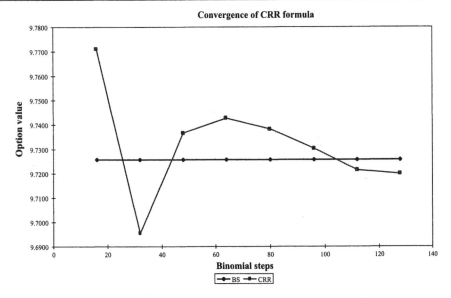

Figure 10.8 CRR tree call value relative to BS formula call value as number of steps increases

For a given number of steps there is a single binomial tree for the share price process. As the number of steps in the tree increases, the relative position of the exercise price changes with respect to the share price nodes. This changes the sign of the error term between the binomial tree approximation and the true Black–Scholes value.

10.7   THE LR TREE

The third set of parameters for developing the share price tree is that proposed by Leisen and Reimer. Their choice has two important advantages over the JR and CRR parameters. Firstly, they suggest better and separate estimates for the $N(d_1)$ and $N(d_2)$ values in the Black–Scholes formula. Secondly, by centring the share price tree at maturity around the exercise price, the oscillation in convergence seen with the JR and CRR trees is removed. The calculations involved in setting up the LR tree and the resulting option value are in the LREuro sheet shown in Figure 10.9.

	A	B	C	D	E	F	G	H	I	J	K
2	LR European Option Value										
3						Leisen & Reimer					
4	Share price (S)			100.00		δt	0.0556			BS	LR
5	Exercise price (X)			95.00		erdt	1.0045				
6	Int rate-cont (r)			8.00%		ermqdt	1.0028		M	4.6202	4.6209
7						d1	0.6102		V	0.0200	0.0185
8	Dividend yield - cont (q)			3.00%		d2	0.4688				
9						p	0.5755		M1	102.532	102.532
10	Time now (0, years)			0.0000		p*	0.4245		M2	10725.1	10708.5
11	Time maturity (T, years)			0.5000		p'	0.5979				
12	Option life (τ, years)			0.5000		u	1.0418		a		5
13	Volatility (σ)			20.00%		d	0.9499		Φ [a:n,p']		0.7290
14										N (d1)	0.7291
15	Steps in tree (n)			9		LR value	9.72			Φ [a:n,p]	0.6803
16	iopt			1						N (d2)	0.6804
17	option type			Call		BS value	9.73				

Figure 10.9   Option details and LR parameters for binomial tree (sheet LREuro)

In the LR model, the parameters are chosen in reverse order to the JR and CRR models, the probabilities being decided first and then the share price moves. The probabilities are derived using an inversion formula that provides accurate binomial estimates for the normal distribution function. The probability p relates to the d_2 term and the probability p' relates to the d_1 term in the Black–Scholes formula. For example, the formula for p in cell G9 is:

$$=\text{PPNormInv(G8,D15)}$$

where G8 contains the actual Black–Scholes d_2 value. The accuracy of the term equivalent to $N(d_2)$ (i.e. the $\Phi[a{:}n, p]$ value in cell K15) can be seen by comparing it with the Black–Scholes $N(d_2)$ value in cell K16. A similar level of accuracy is achieved in the estimation of $N(d_1)$. Note that parameter a takes value $(n + 1)/2$ in the LR tree to ensure that the share price tree is centred around the exercise price.

The up and down price multipliers for the share price moves in the tree take the form:

$$u = bp'/p \quad \text{where } b = \exp[(r - q)\delta t]$$
$$d = b(1 - p')/(1 - p)$$

By changing the exercise price in cell D5, you can confirm that the share price tree at maturity remains centred on X by checking the revised tree in your spreadsheet.

With these parameter choices, valuation in the LR tree proceeds in exactly the same way as in the other tree models (see Figure 10.10). The option payoff is calculated, and its expected discounted value serves as the option's value. Here, the LR tree gives the European call a value of 9.724 (in cell G15), which is very close to its Black–Scholes formula value of 9.726 (in cell G17).

	A	B	C	D	E	F	G	H	I	J	K
19	Share										
20		0	1	2	3	4	5	6	7	8	9
21	9										144.56
22	8									138.76	131.81
23	7								133.19	126.52	120.18
24	6							127.85	121.44	115.36	109.57
25	5						122.72	116.57	110.73	105.18	99.91
26	4					117.80	111.89	106.29	100.96	95.90	91.09
27	3				113.07	107.40	102.02	96.91	92.05	87.44	83.06
28	2			108.53	103.09	97.93	93.02	88.36	83.93	79.73	75.73
29	1		104.18	98.96	94.00	89.29	84.81	80.56	76.53	72.69	69.05
30	0	100.00	94.99	90.23	85.71	81.41	77.33	73.46	69.78	66.28	62.96

Figure 10.10   LR share price tree (sheet LREuro)

10.8   COMPARISON OF CRR AND LR TREES

The next sheet in the OPTION1 workbook uses VBA functions for option valuation to compare call values from the CRR and LR trees with the Black–Scholes value as the number of steps in the binomial trees is increased. Figure 10.11 shows the Compare sheet with the valuation estimates for a call from binomial trees with from 16 up to 128 steps. Column F contains the Black–Scholes value (evaluated from the user-defined function, BSOptionValue). This has been used as a benchmark throughout the chapter and is, of course, independent of the number of steps.

	A	B	C	D	E	F	G	H
2	**Euro Binomial Tree**							
3								
4	Share price (S)	100.00		Steps in tree (n)			BS value	9.7258
5	Exercise price (X)	95.00			9		CRR tree	9.6332
6	Int rate-cont (r)	8.00%					LR tree	9.7242
7								
8	Dividend yield - cont (q)	3.00%						
9					steps	BS	CRR	LR
10	Time now (0, years)	0.0000			16	9.7258	9.7709	9.7253
11	Time maturity (T, years)	0.5000			32	9.7258	9.6954	9.7256
12	Option life (τ, years)	0.5000			48	9.7258	9.7367	9.7257
13	Volatility (σ)	20.00%			64	9.7258	9.7427	9.7257
14					80	9.7258	9.7382	9.7257
15	iopt	1			96	9.7258	9.7303	9.7257
16					112	9.7258	9.7214	9.7257
17	option type	Call			128	9.7258	9.7199	9.7257

Figure 10.11   Comparison of binomial tree valuation with BS value for different tree types

In adjacent columns G and H, a second user-defined function, BinOptionValue, returns option values based on binomial trees, given inputs to specify the tree type, the option type, the number of steps in the tree, etc. For example, the first input for the function imod takes value 1 for a CRR tree or 2 for an LR tree. These binomial tree values are compared with the Black–Scholes value. For the chosen European call, the LR tree with 48 steps matches the Black–Scholes value very closely, in fact to four decimal places.

The code for the BinOptionValue function is in Module0 of the workbook, along with other functions developed to make the binomial tree valuation methods more straightforward to implement. Features of the coding are discussed in section 10.10.

It is also instructive to compare the summary statistics of the share price trees generated by different methods. Figure 10.12 collects together the first and second moments ($M1$ and $M2$) for the terminal share price distributions for the three tree types and also the implied mean and variance (M and V) for each. These summary statistics are for the nine-step valuation of the European call used throughout this chapter and they have been given separately in Figures 10.3, 10.5 and 10.9.

	BS	JRtree	CRRtree	LR tree
S_T is lognormal with:				
$M1$	102.5315	102.5311	102.5315	102.5315
$M2$	10725.08	10724.45	10723.55	10708.48
$\ln(S_T)$ is normal with:				
M	4.6202	4.6202	4.6202	4.6209
V	0.0200	0.0199	0.0199	0.0185

Figure 10.12   Comparison of share price summary statistics for different trees versus BS values

It is interesting to note that the JR and CRR trees match the assumed variability in share price better than does the LR tree, despite the LR tree valuation producing a more precise option value. Thus centring the share price tree at maturity around the exercise price is the key modification with the LR tree.

10.9 AMERICAN OPTIONS AND THE CRR AMERICAN TREE

Because binomial tree valuation can adapt to include the possibility of exercise at intermediate dates and not just the maturity date, it is an extremely important numerical method when pricing American options. In the case of puts, it is frequently the case that the possibility of early exercise increases the value of the put. The sheet CRRTree allows puts to be valued as European options (no early exercise) and also as American options (with early exercise permitted). The results can be compared easily in this format.

To demonstrate this, specify the option in the CRRTree sheet to be a put, that is, enter −1 in cell D16. Figure 10.13 shows that with no early exercise the put's value is 2.40 (cell H15), whereas with early exercise the value rises to 2.54 (cell H17). Even in the absence of dividends, the early exercise feature has an advantage for puts. Since the Black–Scholes formula is for European options, it is a benchmark only for the European put.

	A	B	C	D	E	F	G	H	I	J	K
2	CRR American Binomial Tree										
3											
4	Share price (S)			100.00		Cox, Ross & Rubinstein					
5	Exercise price (X)			95.00							
6	Int rate-cont (r)			8.00%		δt	0.0556				
7						erdt	1.0045				
8	Dividend yield - cont (q)			3.00%		ermqdt	1.0028				
9						u	1.0483				
10	Time now (0, years)			0.00		d	0.9540				
11	Time maturity (T, years)			0.50		p	0.5177				
12	Option life (τ, years)			0.50		p*	0.4823				
13	Volatility (σ)			20.00%							
14											
15	Steps in tree (n)			9		CRR Euro Value		2.40		BS value	2.49
16	iopt			-1							
17	option type			Put		CRR Amer Value		2.54			

Figure 10.13   Values for the put with and without early exercise in sheet CRRTree

The European and American put values are obtained from the CRR share price tree, from which the actual option payoffs are obtained if exercise occurs at any step conditional on each price level.

	A	B	C	D	E	F	G	H	I	J	K
47	Option Payoff										
48		0	1	2	3	4	5	6	7	8	9
49	9										0.00
50	8									0.00	0.00
51	7								0.00	0.00	0.00
52	6							0.00	0.00	0.00	0.00
53	5						0.00	0.00	0.00	0.00	0.00
54	4					0.00	0.00	0.00	0.00	0.00	0.00
55	3				0.00	0.00	0.00	0.00	0.00	4.00	8.19
56	2			0.00	0.00	0.00	0.00	0.00	4.00	8.19	12.19	16.00
57	1		0.00	0.00	0.00	4.00	8.19	12.19	16.00	19.64	23.11
58	0	0.00	0.00	4.00	8.19	12.19	16.00	19.64	23.11	26.42	29.57

Figure 10.14   Option payoff tree for put in CRRTree sheet

Rows 49 to 58 in Figure 10.14 show these option values. Assuming no early exercise, the only relevant option values are those for step 9 (in K49:K58). The value for this European put is obtained (as already described for the European call in section 10.4) by evaluating the expected put payoff and discounting at the risk-free rate. As already stated, the put value is 2.40 as shown in cell H15 (in Figure 10.13).

To value the American option, it is necessary to know the value of the put not only if exercised at step 9, but also the expected value at intermediate stages. From the terminal payoffs shown in column K of Figure 10.15, we evaluate the expected option values at step 8, conditional on level, remembering to discount the expectation at the risk-free rate. We use the CRR probabilities [$p = 0.5177$ and $(1 - p) = p^* = 0.4823$] when calculating the expected value to ensure that the risk-neutral world is preserved. Denoting the option payoff for state i at step 9 as $V_{i,9}$, the expected payoff in state $(i - 1)$ at step 8 is evaluated from the relationship:

$$V_{i-1,8} = [pV_{i,9} + (1 - p)V_{i-1,9}]/\exp(r\delta t)$$

which calculates the expectation and discounts it back to each earlier node. The process of calculating expected values at nodes and discounting is referred to as 'stepping back' through the tree.

	A	B	C	D	E	F	G	H	I	J	K
61	European Option Value										
62		0	1	2	3	4	5	6	7	8	9
63	9										0.00
64	8									0.00	0.00
65	7								0.00	0.00	0.00
66	6							0.00	0.00	0.00	0.00
67	5						0.00	0.00	0.00	0.00	0.00
68	4					0.00	0.00	0.00	0.00	0.00	0.00
69	3				0.10	0.21	0.44	0.91	1.89	3.93	8.19
70	2			0.46	0.84	1.53	2.72	4.69	7.74	11.90	16.00
71	1		1.20	2.01	3.28	5.19	7.89	11.39	15.42	19.34	23.11
72	0	2.40	3.70	5.56	8.06	11.21	14.88	18.75	22.50	26.11	29.57

Figure 10.15   Put valued as European option in CRRTree sheet

With the option payoffs after nine steps in cells K63:72, this stepping back process is best accomplished in Excel by copying the formula in cell J72:

$$=IF(\$A72<=J\$62,(\$G\$11^*K71+\$G\$12^*K72)/\$G\$7,"")$$

throughout the range of the option value tree, that is the range B63 to J72.

The condition within the IF statement ensures that the formula only produces values in cells on or below the leading diagonal, thus mirroring the layout used for the share price tree. The formula within the IF statement evaluates the probability-weighted expected value of the option payoff at each node, discounted then by the one-step risk-free factor in cell G7.

The value of the put based on stepping back through the nine-step CRR tree is 2.40 (cell B72), in fact identical to the value we obtained when calculating the discounted expectation over the terminal payoff distribution. The steps are shown in Figure 10.15.

However, for an American option, at each node there is the possibility of exercising the option. In Figure 10.16, looking at cell J86, the expected put value is 26.42, not the same as the expected value of 26.11 in cell J72 in Figure 10.15. This is because early exercise gives a larger payoff (of 26.42 as can be seen in cell J58 of Figure 10.14). So the cell formula in J86 compares the expected option value (no early exercise) with the option payoff if it were to be exercised and chooses the maximum. The comparison is handled with the Excel MAX functions, as follows:

$$=IF(\$A86<=J\$76,MAX((\$G\$11*K85+\$G\$12*K86)/\$G\$7,J58),"")$$

The formula chooses the maximum of the calculated expected value (as in the European case) and the value from intermediate exercise (given by cell J44). The calculations showing the repeated operation of this formula are shown in Figure 10.16, the final American put value being 2.54 (as displayed in Figure 10.13, cell H17).

	A	B	C	D	E	F	G	H	I	J	K
75	American Option Value										
76		0	1	2	3	4	5	6	7	8	9
77	9										0.00
78	8									0.00	0.00
79	7								0.00	0.00	0.00
80	6							0.00	0.00	0.00	0.00
81	5						0.00	0.00	0.00	0.00	0.00
82	4					0.00	0.00	0.00	0.00	0.00	0.00
83	3				0.10	0.21	0.44	0.92	1.92	4.00	8.19
84	2			0.47	0.87	1.59	2.84	4.92	8.19	12.19	16.00
85	1		1.26	2.11	3.46	5.49	8.39	12.19	16.00	19.64	23.11
86	0	2.54	3.94	5.95	8.68	12.19	16.00	19.64	23.11	26.42	29.57

Figure 10.16   Put valued as American option in CRRTree sheet

This possibility of early exercise also applies to American calls, though in practice if the dividend yield on the share is zero, it is never worth exercising the call early. However, for calls on shares that pay dividends, early exercise can be worthwhile. As an exercise, try changing the put used in this example into a call, then check out how large the dividend yield has to be for early exercise to be worthwhile. You will have to increase the dividend yield substantially before there is a noticeable difference between the American and European call values.

10.10   USER-DEFINED FUNCTIONS IN Module0 AND Module1

The OPTION1 workbook contains the code for several user-defined functions, which implement most of the tree-based valuation methods discussed in this chapter. The main functions to obtain option values using either the CRR or LR binomial trees are in Module0 of the workbook. The most important functions are the BinEuroOptionValue function used on the CRRTheory sheet and the BinOptionValue function used on the Compare sheet.

In the arrays used to hold the option payoffs in the binomial trees we have allowed array dimensions to start from 0 (rather then the more usual 1) as the binomial tree time steps also begin with time period 0. This is done using the statement Option Base 0 at the top of the VBA module sheet. As an additional reminder, we also rename the module sheet to Module0.

The BinOptionValue function can be used to value European or American options using either the CRR (imod=1) or LR (imod=2) binomial trees. The code is most easily understood taking one type of option (a European call say, where iopt=1 and iea=1) and one valuation method (say the CRR tree demonstrated in the CRREuro sheet). The valuation process revolves around the vector array vvec() declared as a variant type with 10 values, vvec(0) to vvec(9), as ensured by the dimensioning statement ReDim vvec(nstep).

The terminal option prices in the share price tree are derived from a formula of the form:

$$\max[S(u^i d^{n-i}) - X, 0] \quad i = 0, 1, 2, \ldots, 9$$

In the VBA statements this is achieved using a loop:

```
For i = 0 To nstep
  vvec(i) = Application.Max(iopt * (S * (u^i) * (d^(nstep - i)) - X), 0)
Next i
```

The subsequent five lines of code drive the process of working backwards through the tree, at each stage discounting the expected option payoff, to calculate the option value:

```
For j = nstep - 1 To 0 Step - 1
  For i = 0 To j
    vvec(i) = (p * vvec(i + 1) + pstar* vvec(i)) / erdt
  Next i
Next j
```

There are two important points to note in the VBA code. By replacing redundant values with new values in the vvec vector as we value the option, we can limit the storage requirements to a single vector with only $n + 1$ elements. The other point is that for American options (iea=2) we just need an additional line of code that chooses the maximum of the European value and the value of immediate exercise.

We describe the hedging parameters in detail in the next chapter, and so limit our comments here regarding the BinOptionGreeks function. Three of the five parameters can be estimated by using an extended binomial tree, while the remaining two parameters require two separate binomial trees to be built. The function uses the more efficient LR tree.

The Module1 sheet contains the code for the BSOptionValue function which computes the Black–Scholes formula. Detailed explanation is given in the following chapter, section 11.7.

SUMMARY

The binomial tree provides a practical way to model the share price process. The resulting discrete distribution of terminal prices can be configured to approximate to the continuous lognormal distribution assumed in the Black–Scholes analysis.

An option on the share is valued via the tree by calculating the expected option payoff (weighting each option payoff by its risk-neutral probability) and discounting the expectation at the risk-free rate.

The efficiency of the binomial method of option valuation (compared to the Monte Carlo sampling approach) comes from the fact that many paths in the tree recombine.

There are several different ways to configure the binomial tree using different sets of parameters (e.g. JR tree, CRR tree, LR tree). The JR tree has equiprobable up and down steps, where size of steps allows for drift and volatility. The CRR tree has related up and down step sizes reflecting volatility but no drift in mean level. To include the drift in prices, the up and down probabilities differ so that (usually) prices drift up. The LR tree at maturity is centred on the exercise price and has quite complex probability and step size parameters.

Experimentation with the different tree types for European options suggests that the LR tree produces estimates close to the Black–Scholes values using only a small number of steps.

The binomial tree method is easily adapted to include the early exercise of an option, thus allowing American options to be valued.

REFERENCES

Cox, J., S. Ross and M. Rubinstein, 1979, "Option Pricing: A Simplified Approach", *Journal of Financial Economics*, **7**, 229–264.

Cox, J. and M. Rubinstein, 1985, *Options Markets*, Prentice Hall, New Jersey.

Hull, J. C., 2000, *Options, Futures and Other Derivatives*, Prentice Hall, New Jersey.

Jarrow, R. A. and A. Rudd, 1983, *Option Pricing*, Richard D. Irwin, Englewood Cliffs, NJ.

Leisen, D. P. J. and M. Reimer, 1996, "Binomial Models for Option Valuation–Examining and Improving Convergence", *Applied Mathematical Finance*, **3**, 319–346.

Wilmott, P., S. Howison and J. Dewynne, 1996, *The Mathematics of Financial Derivatives*, Cambridge University Press, Cambridge.

11
The Black–Scholes Formula

Although the binomial tree provides an easier way to understand option pricing, the analytic Black–Scholes formula remains the central ingredient for European options. Its strength is in providing the option value through a formula and also in determining the hedge ratio for the replicating portfolio. In this chapter, the Black–Scholes formula is derived formally and extended to cover financial assets with a continuous dividend, thus allowing options on currencies and futures to be valued. Hedging parameters can also be derived, and these allow us to create portfolios that are invariant in value to modest changes in share price.

Hull's (2000) textbook on Options is the best reference for most of the topics in this chapter (Chapter 11 for the derivation and explanation of Black–Scholes, Chapter 12 for the adaptation to include continuous dividends and hence how the Black–Scholes formula can be modified to price options on currencies and futures, and Chapter 13 for the 'greeks' and delta hedging). Models illustrating the various Black–Scholes pricing formulas are in the OPTION2.xls workbook, together with a range of useful valuation functions.

11.1 THE BLACK–SCHOLES FORMULA

The Black–Scholes pricing formula for a call option was introduced in section 9.2 and the inclusion of dividends in valuing options was briefly introduced in section 9.7. In this section, the formula of section 9.2 is extended using Merton's approach to allow for continuous dividends.

The argument underlying Merton's extension compares the overall return from a share that pays a continuous dividend yield of q per annum with that for an identical share that pays no dividend. In the risk-neutral world, both shares should provide the same return overall, that is, dividend and capital growth. If the share with the dividend yield grows from S initially to S_T at time T, then the share with no dividends must grow from S initially to $S_T \exp(qT)$. Equivalently, in the absence of dividends it grows from $S \exp(-qT)$ initially to S_T. Thus the same probability distribution for S_T will apply to a share with:

(a)   initial price S paying a continuous dividend yield q or
(b)   initial price $S \exp(-qT)$ paying no dividends.

So when valuing a European option on a share paying a continuous dividend yield rate q, the current share price S is replaced by $S \exp(-qT)$ and the option valued as if the share paid no dividends.

Hence, the Black–Scholes pricing formula for a call option allowing for dividends is:

$$c = S \exp(-qT)N(d_1) - X \exp(-rT)N(d_2)$$

where q is the continuous dividend rate and $N(d)$ the cumulative standard normal probability distribution function with:

$$d_1 = [\ln(S/X) + (r - q + 0.5\sigma^2)T]/\sigma\sqrt{T}$$

$$d_2 = [\ln(S/X) + (r - q - 0.5\sigma^2)T]/\sigma\sqrt{T}$$

Interpreting the terms in the Black–Scholes formula, it helps to think of the call in the form of the replicating portfolio, $c = hS - B$. The multiplier of S in the first term of the formula, the 'hedge ratio', is given by $\exp(-qT)N(d_1)$. The second term of the formula consists of the present value of the exercise price, multiplied by $N(d_2)$. Hence, $N(d_2)$ is interpreted as the probability that the call will be exercised in the risk-neutral world.

Using the put–call parity relationship, the Black–Scholes pricing formula for a put option allowing for dividends can be shown to be:

$$p = -S\exp(-qT)N(-d_1) + X\exp(-rT)N(-d_2)$$

This can be written in the form:

$$p = -[S\exp(-qT)N(-d_1) - X\exp(-rT)N(-d_2)]$$

which apart from the initial minus sign and the minus signs in the cumulative normal functions is the same as the expression for a call.

11.2   BLACK–SCHOLES FORMULA IN THE SPREADSHEET

Figure 11.1 contains the details of the call used as an example throughout the previous chapter, together with the calculations required to evaluate its Black–Scholes value. In early implementations, various polynomial approximations to the cumulative normal probability distribution were used. Now, in the current versions of Excel, the NORMSDIST function takes care of this task. Having evaluated d_1 and d_2, the corresponding cumulative probabilities $N(d_1)$ and $N(d_2)$ are in cells E11 and E16. Since these quantities are probabilities, their values lie between 0 and 1.

	A	B	C	D	E	F	G	H
2	Black-Scholes Formula (extended to allow for continuous dividends)							
3								
4	Share price (S)	100.00			Call			Put
5	Exercise price (X)	95.00		BS value	9.73			2.49
6	Int rate-cont (r)	8.00%						
7				iopt	1			-1
8	Dividend yield (q)	3.00%		BSvalue via fn	9.73			2.49
9	Time now (0, years)	0.0000				via fn		
10	Time maturity (T, years)	0.5000		d_1	0.6102	0.6102		
11	Option life (T, years)	0.5000		$N(d_1)$	0.7291			
12	Volatility (σ)	20.00%						
13								
14	r-q+0.5*σ^2	0.0700						
15	Exp (-rT)	0.9608		d_2	0.4688	0.4688		
16	Exp (-qT)	0.9851		$N(d_2)$	0.6804			

Figure 11.1   Black–Scholes valuation of options in the BS sheet

The Black–Scholes formula in cell E5 is:

$$=B4*B16*E11-B5*B15*E16$$

where the two discounting factors in cells B15 and B16 and the cumulative normals in cells E11 and E16 provide intermediate calculation stages. The call value in cell E5 is 9.73. The Black–Scholes value has also been calculated in cell E8 via the user-defined function, BSOptionValue, whose code is described in section 11.7.

As discussed in the previous section, the hedge ratio is given by the product of $\exp(-qT)$ and $N(d_1)$. Here the hedge ratio has value 0.718 (that is 0.9851*0.7291). The risk-neutral probability that the option will be exercised is $N(d_2)$, which has value 0.680.

For a put on the same share, the Black–Scholes formula in cell H5 is:

$$=B4*B16*(E11-1)-B5*B15*(E16-1)$$

Whereas the call formula has $N(d_1)$ in the first term, the put has $-N(-d_1) = N(d_1) - 1$ because of the symmetry of the normal probability distribution. Hence the E11 term for the call is replaced by (E11 − 1) for the put. Similar remarks apply to the change in the second term. The put value in cell H5 is 2.49. Once again, the Black–Scholes value has been calculated in cell H8 using the same user-defined function BSOptionValue as previously used for the call. The function has the important parameter 'iopt' which takes value 1 for a call, −1 for a put, thus providing one general function in place of two separate ones for call and put respectively. As we have seen, the algebraic expressions for put and call are similar, except for several minus signs.

It is of interest to 'what-if' on details of the underlying share and the option to investigate the effect on the option value. In particular, it will be found that the option value is very sensitive to changes in the volatility of the share. This sensitivity analysis can be implemented easily with one or more Data Tables (as outlined in section 2.7).

11.3   OPTIONS ON CURRENCIES AND COMMODITIES

So far our discussion of option valuation has concentrated on options on equities. However, the Black–Scholes framework with continuously-paid dividends also allows options on foreign currencies and commodity futures contracts to be valued. As we have seen, the Black–Scholes call formula for a share with continuous dividend rate q is:

$$c = S \exp(-qT)N(d_1) - X \exp(-rT)N(d_2)$$

A currency can be treated in the same way as a stock that pays a continuous dividend, with the foreign interest rate R replacing the continuous dividend yield q in the Black–Scholes formula. The domestic interest rate is equivalent to the risk-free rate r. Hence the value of the call on a currency with foreign interest rate R is:

$$c = S \exp(-RT)N(d_1) - X \exp(-rT)N(d_2)$$

This is sometimes known as the Garman–Kohlhagen formula (Garman and Kohlhagen, 1983). Figure 11.2 shows an example in the Currency sheet of valuing a call on a currency with foreign interest rate 4%. The call value is 0.0044 (in cell E11). It has been calculated using the BSOptionValue user-defined function with appropriate inputs.

	A	B	C	D	E	F	G
2	**Valuing Options on Currency Forwards (As shares with a continuous dividend yield)**						
3							
4	Spot rate (S)	**1.6000**		Forward rate (F)	1.6323		
5	Exercise rate (X)	**1.8000**		d_1	-1.3475		
6	Dom Int rate-cont (r)	**8.00%**		d_2	-1.4182		
7							
8	Fgn Int rate (R)	**4.00%**			**Call**		**Put**
9	Time now (0, years)	0.0000		iopt	1		-1
10	Time maturity (T, years)	**0.5000**					
11	Option life (T, years)	0.5000		Garman-Kohlhagen	0.0044		0.1655
12	Volatility (σ)	**10.00%**					
13				Black	0.0044		0.1655
14				Black via fn	0.0044		0.1655

Figure 11.2 Valuing options on currencies in the Currency sheet

Figure 11.2 also illustrates an alternative approach due to Black (1976). He suggested that the option value should be expressed in terms of the forward currency rate, F rather than the spot rate, S. The interest rate parity theorem which states that $S = F \exp[-(r - R)T]$ allows S to be replaced by F in the pricing formula. Hence, Black's formula gives the call value as:

$$c = \exp(-rT)[FN(d_1) - XN(d_2)]$$

where d_1 and d_2 simplify when expressed in terms of the quantity F/X. Black's formula in cell E13 values the call at 0.0044 as before. Once again, a user-defined function called BlackOptionValue has been coded to use Black's approach (see cell E14).

Black's formula can also be used to value options on commodity futures and the Commodities sheet in Figure 11.3 illustrates his approach. We should also notice that a 'put–call–forward' parity relationship holds. One consequence of this is that when the forward or futures price F is equal to the exercise price, then calls and puts will have the same value. (Figure 11.3 illustrates this point.)

	A	B	C	D	E	F	G
2	**Valuing Options on Commodity Futures (As shares with a continuous dividend yield)**						
3							
4	Futures price (F)	**19.00**			**Call**		**Put**
5	Exercise price (X)	**19.00**		iopt	1		-1
6	Dom Int rate-cont (r)	**8.00%**					
7				Black	0.5149		0.5149
8				BS Value	0.5149		0.5149
9	Time now (0, years)	0.0000					
10	Time maturity (T, years)	**0.5000**		via fn	0.5149		0.5149
11	Option life (T, years)	0.5000					
12	Volatility (σ)	**10.00%**					

Figure 11.3 Valuing options on commodity futures in Commodities sheet

11.4 CALCULATING THE OPTION'S 'GREEK' PARAMETERS

The Black–Scholes formula has as its inputs the current share price S, the interest rate r, the option life, and the volatility σ amongst other factors. One way to quantify the impact of changes in the inputs on the option value is to calculate the so-called option 'greeks' or hedge parameters. The most commonly calculated hedge parameters are the first-order derivatives: delta (for change in share price), rho (for change in interest rate), theta (for change in option life) and vega (for change in volatility). The second-order derivative with respect to share price, called gamma, is also calculated. Apart from theta, the hedge parameters are represented by straightforward formulas. The Black–Scholes partial differential equation links theta with the option value, its delta and its gamma.

	A	B	C	D	E	F	G
2	Option Greeks and Hedging						
3							
4	Share price (S)	100.00		d_1	0.6102		
5	Exercise price (X)	95.00		$N(d_1)$	0.7291		
6	Int rate-cont (r)	8.00%		$N'(d_1)$	0.3312		
7	Int rate-annualised	8.33%		d_2	0.4688		iopt
8	Dividend yield (q)	3.00%		$N(d_2)$	0.6804		-1
9	Time now (0, years)	0.0000					
10	Time maturity (T, years)	0.5000			Call		Put
11	Option life (T, years)	0.5000		BSvalue	9.73		2.49
12	Volatility (σ)	20.00%					
13				delta	0.72		-0.27
14	r-q+0.5*σ^2	0.0700		gamma	0.02		0.02
15	Exp (-rT)	0.9608		rho	31.05		-14.59
16	Exp (-qT)	0.9851		theta	-7.43		-3.08
17				vega	23.07		23.07

Figure 11.4 Calculation of the 'greeks' in the Hedge sheet

Figure 11.4 shows the calculation of the 'greeks' for our standard call example, as set out in the Hedge sheet. We see that the call has a delta of 0.72. This means that when the share price changes by a small amount, the call price will change by about 72% of the share price change. Since it is based on $N(d_1)$, the delta for a long position in a call will always have a positive value between zero and one. For a corresponding long position in a put, the delta depends on $[N(d_1) - 1]$ and so is always negative.

The delta given by the formula is the instantaneous rate of change in call value when the share price is 100. It is instructive to use the spreadsheet to explore the actual change in call value for small changes in S. For example, when S is 101, the call value is 10.46, implying an actual delta of 0.73. When S is 110, the call value is 17.85, implying an actual delta of 0.81. As the share price changes, the hedge ratio delta changes and the portfolio will need to be rebalanced.

The gamma of the call is the rate of change of delta with respect to the share price (i.e. the second partial derivative of call value with respect to share price). The formula is identical for calls and puts. If gamma is small, delta changes very little, which is the case in Figure 11.4.

Both calls and puts always have negative values for theta. Theta measures how the value of the option changes as calendar time passes (or equivalently as the option life decreases). As the option life shortens, the value of the option decreases.

On the other hand, increases in volatility add to option value. Vega, the rate of change in the option value as the volatility increases, is always positive. Once again, the formula for vega is the same for calls and puts.

Investment banks typically create hedge portfolios to guard against the risk of options they write. They are interested to know how the value of their overall position will change as share values, volatilities, etc. change. Option sensitivities to changes in the share price and other factors, that is the 'greeks', are used to construct hedge portfolios, as we illustrate in the next section.

11.5 HEDGE PORTFOLIOS

The calculation of the hedge parameters is an essential step in the creation of hedge portfolios. Using the call for which we have calculated 'greeks', we examine how to create two zero-investment hedge portfolios. By zero investment we mean that the portfolio value changes very little with respect to changes in share price. The first is a *delta hedged portfolio*, that is, it is hedged against small changes in share price (called delta risk). The second is a *delta–gamma hedged portfolio* that guards against larger changes in share price and hence changes in gamma (called gamma risk).

Writing the replicating portfolio for a call $(c = hS - B)$ in the form $0 = hS - B - c$ creates a zero-investment portfolio consisting of borrowing an amount in order to purchase a fraction of a share and to sell one call. For the portfolio to require zero investment, these quantities must balance out period-by-period over time for small changes in S. For the portfolio to be delta-neutral, the fraction of the share purchased must equal the delta of the call option in the portfolio. The objective of the delta-neutral portfolio is to offset the change in the stock value by the change in the option value.

	A	B	C	D	E	F	G	H
19	**Creating a delta-neutral portfolio**			**today**			**next week**	
20								
21				n1	-1.00		S1	**102.00**
22				h	0.72			
23				B	-62.10			
24								
25				-1 call	-9.73		-1 call	-11.07
26				h shares	71.83		h shares	73.26
27				cash	-62.10		cash	-62.20
28								
29				total	0.00		total	0.00

Figure 11.5   A delta-neutral portfolio in the Hedge sheet

The spreadsheet extract in Figure 11.5 shows a delta-neutral portfolio constructed from buying some shares and selling a call, the underlying share and call details being those in Figure 11.4 for which the hedge ratios were calculated. The portfolio, shown in cell range E25:E27 of Figure 11.5, involves buying 0.72 shares (the delta shown in cell E22 to two decimal places) and selling a call. The cash required is 62.10 (share cost of 71.83 less income from selling call of 9.73). We can see how the value of the original delta-neutral portfolio will have changed in a week's time for a variety of different future share prices ($S1$ in cell H21). Were $S1$ to equal 102 next week, our portfolio would contain the same 0.72 of a share, now worth 73.26, borrowing of 62.20 (including interest) and a short position in the call now valued at 11.07 (reduced option life offset by the higher share price). For this small change in share price, it would not require new investment and would still be approximately delta-neutral. However, over time with bigger share price changes, the option delta and thus the share element of the portfolio will need to be rebalanced.

To provide a better hedge against larger changes in future share price movements, we can create a delta–gamma neutral portfolio by adding a second different call to the assets making up the delta-neutral portfolio. Thus it would be of the form:

$$0 = hS - c_1 + nc_2$$

with c_1 and c_2 the values of the two calls. Suppose the second call matures in nine months time with an exercise price of 100 as shown in Figure 11.6. The ratio of the gammas for the calls (k=[gamma(call1)/gamma(call2)]) is calculated in cell E37. It transpires that by holding an amount k of this second call option, we eliminate gamma risk from the portfolio. Next, by choosing a suitable fraction h of the share (evaluated in cell E36), we can eliminate the delta risk. The amount of borrowing or lending (in cell E38) ensures that the portfolio requires no net investment. Once again, the performance of the delta–gamma neutral portfolio can be examined in a week's time for a variety of different future share prices ($S1$ from cell H21).

	A	B	C	D	E	F	G	H
					today			next week
33	Creating a delta-gamma neutral position							
34								
35	Call 2			n1	-1.00		S1	102.00
36				h	0.07			
37	Exercise price	100.00		k	1.07			
38	Maturity	0.75		B	-6.38			
39								
40	BSvalue	8.58						
41				-1 call	-9.73		-1 call	-11.07
42	delta	0.61		h shares	6.91		h shares	7.04
43	gamma	0.02		k calls	9.20		k calls	10.40
44	rho	38.97		cash	-6.38		cash	-6.38
45	theta	-6.64						
46	vega	32.26		total	0.00		total	0.00

Figure 11.6   A delta–gamma neutral position in the Hedge sheet

Comparing the overall value in a week's time of the delta hedged and the delta–gamma hedged portfolios projecting a future share price of $S1 = 102$, both the portfolios have a zero value, that is they require no new net investment. We can set up a Data Table to see whether this remains the case as $S1$ varies in a wider range, say between 90 and 110. The results are illustrated in Figure 11.7. This suggests that the simpler delta hedged portfolio will need to be rebalanced more frequently than the more complicated delta–gamma hedged version.

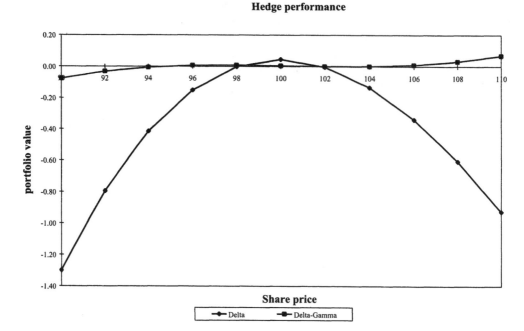

Figure 11.7 Comparison of delta hedged and delta–gamma hedged portfolio performance

11.6 FORMAL DERIVATION OF THE BLACK–SCHOLES FORMULA

The Black–Scholes pricing formula has played a central role in this chapter, so to conclude we set out a simplified explanation of its derivation (using the approach in Nielsen, 1992). As we have stated, the pricing formula for a call option on a share that pays a continuous dividend yield q is:

$$c = S \exp(-qT)N(d_1) - X \exp(-rT)N(d_2)$$

This formula arises from the assumption that log returns on the underlying share at time T are normally distributed. Algebraically, this means that the random variable S_T can be written in a stochastic equation of form $S_T = S \exp(Y_T)$, where Y_T is normally distributed with mean μ_T and standard deviation σ_T.

The call value equals the discounted expectation of the call payoff, under the *risk-neutral probability measure Q*, i.e.:

$$c = \exp(-rT)E^Q[\max(S_T - X, 0)]$$

This expression can be divided into two terms:

$$c = \exp(-rT)E^Q[S_T | S_T > X] - \exp(-rT)E^Q[X | S_T > X]$$

We can express the expectation in the second term as $X \, \mathrm{Prob}[Y_T > \ln(X/S)]$, since $\mathrm{Prob}[S_T > X] = \mathrm{Prob}[S \exp(Y_T) > X] = \mathrm{Prob}[Y_T > \ln(X/S)]$. This simplified expression implies that the option will only be exercised if the value of Y_T is greater than $\ln(X/S)$. Since Y_T is normally distributed with mean μ_T and standard deviation σ_T, where:

$$\mu_T = (r - q - 0.5\sigma^2)T \quad \text{and} \quad \sigma_T = \sigma\sqrt{T}$$

we can convert Y_T into a standard normal variable, Z_T by subtracting its mean and dividing by its standard deviation. Thus the variable:

$$Z_T = [Y_T - \mu_T]/\sigma_T$$

has a standard normal distribution, N(0, 1).

Now the cumulative normal distribution function, $N(d)$, gives the left-hand tail of the distribution, that is Prob$[Z_T < d]$. For the right-hand tail, that is Prob$[Z_T > d]$, we require $N(-d)$ using the symmetry of the N(0,1) distribution.

Thus we can transform Prob$[Y_T > \ln(X/S)]$ into Prob$\{Z_T > [\ln(X/S) - \mu_T]/\sigma_T\}$

$$= \text{Prob}\{Z_T < -[\ln(X/S) - \mu_T]/\sigma_T\}$$

$$= \text{Prob}\{Z_T < [\ln(S/X) + \mu_T]/\sigma_T\}$$

$$= \text{Prob}\{Z_T < [\ln(S/X) + (r - q - 0.5\sigma^2)T]/\sigma\sqrt{T}\}$$

This can be seen by inspection to be the same as $N(d_2)$. We have thus confirmed the second term in the Black–Scholes formula.

The expectation in the first term of the Black–Scholes formula is more complicated to resolve since the random variable S_T appears on both sides within the conditional expectation. To derive the Black–Scholes formula we need to use two standard results, one familiar and one obscure, for lognormal and normal variables.

The first result says that if $\log S_T$ is normal with mean M and variance V then:

$$E[S_T | S_T > X] = E[S_T]N(d) \quad \text{where } d = \sqrt{V} - [\ln(X) - M]/\sqrt{V}$$

where X is a number and $N()$ is the cumulative standard normal probability distribution function. The conditional expectation is replaced by an ordinary expectation multiplied by a normal distribution function. In our case, $\log S_T$ has mean $M = \ln(S) + (r - q - 0.5\sigma^2)T$ and variance $V = \sigma^2 T$:

$$E^Q[S_T | S_T > X] = E^Q[S_T]N\{\sqrt{V} - [\ln(X) - M]/\sqrt{V}\}$$

$$= E^Q[S_T]N\{\sigma\sqrt{T} - [\ln(X/S) - (r - q - 0.5\sigma^2)T]/\sigma\sqrt{T}\}$$

$$= E^Q[S_T]N(\sigma\sqrt{T} + d_2)$$

$$= E^Q[S_T]N(d_1)$$

The next step uses the familiar result concerning the expectation of a lognormally distributed variable. This second result says that if Y_T is normally distributed with mean M and variance V then $E[\exp(Y_T)] = \exp(M + 0.5V)$. Here Y_T is a normal variate with parameters:

$$M = (r - q - 0.5\sigma^2)T \quad \text{and} \quad V = \sigma^2 T$$

$$E^Q[S_T] = SE^Q[\exp(Y_T)]$$

$$= S \exp(M + 0.5V)$$

$$= S \exp[(r - q)T]$$

Thus the first term in the Black–Scholes formula reduces to $S \exp(-qT)N(d_1)$.

By following the derivation through, we see how the link between $d_1(=d_2 + \sigma\sqrt{T})$ and d_2 arises. It stems from the adjustment to reflect the truncation of the share price distribution given that exercise takes place only when the share price is higher than X, and where the scale of the adjustment is linked to the standard deviation of the share price increment.

11.7   USER-DEFINED FUNCTIONS IN MODULE1

The code for VBA functions to calculate the Black–Scholes value for European calls and puts, and the 'intermediate' functions used in the Black–Scholes formula, called descriptively BSDOne and BSDTwo, are stored in this module sheet.

Function BSDOne returns the d_1 value for an option with its current share price S, exercise price X, interest rate r, dividend rate q, time to maturity in years (tyr) and volatility (sigma) all specified as arguments. Function BSDTwo returns the d_2 value for an option in a similar fashion.

These 'intermediate' functions are coded separately from the BSOptionValue function to simplify and clarify the calculation procedure. NDOne uses the Excel function NORMSDIST (and thus is preceded by Application. in the VBA code), where the d_1 value comes from the BSDOne function. There are also statements that try to ensure that inappropriate values (such as a negative share price) are intercepted, and an appropriate error value (here -1) returned.

The code for BSOptionValue has been generalised via the 'iopt' parameter which takes value 1 for a call or -1 for a put. Because of the put–call parity relationship, the Black–Scholes formulas for call and put are identical in the terms contributing, with the exception of differing signs. Variables NDOne and NDTwo change sign from call to put, as do the signs of the two main terms added together in the Black–Scholes formula. Hence the function value given by the code line:

```
BSOptionValue = iopt * (S * eqt * NDOne - X * ert * NDTwo)

Function BSOptionValue(iopt, S, X, r, q, tyr, sigma)
'  returns the Black–Scholes value (iopt=1 for call, -1 for put; q=div yld)
'  uses BSDOne fn
'  uses BSDTwo fn
   Dim eqt, ert, NDOne, NDTwo
   eqt = Exp(-q * tyr)
   ert = Exp(-r * tyr)
   If S > 0 And X > 0 And tyr > 0 And sigma > 0 Then
      NDOne = Application.NormSDist(iopt * BSDOne(S, X, r, q, tyr, sigma))
      NDTwo = Application.NormSDist(iopt * BSDTwo(S, X, r, q, tyr, sigma))
      BSOptionValue = iopt * (S * eqt * NDOne - X * ert * NDTwo)
   Else
      BSOptionValue = -1
   End If
End Function
```

The functions for valuing options on forwards and futures are just variations on the BSOptionValue function, with variable rfgn for the foreign interest rate:

```
Function BlackOptionValue(iopt, F, X, r, rfgn, tyr, sigma)
'  returns Black option value for forwards
'  uses BSOptionValue fn
   Dim S
   S = F * Exp((rfgn - r) * tyr)
   BlackOptionValue = BSOptionValue(iopt, S, X, r, rfgn, tyr, sigma)
End Function
```

The functions for the individual hedge parameters are straightforward replications of the spreadsheet formulas. There is also a composite BSOptionGreeks function that takes advantage of the overlap between calculations for the range of different hedge parameters. The composite function uses individual 'If' statements linked to a chosen integer variable (igreek) for each hedge parameter required:

```
Function BSOptionGreeks(igreek, iopt, S, X, r, q, tyr, sigma)
'  returns BS option greeks (depends on value of igreek)
'  returns delta(1), gamma(2), rho(3), theta(4) or vega(5)
'  iopt=1 for call, -1 for put; q=div yld
'  uses BSOptionValue fn
'  uses BSDOne fn
'  uses BSDTwo fn
'  uses BSNdashDOne fn
   Dim eqt, c, c1, c1d, c2, d, g, v
   eqt = Exp(-q * tyr)
   c = BSOptionValue(iopt, S, X, r, q, tyr, sigma)
   c1 = Application.NormSDist(iopt * BSDOne(S, X, r, q, tyr, sigma))
   c1d = BSNdashDOne(S, X, r, q, tyr, sigma)
   c2 = Application.NormSDist(iopt * BSDTwo(S, X, r, q, tyr, sigma)) .
   d = iopt * eqt * c1
   g = c1d * eqt / (S * sigma * Sqr(tyr))
   v = -1
   If igreek = 1 Then v = d
   If igreek = 2 Then v = g
   If igreek = 3 Then v = iopt * X * tyr * Exp(-r * tyr) * c2
   If igreek = 4 Then v = r * c-(r - q) * S * d - 0.5 * (sigma * S)^2 * g
   If igreek = 5 Then v = S * Sqr(tyr) * c1d * eqt
   BSOptionGreeks = v
End Function
```

SUMMARY

The Black–Scholes formula for valuing European options can be extended to cover options on shares paying a continuous dividend yield rate q. This simply involves replacing the initial share value S with the expression $S \exp(-qT)$ throughout the formula. In practice, shares do not provide continuous dividends. However, several other assets can be considered as shares providing continuous dividends, so this modification extends the range of assets covered by the formula. Hence the Black–Scholes framework also covers the pricing of options on currencies and futures.

The delta of an option is the rate of change of its price relative to the price of the underlying share. By using the delta, it is possible to construct portfolios, for example, of calls and shares that are delta-neutral in the short term. However, because the delta of the portfolio changes over time, the position in the underlying share requires rebalancing.

Option sensitivities to other changes in the inputs, such as volatility, option life and rate of return, are also calculated. Collectively, they are frequently referred to as 'greeks' and their estimation is an important aspect of hedging.

REFERENCES

Black, F., 1976, "The Pricing of Commodity Contracts," *Journal of Financial Economics*, **3**, 167–179.

Garman, M. B. and S. W. Kohlhagen, 1983, "Foreign Currency Option Values," *Journal of International Money and Finance*, **2**, 231–237.

Hull, J. C., 2000, *Options, Futures and Other Derivatives*, Prentice Hall, New York.

Nielsen, L. T., 1992, "Understanding $N(d1)$ and $N(d2)$: Risk-Adjusted Probabilities in the Black–Scholes Model," *INSEAD Working Paper 92/71/FIN*.

Other Numerical Methods for European Options

In this chapter, we look at two numerical methods (Monte Carlo simulation and numerical integration) that can also be used to value European options. They are alternatives to binomial trees for calculating expectation. However, for American options we prefer binomial valuation for standard options.

Monte Carlo simulation is a well-established technique used widely in other fields. However, the ordinary random sampling approach used in Monte Carlo simulation is relatively inefficient for option valuation (especially when compared to binomial tree valuation). For example, to halve the sampling error requires a quadrupling of the number of simulation trials. So, the recent introduction of quasi-random number sequences in finance applications, coupled with enhanced computing power, has boosted the use of Monte Carlo simulation. For valuing path-dependent options, simulation is now considered the best numerical method. Background reading on simulation is in Hull's (2000) text on options, Chapter 16.

In this chapter, we compare the valuation of a European call first using ordinary Monte Carlo simulation, then simulation with antithetic variates and lastly simulation with quasi-random sequences. The aim in using antithetic variables is to improve efficiency of estimation by reducing the standard error of the simulation results. Quasi-random sampling is a further method for effectively controlling the randomness of simulation results. The three simulation approaches are implemented in separate sheets of the OPTION3.xls workbook and their results compared in a fourth sheet.

The chapter continues with an illustration of numerical integration. We have indirectly alluded to the fact that the Black–Scholes option pricing formula is derived from a continuous integral. (As mentioned in Chapter 9, the formula was derived by solving a partial differential equation.) The binomial tree provides one way of generating a discrete approximation, as does the more direct form of numerical integration implemented here using the midpoint rule.

12.1 INTRODUCTION TO MONTE CARLO SIMULATION

At the heart of Monte Carlo simulation for option valuation is the stochastic process that generates the share price. In section 9.2, the stochastic equation for the underlying share price at time T when the option on the share expires was given as:

$$S_T = S \exp(Y_T) = S \exp(\mu_T + \varepsilon \sigma_T)$$

where random variable ε has a standard normal distribution, denoted N(0, 1). Random variable Y_T is normally distributed with mean $\mu_T = (\mu - 0.5\sigma^2)T$ and standard deviation $\sigma_T = \sigma\sqrt{T}$ where μ is the rate of return on the share and σ is the volatility. The associated option payoff depends on the expectation of S_T in the risk-neutral world. It transpires that for risk-neutral valuation, the rate of return on the share (previously μ) is replaced by the risk-free rate r less the continuous dividend yield q, that is by $(r - q)$. Thus the stochastic equation for S_T for risk neutral valuation takes the form:

$$S_T = S \exp[(r - q - 0.5\sigma^2)T + \varepsilon\sigma\sqrt{T}]$$

where ε has the standard normal distribution. The share price process outlined above is the same as that assumed for binomial tree valuation.

Monte Carlo simulation consists of randomly generating a sample of possible values for the terminal share price, S_T, loosely referred to as simulation trials. For each sample value, the option payoff is evaluated and recorded. When sufficient sample values have been generated, the distribution of option payoff values is summarised, usually by calculating the mean and standard deviation. The arithmetic mean of the simulation trials estimates the expectation of the option payoff distribution, which must be discounted back at the risk-free rate to value the call.

Figure 12.1 shows an extract from the MC1 sheet in the OPTION3.xls workbook. The European call valued in the sheet is the standard example of a six-month derivative on a share with a continuous dividend yield of 3%. The sheet contains 36 simulation trials of the option payoff, on the basis of which its discounted expectation is estimated.

	A	B	C	D	E	F	G	H
2	Using Monte Carlo Simulation to Value BS Call Option							
3								
4	Share price (S)	100.00		iopt	1			
5	Exercise price (X)	95.00		option	call			
6	Int rate-cont (r)	8.00%						
7				BS value	9.73			
8	Dividend yield (q)	3.00%						
9	Time now (0, years)	0.0000		MC value	12.85			
10	Time maturity (T, years)	0.5000		MC stdev	2.44			
11	Option life (τ, years)	0.5000						
12	Volatility (σ)	20.00%						
13								
14	Simulations (nsim)	36						
15								
16	mmut	0.0150						
17	sigt	0.1414						
18	Exp(-rτ)	0.9608						
19								
20		simulation	rand	randns		share price		payoff
21								
22		1	0.1032	-1.2634		84.90		0.00
23		2	0.7561	0.6939		111.98		16.98
24		3	0.3048	-0.5106		94.44		0.00
25		4	0.4255	-0.1878		98.85		3.85
26		5	0.0602	-1.5531		81.49		0.00

Figure 12.1   Option details and five (out of 36) simulations of option payoff in sheet MC1

Each simulation trial produces a sample terminal share price (a sample value for S_T) and a sample payoff value. To effect this, a sample of uniform random numbers is chosen using the Excel RAND function as shown in column B. These are converted into random samples from the standard normal distribution using the NORMSINV function as shown in column C. RAND gives random numbers uniformly distributed in the range [0, 1]. Regarding its outputs as cumulative probabilities (with values between 0 and 1), the NORMSINV function converts them into standard normal variate values, mostly between −3 and +3. For example, in the first simulation trial the formula in cell C22 is:

$$=\text{NORMSINV(B22)}$$

which for an input of 0.1032 (or approximately 10%) evaluates as a standard normal variate of −1.2634.

The ε) are then used to generate share prices at call

$$-0.5\sigma^2)T + \varepsilon\sigma\sqrt{T}]$$

to calculate the risk-neutral drift and volatility $\sqrt{T}$ first (as in cells B16 and B17). Hence the

B$16+C22*$B$17)

ll H22 is:

4*(E22-$B$5),0)

oting whether payoffs are for a call or a put. lated (in cell E9) as the discounted value of yoffs. The risk-neutral discount factor [simply

estimate of call value (12.85) is very different rd error for the estimated call value in cell E10, simulated payoffs divided by the square root of hich explains the discrepancy when comparing –Scholes call value). To improve the precision of simulation trials must be increased. generates a further 36 trials and another Monte rd error for the estimate. The cell formulas also he value of the iopt parameter (in cell E4) to of a put, and this can be compared with its

12.2 SIMULATION WITH ANTITHETIC VARIABLES

As well as increasing the number of trials, another way of improving the precision of the Monte Carlo estimate is to use so-called 'antithetic' variables. The antithetic variate approach uses pairs of negatively correlated random numbers that in turn tend to produce pairs of negatively correlated simulation results. If the results from each pair are averaged, the simulation results should be less variable than those produced by the ordinary random sampling.

Figure 12.2 shows some of the simulation results in sheet MC2, where the random normal sample (ε_1 in cell C22) is used to generate two share prices, the share price in cell D22 being from the original $N(0, 1)$ variate ε_1 in column C and the share price in cell E22 from $-\varepsilon_1$, the negative of the normal variate. Since the share prices will be perfectly negatively correlated, in turn the simulation values for payoff1 and payoff2 tend to be negatively correlated. The two option payoffs are averaged to produce the value in cell H22. The simulation trial results in column H should be less variable with this technique.

	A	B	C	D	E	F	G	H
20	simulation	rand	randns	S1	S2	payoff 1	payoff 2	avg payoff
21								
22	1	0.7065	0.5431	109.62	94.01	14.62	0.00	7.31
23	2	0.7676	0.7309	112.57	91.54	17.57	0.00	8.78
24	3	0.5329	0.0825	102.70	100.33	7.70	5.33	6.52
25	4	0.6434	0.3677	106.93	96.37	11.93	1.37	6.65
26	5	0.1782	-0.9221	89.10	115.65	0.00	20.65	10.33

Figure 12.2   Five simulation trials of option payoff using antithetic variables in sheet MC2

The call is valued by averaging all 36 payoffs in column H and discounted using the risk-neutral discount-free rate in cell B18, as in the MC1 sheet.

Everything else in the MC2 sheet is the same as in ordinary Monte Carlo simulation. You should notice that the standard error of the Monte Carlo estimate (with antithetic variables) is substantially lower than that for the uncontrolled sampling approach used in the MC1 sheet.

12.3   SIMULATION WITH QUASI-RANDOM SAMPLING

In practice, uncontrolled random numbers can prove to be too random. For example, a sequence of uniform random numbers often has values clustering together. One way to avoid this clustering is to generate a sequence of numbers that are distributed uniformly across the unit interval instead. Quasi-random sequences preselect the sequence of numbers in a deterministic (i.e. non-random) way to eliminate the clustering of points seen in random numbers. The only trick in the selection process is to remember the values of all the previous numbers chosen as each new number is selected. Using quasi-random sampling means that the error in any estimate based on the samples is proportional to $1/n$ rather than $1/\sqrt{n}$, where n is the number of samples. In the QMC sheet (where we use QMC as shorthand for Quasi-Monte Carlo), we illustrate the result of generating the quasi-random sequence and also an improved method of converting these into standard normal variates. The approach uses the Fauré sequence instead of the uniform random numbers, combined with a revised conversion method due to Moro (1995). Moro suggested his improvement to the traditional Box–Muller transform because some inverse normal distribution functions can scramble the even spacing of the Fauré sequence numbers. The generation of Fauré sequences and their conversion to normal deviates are handled via user-defined VBA functions. The coding of these functions is explained in section 12.7, together with that of the other user-defined functions in Module1. One special point about Fauré sequences is that, in line with common practice, the Fauré sequence begins from 2^4 (here 16) to avoid start-up problems.

Looking at the first simulation trial in row 22 of Figure 12.3, the first quasi-random number in cell B22 uses the FaureBase2 function with input 16. This is converted into a standard normal variate in cell C22 with the MoroNormSInv function. The share price and the option payoff in cells E22 and H22 respectively are generated exactly as in the MC1 sheet, as is the option value labelled 'QMC value' in cell E9. The estimate 8.95 (with standard error of 1.69 in cell E10) is none too close to the Black–Scholes value of 9.73. However, as we shall see in section 12.4, the big advantage of using quasi-random sampling is the much faster convergence to the underlying true value as the number of simulation trials increases.

	A	B	C	D	E	F	G	H
2	Using Monte Carlo Simulation to Value BS Call Option (Quasi-Random Numbers)							
3								
4	Share price (S)	100.00		iopt	1			
5	Exercise price (X)	95.00		option	call			
6	Int rate-cont (r)	8.00%						
7				BS value	9.73			
8	Dividend yield (q)	3.00%						
9	Time now (0, years)	0.0000		QMC value	8.95			
10	Time maturity (T, years)	0.5000		QMC stdev	1.69			
11	Option life (τ, years)	0.5000						
12	Volatility (σ)	20.00%						
13								
14	Simulations (nsim)	36						
15								
16	rnmut	0.0150						
17	sigt	0.1414						
18	Exp(-rτ)	0.9608						
19								
20		simulation	rand	randns		share price			payoff
21								
22		16	0.0313	-1.8627		78.00			0.00
23		17	0.5313	0.0784		102.64			7.64
24		18	0.2813	-0.5791		93.53			0.00
25		19	0.7813	0.7764		113.29			18.29
26		20	0.1563	-1.0100		88.00			0.00

Figure 12.3 Option details and five (out of 36) simulations of option payoff in sheet QMC

Note that pressing the F9 Calculate key in Excel does not produce any change in the spreadsheet. The Fauré sequence is completely deterministic, not random at all, hence the name 'quasi-random' is a misnomer. It is necessary to take a different number of simulation trials to get a different QMC value and standard deviation.

As with the previous sheets, the cell formulas adapt if the option is a put. Changing the value of the iopt parameter (in cell E4) to -1 produces the QMC estimate of a put, and this can be compared with its Black–Scholes value.

Quasi-random sampling can be seen as a development of stratified sampling. For stratified sampling the required interval would be subdivided into a number of smaller intervals, with a small number of observations chosen randomly to lie within each interval. This can lead to there being points clustered within each interval. There is no random element in the sequence of quasi-random numbers, as each number in the sequence is fitted into a pre-ordained position in the required interval.

12.4   COMPARING SIMULATION METHODS

It is informative to examine the convergence of the call value estimates from the different sampling methods described in the three previous sections as the number of simulation trials increases. Figure 12.4 shows results in the Compare sheet as the number of trials increases from 100 to 2000. The true Black–Scholes value (using the BSOptionValue function) provides the benchmark in column F. In column G, the call values from simulations with different numbers of trials using controlled sampling (via antithetic variables) are evaluated from the MCOptionValue function. In column H, the equivalent call values using quasi-random sampling are evaluated from the QMCOptionValue function.

	A	B	C	D	E	F	G	H
2	Comparing Monte Carlo Simulation Methods to Value BS Call Option							
3								
4	Share price (S)	100.00			nsim	BS	MC	QMC
5	Exercise price (X)	95.00						
6	Int rate-cont (r)	8.00%			100	9.73	10.23	9.34
7					200	9.73	9.68	9.50
8	Dividend yield (q)	3.00%			300	9.73	9.28	9.54
9	Time now (0, years)	0.0000			400	9.73	9.84	9.62
10	Time maturity (T, years)	0.5000			600	9.73	9.85	9.62
11	Option life (τ, years)	0.5000			800	9.73	9.48	9.65
12	Volatility (σ)	20.00%			1000	9.73	9.52	9.67
13					1200	9.73	9.71	9.68
14					1400	9.73	9.63	9.68
15	BS Call Option Value	9.73			1600	9.73	9.81	9.68
16					1800	9.73	9.65	9.69
17					2000	9.73	9.73	9.70

Figure 12.4   Monte Carlo random and quasi-random sampling estimates compared with BS

If the data in range E6:H17 is charted, as in Figure 12.5, the relatively erratic convergence of the MC estimate can be compared with more systematic improvement in the QMC value. The QMC values show convergence occurring at a 'quadratic' rate as the number of trials increases, similar to the convergence behaviour shown by the LR binomial tree estimate examined in Chapter 10.

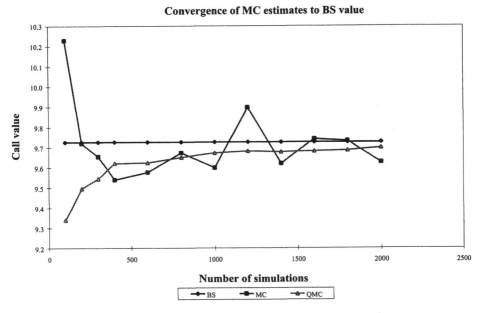

Figure 12.5   Convergence of MC and QMC sampling estimates of call value to BS value

12.5   CALCULATING GREEKS IN MONTE CARLO SIMULATION

Most textbooks suggest that the best way to estimate hedge parameters is by using finite difference approximations, each involving an additional simulation trial where the required input parameter is varied by a small amount. However, this method produces biased estimates and is unnecessarily time-consuming.

Broadie and Glasserman (1996) have shown how to derive direct pathwise estimates within a single simulation run. These estimates are unbiased and rather quicker to obtain than by using the finite difference approach. The user-defined function, QMCOption-Greek135 with parameter 'igreek' contains the code for these formulas and is stored in Module1. The function uses quasi-random normal variates (-qrandns) involving the Faure-Base2 and MoroNormSInv functions. It returns delta (igreek=1), rho (igreek=3) or vega (igreek=5).

12.6   NUMERICAL INTEGRATION

Numerical integration is another well-known mathematical method that can be adapted to value options. Here we illustrate one of the very simplest integration routines, the extended midpoint rule. This uses a set of intervals of equal width h say, with midpoints (z_i) at which the function to be integrated, S_T, together with the associated option payoff is evaluated. The probability of each value of S_T is approximated by calculating the standard normal probability density function for each midpoint and multiplying this by the width of the interval, h. Weighting the option values by their probabilities produces the expected payoff value. Expressed in this way, this form of numerical integration is very similar to the expectation calculated in the binomial tree, except that the normal distribution is retained.

Figure 12.6 shows an extract from the NI sheet. Here the range of possible values for S_T is divided into 36 equal intervals, spanning -6 to $+6$ standard deviations from the mean, each one-third of the standard deviation wide (hence $h = 0.33$). The midpoints of the intervals expressed as multiples of standard deviations away from the mean are in column B and the corresponding risk-neutral share price at maturity is in column C, the first one given by the formula in C21:

$$=\$D\$4^*EXP(\$D\$15+\$D\$17^*B21)$$

	A	B	C	D	E	F	G	H
2	Using Numerical Integration to Value BS Options							
3								
4	Share price (S)			100.00			iopt	1
5	Exercise price (X)			95.00			option	call
6	Int rate-cont (r)			8.00%				
7							BS value	9.73
8	Dividend yield (q)			3.00%				
9	Time now (0, years)			0.00			NI value	9.71
10	Time maturity (T, years)			0.50			via fn	9.71
11	Option life (τ, years)			0.50				
12	Volatility (σ)			20.00%			msd	6
13							-msd	-6
14								
15	$\mu\,\tau$			0.0150			n	36
16								
17	σ Sqrt(τ)			0.1414			h	0.33
18								
19		i	z	S_T		payoff	probability		calc
20								
21		0	-5.83	44.49		0.00	0.0000		0.0000
22		1	-5.50	46.64		0.00	0.0000		0.0000
23		2	-5.17	48.89		0.00	0.0000		0.0000
24		3	-4.83	51.25		0.00	0.0000		0.0000
25		4	-4.50	53.72		0.00	0.0000		0.0000

Figure 12.6   Using the midpoint rule to perform numerical integration in sheet NI

The associated option payoff is in column E. Column F contains probabilities, the formula in cell F21 being:

$$=\$H\$17^*NORMDIST(B21,0,1,FALSE)$$

The FALSE parameter means that the function returns the probability density value, that is, the height of the normal curve when a distance 5.83 standard deviations below the mean. The cell formula gives an approximate probability because the normal probability density function is multiplied by the interval width (h). These probabilities are used in calculating the expected option payoff in exactly the same way as the nodal probabilities in the binomial tree. In column H the product of the payoff and the probability is calculated, and the sum of this column discounted by the risk-free discount factor provides the option value. This 'NI value' in cell H9 is 9.71, which compares favourably with the Black–Scholes value.

For the z-values shown in Figure 12.6, the probabilities shown are effectively zero so the products in column H are also zero. However, when i is in the range 17 to 30, contributions to the expectation are significantly different from zero. Figure 12.6 confirms this, showing the probabilities of S_T at different distances from the mean (in terms of i) and also the corresponding option values, the product of these two components contributing to the expected value.

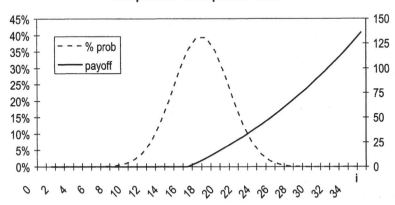

Figure 12.7 Component probability and payoff values, which produce the expected payoff

The example just outlined of applying numerical integration to value a simple option is deliberately very simple. Numerical integration comes into its own when considering the valuation of options with payoffs depending on many assets.

12.7 USER-DEFINED FUNCTIONS IN Module1

To ease spreadsheet computation, user-defined functions have been coded for the main numerical methods discussed in this chapter. We have already met the MCOptionValue and the QMCOptionValue functions in section 12.4, that compared their relative speeds of convergence. The following paragraphs throw some light on their coding.

The MCOptionValue function shown on the MC2 sheet uses a loop structure to run the series of simulation trials. The variable called 'sum' keeps a running total of the option payoff, here derived from two share prices using antithetic variates. The share prices depend on the drift in time 'tyr', a variable called 'rnmut', and another variable called 'sigt' representing the volatility in time tyr. It might be quicker to simulate the log share price, but we retain the share price simulation for clarity. The crucial part of the code is as follows:

```
rnmut = (r - q - 0.5 * sigma^2) * tyr
sigt = sigma * Sqr(tyr)
sum = 0
For i = 1 To nsim
   randns = Application.NormSInv(Rnd)
   S1 = S * Exp(rnmut + randns * sigt)
   S2 = S * Exp(rnmut - randns * sigt)
```

```
   payoff1 = Application.Max(iopt * (S1 - X), 0)
   payoff2 = Application.Max(iopt * (S2 - X), 0)
   sum = sum + 0.5 * (payoff1 + payoff2)
Next i
MCOptionValue = Exp(-r * tyr) * sum / nsim
```

The QMCOptionValue function has a similar format apart from the FaureBase2 and MoroNormSInv functions, which replace the Excel and VBA functions used to generate the random normal samples in MCOptionValue. Thus the main code is:

```
sum = 0
For i = 1 To nsim
   qrandns = MoroNormSInv(Faure1Base2(i + iskip))
   S1 = S * Exp(rnmut + qrandns * sigt)
   sum = sum + Application.Max(iopt * (S1 - X), 0)
Next i
QMCOptionValue = Exp(-r * tyr) * sum / nsim
```

Fauré sequences involve the transformation of integers (base 10) into numbers of a different prime base. Here we have chosen 2 as the base. The digits in the base 2 representation are then reversed and finally expressed as a fraction using powers of $\frac{1}{2}$.

```
Function FaureBase2(n) As Double
'   returns the equivalent first Faure sequence number
   Dim f As Double, sb As Double
   Dim i As Integer, n1 As Integer, n2 As Integer
   n1 = n
   f = 0
   sb = 1 / 2
   Do While n1 > 0
      n2 = Int(n1 / 2)
      i = n1 - n2 * 2
      f = f + sb * i
      sb = sb / 2
      n1 = n2
   Loop
   FaureBase2 = f
End Function
```

The QMCOptionGreek135 function uses the Broadie and Glasserman formulas for three of the greeks (delta, rho and vega). Gamma is not stochastic but deterministic and so can be derived using the same formula as in the BSOptionGamma function in OPTION2.xls. As previously mentioned, theta is best calculated from the simulated option value and the delta and gamma estimates:

```
ert = Exp(-r * tyr)
rnmut = (r - q - 0.5 * sigma^2) * tyr
sigt = sigma * Sqr(tyr)
r1 = (r - q + 0.5 * sigma^2) * tyr
iskip = (2^4) - 1
greek = 0
vg = -1
For i = 1 To nsim
   qrandns = MoroNormSInv(Faure1Base2(i + iskip))
   S1 = S * Exp(rnmut + qrandns * sigt)
   If (igreek = 1 And Sgn(iopt * (S1 - X)) = 1) Then greek = greek + S1
```

```
If (igreek = 3 And Sgn(iopt * (S1 - X)) > = 0) Then greek = greek + 1
If (igreek = 5 And Sgn(iopt * (S1 - X)) > = 0) Then greek = greek + S1 * (Log(S1 / S) - r1)
Next i
If igreek = 1 Then vg = ert * (greek / S) / nsim
If igreek = 3 Then vg = ert * X * tyr * greek / nsim
If igreek = 5 Then vg = ert * (greek / sigma) / nsim
QMCOptionGreek135 = vg
```

The NIOption Value function sets up the share price process and collects the sum for the numerical integration within a loop. Note how the common components (S and h) are inserted after the loop:

```
Function NIOptionValue(iopt, S, X, r, q, tyr, sigma, msd, nint)
' values option using numerical integration
  Dim rnmut, sigt, h, sum, zi, payi
  Dim i As Integer
  rnmut = (r - q - 0.5 * sigma^2) * tyr
  sigt = sigma * Sqr(tyr)
  h = 2 * msd / nint
  sum = 0
  For i = 0 To nint - 1
    zi = -msd + (i + 0.5) * h
    payi = Application.Max(iopt * (Exp(rnmut + zi*sigt ) - X/S), 0)
    sum = sum + payi * Application.NormDist(zi, 0, 1, False)
  Next i
  NIOptionValue = Exp(-r * tyr) * h * S * sum
End Function
```

SUMMARY

In this chapter, we illustrate alternative ways of calculating the expectation of option value, which underlies the Black–Scholes formula for European options.

Monte Carlo simulation consists of using random numbers to sample from the many paths a share price might take in the risk-neutral world. An option payoff is calculated for each path and the arithmetic average of the payoffs, discounted back at the risk-free rate, used to estimate option value.

When compared with the binomial method of valuation, it produces estimates of option value with more estimation error. Many more paths must be generated with Monte Carlo sampling, because unlike the tree, paths do not recombine.

Controlling the random sampling by variance reduction techniques such as using anti-thetic variables can reduce the estimation error. Quasi-random samples preselect the sequence of numbers in a deterministic (i.e. non-random) way, eliminating the clustering of values seen in random numbers. The samples are taken such that they always 'fill in' the gaps between existing samples. This means that the error of estimation is proportional to $1/n$ rather than $1/\sqrt{n}$, where n is the number of simulation samples.

Numerical integration is another method that can be adapted to value options. It is especially useful for options whose payoffs depend on many assets.

REFERENCES

Broadie, M. and P. Glasserman, 1996, "Estimating Security Prices Using Simulation", *Management Science*, **42**(2), 269–285.

Hull, J. C., 2000, "Options, Futures and Other Derivatives", Prentice Hall, New Jersey.

Moro, B. 1995, "The Full Monte", *Risk*, **8**(2), 57–58.

13
Non-normal Distributions and
Implied Volatility

The Black–Scholes formula for valuing options assumes that log share returns follow a normal distribution. First, we emphasise this assumption by showing an alternative form of the Black–Scholes formula expressed in terms of the mean and variance of the normal distribution for log share returns. The Black–Scholes formula can also be expressed in terms of the first two moments of the lognormal distribution for share prices.

In applying the Black–Scholes formula, all the input parameters are known apart from the volatility of the share returns over the life of the option. For a chosen level of volatility, we use the formula to generate an option value. This process works in the reverse direction too. Starting from an observed option price in the market, we can calculate its Black–Scholes *implied* volatility. The process of finding the implied volatility (or ISD for implied standard deviation) can be carried out by manual trial-and-error. An improvement is to automate the process. We discuss various methods of deciding an initial guess followed by a *Newton–Raphson* search to provide a good estimate of the ISD.

Practitioners are interested to know how to allow for departures from strict normality when valuing options. We look at two modifications, the first being an alternative analytic formula and the second an alternative binomial tree. The first approach suggests that share prices follow a reciprocal gamma (RG) distribution rather than the familiar lognormal distribution. The second approach retains the lognormal distribution but instead allows the higher moments (skewness and kurtosis) of log returns to differ from strict normality. This reflects empirical findings that log share returns typically have fat-tails (kurtosis above 3) and may be skewed as well.

Lastly in this chapter, we show how the implied volatility 'smile' seen in option prices from the market may reflect different assumptions regarding the distribution of log returns rather than differing forecasts of volatilities.

With the exception of Hull's discussion of volatility smiles (in Chapter 17), the standard texts do not cover the topics in this chapter. For further details, it is necessary to pursue the individual papers for elucidation. However, most of the calculation routines illustrated in the OPTION4.xls workbook have been coded into user-defined functions.

13.1 BLACK–SCHOLES USING ALTERNATIVE DISTRIBUTIONAL ASSUMPTIONS

The Dist sheet in the OPTION4.xls workbook sheet illustrates alternative ways of generating Black–Scholes option values, stressing the part played by the distributional assumptions. First stressing the normal distribution of log share prices, the mean and variance can be calculated and the Black–Scholes formula reworked from these moments.

Since $M = \ln(S) + (r - q - 0.5\sigma^2)T$ and $V = \sigma^2 T$, and also since $\exp(M + 0.5V)$ can be simplified to $S \exp[(r - q)T]$, the Black–Scholes formula for a European call can be written as:

$$c(\text{LN}) = \exp(-rT)[\exp(M + 0.5V)N(d_1) - XN(d_2)]$$
$$\text{with } d_2 = [M - \ln(X)]/\sqrt{V} = d_1 - \sqrt{V}$$

using the $c(\text{LN})$ notation to imply that distributional moments are used.

From the call details in column B of Figure 13.1, the first two moments (M in cell E4 and V in cell E5) of the normal distribution attributed to the log share price are calculated. The cell formulas for M and V (solely based on the details in cells B4 to B12) are =LN(B4)+(B6−B8−0.5*B12^2)*B11 for the mean and B12^2*B11 for the variance. The value of the call in cell E13 derived from M and V, 9.73, agrees with the Black–Scholes value in cell B17.

	A	B	C	D	E	F	G	H
1	Option4.XLS							
2	Option Values using the LN and RG distributions							
3								
4	Share price (S)	100.00		M	4.6202		M1	102.53
5	Exercise price (X)	95.00		V	0.0200		M2	10725.08
6	Int rate-cont (r)	8.00%						
7				d_1	0.6102		alpha	51.5017
8	Dividend yield (q)	3.00%		d_2	0.4688		beta	0.0002
9	Time now (0, years)	0.00						
10	Time maturity (T, years)	0.50		N (d_1)	0.7291		g1	0.7243
11	Option life (T, years)	0.50		N (d_2)	0.6804		g2	0.6761
12	Volatility (s)	20.00%						
13				LN value	9.73		RG value	9.64
14	iopt	1		via fn	9.73		via fn	9.64
15	option	call						
16								
17	BS option value	9.73					LN value	9.73

Figure 13.1 Black–Scholes valuation with lognormal or reciprocal gamma distributions

The pricing formula (referred to as the lognormal version of Black–Scholes) can also be expressed in terms of the moments of the lognormal distribution attributed to the share price. It takes the form:

$$c(\text{LN}) = \exp(-rT)[M1N(d_1) - XN(d_2)]$$

where d_1 and d_2 are expressed in terms of $M1$ and $M2$. The moments for the lognormal distribution ($M1$ in cell H4 and $M2$ in cell H5) can be calculated from the moments of the normal distribution M and V as follows:

$$M1 = \exp(M + 0.5V) \quad \text{and} \quad M2 = \exp(2M + 2V)$$

The formulas for the moments come from section 7.7. The option value in cell H17 uses $M1$ and $M2$ as inputs in the user-defined function LNOptionValue (whose code is described in section 13.5). In passing, note that the cells labelled 'LN value' in Figure 13.1 all give the Black–Scholes value, although their inputs differ.

The moments $M1$ and $M2$ provide the starting point for an alternative option pricing approach, one that replaces the lognormal assumption with the alternative assumption that share prices follow the RG distribution. Milevsky and Posner (1998) suggested this distribution as appropriate for the valuation of 'so-called' basket options. It is introduced here for the valuation of an ordinary option.

A variable Z is said to have a reciprocal gamma distribution when its reciprocal $(1/Z)$ follows the gamma distribution. The reciprocal gamma version of the pricing formula replaces the normal $[N(d)]$ with the reciprocal gamma distribution function. The gamma distribution depends on the reciprocal of the exercise price $(1/X)$ and two parameters, alpha (in cell H7) and beta (in cell H8). The latter two inputs are calculated from the moments $M1$ and $M2$.

The RG pricing formula for a call option takes the form:

$$c(\text{RG}) = \exp(-rT)[M1g1 - Xg2]$$

where $g1$ and $g2$ replace the normal distribution functions $N(d_1)$ and $N(d_2)$. In the example in Figure 13.1, the RG formula gives the call value as 9.64 (in cell H13), compared to the Black–Scholes value of 9.73. The difference between the RG and Black–Scholes values is only significant when the option is well 'out-of-the money', that is when S is relatively small. To experiment with this, try changing the share price in cell B4 to 75 and note the respective option values. You may need to force the individual formula cells B17, H17, E20 and F20 to recalculate, using the F2 Edit key followed by Enter each time.

13.2   IMPLIED VOLATILITY

Next, we use the Black–Scholes formula to estimate the volatility implied by different option prices in the market. Finding the implied volatility that matches an observed option price is simply a matter of trial and error. There are a number of different approaches: Excel's Goal Seek, Corrado and Miller's (1996) approximation, Manaster and Koehler's (1982) approach or a user-defined function. We examine each in turn.

In Figure 13.2, the details of our standard call are set out (cells B4 to B12), for which the value given by our user-defined function, BSOptionValue in cell B15, is 9.73. Suppose the observed market value for the option is 15.00. Our task is to choose a succession of volatility estimates in cell B12 until the Black–Scholes option value in cell B15 equals the observed price of 15.00. This can be done manually or by applying the Goal Seek command in the Tools part of Excel's menu. Applying the Goal Seek command to 'set cell' B15 to the 'value' 15 'by changing cell' B12, we should find that the true implied volatility is 41.28%.

The above Goal Seek procedure can be replicated by creating a user-defined function called BSOptionISDGoalSeekNR. This Goal Seek function ensures that each new guess of the volatility takes account of the current error (the distance between the current price using the guessed volatility and the observed price) and also the slope of the valuation function with respect to volatility. The slope of the option price with respect to volatility (the first-order derivative $dc/d\sigma$) is available as vega, one of the option 'greeks' discussed in section 11.4. Using the slope to improve the accuracy of subsequent guesses is known as the Newton–Raphson method. It can easily be programmed within a loop until the observed option price is reached, within a certain specified tolerance. The code for BSOptionISDGoalSeekNR, the user-defined function, is described in section 13.5.

	A	B	C	D	E	F	G	H
2	**Estimating Implied Volatility (or ISD) in BS Option Values**							
3								
4	Share price (S)	**100.00**		**ISD Estimate (Corrado & Miller)**				41.10%
5	Exercise price (X)	**95.00**						
6	Int rate-cont (r)	**8.00%**		S * Exp (-q*T)				98.51
7				X * Exp (-r*T)				91.27
8	Dividend yield (q)	**3.00%**		calc0				11.38
9	Time now (0, years)	0.00		calc1				112.88
10	Time maturity (T, years)	**0.50**		calc2				22.01
11	Option life (T, years)	0.50						
12	Volatility (σ)	**20.00%**						
13				**ISD Seed Value (Manaster & Koehler)**				55.24%
14	iopt	**1**						
15	BS Option value	9.73						
16								
17	Observed Option price	**15.00**		**ISD via BSOptionISDGoalSeekNR fn**				41.28%

Figure 13.2   Estimating the implied volatility by matching market prices to BS values

Corrado and Miller (1996) have suggested an analytic formula that produces an approximation for the implied volatility. They start by approximating $N(d)$ as a linear function. The linear approximation is substituted into the Black–Scholes formula, which is equated to the observed call price and then rearranged to derive a quadratic equation. The quadratic equation is then solved to give an approximate formula for implied volatility in terms of the remaining Black–Scholes input parameters and the observed call price. We use Corrado and Miller's approximation as a starting value for the Newton–Raphson search in the BSOptionISDGoalSeekNR function.

This estimate is fairly accurate for a wide range of exercise prices that are relatively close to the current share price. With an exercise price of 95 and an observed option price of 15, the Corrado and Miller estimate of implied volatility is 41.10% in cell H4 compared to 41.28% calculated using the BSOptionISDGoalSeekNR function. However, for some extreme values, the linear approximation approach breaks down. You can demonstrate this by setting the volatility in cell B12 to 20.0%, then setting the observed option price in cell B17 to 7.7. The value of calc1 (one of the intermediate calculations in the Corrado and Miller approximation) in cell H9 becomes negative and the approximation fails.

For such values, Manaster and Koehler (1982) provide an alternative approach that selects a good starting point for the Goal Seek function. Their starting value (called a seed value) is chosen such that one of $N(d_1)$ or $N(d_2)$ equals 0.5. They show that, if a solution exists, then a search that starts from their seed value will find the correct implied volatility. In cases where the Corrado and Miller approach fails (such as for an observed option value of 7.7), the Manaster and Koehler seed value of 55.24% can be used. With this as the start value, the Newton–Raphson search produces successive improved estimates of the implied volatility, eventually reaching the correct value of 9.9%.

13.3   ADAPTING FOR SKEWNESS AND KURTOSIS

There is particular interest from practitioners in option pricing when log returns have different higher moments than the normal distribution assumed in the Black–Scholes formula. Rubinstein (1998) has shown how to adapt the binomial tree method to produce distributions with chosen values of skewness and kurtosis. His approach consists of two steps, which we illustrate for a European option in Figure 13.3 from the Edge sheet. First, a discrete distribution (adapted from the binomial) is generated using the so-called Edgeworth factors, which build in the required skewness and kurtosis. Second, the expectation of the option payoff is calculated using a distribution of share prices (generated from the adapted binomial values) and the Edgeworth probabilities.

	A	B	C	D	E	F	G	H	I	J
2	Generating an Edgeworth distribution							f' & xj		f' & x'j
3										
4	nstep	16			non-neg		Mean	0.00		0.00
5					1		Var	0.91		1.00
6	ξ (skew)	**0.00**			modes		Skew	0.00		0.00
7	κ (kurt)	**5.40**			1		Kurt	3.97		4.85
8										
9						Σ f (xj)		Σ f' (xj)		
10						0.9875		1.0000		
11		init nodes		Bnl probs	Edge facts	init E probs		final E probs		final nodes
12	j	xj		b (xj)	a (xj)	f (xj)		f' (xj)		x'j
13										
14	0	-4.00		0.0000	17.30	0.0003		0.0003		-4.20
15	1	-3.50		0.0002	8.96	0.0022		0.0022		-3.68
16	2	-3.00		0.0018	4.00	0.0073		0.0074		-3.15
17	3	-2.50		0.0085	1.46	0.0124		0.0126		-2.63
18	4	-2.00		0.0278	0.50	0.0139		0.0141		-2.10
19	5	-1.50		0.0667	0.46	0.0304		0.0308		-1.58
20	6	-1.00		0.1222	0.80	0.0978		0.0990		-1.05
21	7	-0.50		0.1746	1.16	0.2018		0.2044		-0.53
22	8	0.00		0.1964	1.30	0.2553		0.2585		0.00
23	9	0.50		0.1746	1.16	0.2018		0.2044		0.53
24	10	1.00		0.1222	0.80	0.0978		0.0990		1.05
25	11	1.50		0.0667	0.46	0.0304		0.0308		1.58
26	12	2.00		0.0278	0.50	0.0139		0.0141		2.10
27	13	2.50		0.0085	1.46	0.0124		0.0126		2.63
28	14	3.00		0.0018	4.00	0.0073		0.0074		3.15
29	15	3.50		0.0002	8.96	0.0022		0.0022		3.68
30	16	4.00		0.0000	17.30	0.0003		0.0003		4.20

Figure 13.3 Generating an Edgeworth distribution with known skewness and kurtosis

We demonstrated (in the JRBinomial sheet of the OPTION1 workbook) how a continuous standard normal distribution could be approximated by a discrete binomial one. We also showed (in the JREuro sheet of the same workbook) how the option could be valued as the discounted expectation of the option payoff values each weighted by its associated nodal probability.

The Edgeworth distribution consists of a sequence of nodes with associated probabilities as shown in Figure 13.3. Since we have chosen to illustrate the process with a 16-step binomial model, the initial nodes range from −4 to +4 standard deviations from the mean. The binomial nodal probabilities in column D are multiplied by the Edgeworth expansion terms in column E to generate the adjusted probability distribution in column F. This adjusted distribution is then rescaled in column H, ensuring that the revised probability distribution now sums to one (confirmed in cell H10). The Edgeworth distribution now has third and fourth moments (in cells H6 and H7 respectively) that should be close to the chosen values in cells B6 and B7. Lastly, the initial node values in column B are adjusted in column J to ensure that the Edgeworth distribution has mean 0 and standard deviation 1. This completes the first step of Rubinstein's approach.

For a symmetric distribution with excess kurtosis (here with skewness $= 0.0$ and kurtosis $= 5.4$), the Edgeworth adjustment increases the probabilities of extreme events (say more than 2 standard deviations away from the mean) at the expense of the more central parts of the distribution. The chart in Figure 13.4 shows the full effect. By redistributing the density from the centre to the extremes, we would expect to see a reduction in the value of the option as compared with the Black–Scholes value.

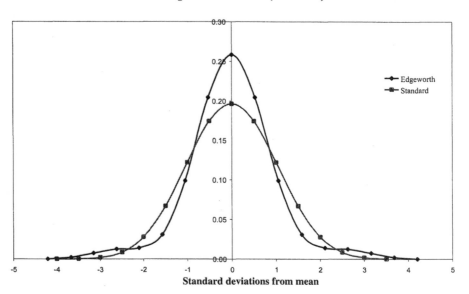

Figure 13.4　An Edgeworth distribution with kurtosis of 5.4 compared to standard normal

So far, we have been working with a standardised distribution with mean 0 and variance 1. We need to adjust it to ensure that the distribution of the share price has the appropriate risk-neutral mean and variance. When the log share price is normally distributed, the annualised drift in mean equals $r - q - 0.5\sigma^2$, in this case 0.03 (as shown in Figure 13.5, cell D44). For departures from strict normality, the appropriate value (here 0.0299) is labelled Edgeworth risk-neutral drift or RNdrift E and calculated in cell D45.

We can now proceed to the second step of option valuation illustrated in Figure 13.5, using the nodes (copied to cells D49 to D65) and the probabilities (in cells H49 to H65) calculated from the first step. The discrete distribution of share prices is in column E, with the call payoffs adjacent in column F. The expectation, using the adjusted Edgeworth probability distribution, is calculated in column J. The resulting call value of 9.37 is given in cell J35. As expected, this is less than the Black–Scholes value of 9.73.

Checking back to earlier results for this call assuming strict normality, if the skewness parameter in cell B6 is set to 0.0 and the kurtosis parameter in cell B7 to 3.0, the Edgeworth call value is seen to be very close to the Black–Scholes value. The slight difference arises because the share price model in this sheet uses only 16 binomial steps to approximate the continuous lognormal distribution.

	A	B	C	D	E	F	G	H	I	J
33	Valuing an Option based on Edgeworth Distribution									
34										
35	Share price (S)			100.00			Edgeworth call value			9.37
36	Exercise price (X)			95.00				via function		9.37
37	Int rate-cont (r)			8.00%						
38	Dividend yield (q)			3.00%			BS call value			9.73
39	Time now (0, years)			0.00						
40	Time maturity (T, years)			0.50						
41	Option life (T, years)			0.50						
42	Volatility (σ)			20.00%						
43										
44		RNdrift LN		0.0300						
45		RNdrift E		0.0299						
46										
47		j	components	x'j	Sj	payoff		f'(xj)		f'(xj)*payoff
48			of expectation	final nodes				final E probs		
49		0	0.0001	-4.20	56.01	0.00		0.0003		0.00
50		1	0.0013	-3.68	60.33	0.00		0.0022		0.00
51		2	0.0047	-3.15	64.99	0.00		0.0074		0.00
52		3	0.0087	-2.63	70.00	0.00		0.0126		0.00
53		4	0.0104	-2.10	75.40	0.00		0.0141		0.00
54		5	0.0246	-1.58	81.22	0.00		0.0308		0.00
55		6	0.0853	-1.05	87.49	0.00		0.0990		0.00
56		7	0.1897	-0.53	94.24	0.00		0.2044		0.00
57		8	0.2585	0.00	101.51	6.51		0.2585		1.68
58		9	0.2202	0.53	109.34	14.34		0.2044		2.93
59		10	0.1149	1.05	117.78	22.78		0.0990		2.25
60		11	0.0385	1.58	126.86	31.86		0.0308		0.98
61		12	0.0189	2.10	136.65	41.65		0.0141		0.59
62		13	0.0183	2.63	147.20	52.20		0.0126		0.66
63		14	0.0116	3.15	158.55	63.55		0.0074		0.47
64		15	0.0037	3.68	170.79	75.79		0.0022		0.17
65		16	0.0005	4.20	183.97	88.97		0.0003		0.02

Figure 13.5 Valuing a call using an Edgeworth distribution for share price in sheet Edge

For reasons of space, we have illustrated the Edgeworth option valuation approach using only 16 steps. Rubinstein suggests that at least 100 steps should be used to give accurate results. This is easily implemented by using the user-defined EdgeworthEuroOptionValue function with the required number of steps specified as an input. The function is used in cell J36.

13.4   THE VOLATILITY SMILE

If the call values obtained assuming the Edgeworth distribution are compared with their Black–Scholes values, we can use the results to illustrate the so-called 'volatility smile'. A volatility smile is a chart of the implied volatility of an option as a function of its exercise price. If the distribution assumptions of Black–Scholes were exactly true, the observed volatility smile would be a straight line. The Smile sheet in the OPTION4.xls workbook illustrates the approach, and Figure 13.6 is an extract from this sheet.

In the previous section, the call value where the share has excess kurtosis and a volatility of 20.0% was shown to be 9.37 based on the appropriate Edgeworth distribution for a 16-step tree. This result is displayed in cell J10 of the Smile sheet and labelled EDGE(S,X,σ) to indicate the valuation method and parameters. Looking at cell J13 in Figure 13.6, we see that the Black–Scholes call value for a volatility of 18.45% is also 9.37. This implied volatility (of 18.45%, labelled EDGE ISD) has been calculated in cell J12 using the BSOptionISDGoalSeekNR function, with the option price set equal to the Edgeworth call value.

	A	B	C	D	E	F	G	H	I	J
2	Estimating Implied Volatility (or ISD) in Edgeworth Option Values									
3										
4	Share price (S)			100.00			iopt			1
5	Exercise price (X)			95.00						
6	Int rate-cont (r)			8.00%			nstep			16
7										
8	Dividend yield (q)			3.00%						
9	Time now (0, years)			0.0000			BS (S,X,σ)			9.73
10	Time maturity (T, years)			0.5000			EDGE (S,X,σ)			9.37
11	Option life (T, years)			0.5000						
12	Volatility (σ)			20.00%			EDGE ISD			18.45%
13							BS (S,X, EDGE ISD)			9.37
14	ξ (skew)			0.00						
15	κ (kurt)			5.40						

Figure 13.6   Similar call values for lognormal and non-lognormal prices in Smile sheet

Thus two different sets of assumptions produce the same call value: either strict normality with share price volatility of 18.45% or excess kurtosis in log returns coupled with a volatility of 20.0%. Hence observed differences in option prices may reflect deviations from strict normality in the process followed by log share returns rather than differences in estimates of future volatilities.

By repeating the calculation of Edgeworth option values and implied volatilities for a range of exercise prices (shown in Figure 13.7, column E), a picture of the volatility smile can be generated from the chosen values for skewness and kurtosis. The chosen exercise values centre on the 'at-the-money' exercise price, that is, the discounted value of X (here 92.65 in cell B22). They range from −2.5 standard deviations to 2.5 standard deviations either side of the 'at-the-money' exercise price of the original option.

	A	B	C	D	E	F	G	H	I	J
19	Illustrating the Volatility Smile									
20					Option Values				Volatility Smile	
21										
22	X at-money	92.65			# sd	X	BS	Edge		BS	Edge
23										
24	# sd	0.00			-2.5	65.06	36.00	36.01		20.0%	23.6%
25					-2.0	69.83	31.43	31.48		20.0%	24.1%
26	X	92.65			-1.5	74.94	26.56	26.67		20.0%	23.7%
27					-1.0	80.44	21.45	21.58		20.0%	22.1%
28					-0.5	86.33	16.26	16.28		20.0%	20.2%
29	BS (S,X,σ)	11.33			0.0	92.65	11.33	11.10		20.0%	18.9%
30	EDGE (S,X,σ)	11.10			0.5	99.44	7.08	6.69		20.0%	18.5%
31					1.0	106.73	3.88	3.58		20.0%	18.9%
32	EDGE ISD	18.9%			1.5	114.55	1.82	1.82		20.0%	20.0%
33	BS (S,X, EDGE ISD)	11.10			2.0	122.94	0.72	0.97		20.0%	21.7%
34					2.5	131.95	0.23	0.53		20.0%	23.6%

Figure 13.7   Comparing volatility under BS assumptions and Edgeworth values

Call values for each exercise price are obtained assuming an Edgeworth distribution (in column G) and then the implied volatility calculated in column J via the BSOption ISDGoalSeekNR function. The chart in Figure 13.8 plots the implied volatility against the exercise price, showing the volatility smile.

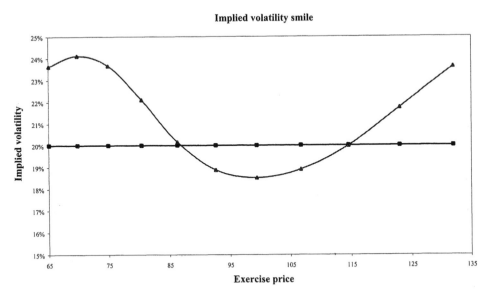

Figure 13.8   Volatility smile from data in Smile sheet

By choosing the particular skewness and kurtosis parameters given in Figure 13.6, in conjunction with the Edgeworth option valuation method, we have produced the smile illustrated in Figure 13.8. By judicious choice of other parameter values combined with the Edgeworth valuation method, we can replicate different shapes of volatility smile.

13.5   USER-DEFINED FUNCTIONS IN Module1

There are two functions that reinforce the assumption of lognormality that underlies the Black–Scholes option valuation. The first, LNOptionValue0, uses the moments of the normal distribution. The second, LNOptionValue, instead uses the moments of the lognormal distribution:

```
Function LNOptionValue0(iopt, M, V, X, r, tyr)
'  returns lognormal option value (iopt=1 for call, -1 for put)
    Dim d1, d2, Nd1, Nd2
    d2 = (M - Log(X)) / Sqr(V)
    d1 = d2 + Sqr(V)
    Nd1 = Application.NormSDist(iopt * d1)
    Nd2 = Application.NormSDist(iopt * d2)
    LNOptionValue0 = Exp(-r * tyr) * iopt * (Exp(M + 0.5 * V) * Nd1 - X * Nd2)
End Function

Function LNOptionValue(iopt, M1, M2, X, r, tyr)
'  returns lognormal option value (iopt=1 for call, -1 for put)
```

```
'  uses LNOptionValue0 fn
   Dim M, V
   M = 2 * Log(M1) - 0.5 * Log(M2)
   V = Log(M2) - 2 * Log(M1)
   LNOptionValue = LNOptionValue0(iopt, M, V, X, r, tyr)
End Function
```

The RGOptionValue function follows in a similar fashion, the prominent difference being the replacement of the lognormal distribution with the reciprocal gamma distribution (the latter using the GAMMADIST function from Excel, where the TRUE parameter ensures that the cumulative distribution function is calculated):

```
Function RGOptionValue(iopt, M1, M2, X, r, tyr)
'  returns reciprocal gamma option value (iopt=1 for call, -1 for put)
   Dim alpha, beta, g1, g2
   alpha = (2 * M2 - M1 ^ 2) / (M2 - M1 ^ 2)
   beta = (M2 - M1 ^ 2) / (M1 * M2)
   g1 = Application.GammaDist(1 / X, alpha - 1, beta, True)
   If iopt = -1 Then g1 = 1 - g1
   g2 = Application.GammaDist(1 / X, alpha, beta, True)
   If iopt = -1 Then g2 = 1 - g2
   RGOptionValue = Exp(-r * tyr) * iopt * (M1 * g1 - X * g2)
End Function
```

The BSOptionISDGoalSeekNR function uses the Corrado and Miller estimate as a close starting point for the Newton–Raphson search (denoted sigmanow below). When the Corrado and Miller method fails (sigmanow $= -1$), the seed value suggested by Manaster and Koehler is used instead:

```
   atol = 0.0001
   sigmanow = BSOptionISDEstimate(iopt, S, X, r, q, tyr, optprice)
'  when above fails, start from Manaster & Koehler seed value
   If sigmanow < = 0 Then sigmanow = Sqr(2 * Abs(Log(S / X) + (r - q) * tyr) / tyr)
   Do
      fval = BSOptionValue(iopt, S, X, r, q, tyr, sigmanow) - optprice
      fdashval = BSOptionVega(iopt, S, X, r, q, tyr, sigmanow)
      sigmanow = sigmanow - (fval / fdashval)
   Loop While Abs(fval) > atol
   BSOptionISDGoalSeekNR = sigmanow
```

The EdgeworthEuroOptionValue function is a little more comprehensive than the corresponding Edge spreadsheet. Tests for the probability density function to have no negative entries (via PDFnonneg) and only a single mode (via PDFmodes) are incorporated. After such a failure, the Edgeworth expansion is replaced by the Gram–Charlier expansion instead. If the tests are not passed at this stage the option valuation method fails, returning a value of -1.

```
   For j = 1 To n
      xvec(j) = (2 * (j - 1) - nstep) / Sqr(nstep)
      bvec(j) = Application.Combin(nstep, j - 1) * ((0.5) ^ nstep)
   Next j
'  Edgeworth expansion used for pdf
   For j = 1 To n
      xj = xvec(j)
      c = 1 + skewco * (xj ^ 3 - 3 * xj) / 6 + (kurtco - 3) * (xj ^ 4 - 6 * xj ^ 2 + 3) / 24
```

```
    c = c + skewco^2 * (xj^6 - 15 * xj^4 + 45 * xj^2 - 15) / 72
    fvec(j) = c * bvec(j)
  Next j
  it1 = PDFnonneg(fvec)
  it2 = PDFmodes(fvec)
  If it1 < 0 Or it2 > 1.5 Then
' use Gram-Charlier expansion for pdf instead
    For j = 1 To n
      xj = xvec(j)
      c = 1 + skewco * (xj^3 - 3 * xj) / 6 + (kurtco - 3) * (xj^4 - 6 * xj^2 + 3) / 24
      fvec(j) = c * bvec(j)
    Next j
    it1 = PDFnonneg(fvec)
    it2 = PDFmodes(fvec)
  End If
  If it1 < 0 Or it2 > 1.5 Or kurtco < 3 Then
' method fails as pdf has non-negative entries or is not unimodal
    ve = -1
  Else
' minor adjustments to fvec and xvec
    frvec = PDFrescale(fvec)
    xsvec = Xvecstd(xvec, frvec)
```

Otherwise, the density function is adjusted and the binomial option value calculated as the discounted expectation of the option payoff. Rubinstein comments that the 100 binomial steps are generally more than adequate for option valuation:

```
' now start option valuation
    sum = 0
    For j = 1 To n
      sum = sum + frvec(j) * Exp(xsvec(j) * sigma * Sqr(tyr))
    Next j
' now calculate rnmu, risk-neutral expectation of ln(Sj/S)
    rnmu = r - q - (Log(sum)) / tyr
    ve = 0
' option value depends on share price (Sj) and risk-neutral pdf (frvec)
    For j = 1 To n
      Sj = S * Exp(rnmu * tyr + xsvec(j) * sigma * Sqr(tyr))
      ve = ve + frvec(j) * Application.Max(iopt * (Sj - X), 0)
    Next j
    ve = Exp(-r * tyr) * ve
  End If
  EdgeworthEuroOptionValue = ve
```

SUMMARY

Of the inputs to the Black–Scholes pricing formula, only the volatility cannot be directly measured. Instead, we can calculate the implied volatility, that is, the volatility which when used in the Black–Scholes formula gives the observed market price for the option. The Goal Seek facility in Excel can be set up to give the implied volatility, but a better approach is to apply a user-defined function.

The Black–Scholes model assumes that the probability distribution of share price S_T is lognormal. In fact, empirical studies suggest that the distribution tends to have fatter tails and possibly some asymmetry (that is, some skewness and kurtosis). Rubinstein has shown how to adapt the binomial tree method to produce distributions with chosen values of skewness and kurtosis. His approach consists of generating a different discrete probability distribution (the Edgeworth distribution) for the share price tree which matches the first four moments.

Whilst the normal distribution remains the cornerstone of option valuation, departures from normality are seen in the markets for traded options. This has given rise to the term volatility smile. When the probability distribution of share price S_T is not lognormal, implied volatilities will differ from those given by Black–Scholes. The plot of the volatility of an option as a function of its exercise price displays the so-called 'volatility smile'.

REFERENCES

Corrado, C. J. and T. W. Miller, 1996, "A Note on a Simple, Accurate Formula to Compute Implied Standard Deviations", *Journal of Banking and Finance*, **20**, 595–603.

Manaster, S. and G. Koehler, 1982, "The Calculation of Implied Variances from the Black–Scholes Model", *Journal of Finance*, **37**(1), 227–230.

Milevsky, M. A. and S. E. Posner, 1998, "Asian Options: The Sum of Lognormals and the Reciprocal Gamma Distribution", *Journal of Financial and Quantitative Analysis*, **33**(3), 409–422.

Rubinstein, M., 1998, "Edgeworth Binomial Trees", *Journal of Derivatives*, **5**(3), 20–27 (also see correction: **5**(4), 6).

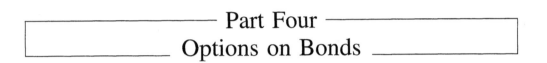

Part Four
Options on Bonds

Introduction to Valuing Options on Bonds

Valuing options on bonds is more complex than valuing derivatives on equities, since we are dealing with the term structure of interest rates. The term structure represents how the pattern of interest rates varies with bond maturity. The term structure is estimated from the prices of all bonds with different maturities that make up the bond market. The process of estimation is complicated in that most traded bonds consist of a stream of coupon payments (typically twice a year) followed by repayment of the face value of the bond at maturity. However some bonds repay the face value only with no intermediate coupons and these are known as zero-coupon bonds.

There are three distinct ways to allow for the term structure when valuing options on bonds: (i) ignore the term structure; (ii) model the term structure; and (iii) match the term structure. Valuing options on bonds has developed from attempts to adapt the Black–Scholes formula (the first way) through continuous models of interest rates (the second way) and is now centred on discrete models of interest rates that match the term structure (the third way).

In this chapter, we start by discussing the term structure of interest rates and the requirement to value coupon bond cash flows using appropriate discount factors. We describe how a simple binomial tree of interest rates can be devised to match the price of a zero-coupon bond in the market. Finally, Black's formula for the valuation of bond options is described. This approach ignores the term structure by assuming instead that the forward price of the bond is distributed lognormally.

Chapter 15 on interest rate models concentrates on the Vasicek model and the Cox, Ingersoll and Ross (CIR) model for the instantaneous short rate. These stochastic models produce a set of interest rates from which 'model-based' prices for zero-coupon bonds of different maturities can be generated. The advantage of such models is that they lead to analytic solutions for the valuation of options on zero-coupon bonds, which in turn allow us to value options on coupon bonds.

The Vasicek and CIR models, in their simplest form, generate a possible term structure but are not capable of matching an observed term structure. Chapter 16 on matching the term structure shows how binomial trees are used to model the distribution of interest rates in such a way as to correctly value zero-coupon bonds (and also the associated term structure of volatilities). Two simple binomial trees are constructed, one assuming lognormally distributed interest rates and the other normal interest rates. The construction of a Black, Derman and Toy (BDT) tree is outlined. The BDT tree, a development of the simple lognormal tree, is the most popular choice amongst practitioners, and we use it to illustrate the valuation of options on zero-coupon bonds.

Although valuing options on bonds is a complex process, the option valuation task should be familiar by now. Valuation involves obtaining the risk-neutral expectation of the option payoff at the time of expiry and employs familiar numerical methods such as binomial trees.

For ease of exposition we limit ourselves to single-factor models of the term structure and to market-derived zero yields and their volatility. We assume that interest rates compound continuously, except in the case of the BDT tree where we introduce rates in discretely compounded form.

The models are implemented in Excel files BOND1 and BOND2. The Excel skills are broadly familiar, with Goal Seek used in the valuation of options on coupon bonds and in the building of short-rate trees. Since many of the formulas are somewhat intricate, it is helpful to implement them via user-defined functions, which are available in the Module sheets of the workbooks.

Some related reading is available in Bodie et al. (1996), Chapters 13 and 14 on bond prices and yields, and the term structure of interest rates, also in Hull's (2000) text, Chapter 21 on interest rate derivatives. An alternative source is Clewlow and Strickland's (1998) text on options. Particular material covered by us that is new to textbooks includes the valuation of bond options using the CIR model (involving the non-central chi-squared distribution function).

14.1 THE TERM STRUCTURE OF INTEREST RATES

Figure 14.1 shows a collection of prices for zero-coupon bonds (or 'zero prices') with maturities between one and 10 years in the Intro sheet of workbook BOND1.xls.

	A	B	C	D	E	F	G	H	I	J
2	Term Structure of Interesr Rates									
3		Maturity		Zero Price		Zero Yields		Forward Rates		Zero Yields
4						(continuous)		(continuous)		(discrete)
5		1		0.941		6.08%		6.08%		6.27%
6		2		0.885		6.11%		6.14%		6.30%
7		3		0.830		6.21%		6.42%		6.41%
8		4		0.777		6.31%		6.60%		6.51%
9		5		0.726		6.40%		6.79%		6.61%
10		6		0.677		6.50%		6.99%		6.72%
11		7		0.630		6.60%		7.20%		6.82%
12		8		0.585		6.70%		7.41%		6.93%
13		9		0.542		6.81%		7.63%		7.04%
14		10		0.502		6.89%		7.67%		7.13%
15						=-LN (D5) / B5		=-LN (D6/D5)		= EXP (F5) -1

Figure 14.1   Prices for zero-coupon bonds, with zero yields and forward rates calculated

Each zero price can be converted into an equivalent zero yield with continuous compounding, because of the relationship:

$$\text{zero price} = (1)\exp(-rt)$$

where t is the bond's time to maturity at which the face value of 1 is repaid and r is the zero yield. (We use the term 'zero yield' for the rate of interest over the period from now, time 0, to time t implied by the relevant zero-coupon bond's price.) Hence the cell formula in cell F5. The collection of zero yields for different maturities is known as the term structure of interest rates. Thus the zero yield for one year is 6.08%, whereas the zero yield for 10 years is 6.89%. Apart from the one-year zero yield, the remainder of the zero yields span multiple time periods.

The information in the term structure can equivalently be expressed as a sequence of forward rates, as in column H. The forward rate of 6.14% in cell H6 represents the implied rate for borrowing during the second year (a single period), and is calculated using the zero prices for maturities of one and two years. The zero yields and forward rates are illustrated in Figure 14.2 (see Chart1 in the workbook). Thus the information found in the term structure of interest rates can be expressed in one of three equivalent ways: using zero prices, zero yields or forward rates.

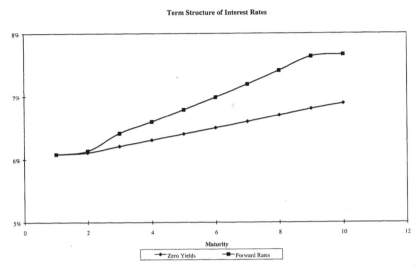

Figure 14.2   Zero yields and forward rates implied by zero-coupon bond prices (Chart1)

14.2   CASH FLOWS FOR COUPON BONDS AND YIELD TO MATURITY

Most traded bonds have regular coupon payments as well as the repayment of their face value at maturity. As an illustration, Figure 14.3 shows the cash flows for a bond with unit face value that matures in 10 years, with annual coupons of 5% (set out in range H25:H34 of the Intro sheet).

	A	B	C	D	E	F	G	H	I	J
17	Valuing Coupon Bonds									
18	0 (nowyr)	0				Bond value		Bond yield		Bond value
19	s (zeroyr)	10				(using zero prices)		to maturity		(using ytm)
20	Bond Face Value (L)	1.00				0.857		6.81%		0.857
21	Bond Coupon (cL)	0.05						(continuous compounding)		
22				Zero Price		PV Bond		Bond Cash Flows		PV Bond
23						Cash Flows				Cash Flows
24		0						-0.86		
25		1		0.941		0.05		0.05		0.05
26		2		0.885		0.04		0.05		0.04
27		3		0.830		0.04		0.05		0.04
28		4		0.777		0.04		0.05		0.04
29		5		0.726		0.04		0.05		0.04
30		6		0.677		0.03		0.05		0.03
31		7		0.630		0.03		0.05		0.03
32		8		0.585		0.03		0.05		0.03
33		9		0.542		0.03		0.05		0.03
34		10		0.502		0.53		1.05		0.53

Figure 14.3   Valuing a coupon bond using zero prices and calculating yield to maturity

With the same set of zero prices defining the term structure (column D), the present value of the bond is simply the sum of the present values of the individual cash flows (in column F). The sum is 0.857 (in cell F20), which should equal the market price of the bond.

Using the market price (as the initial cash outflow in cell H24) and the sequence of cash inflows (as in column H), it is straightforward to calculate the yield-to-maturity for the coupon bond. The yield-to-maturity is defined as the internal rate of return of all the bond's cash flows, including the initial cash outflow. It can be calculated using Excel's IRR function. In fact, the IRR function returns the yield appropriate for discrete compounding. This can be converted into a continuously compounded yield, as done in cell H20 with the formula:

$$=LN(1+IRR(H24:H34))$$

In column J, the bond cash flows are all discounted using the yield-to-maturity, and as can be seen in cell J20, their sum also comes to 0.857.

There is no difficulty in calculating the yield-to-maturity. However, the question is its appropriateness in valuing the cash flows from a bond. In using the yield-to-maturity, we are assuming that payments received at different times can be discounted using a single interest rate. Furthermore, there will be different yield-to-maturity estimates for the different coupon bonds in the market. It is much better to use interest rates that differ according to the time of payments, that is, the term structure of interest rates.

14.3   BINOMIAL TREES

Since bond valuation depends crucially on interest rates that are uncertain, models that incorporate the probabilistic nature of interest rates are required. Just as binomial trees were employed to capture the stochastic nature of share prices in valuing options on shares, we can construct binomial trees to model the uncertain nature of interest rates. Options on bonds can then be valued using these interest rate trees. The approach is illustrated in Figure 14.4. The short rates in the interest rate tree (cells B46:E49) are supposed to reflect the way the zero yields will develop over the next four years. The interest rate for the first period is 6.08% (simply the zero yield on a one-year bond), while for the second period it is assumed to be either 7.17% or 5.11% with equal probability, and so on. The aim is to choose rates in the tree so that the four-year zero-coupon bond price in cell A52 matches the four-year zero price of 0.777 (from cell D8).

In this simplified example, the short rate values in the tree are assumed to be known, up and down moves at any time point being equally probable (cells B39 and B40). The rates can be used to value cash flows, in a similar manner to the process adopted in the valuation of equity options. (In Chapter 16, we discuss how the interest rate values in the tree include assumptions about the volatility of the zero yields. Here we assume this part of the analysis has been completed.)

The cash flow for a four-year zero-coupon bond is its face value (1) at the end of four years whatever the sequence of short rates the bond has experienced. This terminal cash flow (shown in cells E52 to E56 at the conclusion of each path through the tree) is discounted back using the rates relevant to the particular path in the tree.

For example, discounting back one period, the cell formula in cell D52:

$$=(\$B\$39*E52+\$B\$40*E53)/EXP(E46)$$

uses a discount factor depending on the equivalent cell in the interest rate tree (E46) rather than the constant discount factor used for valuing options on equities. Copying the above formula back through the bond valuation tree, the four-year zero price of 0.777 is obtained.

	A	B	C	D	E	F
37	Valuing Zero-Coupon Bonds using Binomial Trees					
38						
39	p		0.5			
40	p*		0.5			
41						
42	Time (years)					
43		0	1	2	3	4
44						
45	Tree for Evolution of Short Rates					
46			6.08%	7.17%	8.64%	10.08%
47				5.11%	6.28%	7.46%
48					4.56%	5.53%
49						4.10%
50				=($B$39*E52+$B$40*E53)/EXP(E46)		
51	Tree for Zero-Coupon Bond Valuation					
52		0.777	0.80	0.84	**0.90**	1.00
53			0.85	0.88	0.93	1.00
54				0.91	0.95	1.00
55					0.96	1.00
56						1.00

Figure 14.4 Using a binomial tree of short rates to value a zero-coupon bond in Intro sheet

The key point to observe at this introductory stage is that it is possible to build a binomial tree for interest rates that is capable of matching the term structure (here in the form of one zero price).

14.4 BLACK'S BOND OPTION VALUATION FORMULA

The first approach to valuing options on zero-coupon bonds was described by Black (1976). We have already encountered his formula, in the context of valuing options on futures (section 11.3). Black assumed that the forward bond price at option maturity was lognormally distributed. This allows the modified Black–Scholes formula to be used.

In Figure 14.5, Black's formula is used to value a four-year option ($T = 4$) on a zero-coupon bond with face value 1 and a 10-year maturity ($s = 10$). The appropriate forward bond price in cell B64 is calculated by multiplying the face value by the ratio of the zero prices for 10 and four years, i.e. the cell formula is =B61*(B63/B62).

The option has an exercise price of 0.6, the short-term interest rate is assumed to be 6% and the volatility of the forward bond price is assumed to be 3%. The formulas for d_1 and d_2 are the same as for options on futures, giving the call a value of 0.038.

Black's formula is included here to illustrate the earliest approach to valuing bond options, and should only be used for options with a short time to expiry relative to the time to maturity of the bond. In the next two chapters, more sophisticated approaches to the valuation of bond options are illustrated.

	A	B	C	D	E
59	**Valuing European Options on Zero-Coupon Bonds (Black 76)**				
60					
61	Bond Face Value (L)	**1.00**		iopt	**1**
62	P(0,T)	0.78		option	call
63	P(0,s)	0.50			
64	Forward Price (F)	**0.65**		value	0.038
65	Exercise Price (X)	**0.60**		via fn	0.038
66	Int rate-cont (r)	**6.00%**			
67					
68	0 (nowyr)	0.00		d_1	1.26
69	T (optyr)	**4.00**		$N(d_1)$	0.90
70	Option life	4.00			
71	s (zeroyr)	**10.00**		d_2	1.20
72				$N(d_2)$	0.89
73	Volatility (σ)	**3.00%**			
74					

Figure 14.5   Black's approach to valuing options on zero-coupon bonds in Intro sheet

14.5   DURATION AND CONVEXITY

For a zero-coupon bond there is an exact link between bond value and yield-to-maturity since, in this special case, the maturity of the bond and the centre of gravity of the bond cash flows coincide. Duration, calculated as the weighted average of the present values of individual cash flows from the bond (the repayment of principal and any coupons), represents the location of this centre of gravity (expressed in years). For coupon bonds there is no longer the exact link between bond value and yield-to-maturity. However, we can then use duration (here viewed as the slope, or first derivative, of the value–yield relationship at the given yield) and convexity (here viewed as the curvature, or second derivative, of the value–yield relationship) to estimate the scale of changes in bond value that would follow from a change in bond yields.

	A	B	C	D	E	F	G	H	I
76	**Calculating Duration of Coupon Bonds**								
77									
78	Bond Face Value (L)	1.00			Year	CFs	PV factor	PV CFs	Year *PV CFs
79	Annual Coupon (cpct)	0.05							
80	0 (nowyr)	0			1	0.050	0.934	0.047	0.047
81	s (zeroyr)	10			2	0.050	0.873	0.044	0.087
82	Coupons per year (coupyr)	1			3	0.050	0.815	0.041	0.122
83	Bond ytm (discrete comp)	7.04%			4	0.050	0.762	0.038	0.152
84					5	0.050	0.712	0.036	0.178
85	Coupon (cper)	0.05			6	0.050	0.665	0.033	0.199
86	Bond value	0.857			7	0.050	0.621	0.031	0.217
87					8	0.050	0.580	0.029	0.232
88	Macaulay duration	7.93			9	0.050	0.542	0.027	0.244
89	Macaulay duration via fn	7.93			10	1.050	0.506	1.532	5.316
90									
91							Sum	0.857	6.795

Figure 14.6   Calculating duration

One important caveat is that such analysis presumes that only parallel shifts in the term structure will take place, and this is a serious weakness to the use of such estimates. Despite this drawback, duration and convexity are much used by practitioners and this is the reason for their inclusion in this chapter. Using the example of the 10-year bond, with an annual coupon of 5% and current yield-to-maturity of 7.04% (using discrete compounding), the calculations are shown in Figure 14.6. The original (Macaulay) measure of duration is calculated as the sum of the time-weighted present values of the individual cash flows (from cell I91) divided by the bond value (from cell H91). This calculation can be replicated in a closed-form formula (due to Chua, 1984) that forms the ChuaBondDuration VBA user-defined function. Practitioners typically use an alternative (Modified) measure of duration that is equal to the Macaulay duration divided by 1 plus the yield-to-maturity. The ChuaBondDuration function returns the Modified measure of duration when the parameter imod takes the value 1 (as used in cell B95).

We go on to illustrate how to estimate changes in bond value for a given change in yield-to-maturity, using modified duration (from cell B95) and convexity (from cell B97), as shown in Figure 14.7. The calculation of convexity is a little more complicated than duration, but can be found by using the closed-form formula (due to Blake and Orszag, 1996) that is used in the BlakeOrszagConvexity user-defined function. The formula in cell B101 presumes that the percentage change in bond value can be estimated as the change in yield-to-maturity times minus modified duration plus the change in yield squared times one-half convexity. For an increase in yield of 0.01 (in cell B99) the bond price would be estimated to fall by 7.06% to the new value of 0.7963 (in cell B103). This approximation compares with the actual value of 0.7962 (from cell H110, as the sum of the present value of bond cash flows using the revised yield-to-maturity of 8.04% from cell G95). Thus, where we are happy to assume that parallel changes in the yield curve are appropriate, the combination of duration and convexity provides a very good estimate of the likely change in bond value.

	A	B	C	D	E	F	G	H
93	Using Duration and Convexiry to Estimate Impact of Change in YTM							
94								
95	Modified duration via fn	7.41				New ytm	8.04%	
96								
97	Convexiry via fn	70.09			Year	CFs	PV factor	PV CFs
98								
99	Change in yield	0.01			1	0.05	0.926	0.047
100					2	0.05	0.857	0.043
101	Bond price % change	−7.06%			3	0.05	0.793	0.040
102					4	0.05	0.734	0.037
103	New bond value (estimate)	0.7963			5	0.05	0.679	0.034
104					6	0.05	0.629	0.031
105					7	0.05	0.582	0.029
106					8	0.05	0.539	0.027
107					9	0.05	0.498	0.025
108					10	1.05	0.461	0.484
109								
110							New bond value (actual)	0.7962

Figure 14.7 Estimating the impact on bond value of changes in yield

14.6 NOTATION

So far, the simple models in the Intro sheet have not required much additional notation. However, in Chapter 15 and the remaining sheets of the BOND1.xls workbook, some simplifying notation is necessary. In particular, the time structure involves time to maturity for bonds and time to exercise for options on bonds.

Generally it is assumed that time now is equivalent to $t = 0$, with options expiring at time $t = T$ and zero-coupon bonds maturing at time $t = s$.

$P(0, s)$ denotes the price at time 0 of a zero-coupon bond maturing at time s (that is, paying 1 at time s), which is also called the zero price. Note that $P(0, s)$ can also be thought of as a discount factor, the discount factor being $\exp(-rs)$ assuming continuous discounting at fixed interest rate r.

$R(0, s)$ denotes the zero-coupon bond yield over the period from time 0 to time s. Unless otherwise stated, this rate will be the continuously-compounded annual rate.

SUMMARY

In this chapter, we use the word 'yield' to describe the rate per annum over a specified time period. A numerical example shows how the yields for zero-coupon bonds are obtained from their current prices (the 'zero prices'). These are the so-called 'zero yields' and are estimates of the term structure of interest rates.

Usually, bonds have coupons and their current prices reflect the value of the expected stream of cash flows (that include periodic coupon payments and ultimately the repayment of the face value). In the past, the yield-to-maturity (or internal rate of return) of the cash flows has been regarded as a valuation measure. However, the discounting of cash flows should use the zero yields, not the somewhat arbitrary yield-to-maturity.

The earliest approach to the valuation of options on bonds is due to Black, whose formula is an extension of the famous Black–Scholes formula using the forward price of the bond. However, the assumptions underlying the approach are regarded as unlikely to hold for bonds, except in somewhat restricted circumstances.

In preparation for Chapter 16, we have shown how binomial trees of interest rates can match a given term structure. Assuming that such interest rate trees can be built, they provide a familiar numerical method for valuing options on bonds.

REFERENCES

Black, F., 1976, "The Pricing of Commodity Contracts", *Journal of Financial Economics*, **3**, 167–179.

Blake, D. and J. M. Orszag, 1996, "A Closed-Form Formula for Calculating Bond Convexity", *Journal of Fixed Income*, **June**, 88–91.

Bodie, Z., A. Kane and A. Marcus, 1996, *Investments*, 3rd edition, Richard D. Irwin, Englewood Cliffs, NJ.

Chua, J. H., 1984, "A Closed-Form Formula for Calculating Bond Duration", *Financial Analysts Journal*, **May/June**, 76–78.

Clewlow, L. and C. Strickland, 1998, *Implementing Derivatives Models*, John Wiley & Sons, Chichester.

Hull, J. C., 2000, *Options, Futures and Other Derivatives*, Prentice Hall, New Jersey.

Interest Rate Models

This chapter concentrates on the valuation of zero-coupon bonds using an interest rate model. In this approach, changes in the short rate are captured in a stochastic model which generates a term structure of zero-coupon prices. This approach via an interest rate model produces analytic solutions for zero-coupon prices. Jamshidian (1989) has suggested how the zero prices can be used to value options on zero-coupon bonds and additionally options on coupon bonds.

We look at two leading interest rate models, those of Vasicek (1977) and of Cox, Ingersoll and Ross (CIR; Cox et al., 1985). Both models assume that the risk-neutral process for the (instantaneous) short rate r is stochastic, with one source of uncertainty. The stochastic process includes drift and volatility parameters which depend only on the short rate r, and not on time. The short rate model involves a number of variables, and different parameter choices for these variables will lead to different shapes for the term structure generated from the model.

Both of the interest rate models feature 'so-called' mean reversion of the short rate, that is, a tendency for the short rate to drift back to some underlying rate. This is an observed feature of the way interest rates appear to vary. The two models differ in the handling of volatility. We start with Vasicek's model, and then consider the CIR model. Both the accompanying spreadsheets (the Vasicek and the CIR sheets) in the BOND1 workbook have the same format and use the same numerical example.

15.1 VASICEK'S TERM STRUCTURE MODEL

Vasicek's model for the changes in short rate r is stochastic and of the form:

$$\mathrm{d}r = a(b - r)\,\mathrm{d}t + \sigma_r\,\mathrm{d}z$$

Thus a small change ($\mathrm{d}r$) in the short rate in time increment $\mathrm{d}t$ includes a drift back to mean level b at rate a for the short rate. The second volatility term involves uncertainty, $\mathrm{d}z$ representing a normally distributed variate with zero mean and variance $\mathrm{d}t$. The short rate r (strictly $r(t)$) is assumed to be the instantaneous rate at time t appropriate for continuous compounding.

When valuing options on equities, the underlying approach is to obtain the discounted expected value in a risk-neutral world of the option payoff. Equivalently, the current value of a share can be viewed as the discounted value in a risk-neutral world of its future expected value. Exactly the same principle applies to bonds and bond option payoffs. In the case of an option on a zero-coupon bond, the value at time t of 1 to be received at time s can be expressed as:

$$P(t, s) = E^Q \left[\exp\left(- \int r(u)\,\mathrm{d}u \right)1 \right]$$

where the integral is over the time interval from lower limit t to upper limit s and the notation E^Q denotes risk-neutral expectation.

For equity options, interest rates are assumed to be constant so the term involving the integral of the short rate can be taken outside the expectation, in that it reduces to the discount factor $\exp[-r(s - t)]$. Therefore for equity options, valuation depends on calculating the risk-neutral expected value of the appropriate payoff, the interest rate term $\exp[-r(s - t)]$ being the constant discount factor.

For options on zero-coupon bonds, the model equation for the short rate has to be combined into the expectation expression for $P(t, s)$. Because of the probabilistic short rates, the interest rate term can no longer be factored outside the expectation.

Given Vasicek's choice of model for the short rate, an analytic solution can be found for the integral and thus for the price of the zero-coupon bond, namely:

$$P(t, s) = A(t, s)\exp[-B(t, s)r(t)]$$

where $r(t)$ is the value of the short rate r at time t

$$B(t, s) = \{1 - \exp[-a(s - t)]\}/a$$

$$A(t, s) = \exp(\{[(B(t, s) - (s - t)](a^2 b - \sigma_r^2/2)\}/a^2 - \sigma_r^2 B(t, s)^2/4a)$$

In the special case when $a = 0$, the expressions for A and B simplify to:

$$B(t, s) = (s - t) \quad \text{and} \quad A(t, s) = \exp[\sigma_r^2(s - t)^3/6]$$

These quantities are most easily calculated in a spreadsheet. Figure 15.1 shows an extract from the Vasicek sheet of the BOND1.xls workbook.

	A	B	C	D	E
2	Vasicek Model : see Hull (4th Edition) p567-9				
3	RN model	dr = a(b-r) dt + σ_r dz			
4					
5	a	0.1779		Zero-coupon bond price	
6	b	0.0866		P(0,s)	0.4867
7	r	6.00%		via fn	0.4867
8	0 (nowyr)	0.00			
9	s (zeroyr)	10.00		Zero yield	
10	zero life	10.00		R(0,s)	7.20%
11	σ_r	2.00%		via fn	7.20%
12					
13	B(0,s)	4.6722		Zero yield (infinite maturity)	
14	A(0,s)	0.6442		R(∞)	8.02%
15					
16				Volatility of zero yield	
17				σ_R(0,s)	0.93%

Figure 15.1 Zero-coupon bond prices, zero yields and volatilities for Vasicek

Vasicek's model requires the current value of the short rate (r) supplemented with three parameters (a, b and σ_r) that must be estimated from historic data. As our base case, we use the parameter values for a, b and σ_r that match those for the one-month treasury bill yield, estimated using US data from 1964 to 1989 by Chan et al. (1992).

In the Figure 15.1 example, the initial short rate is 6%, with the underlying rate to which r reverts of 0.0866 (8.66%) in cell B6. The model is set up to give zero-coupon bond prices for up to 10 years ahead (in general s). Cells B13 and B14 contain the formulas for $B(0, s)$ and $A(0, s)$ from which the price of the zero-coupon bond with maturity s years, $P(0, s)$ in cell E6, is constructed. This means that Vasicek's model evaluates the present value of each unit to be received in s years time (currently $s = 10$ years) at 0.4867. From the zero price, the associated zero yield can be derived, here equal to 7.20%.

The yield for a bond with an infinite maturity, denoted $R(\infty)$ in cell E14, is 8.02%. This value is lower than, though connected to, the chosen value for the parameter b (the level to which the short rate reverts). The formula for the volatility of the short rate is given in cell E17, showing that the 10-year zero yield has a volatility of 0.93% compared to the chosen short rate volatility of 2%.

It is informative to construct a Data Table, evaluating the zero yield and its volatility for different values of s from 0 up to 30 say. The column of zero yields representing the term structure when charted should correspond to the lowest curve in Figure 15.2 (also see Chart 2 in the workbook).

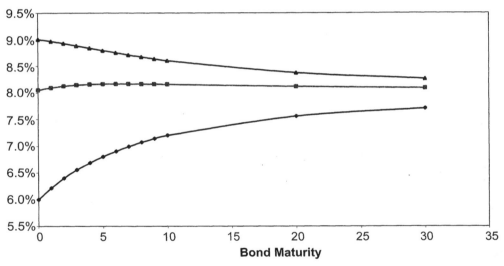

Figure 15.2   Term structure for different values of r

As in Figure 15.2, the term structure of zero yields can take one of three possible shapes, depending on the value of the current short rate in cell B7. The possible shapes are monotonically increasing (when r is less than $R(\infty)$), humped or monotonically decreasing (when r is greater than b). You can check this by changing the value of r and switching to Chart 2 in the workbook. For example, by changing the value of r in cell B7 to 9% the chart should display a monotonically decreasing term structure, whilst a value of 8.05% for r should produce a humped term structure.

One problem with Vasicek's interest rate model is that sometimes it gives rise to negative short rates. See an example in Figure 15.3 which shows a simulation of Vasicek's model with $a = 0.3$ in cell B5. This problem does not arise with the CIR interest rate model. However, before investigating this alternative model for interest rates, the valuation of options on zero-coupon bonds is explored.

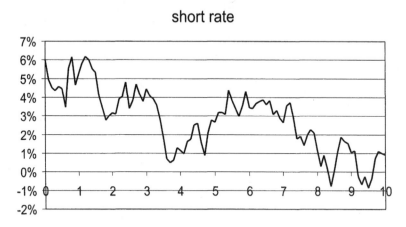

Figure 15.3   One simulation of short rates given by Vasicek's model

15.2   VALUING EUROPEAN OPTIONS ON ZERO-COUPON BONDS, VASICEK'S MODEL

The formula for the valuation of options on zero-coupon bonds in the Vasicek sheet is due to Jamshidian (1989). Jamshidian's formula is best viewed as an application of the lognormal option formula seen previously in section 13.1. [The only difference in the formula is the replacement of the discount factor $\exp(-rT)$ with the equivalent zero-coupon bond price $P(0, T)$.] His contribution was to determine formulas for M and V corresponding to the forward bond price on which the option is based.

The price at time 0 of a European call with exercise price X expiring at time T on a zero-coupon bond with maturity s and principal L is:

$$c = P(0, T)[\exp(M + 0.5V)N(d_1) - XN(d_2)]$$

where:

$$M = \ln[LP(0, s)/P(0, T)] - 0.5\sigma_p^{\,2}$$

$$V = \sigma_p^{\,2}$$

$$d_2 = [M - \ln(X)]/\sqrt{V}$$

$$d_1 = d_2 + \sqrt{V}$$

$$\sigma_p = v(0, T)B(T, s)$$

$$v(0, T) = \sigma_r \sqrt{\{[1 - \exp(-2aT)]/2a\}}$$

$$B(T, s) = \{1 - \exp[-a(s - T)]\}/a$$

Note that when $a = 0$, the volatility component $v(0, T)$ simplifies to $\sigma_r\sqrt{T}$ and $B(T, s)$ to $s - T$.

Figure 15.4 shows the calculations to get the option value. The two prices for zero-coupon bonds $P(0, T)$ and $P(0, s)$ have been evaluated in cells E27 and E28, here via the user-defined function VasicekCIRZeroValue. (They can also be obtained from cell E6 with the appropriate maturity times.) There are intermediate calculations for volatility σ_P and for M and V in the spreadsheet. The resulting value of the call maturing in four years on the 10-year zero-coupon bond is 0.037 in cell H26. In H27, the same result is obtained via a second user-defined function.

	A	B	C	D	E	F	G	H
21	Valuing European Options on Zero-Coupon Bonds (Jamshidian)							
22								
23	a	0.1779		Bond Face Value (L)	1.00		iopt	1
24	b	0.0866		Option Exercise Price (X)	0.60		option	call
25	r	6.00%						
26							Option value	0.037
27	0 (nowyr)	0.00		P(0,T)	0.7652		via fn	0.037
28	T (optyr)	4.00		P(0,s)	0.4867			
29	s (zeroyr)	10.00		v(0,T)	0.0292		M	-0.4583
30				B(T,s)	3.6880		V	0.0116
31	σ_r	2.00%		σ_P	10.77%			
32							d_1	0.5953
33							d_2	0.4876
34								
35							N (d_1)	0.7242
36							N (d_2)	0.6871

Figure 15.4 Jamshidian's valuation for a zero-coupon bond

Increasing the short rate volatility (in cell B11) from 2% up to 4% increases the option value to 0.076.

15.3 VALUING EUROPEAN OPTIONS ON COUPON BONDS, VASICEK'S MODEL

Jamshidian also derived a more general method for valuing options on coupon bonds. The key insight is that an option on a coupon bond can be decomposed into separate zero-coupon options on each of the cash flows from the bond due after the expiry of the option. With our example of a four-year option on a 10-year bond with annual coupons, there will be coupons for years 5 to 10 to consider, together with the return of the bond face value in year 10. In Figure 15.5, the relevant cash flows (Lj) are shown in cells E51 to E56, in total 1.30 (the sum of the face value and the six coupons from the bond after the expiry of the option). We need to find an interest rate (say r^*) that reduces the present value of these payments to match the exercise price of the option (0.6 in cell E43). Finding the value of r^* is a matter of trial and error, here accomplished with the user-defined function named Jamshidianrstar.

	A	B	C	D	E	F	G	H
39	**Valuing European Options on Coupon-Bearing Bonds (Jamshidian)**							
40								
41	a	0.1779		Bond Face Value (L)	**1.00**		iopt	1
42	b	0.0866		Bond Coupon (cL)	**0.05**		option	call
43	r	6.00%		Option Exercise Price (X)	**0.60**			
44	0 (nowyr)	0.00					Option value	0.206
45	T (optyr)	4.00					via fn	0.206
46	s (zeroyr)	10.00		r* via fn	18.30%			
47	(coupyr)	1.00		r* exercise price	0.60			
48	σ_r	2.00%						
49								
50			T	sj	P(r*,T,sj)	Lj	Strike (Xj)	Option values
51		1	4.0	5.0	0.8396	0.05	0.0420	0.00
52		2	4.0	6.0	0.7154	0.05	0.0358	0.01
53		3	4.0	7.0	0.6172	0.05	0.0309	0.01
54		4	4.0	8.0	0.5382	0.05	0.0269	0.01
55		5	4.0	9.0	0.4735	0.05	0.0237	0.01
56		6	4.0	10.0	0.4198	1.05	0.4408	0.17

Figure 15.5   Valuing options on coupon-paying bonds using Jamshidian's approach

You can confirm that the calculated value for r^* (18.30% in cell E46) does ensure that the present value of the bond payments (summed in cell E47) agrees with the chosen strike price for the option in cell E43. The value of the option on the coupon bond is simply the sum of the values of the separate zero-coupon options–the separate options use the appropriate values of Lj, Xj and sj in the VasicekZeroOptionValue function. Note though that the interest rate used for the separate option values is the original short rate (here 6%) rather than r^*.

15.4   CIR TERM STRUCTURE MODEL

The main difference between the Vasicek and the CIR models is the way that the volatility of the short rate is modelled. In the CIR model, volatility depends also on the square root of the short rate and this ensures that the short rate does not go negative.

Hence in the CIR model, the risk-neutral process for the short rate is a stochastic process of the form:

$$dr = a(b - r)\,dt + \sigma\sqrt{r}\,dz$$

Here we see that the volatility of the short rate [$\sigma_r = \sigma\sqrt{r}$] increases with the square root of the level of the short rate. This model prevents the occurrence of negative interest rates (as long as the parameter values satisfy the relationship $2ab \geqslant \sigma^2$).

Figure 15.6 shows the CIR model for pricing zero-coupon bonds in the CIR sheet. As can be seen, the layout here and throughout the sheet is similar to the Vasicek sheet.

	A	B	C	D	E
2	Cox, Ingersoll and Ross Model : see Hull (4th edition) p570				
3	RN model	dr = a(b-r) dt + σ sqrt(r) dz			
4					
5	a	0.2339		Zero-coupon bond price	
6	b	0.0808		P(0,s)	0.4926
7	r	6.00%		via fn	0.4926
8	0 (nowyr)	0.00			
9	s (zeroyr)	10.00		Zero yield	
10	zero life	10.00		R(0,s)	7.08%
11	σ	0.0854		via fn	7.08%
12					
13	γ	0.2633		Zero yield (infinite maturity)	
14	exp(γ(s-0))-1	12.9108		R(∞)	7.60%
15	B(0,s)	3.7178			
16	A(0,s)	0.6156		Volatility of zero yield	
17				σ_R(0,s)	0.78%

Figure 15.6   Zero-coupon bond prices, zero yields and volatilities for CIR model

Cox, Ingersoll and Ross showed that bond prices have the same general form as in Vasicek, the formula for the price of a zero-coupon bond paying 1 at time s, $P(t, s)$, being:

$$P(t, s) = A(t, s) \exp[-B(t, s)r(t)]$$

where $r(t)$ is the value of r at time t. The functions $B(0, s)$ and $A(0, s)$ have somewhat different forms, which involve a new parameter, γ. Using the CIR interest rate model, the 10-year zero-coupon bond is valued at 0.4926, the 10-year zero yield being 7.08%. Once again, via a Data Table the zero yields can be plotted for different values of s, as in Chart3 of the workbook. The same range of possible shapes for the term structure can be achieved as with Vasicek.

15.5   VALUING EUROPEAN OPTIONS ON ZERO-COUPON BONDS, CIR MODEL

To value a CIR zero-coupon option requires the calculation of the distribution function of the non-central chi-squared distribution (instead of the normal distribution used in Black–Scholes and in Vasicek's pricing formula). Since the CIR formula is rather complicated and thus normally omitted from textbooks, we prefer to see our main task as ensuring that the formulas in the spreadsheet and the associated function return the correct values. Those of a brave disposition are very welcome to delve into the original CIR paper, as well as the paper by Schroder (1989) in which he gives an approximation for the necessary distribution function. Figure 15.7 shows the procedures for valuing options on zero-coupon bonds, the value of the four-year call on the 10-year zero-coupon bond being 0.040 (in cell H26). This same value is obtained in cell H27 via a user-defined function.

	A	B	C	D	E	F	G	H
21	Valuing European Options on Zero-Coupon Bonds (CIR)							
22								
23	a	0.2339		Bond Face Value (L)	1.00		iopt	1
24	b	0.0808		Option Exercise Price (X)	0.60		option	call
25	r	6.00%						
26							Option value	0.040
27	0 (nowyr)	0.00		P(0,T)	0.7660		via fn	0.040
28	T (optyr)	4.00		P(0,s)	0.4926			
29	s (zeroyr)	10.00					chi1	0.8079
30				calc1	2.4421		chi2	0.7794
31	σ	0.0854		A(T,s)	0.8012		c11	20.14
32				B(T,s)	3.1555		c2	10.36
33	γ	0.2633		φ	38.6449		c31	4.67
34				ψ	68.1050		c12	19.56
35				r*	0.0916		c2	10.36
36							c32	4.81

Figure 15.7   Valuing options on zero-coupon bonds using CIR model

15.6   VALUING EUROPEAN OPTIONS ON COUPON BONDS, CIR MODEL

We value options on coupon bonds with the CIR model using the approach suggested by Jamshidian, used earlier in the chapter with the Vasicek model. Again, the option on the coupon bond can be viewed as separate options on the cash flows between option expiry and bond maturity. Each of the separate options can be valued as an option on a zero-coupon bond. Jamshidian's contribution is in finding an interest rate r^* such that the sum of the exercise prices of the separate options equals the exercise price of the option on the coupon bond.

Figure 15.8 shows the procedure. The interest rate in cell E47 is 20.31%, evaluated using the Jamshidianrstar function. The value of the option on the coupon bond is the sum of the individual options on the separate zero-coupon bonds, the final call value being 0.212 in cell H44. (Under Vasicek's model, the option value was slightly lower at 0.206 in Figure 15.5.)

	A	B	C	D	E	F	G	H
39	Valuing European Options on Coupon-Bearing Bonds (Jamshidian)							
40								
41	a	0.2339		Bond Face Value (L)	1.00		iopt	1
42	b	0.0808		Bond Coupon (cL)	0.05		option	call
43	r	6.00%		Option Exercise Price (X)	0.60			
44	0 (nowyr)	0.00					Option value	0.212
45	T (optyr)	4.00		γ	0.2633		via fn	0.212
46	s (zeroyr)	10.00						
47	(coupyr)	1.00		r* via fn	20.31%			
48	σ	0.0854		r* exercise price	0.60			
49								
50			T	sj	P(r*,T,sj)	Lj	Strike (Xj)	Option values
51		1	4.0	5.0	0.8273	0.05	0.0414	0.00
52		2	4.0	6.0	0.7008	0.05	0.0350	0.01
53		3	4.0	7.0	0.6051	0.05	0.0303	0.01
54		4	4.0	8.0	0.5306	0.05	0.0265	0.01
55		5	4.0	9.0	0.4710	0.05	0.0236	0.01
56		6	4.0	10.0	0.4222	1.05	0.4433	0.18

Figure 15.8   Valuing options on coupon-paying bonds using Jamshidian's approach

15.7   USER-DEFINED FUNCTIONS IN Module1

Since the Vasicek and CIR models share common elements, it makes sense to write a single function, allowing both the Vasicek (with imod=1) and the CIR (with imod=2) calculations. In common with the spreadsheet, the function also allows for the case when $a = 0$ by using If statements:

```
Function VasicekCIRZeroValue(imod, a, b, r, nowyr, zeroyr, sigma)
'  returns the Vasicek (imod=1) or CIR (imod=2) zero-coupon bond value
   Dim syr, sig2, Asyr, Bsyr, rinf, gamma, c1, c2
   syr = zeroyr - nowyr
   sig2 = sigma^2
   If imod = 1 Then
     If a = 0 Then
       Bsyr = syr
       Asyr = Exp((sig2 * syr^3) / 6)
     Else
       Bsyr =(1 - Exp(-a * syr)) / a
       rinf = b - 0.5 * sig2 / (a^2)
       Asyr = Exp((Bsyr-syr) * rinf - ((sig2 * Bsyr^2) /(4 * a)))
     End If
   ElseIf imod = 2 Then
     gamma = Sqr(a^2 + 2 * sig2)
     c1 = 0.5 * (a + gamma)
     c2 = c1 * (Exp(gamma * syr) - 1) + gamma
     Bsyr = (Exp(gamma * syr) - 1) / c2
     Asyr = ((gamma * Exp(c1 * syr)) / c2)^(2 * a * b / sig2)
   End If
   VasicekCIRZeroValue = Asyr * Exp(-Bsyr * r)
End Function
```

The following function incorporates the required zero prices using the above function and then proceeds to calculate the lognormal parameters M and V. The subsequent lines of code are the same as for the LNOptionValue0 function in OPTION2.xls, with the zero price replacing the discount factor:

```
Function VasicekZeroOptionValue(iopt, L, X, a, b, r, nowyr, optyr, zeroyr, sigma)
'  returns the Vasicek zero-coupon bond option value
'  uses VasicekCIRZeroValue fn
   Dim P0T, P0s, v0T, BTs, sigmap, M, V, d2, d1, Nd1, Nd2
   P0T = VasicekCIRZeroValue(1, a, b, r, nowyr, optyr, sigma)
   P0s = VasicekCIRZeroValue(1, a, b, r, nowyr, zeroyr, sigma)
   If a = 0 Then
     v0T = sigma * Sqr(optyr - nowyr)
     BTs = zeroyr - optyr
   Else
     v0T = Sqr(sigma^2 * (1 - Exp(-2 * a * (optyr - nowyr))) /(2 * a))
     BTs = (1 - Exp(-a * (zeroyr - optyr))) / a
   End If
   sigmap = v0T * BTs
   M = Log(L * P0s / P0T) - 0.5 * sigmap * 2
   V = sigmap^2
   d2 = (M - Log(X)) / Sqr(V)
   d1 = d2 + Sqr(V)
   Nd1 = Application.NormSDist(iopt * d1)
```

```
Nd2 = Application.NormSDist(iopt * d2)
VasicekZeroOptionValue = P0T * iopt * (Exp(M + 0.5 * V) * Nd1 - X * Nd2)
End Function
```

The following function is attempting to vary the interest rate when used to value the payments from the coupon bond payable after the option matures in order to match the exercise price of the option. In the absence of an analytic formula for the slope, we approximate the slope by using a difference formula:

```
Function Jamshidianrstar(imod, L, cL, X, a, b, rtest, optyr, zeroyr, coupyr, sigma, radj)
' replicates Goal Seek to find rstar in Vasicek or CIR coupon option value
' uses VasicekCIRBondnpv fn
  Dim atol, rnow, fr1, fr, fdashr
  atol = 0.0000001
  rnow = rtest
  Do
    fr1 = VasicekCIRBondnpv(imod, L, cL, a, b, rnow + radj, optyr, zeroyr, coupyr, sigma) - X
    fr = VasicekCIRBondnpv(imod, L, cL, a, b, rnow, optyr, zeroyr, coupyr, sigma)-X
    fdashr = (fr1 - fr) / radj
    rnow = rnow - (fr / fdashr)
  Loop While Abs(fr) > atol
  Jamshidianrstar = rnow
End Function
```

The formula underlying the approximation of the distribution function for the non-central chi-squared distribution can be seen in the Schroder paper. [However, note that his equation (10) gives $c3$ in the function rather than the correct $N(c3)$.]

```
Function CIRSankaranQ(z, nu, kappa)
' component for CIR Option Valuation (see Schroder)
  Dim n, k, h, p, m, c1, c2, c3
  n = nu
  k = kappa
  h = 1 - (2 / 3) * (n + k) * (n + 3 * k) / (n + 2 * k)^2
  p = (n + 2 * k) / (n + k)^2
  m = (h - 1) * (1 - 3 * h)
  c1 = 1 - h + 0.5 * (2 - h) * m * p
  c2 = 1 - h * p * c1 - (z / (n + k))^h
  c3 = c2 / (h * Sqr(2 * p * (1 + m * p)))
  CIRSankaranQ = Application.NormSDist(c3)
End Function
```

SUMMARY

The interest rate models of Vasicek and CIR were the earliest attempts to model interest rates and so generate a possible term structure (via analytic solutions for zero-coupon bond prices). The ultimate goal was to provide analytic solutions allowing the valuation of options on zero-coupon bonds, and thereby improve on adaptations of the Black–Scholes approach that essentially ignored the term structure. By varying the choice of parameters, both the models can generate a variety of patterns for the term structure. The CIR model explicitly links the volatility of interest rates to their level, a feature that is missing in Vasicek's model. Jamshidian showed how the formulas for options on zero-coupon bonds could be extended to allow for options on coupon bonds. These models remain important for their analytic solutions, but have to a great extent been superseded by the approach of matching the term structure, to be covered in the next chapter.

REFERENCES

Chan, K. C., G. A. Karolyi, F. A. Longstaff and A. B. Sanders, 1992, "An Empirical Comparison of Alternative Models of the Short-Term Interest Rate", *Journal of Finance*, **47**, 1209–1227.

Cox, J. C., J. E. Ingersoll and S. A. Ross, 1985, "A Theory of the Term Structure of Interest Rates", *Econometrica*, **53**, 385–407.

Jamshidian, F., 1989, "An Exact Bond Option Formula", *Journal of Finance*, **44**, 205–209

Schroder, M., 1989, "Computing the Constant Elasticity of Variance Option Pricing Formula", *Journal of Finance*, **44**, 211–219.

Vasicek, O. A., 1977, "An Equilibrium Characterisation of the Term Structure", *Journal of Financial Economics*, **5**, 177–188.

16
Matching the Term Structure

In the previous chapter, the starting point was the continuous stochastic models for the short rate of Vasicek and Cox, Ingersoll and Ross. From these models, analytic solutions were obtained for zero-coupon bond prices and subsequently methods developed for valuing options on bonds. In this chapter by contrast we model the short rate using a discrete binomial tree. By so doing, we can match a given term structure of zero-coupon prices and subsequently derive tree-based values for options on bonds.

In section 14.3, we used an example of an interest rate tree that allowed the matching of zero prices. In this chapter, we describe how such a rate tree can be calculated so that it matches the term structure and the associated volatilities. The price we pay, in computational terms, is that analytic solutions are no longer available and an iterative approach is needed to develop the binomial tree for the short rate.

When building binomial trees for equity options, the starting point involves two known values, the current share price S and the (risk-free) interest rate r, from which a distribution of share prices at the expiry date for the option is generated. The binomial tree is then used to value options, or indeed any pattern of cash flows that can be associated with the nodes in the tree.

With binomial trees for interest rate options, the two known values are the current zero-coupon value P and the cash flow at maturity (equal to 1) from which a binomial tree of interest rates is to be generated. The binomial tree is built up from the current short rate and at each subsequent time step an iterative process ensures that the tree up to and including the present time step can be used to match the appropriate zero-coupon bond price seen in the market. At each time step in the tree, the rates in the cross-section are linked together by a formula that reflects the local volatility. We can then solve for the remaining unknown rate to ensure that the interest rate tree correctly prices the zero-coupon bond corresponding to that time step in the tree. Thus the tree, unlike share price trees, has a drift that varies at each time step. This solution process is done in time-series fashion with increasing time steps until bond maturity is reached.

The associated models are in the BOND2.xls workbook. There are two relatively simple sheets (LnNormal and Normal) and two using the more complicated Black, Derman and Toy tree (one illustrating the building of the tree and the second using the tree to value a zero-coupon option). The simple trees use continuously-compounded interest rates while the BDT trees use discretely-compounded interest rates.

16.1 TREES WITH LOGNORMALLY DISTRIBUTED INTEREST RATES

Figure 16.1 shows the zero-coupon bond prices for different maturities (and hence the current term structure of interest rates) and also volatilities. The rate tree which has been calculated to be consistent with the zero prices and short-rate volatilities is shown in range B48:E51. In fact, the bond prices and volatilities shown in columns H and J have been derived from this rate tree as a demonstration of consistency. We now explain how the rate tree has been obtained.

	A	B	C	D	E	F	G	H	I	J	K
47	Short-rate tree via fn		LnNormally distributed short rates					Zero Price		Ln Short Rate Volatility	
48		6.08%	7.17%	8.64%	10.08%		1	0.941			
49		0.00%	5.11%	6.28%	7.46%		2	0.885		0.1700	
50		0.00%	0.00%	4.56%	5.53%		3	0.830		0.1600	
51		0.00%	0.00%	0.00%	4.10%		4	0.777		0.1500	

Figure 16.1 Final rate tree, demonstrated to be consistent with zero prices and volatilities

Figure 16.2 shows the same initial market information on zero prices and short-rate volatilities together with a two-period short-rate tree and a two-period price tree for a two-year bond, face value 1. The periods are of length one year.

	A	B	C	D	E	F	G	H	I	J	K
2		Binomial Term Structure Models									
3		LnNormally distributed short rates									
4								Ln Short Rate			
5		Maturity		Zero Price		Zero Yield		Volatility		Face (L)	1.00
6		1		0.941		6.08%				delt	1.00
7		2		0.885		6.11%		0.17		p	0.50
8		3		0.830		6.21%		0.16		p*	0.50
9		4		0.777		6.31%		0.15			
10											
11	Short-rate tree : two periods										
12		6.08%	7.00%	=ru						Using Goal Seek	
13			4.98%	=rd						Set cell	B18
14				=C12*EXP(-2*$H$7)						To value	0.00
15	Zero price tree : two periods			=($K$7*D16+$K$8*D17)/EXP(C12)						Changing	C12
16		0.886	0.93	1.00							
17			0.95	1.00							
18	test value	0.132		1.00							
19				=100*(B16-D7)							

Figure 16.2 Prices and yields for zero-coupon bonds with volatilities for short rates

In the lognormal tree, the cross-sectional relationship to be satisfied by the interest rates in adjacent cells at each time step i is:

$$\ln(r_u/r_d) = 2\sigma(i)$$

This relationship can be rewritten as $r_d = r_u \exp[-2\sigma(i)]$ which explains the formula in cell C13. We then use the two-period short-rate tree to value the cash flows of a two-period zero-coupon bond. Bonds are priced in the zero price tree assuming that up and down interest rates are equally likely and discounting using the respective rates in the short-rate tree.

For example, starting with the one-year rate r of 6.08% in cell B12, the short rate has an equiprobable chance of increasing to r_u or decreasing to r_d in the following period. With a trial value of 7% for r_u in C12, the formula in cell C13, linking to the interest rate in cell C12 and the short-rate volatility in cell H7, produces a value for r_d of 4.98%. When these rates are used to price the bond in the two-period price tree, the two-year zero price is 0.886. Note the formula in cell C16, which is the discounted expected value of the bond one year before maturity if the rate increases, discounted using the C12 (here 7%) rate.

The problem now involves one unknown element (C12, currently 7%) in the per period rate tree and one known bond price (here the two-year zero price of 0.885 in cell D7).

For consistency, the value in cell C12 needs changing such that the B16 cell formula evaluates to 0.885, or a better way, the B18 test value (which is the difference between the two-year zero price and cell B16, multiplied by 100 to aid convergence) needs to be zero. To do this, we use Goal Seek in the bond price tree, by setting cell B18 to a value of 0 by changing the value of C12 in the rate tree. As Figure 16.3 shows, the value in cell C12 changes from 7% to 7.17%. The price tree incorporates equal probabilities for up and down moves and a valuation formula at each node that is very similar to that used in trees for equity option valuation.

The rate tree is built forwards in time, starting with time step 2 (since the first zero yield can be used at step 1) and ending with the time step representing the maturity of the bond on which we wish to value the option, with the Goal Seek operation carried out at each step. The Goal Seek operation ensures that the drift of the tree at each time step matches the drift implied by the equivalent market zero-coupon price.

	A	B	C	D	E	F	G	H	I	J	K
11	Short-rate tree : two periods									**Using Goal Seek**	
12		6.08%	**7.17%**	=ru						Set cell	B18
13			5.11%	=rd						To value	0.00
14					=C12*EXP(-2*$H$7)					Changing	C12
15	Zero price tree : two periods				=($K$7*D16+$K$8*D17)/EXP(C12)						
16		0.885	**0.93**	1.00							
17			0.95	1.00							
18	test value	**0.000**		1.00							
19					=100*(B16-D7)						

Figure 16.3 Finding short-rate tree entries with Goal Seek to produce correct zero price of 0.885

The complete four-period rate tree, shown in Figure 16.4, can be achieved in this step-by-step manner. However, it is easier to use the BinZeroRateTree function, shown initially in Figure 16.1. The zero prices (in H48:H51) and short-rate volatilities (in J48:J50) resulting from the rate tree exactly match the prices and volatilities used to build the tree.

	A	B	C	D	E	F	G	H	I	J	K
21	Short-rate tree : three periods									**Using Goal Seek**	
22		6.08%	7.17%	8.64%	=ruu					Set cell	B29
23			5.10%	6.28%	=rud					To value	0.00
24				4.56%	=rdd					Changing	D22
25											
26	Zero price tree : three periods										
27		0.830	0.86	**0.92**	1.00						
28			0.90	0.94	1.00						
29	test value	**0.000**		0.96	1.00						
30					1.00						
31											
32											
33	Short-rate tree : four periods									**Using Goal Seek**	
34		6.08%	7.17%	8.64%	10.08%	=ruuu				Set cell	B42
35			5.10%	6.28%	7.46%	=rudu				To value	0.00
36				4.56%	5.53%	=rddu				Changing	E34
37					4.10%	=rddd					
38											
39	Zero price tree : four periods										
40		0.777	0.80	0.84	**0.90**	1.00					
41			0.85	0.88	0.93	1.00					
42	test value	**0.000**		0.91	0.95	1.00					
43					0.96	1.00					
44						1.00					

Figure 16.4 Completing short-rate tree with Goal Seek to ensure consistency with zero prices

A more concise way to summarise the short-rate tree uses just two vectors. The **x** vector contains the highest interest rate for each of the time steps in the short-rate tree. The **k** vector contains the multiplicative link between the cross-sectional cells, corresponding to $\exp[-2\sigma(i)]$.

The process of building the tree by matching the sequence of bond prices would normally be made more efficient by instead calculating a tree of so-called Arrow–Debreu prices. However, the repeated applications of Goal Seek used here provide an easier route to understanding the process of building the tree.

We now have a short-rate binomial tree (matching the current term structure of zero prices and associated volatilities) that can be used to value options bonds.

16.2   TREES WITH NORMAL INTEREST RATES

The only difference between the calculations in the LogNormal sheet just described and the Normal sheet that follows is in the specification of the volatility relationship linking the short rates in the binomial tree. In the normal tree, the cross-sectional relationship to be satisfied by the interest rates in adjacent cells at each time step i is:

$$r_u - r_d = 2\sigma(i)$$

which can be rewritten as $r_d = r_u - 2\sigma(i)$ which explains the formula in cell C13 that sets up the additive link. Note that we are now trying to match the volatility of the short rate (in cells H7:H9). Thereafter the process of building the rate tree follows in exactly the same way as in the previous sheet (Figure 16.5).

	A	B	C	D	E	F	G	H	I	J	K
2		Binomial Term Structure Models									
3		Normally distributed short rates									
4								Short Rate			
5		Maturity		Zero Price		Zero Yield		Volatility		Face (L)	1.00
6		1		0.941		6.08%				delt	1.00
7		2		0.885		6.11%		0.0100		p	0.5
8		3		0.830		6.21%		0.0095		p*	0.5
9		4		0.777		6.31%		0.0090			
10											
11	Short-rate tree : two periods									Using Goal Seek	
12		6.08%	10.00%	=ru						Set cell	B18
13			8.00%	=rd						To value	0.00
14					=C12-2*$H$7					Changing	C12
15	Zero price tree : two periods				=($K$7*D16+$K$8*D17)/EXP(C12)						
16		0.860	0.90	1.00							
17			1.92	1.00							
18	test value	-0.025		1.00							
19					=B16-D7						

Figure 16.5   Building the short-rate tree assuming normally distributed short rates

The result is the rate tree as shown in Figure 16.6. The rate tree has been produced from the same BinZeroRateTree user-defined function. (The initial parameter in the function specifies whether rates are assumed normally or lognormally distributed.)

	A	B	C	D	E	F	G	H	I	J	K
47	Short-rate tree via fn		Normally distributed short rates					Zero Price		Short Rate Volatility	
48		6.08%	7.14%	8.33%	9.34%		1	0.941			
49		0.00%	5.14%	6.43%	7.54%		2	0.885		0.0100	
50		0.00%	0.00%	4.53%	5.74%		3	0.830		0.0095	
51		0.00%	0.00%	0.00%	3.94%		4	0.777		0.0090	

Figure 16.6   Interest rate tree calculated assuming normally distributed short rates

16.3   THE BDT TREE

The Black, Derman and Toy (BDT) tree follows on from the simplified lognormal tree, but with the difference that the short-rate tree now has to match the volatility of the zero yields as opposed to the volatility of the log short rates.

The LnNormal sheet contained the relationship:

$$\ln(r_u/r_d) = 2\sigma(i)$$

as the cross-sectional link between the short rates in the binomial tree and the short-rate volatility. In the BDT sheet, the BDT version of the lognormal tree is constructed, where the relationship:

$$\ln(y_u/y_d) = 2\sigma_R(i)$$

is the cross-sectional link between the yields in the BDT tree and the zero-yield volatility.

There are two implications: first, the sequential process of setting the short rate volatility then matching the drift is replaced by a single optimisation that attempts to simultaneously match the volatility and drift in the tree; second, the single optimisation does not give us an exact match to zero-coupon prices.

In Figure 16.7 the implementation of Jamshidian's (1991) method for fitting the BDT tree to zero yields and volatility is illustrated. The BDT sheet has two distinct sections: the entries in columns E to H match the zero-coupon yields while the entries in columns K to N match both the zero yields and the yield volatilities. Interest rates change from the continuously-compounded form used in previous sheets to the discretely-compounded form.

	A	B	C	D	E	F	G	H	I	J	K	L	M	N	O	P
2				Black, Derman & Toy Short-rate Tree (Jamshidian)												
3	delt	1.00		0	1	2	3	4								
4												1	2	3	4	
5	Zero yields, given				6.27%	6.30%	6.41%	6.51%								
6																
7	Zero prices, from given yields				0.9410	0.8850	0.8300	0.7770								
8																
9	Pu (guess / goal seek)					0.9000	0.8000	0.7500			Pu (solution) via fn		0.9310	0.8650	0.8029	
10	Pd					0.9810	0.9641	0.9014			Pd (solution)		0.9499	0.8991	0.8486	
11																
12	Zero prices, from Pu and Pd					0.8850	0.8300	0.7770								
13																
14																
15	Yield volatilities (σR(i)), given					17.00%	16.00%	15.00%								
16																
17	yu (from Pu)					11.11%	11.80%	10.06%			yu (solution)		7.41%	7.52%	7.59%	
18	yd (from Pd)					1.94%	1.85%	3.52%			yd (solution)		5.27%	5.46%	5.63%	
19																
20	Yield volatilities, from yu and yd					87.29%	92.77%	52.53%			Yield volatilities		17.00%	16.00%	15.00%	
21																
22	y test					-702.8561	-767.7268	-375.3433								
23																
24																
25	Kvec					5.7300	7.1321	0.9593			Kvec (solution)					
26	via fn					5.7300	7.1321	0.9593			via fn		1.4049	1.3511	1.2997	
27																
28	Xvec					10.77%	20.39%	6.40%			Xvec (solution)					
29	via fn					10.77%	20.39%	6.40%			via fn		7.39%	8.75%	9.85%	
30																
31	Short-rate tree										Short-rate tree (solution)					
32					6.27%	10.77%	20.39%	6.40%				6.27%	7.39%	8.75%	9.85%	
33						1.88%	2.86%	6.68%					5.26%	6.48%	7.58%	
34							0.40%	6.96%						4.80%	5.83%	
35								7.26%							4.49%	
36																
37	Zero price tree										Zero price tree (solution)					
38					0.7837	0.7627	0.7797	0.9398	1.0000			0.7776	0.8036	0.8459	0.9103	1.0000
39						0.9031	0.9102	0.9374	1.0000				0.8491	0.8802	0.9295	1.0000
40							0.9299	0.9349	1.0000					0.9075	0.9449	1.0000
41								0.9324	1.0000						0.9571	1.0000
42									1.0000							1.0000

Figure 16.7   Short rates given by BDT approach

A more detailed description of the tree-building process is given in Clewlow and Strickland (1998) using Arrow–Debreu state prices. Instead, we concentrate firstly on illuminating the differences between the BDT tree and the simple lognormal tree and secondly on confirming the close match of the term structure of zero prices and yield volatilities.

Using the layout in Figure 16.7, we build a four-period BDT tree to match the zero-coupon price in cell H7 of 0.7770. For comparison, the initial tree (using guesses for the values of P_u in the range F9:H9) values the four-year zero-coupon bond at 0.7837 (in cell E38) whilst the solution tree using Jamshidian's approach values the bond at 0.7776 (from cell L38).

The P_u and P_d vectors are necessary and sufficient for the matching of both the zero prices and the yield volatilities. The P_u and P_d vectors represent the zero-coupon bond value at the time step 1 (when the bond has three years to maturity) at the up step and down step respectively. Here the exact values of P_u and P_d are 0.8029 and 0.8486 (from cells O9 and O10), compared to the Jamshidian tree values of 0.8036 and 0.8491 (from cells M38 and M39).

Concentrating on the numbers in the first section in column F to H, note that the exact zero prices in row 7 (derived from the zero yields in row 5) agree with the estimated zero prices in row 12 (which depend principally on the values of P_u in row 9). However the estimated yield volatilities in row 20 do not yet match the exact zero yield volatilities given in row 15. We can use Goal Seek three times (column F, G then H), setting the y test value in row 22 to equal 0 by changing the P_u value in row 9. This should ensure that the yield volatilities are now matched. The resulting short-rate and zero price solution trees are given between rows 32 and 42 in columns L to P.

The zero price tree built using Jamshidian's method and annual time steps does not give an exact fit for the price of the four-year zero-coupon bond (0.7770 in cell H7), with 0.7837 in cell E38 from the initial values for P_u and 0.7776 in cell L38 from the solution. Bjerksund and Stensland (1996) show how greater accuracy can be achieved using additional iterations.

16.4   VALUING BOND OPTIONS USING BDT TREES

The purpose of building a binomial tree for the short rate is to allow us to build a tree for the associated zero price and subsequently to value options on the zero-coupon bond. The ZCBOption sheet uses the BDT tree to value European and American put options with expiry in four years on a zero-coupon bond with maturity in 10 years.

As shown in Figure 16.8, we continue using the sequence of zero-coupon yields (zvec in row 8) and yield volatilities (sigvec in row 9) extending out to year 10. We employ the user-defined array functions BDTKvec (in row 15) and BDTXvec (in row 16) to generate the short-rate tree. The values for steps 0 to 3 agree with the solution values seen in the short-rate tree from the previous BDT sheet. We then use the short-rate tree to build a price tree for the asset on which the option is written, a 10-year zero-coupon bond (Figure 16.9). This gives the bond a current value of 0.5042 (in cell B36) compared to the market price of 0.5020 (in cell L13).

The options are then valued in a similar way to equity options. The option payoffs at maturity (four years) are calculated from the zero prices and the option exercise price, and the option value is found by rolling back within the binomial tree to the current time.

	A	B	C	D	E	F	G	H	I	J	K	L	M
2	Pricing Options on Zero-Coupon Bonds using BDT Tree (Jamshidian)												
3													
4	delt	1.00			X	0.80							
5	r0	6.27%			iopt	-1							
6													
7													
8	Zvec		6.27%	6.30%	6.41%	6.51%	6.61%	6.72%	6.82%	6.93%	7.04%	7.13%	
9	Sigvec			17.00%	16.00%	15.00%	14.00%	13.00%	12.00%	11.00%	10.00%	9.00%	
10													
11	P_u vec via fn			0.9310	0.8650	0.8029	0.7445	0.6897	0.6384	0.5903	0.5453	0.5044	
12	P_d vec			0.9499	0.8991	0.8486	0.7985	0.7492	0.7006	0.6530	0.6066	0.5626	
13	P vec	1.0000	0.9410	0.8850	0.8300	0.7770	0.7260	0.6770	0.6300	0.5850	0.5420	0.5020	
14													
15	Kvec		1.4049	1.3511	1.2997	1.2509	1.2045	1.1604	1.1185	1.0786	1.0368		
16	Xvec		7.39%	8.75%	9.85%	10.72%	11.28%	11.47%	11.26%	10.67%	9.36%		
17													
18													
19	Short-rate tree												
20		0	1	2	3	4	5	6	7	8	9	10	
21	0	6.27%	7.39%	8.75%	9.85%	10.72%	11.28%	11.47%	11.26%	10.67%	9.36%		
22	1		5.26%	6.48%	7.58%	8.57%	9.36%	9.88%	10.07%	9.90%	9.03%		
23	2			4.80%	5.83%	6.85%	7.77%	8.51%	9.00%	9.18%	8.71%		
24	3				4.49%	5.48%	6.45%	7.34%	8.05%	8.51%	8.40%		
25	4					4.38%	5.36%	6.32%	7.19%	7.89%	8.10%		
26	5						4.45%	5.45%	6.43%	7.31%	7.81%		
27	6							4.70%	5.75%	6.78%	7.54%		
28	7								5.14%	6.29%	7.27%		
29	8									5.83%	7.01%		
30	9										6.76%		
31	10												

Figure 16.8 The short-rate tree for valuing bond options in the ZCBOption sheet

	A	B	C	D	E	F	G	H	I	J	K	L
34	Zero price											
35		0	1	2	3	4	5	6	7	8	9	10
36	0	0.5042	0.5069	0.5180	0.5402	0.5737	0.6194	0.6775	0.7475	0.8275	0.9144	1.0000
37	1		0.5647	0.5707	0.5866	0.6130	0.6510	0.7010	0.7630	0.8358	0.9172	1.0000
38	2			0.6181	0.6288	0.6491	0.6802	0.7229	0.7776	0.8438	0.9199	1.0000
39	3				0.6668	0.6819	0.7070	0.7432	0.7913	0.8514	0.9225	1.0000
40	4					0.7115	0.7315	0.7620	0.8041	0.8586	0.9251	1.0000
41	5						0.7538	0.7794	0.8162	0.8654	0.9275	1.0000
42	6							0.7954	0.8275	0.8719	0.9299	1.0000
43	7								0.8380	0.8781	0.9322	1.0000
44	8									0.8840	0.9345	1.0000
45	9										0.9367	1.0000
46	10											1.0000
47												
48												
49	European Zero Option Value											
50		0	1	2	3	4						
51	0	0.1179	0.1360	0.1587	**0.1881**	**0.2263**						
52	1		0.1146	0.1334	0.1570	0.1870						
53	2			0.1078	0.1271	0.1509						
54	3				0.0989	0.1181						
55	4					0.0885						
56	5											
57	6											
58												
59												
60	American Zero Option Value											
61		0	1	2	3	4						
62	0	0.2958	0.2931	0.2820	**0.2598**	**0.2263**						
63	1		0.2353	0.2293	0.2134	0.1870						
64	2			0.1819	0.1712	0.1509						
65	3				0.1332	0.1181						
66	4					0.0885						
67	5											
68	6											

Figure 16.9 Zero option values using zero price tree (and short-rate tree) in ZCBOption sheet

The valuation tree uses probabilities of 0.5 for the up and down steps with the discount rate taken from the corresponding cell in the short-rate tree.

The European put with an exercise price of 0.8 has a value of 0.1179 (in cell B51), while the American put has a higher value of 0.2958 (in cell B62).

The BDT tree builds on the simple lognormal tree and its popularity is due to the ease with which the term structure of zero prices and yield volatilities can be derived from market prices. With a small number of additional iterations, as suggested by Bjerksund and Stensland, a more accurate match to the term structure can be achieved.

16.5   USER-DEFINED FUNCTIONS IN Module1

The function allows spot rate trees with both normal and lognormal rates by incorporating the parameter imod. The Newton–Raphson (NR) search uses a finite difference approximation to the required derivative (slope):

```
Function BinZeroRateTree(inorm, zpvec, volvec, L, delt)
'  generates binomial spot rate tree
'  inorm = 1 for normal rates, 2 for ln-normality
'  continuous interest rates only
'  uses BinZeroPrice fn
   Dim radj, atol, zpk, vkd, rk, fr1, fr, fdashr
   Dim i As Integer, j As Integer, k As Integer, n As Integer
   Dim RTmat() As Variant
   n = Application.Count(zpvec)
   ReDim RTmat(n, n)
   radj = 0.001
   atol = 0.0000001
   RTmat(1, 1) = -(Log(zpvec(1) / L)) / delt
'  solve for RTmat column-by-column
   For k = 2 To n
   zpk = zpvec(k)
   vkd = 2 * volvec(k - 1) * Sqr(delt)
'  use NR search to solve for rk, with finite difference fr1
   rk = RTmat(1, k - 1)
   Do
      RTmat(1, k) = rk + radj
      For i = 2 To k
         If inorm = 1 Then RTmat(i, k) = RTmat(i - 1, k) - vkd
         If inorm = 2 Then RTmat(i, k) = RTmat(i - 1, k)*Exp(- vkd)
      Next i
      fr1 = BinZeroPrice(L, RTmat, k, delt) - zpk
      RTmat(1, k) = rk
      For i = 2 To k
         If inorm = 1 Then RTmat(i, k) = RTmat(i - 1, k) - vkd
         If inorm = 2 Then RTmat(i, k) = RTmat(i - 1, k) Exp(- vkd)
      Next i
      fr = BinZeroPrice(L, RTmat, k, delt) - zpk
'  finite difference approximation to derivative
      fdashr = (fr1 - fr) / radj
      rk = rk - (fr / fdashr)
   Loop While Abs(fr) > atol
   Next k
   BinZeroRateTree = RTmat
End Function
```

Here the NR search uses an analytic formula for the required derivative:

```
Function BDTPUvec(z0, zvec, sigvec, delt)
'  replicates Goal Seek to find initial PU vector in BDT
'  discrete interest rates only
'  see Jamshidian (1991)
   Dim atol, r0, jdt, zpj, puj, sigj, pdj, yuj, ydj, fval, fdashval
   Dim j As Integer, n As Integer
   Dim puvec() As Variant
   n = Application.Count(zvec)
   ReDim puvec(n)
   atol = 0.000001
   r0 = (1 + z0)^(delt) - 1
   For j = 1 To n
     jdt = j * delt
     zpj = (1 + zvec(j))^-((j + 1) * delt)
     puj = zpj * (1 + r0)
     sigj = sigvec(j)
     Do
       pdj = 2 * zpj * (1 + r0) - puj
       yuj = (puj^(-1 / jdt)) - 1
       ydj = (pdj^(-1 / jdt)) - 1
       fval = 0.5 * Log(yuj / ydj) - sigj * Sqr(delt)
       fdashval = -(0.5 / jdt) * ((puj^-(1 / jdt + 1)) / yuj + (pdj^-(1 / jdt + 1)) / ydj)
       puj = puj - (fval / fdashval)
     Loop While Abs(fval) > atol
     puvec(j) = puj
   Next j
   BDTPUvec = puvec
End Function
```

The PU vector is then used to form the K and X vectors that generate the short-rate tree:

```
Function BDTKvec(puvec, pdvec)
'  from Pu and Pd vectors to approximation vector K in BDT
'  see Jamshidian (1991)
   Dim i As Integer, n As Integer
   Dim kvec() As Variant
   n = Application.Count(puvec)
   ReDim kvec(n)
   kvec(1) = ((1 / puvec(1)) - 1) / ((1 / pdvec(1)) - 1)
   For i = 2 To n
     kvec(i) = ((puvec(i - 1) / puvec(i)) - 1) / ((pdvec(i - 1) / pdvec(i)) - 1)
   Next i
   BDTKvec = kvec
End Function
```

```
Function BDTXvec(puvec, pdvec, kvec)
'  from Pu and Pd vectors to approximation vector X in BDT
'  see Jamshidian (1991)
   Dim pvec0
   Dim i As Integer, n As Integer
   Dim xvec() As Variant
   n = Application.Count(puvec)
   ReDim xvec(n)
   xvec(1) = ((1 / (0.5 * (puvec(1) + pdvec(1)))) - 1) / (0.5 * (1 + 1 / kvec(1)))
   For i = 2 To n
```

```
xvec(i) = (((puvec(i - 1) + pdvec(i - 1)) / (puvec(i) + pdvec(i))) - 1) / ((0.5 * (1 + 1 / kvec(i)))^i)
Next i
BDTXvec = xvec
End Function
```

SUMMARY

The process needed to build binomial trees explains why bond options are much more difficult to value than equity options. But matching the term structure is a prerequisite for the practical valuation of bond options in financial markets today. Fortunately, we have used risk-neutral valuation and binomial trees extensively when valuing equity options. Thus our focus in this chapter has been on the iterative methods needed for the building of binomial trees for interest rates. The BDT tree used to illustrate the valuation of zero-coupon options is popular with practitioners.

REFERENCES

Bjerksund, P. and G. Stensland, 1996, "Implementation of the Black–Derman–Toy Interest Rate Model", *Journal of Fixed Income*, **6**, 67–75.

Black, F., E. Derman and W. Toy, 1990, "A One-Factor Model of Interest Rates and its Application to Treasury Bond Options", *Financial Analysts Journal*, **46**, 33–39.

Clewlow, L. and C. Strickland, 1998, *Implementing Derivatives Models*, John Wiley & Sons, Chichester.

Jamshidian, F., 1991, "Forward Induction and Construction of Yield Curve Diffusion Models", *Journal of Fixed Income*, **1**, 62–74.

Appendix
Other VBA Functions

This appendix provides additional examples of user-defined functions for short-term fore-casting, ARIMA modelling, calculating splines and eigenvalues and eigenvectors. There is a brief introduction on each application. The spreadsheets themselves are less impor-tant than the associated VBA functions, whose code can be examined in the VBE Code window. The associated workbook is called OTHERFNS.xls.

FORECASTING

The functions associated with the 4Cast sheet are based on time-series analysis typically applied to past monthly sales data for a product or a product group. Time-series forecasting methods assume that existing sales patterns will continue into the future, hence they give better results in the short term than the long. Sales data is 'averaged' in different ways, which ensures that recent data is given more weight in the average than data way back in the past. Short-term forecasts are constructed by projecting most recent averages one period ahead.

Firstly, visual inspection and other techniques suggest the appropriate underlying model for the data generating process. If the data oscillates randomly about an average 'level', the model is assumed to be of the form:

$$\text{data} = \text{level} + \text{error} \qquad \text{(type A)}$$

If the data displays trend (an average level that changes systematically over time), the model is assumed to be of the form:

$$\text{data} = \text{level} + \text{trend} + \text{error} \qquad \text{(type B)}$$

If it oscillates regularly with a fixed frequency related to a seasonal effect, the model is assumed to be of the form:

$$\text{data} = (\text{level} + \text{trend})*\text{seasonal\_factor} + \text{error} \qquad \text{(type C)}$$

where the seasonal factors average to one.

Having decided the appropriate data-generating model for a data series, choose a method together with its required parameters and get period-by-period forecasts. These are esti-mates of the 'average' size of series next period, based on past data up to the most recent observation. For type A data, these forecasts can be moving averages. Alterna-tively, 'averaging' past data can involve exponentially weighted averages. Exponential smoothing methods can be crafted to apply for all three types of series. The user-defined functions ESvec, ESHoltvec and ESWintervec return exponentially smoothed forecasts for the different data series types, each requiring the data (referred to as dvec) and different input parameter values.

The underlying updating equation for exponentially smoothed forecasts is:

$$\text{new forecast} = \alpha^*\text{data} + (1 - \alpha)^*(\text{old forecast})$$

The smoothing constant α (between 0 and 1) determines how quickly the forecast responds to changes.

The 4Cast sheet contains three sales series of different types (type A in column B, type B in column I and type C in column O).

Looking first at the sales data of type A, six-period moving average forecasts of sales are given (column D) and also forecasts from simple exponential smoothing with alpha $= 0.1$ (column F). The function MAvec(B11:B34, D3) returned the entries in column vector D11:D34, after using the transpose function to get column vector output. The entries in column F are from the functions ESvec(B11:B34, F5, F3), again after transposing.

The coding of the user-defined functions, such as MAvec, ESvec, etc. starts with initialisation of variables, then continues with updating of the 'average'. The main variables in the code are dvec (data) and fvec (forecasts). These vectors are declared as variants with names incorporating 'vec'–fvec for forecasts, lvec for period-by-period 'level', tvec for period-by-period trend values. The vectors are dimensioned to hold n values, the updated values (one for each time period or data point). For seasonal data, we need to convert period i to the appropriate season and the user-defined function MMod does this.

All these methods assume that the future level of sales can be forecast using combinations of past data points. For example, the moving average is a weighted average of a limited number of data points, the weights being equal (or zero) in this case. In exponential smoothing, it can be demonstrated that the forecast is a weighted average of past data in which the weights decrease in a geometric series. In both cases, a combination of past data is used to produce the forecast, but the weights themselves depend on the particular method applied. In contrast, the Box–Jenkins approach (illustrated in the next section under the title ARIMA) aims to determine the optimal set of weights for the past data points and makes forecasts ahead from the resulting combination.

ARIMA MODELLING

Some of the simpler autoregressive integrated moving average models referred to as ARIMA models can be implemented in Excel, in combination with Solver optimisation. Usually, the estimation of such models is of the black box variety–present the data to the software package, wait, then receive the answers–with few clues as to the mechanics used by the software. In developing Excel implementations, it is necessary to take a closer look at the computations, paying attention to the production of good first-stage parameter estimates so as to ensure that the second-stage (using Solver) proceeds smoothly. The first-stage estimates can be coded as VBA functions while the second-stage requires Solver, so this has been automated in the form of macros.

The procedure for ARIMA modelling that we describe follows the process used by Box and Jenkins (and described in Pecar, 1994). The first step is to check whether or not the data is stationary, and if not to transform it to achieve stationarity, usually by differencing. This turns the problem from choosing an ARIMA model for the original data into choosing an ARMA model for the transformed data. The second step is to estimate the parameters of the ARMA model, generally using non-linear least squares (NLS). The choice of order (p, q) for the ARMA model is usually decided on the basis of the autocorrelation and partial autocorrelation functions of the data to be modelled. The third step is to check that the residuals from the ARMA model resemble white noise, using an appropriate test (usually the Q-test). Steps 2 and 3 can be cycled through as various combinations of p and q are tried. The process combines art and science in equal measure, though there are also some 'goodness of fit' criteria available to help in choosing the best model. A selection of diagnostic tools is provided in the workbook, starting with functions for calculating sample autocorrelations and partial autocorrelations functions, including functions for the Q-tests from Box–Pierce and from Box–Ljung.

The first steps in applying ARIMA modelling in Excel include checking on stationarity by inspecting a chart of the series and then differencing the series where required. In the second step, charts of the autocorrelations and partial autocorrelations at different lags can be constructed from the user-defined functions ACFk and PACFk which return the correlations at lag k. Inspection of these charts directs the choice of AR and/or MA terms to be estimated in the ARMA model. In the ARMA sheet, we illustrate the estimation procedure for three different series in columns D, G and N, row 34 and below. Inspection of the AC and PAC functions for these three series computed in rows 7 to 18 suggests fitting an AR model to series 1, an MA to series 2 and an ARMA model to series3. We illustrate in turn the estimation of a first-order autoregressive model (denoted AR(1)), a second-order moving average model (MA(2)) and an ARMA(1,1) model, using functions and macros. There is also a user-defined function which returns initial parameter estimates for any ARMA(p, q) model ready for presentation to Solver.

The estimation of ARMA models with only autoregressive (AR) terms requires ordinary least squares regression and thus exact parameter estimates are obtained in a single stage. The function ARpvec returns the results of a multiple linear regression of the data series on its lagged values using the LINEST function. In the ARMA sheet, the ARpvec function is used to estimate the parameters of an AR(1) process.

The inclusion of moving average (MA) terms in an ARMA model forces the estimation procedure to involve two stages, with initial estimates used as starting values for an optimisation routine to generate the final estimates. Box and Jenkins (1984) suggest how to find good initial estimates for the MA parameters and their idea is implemented in the MAqvec0 function. They start by calculating ($q + 1$) autocovariances for the data series, and then use an iterative process, starting with the MA parameter estimates set to zero, until the residual variance is minimised. In the spreadsheet these initial estimates (in cells G26:G28) are then used to give a series of residuals (errors) for the MA(2) process. Note that the residual for a particular time period depends not on the data series, but instead on the residuals for the previous two periods (see formula in cell I34). With the chosen initial estimates the residual sum of squares (in cell G30) has a value of 1.067. We now use Solver to search through alternative combinations of parameters whilst trying to reduce the ensuing residual sum of squares. This can be achieved through Excel commands or automated in a VBA macro, (which is invoked with the Ctrl+Shift+B keystroke combination). The code for this subroutine (called MA2qvec) is set out in ModuleBM. The improved parameter estimates are shown in cells I26:I28 and these model values reduce the size of the residual sum of squares to 1.053.

For an ARMA model, we require initial estimates for the AR parameters and these are obtained from the Yule–Walker equations that link the autocovariances with the theoretical parameters. The initial AR parameter estimates are obtained (using the ARMApqvec0 function) (see cells N26:N28). In the spreadsheet, these initial estimates are then used to generate a series of residuals for an ARMA(1,1) process. Note that for an ARMA(1,1) model, the residual for a particular time period now depends both on the series and the residual from the previous period (as shown in the formula in cell P35). The residual sum of squares, from the initial estimates, is 27.047 (cell N30). Exactly as for the MA2 process, Solver is applied to produce improved parameter estimates (in cells P26:P28). The Solver optimisation can be controlled by subroutine ARMA11pqvec, which is invoked using the Ctrl+Shift+C keystroke combination.

SPLINES

Splines provide a useful way of generating a smooth curve to represent some $x-y$ data points. The purpose could be interpolation (where the curve is required to pass through all the data points) or a more general fitting process (where the curve aims to best fit but not necessarily pass through all the points). In contrast to alternatives such as fitting high-order polynomials, one advantage of splines is that they require only a small number of parameters. Low-order polynomials are fitted piecewise to the intervals between successive data points, the parameters of the polynomials being chosen to produce a smooth curve by matching up values and slopes at the interval ends. We concentrate on cubic splines, ensuring that the fitted function and its first and second derivatives are continuous. The functions developed in this module (ModuleC1) implement the calculations for the standard (interpolating) cubic spline. In addition, we have included a function for the generation of a set of cubic basis splines that can then be used in deriving a curve of best fit.

Starting with a set of data points, in the terminology of splines the x values are referred to as knots, and the y values as function values associated with the knots. Fitting the spline involves linking each pair of adjacent knots with a cubic polynomial such that the resulting spline function is smooth. For a cubic spline, this is achieved by constraining the polynomials on either side of each knot to share the same second derivative value. The function CubicSplinezvec returns the vector of second derivative values (called zvec) at each of the knots, using the vectors of knots (kvec) and function values (ykvec) as input arrays. The function calculates two arrays, a tridiagonal matrix (Tmat) and a vector (vvec), then combines these by matrix multiplication to produce the vector of second derivative values (zvec). The derivative values returned by function CubicSplinezvec are used in the second function, CubicSplineValuey. This interpolates for a specific value of x (called xstart) producing the 'y value' from the appropriate fitted spline segment. For a *natural* cubic spline function, the second derivative of the spline function at each end of the x range must equal zero. For a specific value of xstar, the first step is to determine the pair of knots between which it lies before selecting the appropriate cubic polynomial joining the knots and finally calculating the spline value for xstar. The spline value uses a multiplication formula with variable references to the first (br) and second (nzvec) derivatives.

The CubicSplineValuey function returns one spline value for each specific value of xstar. As a consolidation exercise, think out how you would write a function that generates spline values for a range of x values within the series of knot points.

While standard splines are very useful, one potential drawback is that changing the value of a single point on the function to be interpolated has a global effect on the spline function chosen. For instance, change the value in cell C20 (Spline sheet) from

1.59 to −5.00 and note that the vector of second derivatives changes throughout. Note also though (Chart1 sheet) that the amended spline function has retained the smoothness to the eye.

In contrast, basis splines have the advantage of adapting locally but not globally if a data point changes. The approach consists of defining a 'basis of splines' where each basis spline takes positive values over a number of intervals between adjacent knots but is zero elsewhere. Each basis spline is centred on a different knot. By using a number of different basis splines as building blocks, we create a single function by adding together the values of all the splines at any point. The user chooses where to place the knots (including some outside the range to be estimated) and can then use regression to find weights for each of the basis splines to best fit the data points. Notice that the basis spline approach is a more general fitting task (an optimal fit over all points), whereas the cubic splines produce a function that fits the data points perfectly. Basis splines are used as one approach to fitting the term structure of interest rates.

As with standard splines, we illustrate only the cubic form of basis splines, where each of the cubic splines is positive over four consecutive intervals. For a given value of xstar, we need to find values for each of the four basis splines (indexed by integer istar) with positive values. The function CubicBSplineValuei, with the matrix IKmat containing knot values as additional input, uses the recurrence relationship of Powell to generate the value of the (istar) basis spline. The recurrence relationship proceeds by first calculating three basis splines of degree one, then the two splines of degree two, thus allowing the calculation of the single cubic spline of degree three.

EIGENVALUES AND EIGENVECTORS

Although eigenvalues play an important role in physics and engineering, they also serve in finance for the estimation of principal components. A typical application is to decompose risk (represented by a covariance or correlation matrix from asset returns) into a number of linearly independent variables (the principal components or eigenvectors). The eigenvalues give the proportion of risk due to each of the eigenvectors.

Although there are more efficient methods for larger matrices, the Jacobi method is foolproof for all matrices that are real and symmetric (as are covariance and correlation matrices). This method seeks to nudge the input matrix towards diagonal form by a sequence of transformations or matrix rotations. Each transformation preserves the sum of the diagonal elements (which will in due course become the eigenvalues), whilst decreasing monotonically the sum of squares of the off-diagonal elements. The process continues until the sum of squares falls below a certain value. (We have used a tolerance of 10^{-19} for the loop to terminate.)

The function Eigenvaluesevec (in ModuleD1) is the main program, calling the intermediate functions that form each Jacobi rotation. First, the rotation angle is calculated (with the Jacobirvec function), then the rotation matrix constructed (in the JacobiPmat function) and finally the current input matrix is updated (in the JacobiAmat function). Within each loop of the main program, a new input matrix is generated and the sum of its off-diagonal elements calculated. When the tolerance level is reached, the eigenvalues are taken as the diagonal elements of the transformed input matrix.

The calculation of the associated eigenvectors (in the EigenvectorsEmat function) follows the same pattern, except that an additional matrix (starting as the identity matrix) that captures the cumulative effect of the transformations is also updated. When the tolerance level is reached, the eigenvectors are the columns of this additional matrix.

REFERENCES

Box, G. E. P. and G. M. Jenkins, 1984, *Time Series Analysis: Forecasting and Control*, Molden Day, San Francisco, CA.

Pecar, B., 1994, *Business Forecasting for Management*, McGraw-Hill, Maidenhead.

INDEX